Hallowed Stewards

SOCIETAS: HISTORICAL STUDIES IN CLASSICAL CULTURE

Celia E. Schultz and Sara Forsdyke, Series Editors

Hallowed Stewards: Solon and the Sacred Treasurers of Ancient Athens
William S. Bubelis

A Family of Gods: The Worship of the Imperial Family in the Latin West
Gwynaeth McIntyre

Hallowed Stewards

SOLON AND THE SACRED TREASURERS OF ANCIENT ATHENS

William S. Bubelis

UNIVERSITY OF MICHIGAN PRESS
ANN ARBOR

Published in the United States of America by the
University of Michigan Press
Manufactured in the United States of America
♾ Printed on acid-free paper

2019 2018 2017 2016 4 3 2 1

A CIP catalog record for this book is available from the British Library.

Library of Congress Cataloging-in-Publication Data

Bubelis, William Stanley, author.
Hallowed stewards : Solon and the sacred treasurers of ancient Athens / William S. Bubelis.
pages cm.(Societas : historical studies in classical culture)
Includes bibliographical references and index.
ISBN 978-0-472-11942-4 (hardback)
1. Finance, Public (Greek law) 2. Temples—Economic aspects—Greece—History—To 1500. 3. Constitutional history—Greece—Athens—To 146 B.C. I. Title.
KL4378.B83 2014
938'5—dc23

2014044023

For my Mother and Father

Preface

In a formal sense, this project originated in a dissertation, completed in 2007 at the University of Chicago under the able direction of Professor Jonathan Hall, but it also possesses a prehistory of sorts. While lodged academically in Chicago's now disbanded Committee on the Ancient Mediterranean World, I split my efforts between Assyriology and all things Hellenic. At Chicago, I benefited greatly from a compelling environment in which I was encouraged to develop as independent a scholarly voice and discipline as I could imagine, and did so particularly under professors Hall, James Redfield, and Christopher Faraone. Professors Walter Kaegi, Elizabeth Asmis, and Elizabeth Gebhard provided sound advice, opportunities, and encouragement that did much to alleviate the doubt that afflicts us when pursuing so new a path as that which has led to this book.

In tandem with a rigorous education in Classics and ancient Mediterranean history, while I labored at the Oriental Institute under Professor Matthew Stolper and my other teachers there, especially Professor Walter Farber, I acquired knowledge of signal value. Although the reader may see no overt trace of it in the following pages, my study of Neo-Babylonian and Achaemenid cuneiform texts under Matt Stolper greatly informed my approach to legal and administrative documents of any description. A year as the John Williams White Fellow at the American School of Classical Studies at Athens in 2002–03 was crucial in all respects. The community of scholars in Athens has been for me a kind of second family, whose intellectual acuity and curiosity, as well as abiding friendship, amply mirrors what it means to study holistically Hellenic history and culture in all of its rigor and beauty. But my interest in the sacred treasurers of Athens had already coalesced when, while attending my alma mater the University of Washington in Seattle, I had composed under the direction of Professor Merle Langdon a senior thesis on Athena's finances in the year 434/3. Study at Chicago and in Athens, nevertheless, was to those interests as the sun is to the summer fruit as it ripens for an autumn harvest.

Saint Louis saw the birth of the book from those early beginnings and nourished it with an industry and character that can only come from a city so uniquely endowed with both. Washington University in Saint Louis has proven itself to be a place of remarkable opportunity. At an early stage in the book's composition, Professor Susan Rotroff cheerfully volunteered to read a version of what is now chapters 4 and 5, to which she deftly applied her sharp eye and practical acumen. To have the encouragement of an archaeologist so steeped in all things Athenian as Susan is, and to have the support of other colleagues at Washington University in Saint Louis, especially Cathy Marler, was to have a following wind in my sails. Heartfelt thanks are owed to Professor Timothy Moore for checking without hesitation the manuscript for errors of grammar and sense, of which he found many that I could no longer see for myself. Likewise, two readers for the Press have my thanks for challenging me to justify my arguments more clearly at nearly every turn. Ellen Bauerle has earned special respect and gratitude not only for having faith in a project that, I feared, risked being let adrift but also for piloting the book through the Skylla and Kharybdis of academic publishing.

But what could have been accomplished without my family and friends? My friend, Jon Berliner, has helped to shape the book at so many turns by his keen insight, unflagging interest, probing questions, and companionship in all things great and small; as a great craftsman of knowledge in his own right, he knows this book, I suspect, better than I do. When completion of the book seemed so unattainable, Katy Keich provided such resolute courage, faith, good humor, and hope as to drive away the fears of academic night. My beloved parents, to whom I gratefully dedicate the book, are owed more than can possibly be expressed since they have been my greatest of teachers and most steadfast of supporters. Without them, and without our larger family, this book would never have been started much less completed, and I could only wish that more were still present with us to celebrate what has come to pass.

On the Banks of the Mississippi at Saint Louis, September 2013

Contents

Abbreviations

The names and works of ancient authors are abbreviated in the notes according to *LSJ* (and *LSJ* Suppl.), even where their full names appear in the text as transliterated from the Greek directly. The exceptions are the slightly expanded forms "Dem." for Demosthenes ("D." in *LSJ*), "Xen." for Xenophon ("X." in *LSJ*), and as noted below "*Ath.Pol.*" for the Aristotelian *Constitution of the Athenians* ("*Ath.*" in *LSJ*). I have retained the familiar Latin spelling only for those authors (e.g., Thucydides), proper names, and toponyms for which such full transliteration from the Greek might prove distracting to the reader. In addition, citations of particular editions of ancient authors are abbreviated also according to *LSJ*, except in the few cases noted below. Journals are abbreviated in accordance with *L'Année Philologique* and are not listed here.

Agora	The American School of Classical Studies at Athens. *The Athenian Agora* (Princeton, NJ: 1961–).
Aleshire "Demos"	Sara B. Aleshire. "The Demos and the Priests: The Selection of Sacred Officials at Athens from Cleisthenes to Augustus," in *Ritual, Finance, and Politics: Athenian Democratic Accounts Presented to David Lewis* Robin Osborne and Simon Hornblower, eds. (Oxford: 1994), 325–37.
Aleshire "State Cult"	Sara B. Aleshire. "Towards a Definition of 'State Cult' for Ancient Athens," in Hägg (1994), 9–16.
Ath.Pol.	[Aristotle]. *Athênaiôn Politeia* M. Chambers, ed. (Leipzig: 1994).

ATL	Benjamin Dean Meritt, H. T. Wade-Gery, and Malcolm Francis McGregor. *The Athenian Tribute Lists* 4 vols. (Cambridge, MA, and Princeton, NJ: 1939–53).
Busolt/Swoboda	Georg Busolt. *Griechische Staatskunde. Erste Hälfte. Allgemeine Darstellung des griechischen Staates. Zweite Hälfte. Darstellung einzelner Staaten und der zwischenstaatlichen Beziehungen. Bearbeitet von H. Swoboda* 3rd rev. ed. (Munich: 1920–26).
Conomis *Din.*	N. C. Conomis, ed. *Dinarchus. Orationes cum Fragmentis* (Leipzig: 1975).
Conomis *Lyc.*	N. C. Conomis, ed. *Lycurgus. Oratio in Leocratem* (Leipzig: 1970).
DAA	Antony E. Raubitschek, ed. *Dedications from the Athenian Akropolis. A Catalogue of the Inscriptions of the Sixth and Fifth Centuries B.C.* (Cambridge, MA: 1949).
D-K	Hermann Diels and Walter Kranz, eds. *Die Fragmente der Vorsokratiker* 6th ed. 3 vols. (Berlin: 1952).
Dilts	M. R. Dilts, ed. *Scholia Demosthenica* vol. II: *Scholia in Orationes 19–60 Continens* (Leipzig: 1986).
EG	Margherita Guarducci, ed. *Epigrafia Graeca* (Rome: 1967–68).
Fortenbaugh	W. W. Fortenbaugh et al., eds. *Theophrastus of Eresus. Sources for his Life, Writings, Thought and Influences. Part Two. Psychology, Human Physiology, Living Creatures, Botany, Ethics, Religion, Politics, Rhetoric and Poetics, Music, Miscellanea* (Leiden: 1992).
I.Eleusis	Kevin Clinton, ed. *Eleusis. The Inscriptions on Stone. Documents of the Sanctuary of the Two Goddesses and Public Documents of the Deme* 2 vols. Vivliotheke tes en Athenais Arkhaiologikes Hetaireias 259 (Athens: 2005–8).
I.Oropou	B. C. Petrakos, ed. ʿΟι Επιγραφὲς τοῦ ʾΩρωποῦ Vivliotheke tes en Athenais Arkhaiologikes Hetaireias 170 (Athens: 1997).
FGrH	Felix Jacoby, ed. *Fragmente der griechische Historiker* (Berlin: 1923–40; Leiden: 1940–).

Holwerda	D. Holwerda, ed. *Scholia in Aristophanem. Pars II. Scholia in "Vespas;" "Pacem;" "Aves" et "Lysistratam." Fasc. II continens Scholia Vetera et Recentiora in Aristophanis "Aves"* (Groningen: 1991).
ID	Jacque Coupry, ed. *Inscriptions de Délos. Période de l'Amphictyonie attico-délienne. Actes administratifs nos. 89-104-33* (Paris: 1972).
IGBulg	Georgius Mihailov, ed. *Inscriptiones Graecae in Bulgaria Repertae* (Sofia: 1956–97).
IG	*Inscriptiones Graecae* (Berlin: 1873–).
IScM	*Inscriptiones Scythiae Minoris* (Bucharest: 1983–; vol. 3: Bucharest and Paris: 1999).
IvEphesos	Hermann Wankel, ed. *Die Inschriften von Ephesos* vol. 1: *Inschriften griechischen Städte aus Kleinasiens* 11 (Bonn: 1979).
Jensen	Christianvs Jensen, ed. *Hyperidis Orationes Sex* (Leipzig: 1917).
Koster-Holwerda	W. J. W. Koster and D. Holwerda, eds. *Scholia in Aristophanem. Pars II. Scholia in* Vespas; Pacem; Aves *et* Lysistratam. *Fasc. I. Continens Scholia Vetera et Recentiora In Aristophanis* Vespas (Groningen: 1978).
Lambert "Calendar"	Stephen D. Lambert. "The Sacrificial Calendar of Athens," *ABSA* 97 (2002), 353–99, pls. 31–36.
Lambert "Genesia"	Stephen D. Lambert. "Parerga III: The Genesia, Basile and Epops Again," *ZPE* 139 (2002), 75–82.
Lambert "Nemean"	Stephen D. Lambert. "Parerga II: The Date of the Nemean Games," *ZPE* 139 (2002), 72–74.
LGPN Aegean	P. M. Fraser and E. Matthews, eds. *A Lexicon of Greek Personal Names vol. I: The Aegean Islands, Cyprus, Cyrenaica* (Oxford: 1987).
LGPN Attica	M. J. Osborne and S. G. Byrne, eds. *A Lexicon of Greek Personal Names vol. II: Attica* (Oxford: 1994).
LGPN Central Greece	P. M. Fraser and E. Matthews, eds. *A Lexicon of Greek Personal Names vol. III.b. Central Greece: From the Megarid to Thessaly* (Oxford: 2000).
LSJ	H. G. Liddell, Robert Scott, H. Stuart Jones, and Roderick McKenzie, eds. *Greek-English Lexicon* 9th ed. rev. H. Stuart Jones (Oxford: 1940).

LSJ Suppl.	P. G. W. Glare, ed. *Greek-English Lexicon. Revised Supplement* (Oxford: 1996).
Meiggs/Lewis	Russell Meiggs and David Lewis, eds. *A Selection of Greek Historical Inscriptions: To the End of the Fifth Century B.C.* (Oxford: 1969).
NGSL	Eran Lupu. *Greek Sacred Law: A Collection of New Documents (NGSL)* (Leiden: 2005).
Nouveau choix	*Nouveau choix d'inscriptions grecques* (Paris: 1971).
Parker "Law"	Robert Parker. "Law and Religion," in Gagarin and Cohen (2005), 61–81.
Parker "Polytheism"	Robert Parker. *Polytheism and Society at Athens* (Oxford: 2005).
PatmLex.	Sakkélion, ed. "Εκ των συνεκδότων της Πατμιακής Βιβλιοθήκης. *Scholies de Démosthène et d'Eschine d'après un manuscrit inédit de Patmos,*" *BCH* 1 (1877), 1–16, pl. 6.
PCG	R. Kassel and C. Austin, eds. *Poetae Comici Graeci* (Berlin: 1983–2001).
Petrakos Ὁ Δῆμος τοῦ Ραμνοῦντος	B. C. Petrakos, ed. Ὁ Δῆμος τοῦ Ραμνοῦντος. II. Ὁι Επιγραφές Vivliotheke tes en Athenais Arkhaiologikes Hetaireias 182 (Athens: 1999).
Preller	L. Preller, ed. *Polemonis Periegetae Fragmenta* (Leipzig: 1838).
Raubitschek "Leagros"	A. E. Raubitshek. "Leagros," *Hesperia* 8 (1939), 155–64.
Raubitschek "Votive"	A. E. Raubitshek. "Early Attic Votive Monuments," *ABSA* 40 (1939) [1943], 17–37, pls. 7–13.
Raubitschek "Weihinschriften"	A. E. Raubitschek. "Zu altattischen Weihinschriften," *JÖAI* 31 (1939), Beiblatt cols. 21–67.
RE	*Paulys Realencyclopädie der classischen Altertumswissensschaft* (Stuttgart: 1894–1972).
Rhodes/Osborne	P. J. Rhodes and Robin Osborne, eds. *Greek Historical Inscriptions, 404–323 B. C.* (Oxford: 2003).
Ruschenbusch	Eberhard Ruschenbusch, ed. ΣΟΛΩΝΟΣ ΝΟΜΟΙ (Wiesbaden: 1966).
SEG	*Supplementum Epigraphicum Graecum* (Leiden: 1923–).
*SIG*³	Wilhelm Dittenberger, ed. *Sylloge Inscriptionum Graecarum* 3rd ed. (Leipzig: 1915–24).

Slater	William J. Slater, ed. *Aristophanis Byzantii Fragmenta* (Berlin: 1986).
Strecker	Carolus Strecker, ed. *De Lycophrone Euphronio Eratosthene Comicorum Interpretibus* (Greifswald: 1884).
Wehrli *Dem.*	F. Wehrli, ed. *Die Schule des Aristoteles.* Vol. IV. *Demetrios von Phaleron* 2nd rev. ed. (Basel and Stuttgart: 1968).
Wehrli *Phain.*	F. Wehrli, ed. *Die Schule des Aristoteles.* Vol. IX. *Phainias von Eresos,* 2nd rev. ed. (Basel and Stuttgart: 1969).

Introduction

In the far corner of modern Athens' Epigraphic Museum, past so many significant monuments of antiquity, lies one particular votive dedication whose importance may hardly be obvious. Deceptively simple in appearance, it consists of a single, massive block of ochre-colored *poros* limestone that is whole for most of its impressive length (c. 2.75m, originally) despite having been broken in half long ago. Quite unlike the altars of later ages that so often boast delicate proportions and ornament, this altar confronts the viewer with its singularly impressive bulk and an almost primitive quality. The form that the altar takes is that of a *trapeza*, in which the single main block rests on two smaller stones, rendering the simple shape of a bench or table. Just below the upper edge of its front side, the altar proclaims in unusually large letters of retrograde script that must once have been painted (*IG* I³ 590):

[------- ἀνέθ]εκεν ⁝ 'Αθεναίαι ⁝ Χα[ι]ρίον ⁝ ταμιεύον ⁝ Κλε[δ]ί̣[ϙο ⁝ *h*υιός] ←.

[Khairion, while serving as *tamias*, the son of Kleidiqos, dedicated to Athena . . .]

The monument lacks an original context, since it was discovered in the course of the 1889 season of excavation on the Athenian akropolis amid other, much later, inscriptions used as fill for terracing the akropolis' southeast edge. Even without an identifiable site for its original placement on the akropolis, the altar is striking for its great size. Most plausibly dated to c. 565–50 on the basis of the letter-forms employed by other surviving dedications, concerning all details of which see the appendix, Khairion's altar stands as the akropolis' earliest inscribed religious monument.

The altar is all the more worthy of note, however, because it possesses an implicitly political character as well as a religious one. Whereas almost all other Athenians identify themselves by no more than name and patronymic, Khairion stipulates that he offered the altar while serving as a *tamias*. While Khairion could depend on his fellow Athenians to know exactly what a *tamias* was and why his tenure as one was remarkable, we confront our own collective ignorance. If pressed to articulate just what the *tamiai* were, most students of Athenian history may conjure only a hazy image of them as bureaucratic scriveners. After all, it was the *tamiai* who were responsible for the extensive inventories of the classical centuries that document the various possessions of Athena and other gods. But neither those inventories nor the common misperception square easily with the grandiosity of Khairion's altar and much less so with the individuality that its dedicatory text bespeaks. By the act of dedication, Khairion converted some of his own wealth into the property of Athena, thereby magnifying the goddess. This is hardly the action of a demure clerk. Khairion's very office was the subject of major legislation a generation earlier, moreover. The pseudo-Aristotelean *Constitution of the Athenians* (*Ath.Pol.*, hereafter) credits the early Athenian lawgiver Solon with establishing in 594/3 a law that not only detailed procedures for the selection of *tamiai* but also stipulated that only the wealthiest of Athenians could hold that office.[1] The massive dimensions of Khairion's altar are evidence enough of his substantial wealth, but his self-promotion as a *tamias* made his position at the apex of Athenian society apparent to all. No one could have been mistaken about Khairion's preeminence, and for some reason this was just as he wished. But was this in keeping with Solon's intentions? Given that the law combines restrictive procedural rules with a measure of dignity granted to the wealthy, the answer may be a complicated one. Solon's objectives are indeed important, but it is nevertheless the law's history after its passage that is most relevant to making sense of Khairion and his altar.

That history is primarily a history of institutions. Broadly, there is the system of government itself. At its heart lie the constitutional rules, laws, and procedures that governed how *tamiai* and many other magistrates entered office, completed their duties, and exited. By extension, it also encompassed the lines of authority that connected or subordinated one college of magistrates to another, all under the supervision of such supreme bodies as the Areiopagos and

1. *Ath.Pol.* 47.1 (= Harpokration, s.v. ταμίαι; Souda s.vv. ταμίαι); 8.1; cf. 7.3.

Boule. But the purpose of this superstructure of magistrates and laws was to manage property, be it money or ritual implements of bronze and gold. It was by deploying this property in accord with their laws and subject to their magistrates that the Athenians met their communal religious aims. It is impossible, after all, to imagine classical Athens without its festivals of the Panathenaia or its Dionysia, or bereft of its many temples and great sacrificial feasts, all of which required public resources and public magistrates.

The central argument of this book is that Solon's law and other measures related to it unintentionally catalyzed a long-term transformation in these offices that shaped the future growth of the *polis* itself. From a relatively simple state apparatus in Solon's time, the Athenians created, piece by piece, an administrative superstructure of magistracies devoted to handling public resources for religious ends that by the late fourth century represented a significant proportion (perhaps two-fifths) of the total number of magistracies within the *polis*.[2] Likewise, the sheer cost of public treasure devoted to religion also grew, along with the political commitment to maintain those outlays. In his Funeral Oration, Thucydides has Perikles say that the athletic contests and sacrifices held throughout the year in Athens provided a respite from labors not available to the Demos of other cities.[3] The Old Oligarch even claims that the Athenian poor took a share in the rituals and festivals staged by the whole *polis* because they could not afford to offer victims in their own right (that is, like wealthier Athenians).[4] It was not lost on the Athenians that their public commitments were costly. In a trial from the 390s, for example, a prosecuting citizen accused Nikomakhos, who was one of those responsible for re-drafting the *polis*' calendar of sacrifices (attributed to none other than Solon), with being nothing short

2. *pace* Allen (2000), 305–16, Hansen (1980) argues that the total number of magistracies in fourth-century Athens likely did approach the 700 mentioned by *Ath.Pol.* (24.3), which nevertheless provides detail (42.2–62.2) on only a small proportion of those (of those noted, fully fifty-seven out of the total 319 are sacred treasurers). Moreover, Hansen, 164, emphasizes that the number of "sacral officials" (i.e., sacred treasurers) was probably far higher than can be known from extant sources, since inscriptions are often our only source of information that a particular board ever existed; epigraphic data (and some oratory) provides for another forty-four to seventy-nine sacred treasurers on Hansen's examination, 156–63, of the evidence. Working from Linders' data (1975), 14–16, Hansen suggests that there were another one hundred to two hundred pan-Athenian sacred treasurers unattested by any source, in which case out of the total of approximately seven hundred magistrates as many as c. 205–340 might have been sacred treasurers.

For the demes and tribes, that proportion is likely higher still because they are not known to have had their own equivalent of most pan-Athenian magistrates (such as the *sitophylakes* and the Eleven) but did have *hieropoioi* and in at least some cases, *tamiai*; cf. Hansen (1990), 230–40.

3. Thuc. 2.38.
4. [Xen.] *Ath.Pol.* 2.9.

of a temple-robber who had ostensibly admitted, "I made my transcriptions out of piety, not cheapness."[5] And in the *Areopagitikos* of c. 355, Isokrates also claims that the ancestral rites (*ta patria*), though simple and necessary, were being neglected in favor of major expenditures on supplementary sacrifices (*ta epitheta*).[6] Public money spent annually in the 330s on regular sacrifices reached a *minimum* of eighteen to twenty-four *talents*. So important were those sacrifices to the fabric of the democracy that that figure compares favorably with the twenty-two to thirty-seven *talents* spent on paying citizens to serve as jurors, for example.[7] The Athenians were then sacrificing cattle alone on the order of c. 1,400–1,700 head per annum, and on J. Mikalson's calculations, the number of festival days in the Athenian calendar amounted to about half of the year.[8] But democratic expenditures and budgetary priorities did not commence *ex nihilo* with Kleisthenes' democratizing reforms of 508/7. Their prehistory lies with Solon and even with the Peisistratid tyrants that followed Solon.

The key development, I argue, lay in the creation of new forms of sacred property that could better meet the expanding economic needs of Athenian religious life. This process appears to have commenced in the sixth century, perhaps under the Peisistratidai and on a blueprint, if you will, provided by Solon's laws. In tandem with the new property came new managerial techniques that, in turn, required wholly new magistracies, especially under the democracy. Yet the older type of office, whose paradigm was none other than the *tamiai* of Athena, did not disappear but, to the contrary, remained vital. With the creation of financial offices to oversee an increasingly monetized form of sacred wealth, the Athenians instigated what was in effect a loosely bifurcated system. Each type of office oversaw a distinct class of property that had its own role to play in religious life. For every cult the particular constellation of

5. Lys. 30.21: κᾆθ ᾽ οὑτὸς ὁ ἱερόσυλος περιτρέχει, λέγων ὡς εὐσέβειαν ἀλλ ᾽ οὐκ εὐτέλειαν ἀνέγραψε.
6. 7.29–30.
7. On these nonsacrificial costs, see Hansen (1991), 189, 255, 315–16. For sacrificial costs, I base my estimate on the figures for prices of sacrificial animals culled from six surviving Athenian sacrificial calendars (all but one from c. 400–350), as well as the *dermatika* accounts from the late 330s (Rosivach [1994]). The minimum and maximum figures cited above thus reflect only the range of values pegged to Rosivach's low estimate and also excludes sacrifices of swine (too few data) and piglets (usually sacrificed as holocaust not as alimentary offerings). This calculation also excludes large, one-time supplements or sacrifices, such as the extra 261 oxen sacrificed to Zeus Soter in 332/1, for which see Rosivach, 53.
8. Rosivach (1994), 156–57, also estimates that the high end of the aggregate number of oxen purchased at public expense (i.e., those supplements, and only at *polis* expense) as c. 1,400 (as the low end of Jameson's [1988], 107–12, estimate of 1,400–1,700 oxen based on the *dermatika* accounts [implying a cost of eighteen to twenty-one *talents* alone]). Calendar: Mikalson (1975), 201–03. Rosivach (1994), 3, aptly terms the effect of such calendars a "complex accumulation of sacrifices."

offices and property was different, but there are broad patterns and developments that deserve to be charted. Therefore, while this book is a history of institutions, that is, the magistrates and the apparatus of laws and procedures of which they were an integral part, it also offers what amounts to a chapter in the history of sacred property among the Greeks.

Sacred Property between Priests and Sacred Treasurers

To define the relationship between magistrates and the property that they handled, one ought first to delineate the general parameters by which a history such as this ought best to proceed. The nomenclature by which the Athenians, nonetheless, described these various magistrates presents an interesting problem, for they did not conceive of them as constituting a particular class. One served merely as a *hieropoios* of Apollo or a *naokoros* of Poseidon at a particular sanctuary, and only for a given year, at that. While such words as "sexton" and "sacristan" or even merely "warden" would appear to offer a ready-made rubric for that purpose, to invoke any particular term from Western ecclesiastic history presupposes a certain division of labor between sacred and secular tasks that should not be assumed too readily. It seems sensible, therefore, to designate simply by "sacred treasurer" all those magistrates who possessed a reasonably significant degree of authority over some kind of sacred property or another.[9] This phrase necessarily excludes those magistrates whose stewardship of property had little to do with the gods. This is an important distinction, for when the Athenians created new financial magistracies they habitually borrowed for them the nomenclature that had long been traditional for the more expressly religious offices.[10] The phrase "sacred treasurer" also excludes any Athenian whose functions, however religious, had little to do with property. But this demarcation between sacred treasurer and anyone possessing a merely sacred task raises a question that is critical to resolve before moving ahead: why should there be any distinct treasurer, and a magistrate at that, in a cult alongside and yet separate from those who conducted its rituals?

9. On the question of nomenclature, see especially chapter 5, n. 2.
10. From the mid-fifth century onward, beginning with the *hellenotamiai*, the Athenians applied the nomenclature of the *tamiai* to unmistakably financial offices such as the *tamias* of the Stratiotic Funds, the *tamias* of the Demos, and so on. But in 363/2 the Athenians did attach pronounced ritual duties to an office, that of the *tamiai* of the two sacred triremes, for which see Bubelis (2010).

The answer involves several problems of method and approach that elucidate the essential contours of this book. Habitually neglected as historical subjects in their own right by modern scholarship, sacred treasurers have often been mistakenly subsumed in a narrative whereby the Athenian state's ability to organize religious life grew at the expense of other parties, especially those whose claim was intrinsically ritual in nature.[11] While those scholars working to uncover the early political history of Athens have often glanced at the property that the *polis* deployed in pursuit of communal religious ends, that property has played at most only a marginal and somewhat nebulous role in their larger effort to establish that the state's historical development occurred at the expense of other, private, stakeholders in Athenian rites. That history, indeed, the history of Solon himself and his laws, has been interpreted almost solely through the lens of politics and religion, or rather through a particular understanding of how politics and religion might intersect.

In this vein lies principally F. Jacoby's well-known claim (1944) that Solon's creation of the religious festival known as the Genesia (that is, a public festival for all Athenian ancestors) initiated a hostile approach by the *polis* toward the affairs and powers of familial religious bodies (particularly the *genê*) and their priests. According to that interpretation, the *genê* were more closely bound up with certain elite families of Athens, the so-called Eupatridai, than any others and were sometimes even thought to be synonymous with the elite as a whole.[12] These claims are especially relevant since, as I discuss in chapter 3 and the Appendix, none other than Khairion is identified as a member of the Eupatridai on his tombstone (of c. 540). Of course, the Genesia itself bears strongly on how Solon might have shaped Athenian religious life and its administration. If correct, Jacoby's thesis would permit us to view Khairion's altar as an anti-Solonian gesture to some degree. Jacoby, in any event, went so far as to argue that along

11. By the term "state," I mean that dimension of the *polis* that consisted in the aggregate collection of offices, duties, laws, and powers that claim exclusive authority to make decisions and carry them out within the *polis*. The state is thus only a dimension of the *polis*, which I take to encompass a community's totality with regard to territoriality, identity, and citizenship. I use the term mostly in the introduction so as to avoid confusion with the *polis* as I seek to probe and undercut the secularization hypothesis, for which the notion of the state as intrinsically separate from civil society and private life is a *sine qua non*. In the rest of the book, I usually employ *polis* to cover the sovereign authority of laws, offices, and institutions (or totality thereof) since this is the appropriate Athenian term and therefore less prejudicial to our understanding. For an incisive and useful examination of the *polis* with regard to concepts of state, see Hansen (1998).

12. Jacoby (1944), 69–70. For the equation of the Eupatridai and the *genê*, see, for example, Ferguson (1938), 51; Wade-Gery (1958), 86–110; Jacoby (1949), 263–64; Feaver (1957), 128; cf. J. Oliver (1950), 32 and n. 17.

with the Genesia Solon created *ex nihilo* a number of cults whose mass appeal would have cemented popular commitment to the state as well as to the laws that he promulgated against the elite.[13] Jacoby can be read to argue, therefore, that not only did the *polis* take over certain religious prerogatives of the elite and share them among all citizens but the *polis* also prevented the elite from instituting new privileges that might remain under their control exclusively. In effect, Jacoby's argument stands as a "secularization" hypothesis in which Solon magnified the religious power of the *polis* at the expense of the elite.

That argument assumes, of course, that the elite were homologous with the *genê*, which is a doubtful proposition for several reasons that bear manifestly both on the duties and powers of sacred treasurers like Khairion and also on the subsequent development of their duties relative to those of the *genê* and their priests. First, the sources at issue might well have confused the situation in archaic Athens for that of Roman Athens, when this equation of elite and *genê* did hold largely true.[14] Second, even if a substantial proportion of the elite did in fact belong to such groups, there is no evidence to suggest that Athenians of lower status did not also belong to them.[15] To deprive the *genê* of the privilege of conducting private rites might well have denied a broad swath of Athenian society its right to participate in its own religious life. Therefore, the motive attributed to Solon, namely, to break the religious influence of the elite, is not compelling. Some purpose other than to abrogate the elite's hereditary hold on religion might therefore have lain behind Solon's expansion of the *polis*' financial and administrative commitment to religious life. Solon might have created the Genesia, but there is little to recommend Jacoby's unsubstantiated claim that the Genesia replaced or excluded private celebrations and rites.[16] Intrigu-

---

13. Jacoby (1944).
14. Elite families like the Alkmaionidai could, until perhaps the end of the fourth century, also be described by the term *genos* even when they had no exclusive claim on rites in a religious cult: Ismard (2010), 58–61; Duplouy (2003), 13–17; Duplouy (2002), 6–10; Figueira (1984); Bourriot (1976), 553–60; Dickie (1979); cf. Roussel (1976), 51–78*bis*. Dittenberger (1885), 3, may have been the first to question the idea that the elite and the *genê* were one and the same. On *genê* in Roman sources see, for example, J. Oliver (1970) and (1980).
15. A closely allied notion is that possession of wealth acquired by means other than mere birth might already have been an important factor in determining the make up of the elite. On wealth as the defining feature of the archaic elite, see Duplouy (2003) and (2002); Van Wees (2000); Stein-Hölkeskamp (1989), 57–138; Stahl (1987), 79–105; Forsdyke (2005), 11–12.
16. Parker (1996), 48–49, finds Jacoby's essential argument plausible but points out that it gives short schrift to the extent of public religion prior to Solon and that it remains difficult to associate with Solon the bevy of other cults or religion institutions Jacoby attributes to him; cf. Parker "Polytheism" (2005), 23–32; Blok (2006), 213 n. 46. Humphries (2004), 134–39, argues that the mere presence of the state cannot be allowed to obscure local initiative as if the state were merely the pan-Athenian

ingly, Jacoby cited as pivotal evidence two lexicographical sources (one claiming the authority of Solon himself in the *axones* that contained his laws) that indicate that, as established by Solon, the sacrifices held for the Genesia were given by the *polis* at public expense.[17] Those sources perhaps offer a critical window into the workings of the early *polis*, but Jacoby was regrettably uninterested in what it meant for Solon to commit the *polis* in this way to a permanent administrative and financial obligation beyond serving his claim that these publicly funded festivals must have either absorbed or displaced those of the *genê* alone. A simpler hypothesis is that Solon merely endowed a preexisting Genesia with public funds for the first time. This would have been no small step, possibly rendering the public celebration far grander (by virtue of great expenditure and mass audience) than all of the other competing private celebrations held by *genê*, if, of course, one grants the conflict of state and *genê* much credit at all.

That alternative reading of the evidence raises, paradoxically perhaps, an intriguing facet of the "secularization" hypothesis, namely, that the momentary intervention of the state, through Solon or anyone else in the sixth century, ought to have catalyzed some of those features of Athenian government that tended to persist across the centuries. Events such as a sweeping reform of laws might offer a relatively efficient explanation both for the long-term growth in the state's relative complexity and also the numerous magistrates who were responsible for sacred property. Such an argument has long been attractive and some scholars have invoked it to explain the process as one in which the state grew at the expense of those religious institutions that were no longer politically efficient, especially with respect to the advent of the democracy.[18] That

polis and points especially to the case of Eleusis as evidence for initiative coming from a highly autonomous pair of *genê*, the Kerykes and Eumolpidai.

17. Jacoby (1944), 67 n. 8, on *Anecd.Bekk.* vol. 1, Lex. Rhet. p. 240 no. 28, of which the key passage is τὰ μὲν δημοτελῆ θύματα ἡ πόλις δίδωσιν (the other source is Harp. s.v. δημοτελῆ καὶ δημοτικὰ ἱερὰ). Lex. Rhet. employs the present tense and thus indicates continued funding by the *polis* well after Solon, but Jacoby, 70, claims that Solon had abolished the practice of *genê* funding their own festivals for ancestors (followed, for example, by Roussel [1976], 67). Schlaifer (1940), 237–38, had already argued against this idea as being simply baseless, founded as it was on Plutarch's statement (*Thes.* 25.2) that Theseus had granted to the Eupatridai a monopoly of political and religious offices as well as the power to interpret laws and exegetical matters. Deubner (1932), 214, argued that the cult of the Semnai was the onetime province of the Eupatridai by virtue of their genealogical(!) connection to Orestes (based on Sophokles' *Elektra*). See now also Duplouy (2003), 19–21, Connor (1988), 169, and Rhodes (1993), 67–68 and 71–73, on that and related texts positing some ancestral distribution of powers among the populace (e.g., Strabo [8.7.1 C383] claims also that Ion divided the population into four parts, and to one granted the sole power to act as *hieropoioi*).

18. Davies' (1988) argument that the state made religious institutions more efficient as it "emancipated"

notion would on its surface appear more inherently plausible, if only because it encourages us to move beyond lone personalities like that of Solon, whose legendary status might too easily cloud our understanding. But it is not altogether clear how strife on the order of state and elite would be sufficient to create so self-aggrandizing a state as Jacoby envisaged, much less lead to the robust sacral administration of the fourth century. Such conflict hardly seems implicit in *Ath.Pol.*'s straightforward statement that in 508/7 Kleisthenes allowed the *genê*, *phratriai*, and priests to conduct their affairs and hold their privileges just as before.[19] Why Kleisthenes should have missed the opportunity to strike at elite adversaries and grant some of their religious power to the Demos when he had the opportunity to do so is difficult to explain.

Of course, such a hypothesis resolves nothing with regard to Solon himself. One can hardly ignore, moreover, how it is mainly the later, post-Kleisthenic, evidence that some have adduced to give substance to claims such as those advanced by Jacoby. Indeed, the fourth-century evidence alone manifests such a variety of ritual groups enjoying what can only be described as full autonomy over the plethora of cults and rites in which they had an interest that one might hardly consider Jacoby's thesis to have any warrant for this later era, so far removed from Solon's time as it might seem to be.[20] Mere "lateness" of evidence,

---

itself from them has proven especially influential in this regard and retains wide enough acceptance, for example, by Harrison (2006), 139, and Garland (1990), 86. The debate has largely concentrated on elucidating the historical development of Athenian priesthoods, especially the establishment of (a very few) allotted priesthoods under the democracy (e.g., Blok and Lambert [2009]; Lambert [2010]; Blok [2009]; Feaver [1957]); I address these issues further in a paper currently in progress. But the historiographic position taken up by Davies and Jacoby has other antecedents also, some of which, like that of Wade-Gery (1933), 26–27, were perceived as so extreme as to occasion special criticism from Jacoby (1949), 258–59; cf. Finley (1983), 95; J. Oliver (1950), 47 n. 25. Ismard (2010), 122–38, is the most recent critic of that hypothesis (framed more in terms of centralization by the *polis*, especially in the Lykourgan era), but his misgivings arise partly from the notion that the state itself hardly existed as a distinct entity and thus that there could be no real conflict between it and other elements of society such as the *genê*.

19. *Ath.Pol.* 21.6: τὰ δὲ γένη καὶ τὰς φρατρίας καὶ τὰς ἱερωσύνας εἴασεν ἔχειν ἑκάστους κατὰ τὰ πάτρια. Where Feaver (1957), 143, suggests that the reforms shunted aside the *genê* to the degree that they were not made essential to the new form of state, Kearns (1985), 206, posits that the creation of the ten tribes created broadly mixed groups of people that cut across the highly atomized religious landscape of old Attica and "destroyed the uniqueness of such types of special relationships without removing the particular privileges of the *genê*." Cf. Wade-Gery (1933), 26–27.

20. Connor (1988), 184–85, notes that an opposition between cult and state under the democracy is misconceived because secularization of cult by the *polis*—*if* it ever occurred—had occurred well *before* Kleisthenes' reforms. Connor also notes, 184, that it would be difficult to show how the Athenians were less religious in the fifth and fourth centuries than in the archaic period. In this vein, Whitehead (1986), 174, suggests that in Athens the trend is more accurately described as one in which public cults dominate our evidence (i.e., the sixth century) to one in which private ones appear prominently (i.e., the fourth century and beyond); cf. Blok (2010), 91 n. 86.

nevertheless, is not a cogent reason to reject its usefulness if it meets other standards of relevance and accuracy, as Jacoby's own citation of the lexicographers affirms. The abiding merit to Jacoby's thesis is that it forces one to consider just why the state apparatus should have grown as it did in the sphere of religion. In no way are we compelled to assume that because that apparatus was as extensive as it was in the fourth century, when sacred treasurers are among the most numerous of all Athenian magistrates, that this was always so, much less that it was historically inevitable. Putting it another way, Jacoby might well have asked: why is it that there should be so many sacred treasurers when the *genê* and other groups would seem to have been in a position to provide that service naturally?

In seeking an alternative to the hypothesis of state growth through conflict, M. Jameson (1988) sketched out a larger process in which the growth of the state's share in sacrifice grew largely in cooperation with the *genê* and other ritual groups, such that the whole of the sacrificial community acquired greater complexity over time. On Jameson's reading of the evidence, this process required still more magistrates to carry out the state's contribution and so ensure that the needs and demands of that enlarged community could be met in a more or less satisfactory way, and likely commenced at a very early date, also. Jameson's argument is important alone for his observation that the institutions of the *polis* might have grown merely in response to growing demand for religious rites and celebrations. His hypothesis, however, does not articulate how the state, and not ritual groups, should thus have gained so great a share of responsibility, nor does it offer an account for the property at issue. An alternative approach is to deny the potential for conflict altogether, and others have painted an expansive picture of Athenian polytheism as occupying many different forms at any given moment, and with seemingly every degree of the *polis*' official involvement—or absence thereof—in concert with *genê* and other ritual groups.[21] The old binary of "state cult," which denotes those cults equipped with public funding and sacred treasurers, over and against the *genê* and other essentially private groups, thus appears grossly inadequate because it does not capture the complexity of organization found in any one cult, and because it partakes of the same assumptions that guide the "secularization" hypothesis.[22] But we should not be confused about the fundamental relationship between

21. E.g., Parker (1996) and (2005).

22. Proponents of "state cult" include Aleshire "State Cult" (1994); Feaver (1957), 152 n. 112; Schlaifer (1943).

these entities and the *polis*. Even if these groups enjoyed an unquestioned position of ritual authority within a given cult, as usually seems to be the case, it was the *polis* alone that recognized or accorded those privileges in a manner perhaps broadly similar to a public trust, and it was the *polis* alone that retained ultimate judicial and executive authority over sacred property.[23]

Property is never far removed from the question that seemed implicit in Jacoby's work, that is, where the limits of sacred treasurers' authority lie relative to that of the priests. Wherever the *polis* supplied sacred treasurers to manage the property relating to a given cult it also endowed them with an exclusive authority to do so. In short, priests and magistrates did not enjoy equal power to extract taxes or fees, to sell goods or collect rents from sacred land, or to spend those proceeds in turn. In the *Politics*, for example, Aristotle envisions treasurers as ubiquitous, and, except for small *poleis* whose resources and needs might be very limited, he treats them as quite separate from any priesthood. The power that certain magistrates held over public sacrifices both constituted the highest levels of state and also derived in no way from priestly right (1322b22–25):

> συμβαίνει δὲ τὴν ἐπιμέλειαν ταύτην ἐνιαχοῦ μὲν εἶναι μίαν, οἷον ἐν ταῖς μικραῖς πόλεσιν, ἐνιαχοῦ δὲ πολλὰς καὶ κεχωρισμένας τῆς ἱερωσύνης, οἷον ἱεροποιοὺς καὶ ναοφύλακας καὶ ταμίας τῶν ἱερῶν χρημάτων. ἐχομένη δὲ ταύτης ἡ πρὸς τὰς θυσίας ἀφωρισμένη τὰς κοινὰς πάσας, ὅσας μὴ τοῖς ἱερεῦσιν ἀποδίδωσιν ὁ νόμος, ἀλλ ' ἀπὸ τῆς κοινῆς ἑστίας ἔχουσι τὴν τιμήν· καλοῦσι δ ' οἱ μὲν ἄρχοντας τούτους οἱ δὲ βασιλεῖς οἱ δὲ πρυτάνεις.

> [It sometimes comes to pass, as for example in small *poleis*, that there is a single magistracy with responsibility, and sometimes that there are a number of others separate, in fact, from a priesthood, such as *hieropoioi*, *naophylakes*, and *tamiai* of *hiera* (sacred) property. Next, there is the magistracy that is responsible for all public sacrifices, however many the law does not give over to the priests, but (those who serve in this position) possess their honor from the common hearth. Some call these *arkhontes*, and others *basileis*, and others still *prytaneis*.]

For Aristotle, schematic as his formulation is, the state represents authority that effectively outranks that of priests and the like, and much of that authority is

23. For a fuller exploration of this issue, see Ismard (2010) and my review in Bubelis (2012).

invested, at the managerial level, in the various sacred treasurers (that is, the *hieropoioi*, *naophylakes*, and *tamiai*) and at the executive level in officers such as the *arkhontes*, *basileis*, and *prytaneis* to whom the privilege of conducting certain sacrifices is granted. It is impossible to imagine how even the most influential *genos* could on its own authority mandate anything like the tax that the Athenians imposed (c. 432) in the name of Apollo on all maritime traders entering the port at Phaleron, in an act probably meant to support eventual construction of a temple there.[24] More directly, the Athenians took the property of condemned criminals, auctioned it off to benefit the *polis*' public treasury (*dêmosion*), and subsequently gave a tithe (an *epidekaton*) over to Athena. While this seizure was made in the goddess' name, her treasurers—not her priestesses—had responsibility for the proceeds.[25] This is to say nothing of all the other measures that the *polis* might employ in order to increase the resources that the *polis* could devote to one religious purpose or another, the budget for which must surely have exceeded the collective wealth of the *genê* by a significant magnitude.

Parallel to such exclusive power over the management of resources, the classical *polis* also possessed an absolute judicial authority such as would be necessary for the sacred treasurers to exercise the fullest control possible. Again, there is no evidence that the *polis* aggrandized its authority with the express purpose of depriving priests of any special, legitimate claim to some element of state power. As pointed out earlier, on occasion the *polis* might concede or delegate that authority to a particular group as a kind of public trust, but there is no evidence that it surrendered any and all claims to it. No example of an Athenian sacred law attributes any judicial authority to priests.[26] Rather, by default it is the *polis* that must enforce all the laws that relate to sacred affairs. For that reason alone, one should doubt whether Khairion was under any compulsion whatsoever to consult with the priestess of Athena concerning the propriety of his own gift.

Moreover, little evidence survives to suggest that Athenian priests in and of

---

24. *IG* I[3] 130.

25. E.g., And. 1.96; *IG* I[3] 46, *ll.* 28–29. For further discussion, see chapter 2.

26. What are commonly called "sacred laws" include various rules, prohibitions, and penalties that are almost always known solely from inscriptions (see *NGSL*) and often do not specify which particular entity established them and by what entity they are to be enforced. With regard to their legal sanction, both Naiden (2006) and Parker "Law" (2005) show that while such laws rested on deeply held beliefs that divine punishment was inevitable and severe, they also dovetailed with the regular judicial structure (i.e., without need of special religious courts or authorities); cf. Todd (1993), 307–10.

themselves typically served as their own treasurers in place of magistrates, even where the cult was so small or lacking in popularity that it would likely have no benefit of magistrates whatsoever. The only Athenian example of priests who did act as their own *tamiai* is that of the priests of Asklepios, who came not from an ancestral *genos* but were chosen by allotment from the general citizenry once, it appears, the cult's founding family died out in the mid-fourth century.[27] Of special interest here is a much earlier law of c. 460 by which the *polis* regulated how the *genê* of the Eumolpidai and Kerykes, and the priestess of Demeter (drawn from the *genos* of the Philleidai), collected fees for their services from prospective initiates into the Eleusinian Mysteries. By this measure, the *polis* did assume an umbrella of authority over property insofar as it stipulated the value of the fees involved and which parties had the right to collect them. Moreover, the *polis* thus directed its principal sacred treasurers for Eleusis (the *hieropoioi*) to safeguard upon the akropolis the proceeds, which appear to have remained the property of Demeter and Kore.[28] Why the Athenians collectively stepped in to regulate how the *genê* collected these fees, and why they should thereafter have been managed by *hieropoioi* from the *polis* is hardly clear but the precision of the law's fragmentary text suggests a correspondingly specific circumstance, and not at all a general move against these two or any other *genê*. Moreover, the text might even support a reading in favor of the *genê*, namely, that the law protects their privileges from competing *genê* who might advance their own claim to the money in question.

In any case, the law establishes that the *polis*' magistrates shall act as the exclusive treasurers of the relevant funds. One might take the law as evidence in support of the "secularization" hypothesis, whereby the *genê* were stripped of what had been their unquestioned domain. But the richer and more complete evidence of the fourth century reveals these *genê* as actively cooperating in the management of resources for the cult of Demeter and Kore, almost as if they themselves were magistrates but apparently not subject to the same level of accountability.[29] Priests and their ritual assistants might well have fallen outside

27. Priests: Aleshire (1989), 82–83. If Aleshire is correct in suggesting, 74–75, that as early as the fourth century the priesthood of Asklepios amounted to a kind of liturgy then this post would be even more of an outlier. More typical is the priestess who handed votives over to the *epistatai* of the cult of Artemis Brauronia (*IG* II^2 1524, of 353/2), for which see Linders (1972), 52 (cf. 72).

28. *IG* I^3 6 C (= *I.Eleusis* 19), *ll.* 20–31.

29. The *genê* not only controlled some proportion of the gods' property but also administered their own affairs in an unusually corporate sense, and, at least in the late fourth century, possessed "magistrates" *(arkhontes)* of their own. Strikingly, these *arkhontes* are attested in 329/8 as collecting on behalf of the Two Goddesses an odd type of rent from peculiar plots of land, the proceeds of which they

of the liabilities imposed on magistrates altogether precisely because they did not customarily exercise authority over property (that is, beyond a very limited array of ritual objects and the like).[30] For the Athenians, priests and magistrates constituted two different kinds of authority.

A sundry of ritual groups were, furthermore, in full possession of their own wealth and had the legal capacity to manage it accordingly. Surviving documents from some of these groups, which are very similar to those of the *polis* and its demes in style and content, suggest that property belonged to them exclusively as a corporate group. In turn, ritual groups might collect income from that property by employing financial techniques closely parallel to, but entirely separate from, a number of those deployed by the state.[31] Such groups might direct funds to whatever end they saw fit, even to the particular sacrifices or rituals with which they and the *polis* were jointly concerned or to some purpose of entirely their own undertaking.[32] Such autonomy, of course, encourages the view that where the *polis* intervened it did so where matters concerned it directly and unavoidably, and thus left these groups to develop their own finan-

---

termed "first-fruits" (*aparkhai*) as if it were *hiera* wealth and not *hosia* as one might expect (as per my discussion in later chapters of this book): *IG* II^2 1672 add. p. 812, *l.* 252 (= *I.Eleusis* 177). The plot of land at issue here is a special area known as the Rharia, concerning which see now Papazarkadas (2011), 34 n. 83, 39–40, 60–61, 207.

30. The key text cited in support of priests being subject to procedures of accountability used for magistrates (*euthynai*) is often made to prove what it does not, in fact, show. Aeschines (3.18) merely claims that those particular members of the *genê* who took sacrificial perquisites (*gera*) or offered prayers on behalf of the *polis* were subject to *euthynai* (i.e., as if regular magistrates), which Dittenberger (1885), 32, and Ferguson (1932), 33 n. 5, took to apply to the money and victims supplied by the *polis* for these rites. But there is no independent evidence for such a procedure as applied to a whole *genos* (*pace* Garland (1990), 86). In a variation of the "secularization" hypothesis, Aleshire "Demos" and now Blok and Lambert (2009) argue that under the Athenian democracy priesthoods were often chosen by means of allotment from an approved list (*prokrisis*), and that all were subject to the *euthyna* as were all other magistrates. But Aeschines' statement applies only to those whom he identifies, not to all (prospective) priests. The legal reason behind what Aeschines describes is that the *euthyna* can only apply to those members of a *genos* who were serving with the authority of regular magistrates in specific situations where the presence of such men was ritually required in a manner that circumvented the adlection of normal magistrates, namely, those involving sensitive matters of cult, such as those described in *Ath.Pol.* (57.1) and the epigraphic record (e.g., *I.Eleusis* 138).
31. For example, at least some *genê* in the fourth century advanced monetary loans, as shown by one *horos* (*IG* II^2 2670; = Finley [1951] no. 146) that marks land hypothecated to a *genos*, a tribe, and a deme for a woman's dowry. This grouping of creditors suggests that the *genos* in question (the Lykomidai) advanced part of a loan in concert with a tribe and deme. Some *genê* also let out property, as for example the Salaminioi in their arbitrated separation agreement of 363/2 (Rhodes/Osborne 37, *ll.* 24, 58–61, 84, 94–95).
32. There is, therefore, a clear distinction between property owned outright by a *genos* and that controlled by it within the framework of a cult to which the *polis* also supplied magistrates, as Schlaifer (1940), 238, correctly observes. That the two had been at one time mixed or otherwise indistinguishable appears implicit in the arguments of Jacoby and others, for which see the discussion above.

cial machinery as they saw fit. In accord with Jameson's hypothesis, then, the *polis* perhaps created more magistracies and took on more financial responsibility through a long series of legal acts that seemed necessary only when the circumstances of a given cult's management appeared in need of reform. Such growth need not betoken systemic conflict, much less aggression, on the part of the *polis*.

We return, nonetheless, to a central point. Judicial authority over whatever property was earmarked for communal religious life but which was not owned outright by a *genos*, similar group, or an individual lay ultimately with the state. While some magistrates possessed special legal powers above that of ordinary citizens, in classical Athenian law priests do not seem to have possessed any authority to act on their own initiative beyond the same capacity to arrest or denounce that was available to every citizen.[33] If any priest invoked the very serious charges of impiety (*asebeia*), whose penalty was capital, then determination by a court made up of regular citizens was required.[34] Modern attempts to define lexically what makes a Greek (or at least an Athenian) priest a priest founder on the very question of property, as if we are uncomfortable with the notion that ritual could be so dependent on the provision of money and other resources.[35] In recent accounts, the various subsidiary priests or ritual attendants are often termed cultic or sacral "personnel," or even "officials."[36] This difficulty suggests that there still remains some uncertainty as to how best to categorize the various actors since no clear comprehensive exposition of sacral administration has yet been produced, and understandably so in light of the "secularization" hypothesis. We cannot forget, however, that while the rest of

33. Migeotte (2006) shows that priestly and political authority were separated from one another in most communities and that this division persisted well past the classical era. Dignas (2002) demonstrates that such division holds less true in the Hellenistic and Roman eras in those regions (of Anatolia, in her study) where the *polis* was not always the relevant political unit. In his comments to Migeotte, Dreher (2006), 249–51, also suggests that this pattern finds its fractal in the role of Greek priests as occasional or partial caretakers of sanctuaries and property, but within and under the authority of the *polis*.

34. Of note is the trial and execution of Arkhias the Eleusinian *hierophantês* for performing at the Haloa festival a sacrifice that, because the rites belonged exclusively to the priestess of Demeter, constituted an act of *asebeia*: [Dem.] 59.116. In essence, the court convicted one priest for violating the sacral privileges of another.

35. Chaniotis (2008) argues that the running of a sanctuary did not require ritual experience, and that this is a key element in what defined Greek priests (i.e., they were not drawn from a schooled, priestly caste as in other ancient and modern religions). This argument, however, undercuts the imperative to discover where in the life of a sanctuary experience *was* necessary, that is, among at least some of its magistrates (and potentially its priests, too). Cf. Dignas and Trampedach (2008).

36. E.g., Cole (2008), 66; Clinton (1974).

the *polis* deeply respected the religious primacy of priestly figures and their ritual obligations, it was the *polis* that exercised ultimate authority, and not they.

History and the Sacred Treasurers

As to what sort of history of property and institutions this book aims to be, at all times the anchor is the sacred treasurers, concerning whom there is a pressing need for an accurate description. Syntheses that were compiled over the last century and beyond were meant to fulfill basic encyclopedic aims and at best they provide only a brief survey of the evidence then known. These treatments, furthermore, often aimed to provide a synchronic picture of a given office and its customary tasks as if what could be achieved from mixing evidence pertaining to various cults and periods, and even whole cities, would amount to an accurate enough picture of the timeless, indeed universal, essentials.[37] Beyond the encyclopedic sketches, nonetheless, what scholarship there is on the sacred treasurers has focused almost exclusively on some or another constricted aspect of the general apparatus of institutions in which they operated but has failed to see the bigger picture and tackle the important questions surrounding those institutions. Moreover, such efforts have confined themselves to elucidating from a technical point of view a generally narrow but relatively abundant stream of epigraphic evidence from the fifth and fourth centuries and to the very limited financial questions that it best serves. This book also aims to contribute to those questions, and its arguments concerning such matters as the *polis*' budget and the origins of *hosia* wealth offer what I hope are useful contributions to knowledge; but it does so from a novel, wider perspective and with different aims than anything currently available.[38]

Otherwise, the few monographs or articles of any size that have attempted to treat this topic in some manner have remained firmly within the framework offered by the inscribed inventories of the treasuries atop the Athenian akropolis and dating solely to the fifth and fourth centuries. W. Ferguson (1932) on the

37. E.g., Schwahn (1932); Oehler (1913), Hannel (1901).

38. Only after the completion of the manuscript for this book (spring 2013) did I become aware of a new monograph on Athenian public finance by H. van Wees (*Ships and Silver, Taxes and Tribute: A Fiscal History of Archaic Athens* [London: 2013]). While I have been completely unable to respond to his ideas and arguments, van Wees' book is a most welcome development, and I anticipate that it will stimulate much in the way of productive discussion and work in the coming years.

tamiai of Athena, T. Linders on the *epistatai* of Artemis Brauronia (1972), and M. Cavanaugh on the *hieropoioi* and *epistatai* of Eleusis (1996) are especially noteworthy in this regard. Tellingly, however, the best monograph on sacred treasurers of any kind, Linders' (1975) work on the board known as the *tamiai* of the Other Gods (created in 433/2), was written in part so as to refute a version of the "secularization" hypothesis advanced by G. Busolt (1920 and 1926).[39] Anchored to that hypothesis for so long, our knowledge of the treasurers and the property under their control has thus advanced only by fits and starts. One further reason for that laggard progress is that study of the sacred treasurers has traditionally been undertaken only to advance other subjects. This is particularly true with regard to the epigraphy of fifth-century imperial Athens and its Delian League. Although surprisingly rich in number and quality, and hardly exhausted with respect to their potential knowledge, the surviving texts are usually made to answer questions far removed from the fact that they were either produced by sacred treasurers or directly relevant to their service. As a consequence, these texts have weighed so heavily in what little study of sacral property there has been as to obscure the actual state of our knowledge. This deficiency still holds true even for V. Chankowski (2008), B. Dignas (2002), L. Samons (2000), and others, all of whom have recently done much to elucidate the structure of sacral finance (though, of course, their focal points lie elsewhere).[40] Yet, these particular treatments rely heavily for their contextual discussion of Athens' emblematic sacred treasurers on the accounts of Ferguson, Linders, and the few others who have touched on the subject. By virtue of their illuminating treatments, nonetheless, it may be fairly said that these studies also demonstrate that the exploration of the larger institutional context of sacred property can profit our general knowledge of Athens considerably.

In order to help fill the outstanding deficit left by such accounts, this book attempts to do several things. First, it offers what amounts to the fullest description of the treasurers to appear, but does so selectively. The *tamiai* of Athena are

39. On nothing less than the second line of her own treatment, Linders (1975), 1, cites Busolt's definition (Busolt/Swoboda [1926], 1138–39, of the treasurers; cf. Schwahn (1932), col. 2113. In Busolt's version, the *tamiai* were always secular officials, first serving the Homeric kings as (female and servile!) household administrators until the rise of the aristocratic state turned them into (male) municipal magistrates, for which see the fuller version in Busolt/Swoboda (1920), 588–90; cf. Schwahn (1932), col. 2100. The connection between the female figures of Homeric myth (e.g., Eurykleia, *Od.* 2.345), other mythical (male, high-status) figures (e.g., Aiolos, *Od.* 10.1–79), and the high-status male office of historical Athens appears to be one only of broad linguistic affinity, for which see chapter 4, n. 1.

40. E.g., Chankowski (2008), 134–46; Dignas (2002), 30–35 (citing also, 15 n. 11, Solon 4 West). Samons (2000), 28–83; cf. Hamilton (2000), 247–76.

awarded pride of place because they are the key to understanding the whole system, and others are discussed only where particularly relevant.[41] The express purpose of the book, after all, is to expose the main lines of historical development for the institutions surrounding sacred property going back to Solon and his laws, not to offer anything like a catalogue or a merely synoptic description. Second, by elucidating the nature of that property and its likely development, this book presents a significant reappraisal of the Athenian public economy that does not simply move past the debates and intellectual stalemate of prior efforts but moves in an altogether new direction. Just as sacral finance and its administration figured so conspicuously in the *polis*' constitutional structures, politics, religion, and economy, so too they ought to occupy a central place in scholars' efforts to understand that *polis*. Third, my account of Solon and particular dimensions of his laws is intended to open up new horizons on this seminal figure and his legacy. This book cannot explore at length the whole of Solon's reforms but rather it aims to illuminate only a discrete part thereof whose effects on the Athenian body politic were far more consequential than one might at first suspect. Far beyond the momentary political crisis that occasioned his reforms, Solon emerges from this study as the unwitting catalyst behind significant development in the *polis*' institutions over the ensuing centuries.

The book's fundamental arc transits the highly personal politics of the early sixth century, to which Solon's laws were a response, to the less personal and more abstract protocols, property arrangements, and magistracies of the fourth-century democracy. Across that arc I have worked to reconstruct not only Solon's key law on the *tamiai* of Athena and his related measures pertaining to other magistrates but also many other elements of Athenian history, ranging from the electoral dynamics of the archaic period to magistrates' use of the gods' precious vessels and equipment for sacrificial meals. At every juncture I have hewn assiduously to the evidence, whether documentary, literary, or archaeological in nature, and the method that I employed was fundamentally inductive in origin. While I have asked hard questions of the evidence such as to account best for its patterns and detail, inevitably for many of the critical issues that we would like to have answered there is simply no evidence available. Accordingly, the reader should bear in mind that what I offer is an historical

41. The sacred treasurers of the Attic demes have already benefited from good, though by no means exhaustive, treatment from Whitehead (1986) and Georgoudi (2007).

reconstruction, especially for sixth-century Athens, even where my presentation of particular matters may rightfully stand as authoritative. A single discovery, such as an inscription, may radically re-shape our understanding of a specific problem, and perhaps even of the thesis that I present. Pending any such breakthroughs, however, the book must advance an historical account that is internally coherent such that not only are its gaps clearly visible but that its thesis can accommodate those new discoveries. The book's argumentation thus stands as a tissue of many interlocking responses to specific problems in the evidence as much as to an overarching one, and for which I proffer what I believe to be the most plausible solutions. In sum, if I am at all successful in this effort no account of Athenian history or society can henceforth neglect to consider the centrality of sacral property and its institutions, whether that involves the staging of dramatic festivals or the operations of the Delian League.

Chapter 1 explicates Solon's law on the *tamiai* of Athena and situates it historically as a major piece of legislation by which Solon sought to balance the interests of the *polis* with politically ambitious men. Not only did the law establish procedural limits on electioneering by those seeking office as a *tamias* but conceded to the elite that this post would only draw its members from the wealthiest of Athenians, which the law defined henceforth as the census class of *pentakosiomedimnoi*. Chapter 2 extends that analysis to the more fragmentary evidence for other laws of the same type, all of which appear to have stipulated the duties of sacred treasurers and other important magistrates with respect to sacrifices, festivals, and the like. While Solon's laws were likely intended to render magistrates more accountable to the Areiopagos, for which the census classes were indispensable, they had the effect of establishing a positive standard that magistrates could use in turn to elicit further resources from the *polis* in pursuit of their duties.

In chapter 3, I turn to examine such monuments as Khairion's altar as indicators, even after Solon, of a highly competitive milieu in which personal power and influence especially mattered. In addition, I examine the classical evidence for electoral patronage and argue that it echoes a robust dynamic of the archaic period in which wealthy Athenians deployed their own fortunes and resources to stage sacrifices and the like in hopes of winning favor with their tribal electorate. There was a strong incentive, therefore, to acquire an office whose responsibilities and resources could in turn be used to elevate one's electoral superiority. Notwithstanding the straitened political environment of Athens under the Peisistratidai, electoral banqueting likely thrived. As the tyrants and their allies pursued offices and prestige, they placed great demands on the *polis* to provide those resources of money, property, and manpower that were the lifeblood of Athenian religious and political life. Even as it altered some important features of the *polis*' institutions, the early democracy nonetheless affirmed the essential calculus governing sacred property and, in turn, accelerated a transformation that was probably underway already.

The second half of the book provides a thorough treatment of that metamorphosis. Through the course of the democracy, the Athenians retained and fully supported a particular kind of property (*hiera*) that was by nature as fiscally static as it was ritually sacred. As I explore in chapter 4, the *tamiai* of Athena continued to steward the goddess' *hiera* wealth as they likely had in the archaic period, and they maintained a corresponding measure of dignity and prestige. Although *hiera* encompassed cult-statues and votives of all sorts, a sizeable portion of it consisted of equipment for sacrifice and banqueting, which the *tamiai* dispensed both for use as ritual pomp and also to serve at special meals enjoyed by the *polis*' most senior magistrates. But the Athenians also created a new form of sacred property (*hosia*) that could aid them in funding their various religious needs better than existing properties and institutions could.

Chapter 5 illuminates the archaic origins of *hosia* wealth and the likely budgetary structures of pre-democratic Athens, in which the *polis* maintained a fairly simple public treasury that funded religious expenditures directly. Chapter 6, finally, shows how the Athenians used *hosia* wealth to generate cash income on a continuous basis and that it was independent of the public treasury except where an initial allocation of money was required. But where it came to the major expenditures for religious life, the Athenians created new budgetary structures and procedures because the cost of events like the Panathenaia far outstripped what *hosia* could normally provide. This system, nevertheless, required the attention and labor of many more magistracies than had existed at its dawn, few of whom possessed the kind of visible prestige that was a hallmark of the *tamiai* of Athena and so tangible in Khairion's great altar.

CHAPTER 1

Solon's Law on the *Tamiai*

This chapter examines a law of Solon regarding the single most important college of sacred treasurers, the *tamiai* of Athena, and which appears to be of much greater importance than previously understood. The law was a seminal innovation for several reasons. Solon exercised a trade-off in which he subordinated certain elite interests to those of the *polis* in return for assuring the elite that to be a *tamias* would remain their exclusive privilege. The law's restrictive feature was that it combined the traditionally open election of magistrates at a tribal level with a second, but randomized, procedure at the pan-Athenian one. The law ensured that men could compete at the level of their tribes, whose importance should not be underestimated, even as it precluded the sort of pan-Athenian competition that proved disruptive in the case of the highest offices of state. But because the law also mandated that *tamiai* could only come from a wholly new census class that henceforth consisted solely of the wealthiest Athenians, it guaranteed its members political and social preeminence. Established by Solon as the chief authority over the *polis*' magistrates, the Council of the Areiopagos acquired control over the *tamiai* and by extension over all lesser magistrates that necessarily fell into the lower classes. The census classes offered the Areiopagos a useful instrument by which it could maintain its control without overt demonstrations of power. While membership in a given class established one's ability to obtain a certain level of office, and hence to enjoy a corresponding level of prestige, an official determination of what property one possessed likely served as the basis for payment of fines if the Areiopagos should condemn one for offenses committed while in office.

By virtue of that constitutional mixture, the law served as the key model by which the Athenian democracy would eventually reform the highest office of all in the *polis*, that of the nine *arkhontes*. To unravel the relationship of the law to that later measure illuminates much of the course of early Athenian constitutional and political history. Because Solon's law on the *tamiai* established the parameters of that office for centuries to follow and ensured that the office would remain among the most senior magistracies of the *polis*, its repercussions for the history of sacred property and its management cannot be ignored.

Selection and Its Mechanics in Solon's Law: The Evidence of The Constitution of the Athenians *(*Ath.Pol.*)*

For our direct knowledge of the law, we are almost entirely dependent on several quotations of it in *Ath.Pol.*, notwithstanding those passages from Aristotle, the Attic orators, and inscriptions that provide critical help. For *Ath.Pol.*'s author, the law's significance lay principally in how it arranged for the Athenians to choose certain men to fill a whole college of *tamiai*. Although *Ath.Pol.* does not provide a complete text of this law, it does provide critical information about the law when first invoking it to explain a similar measure pertaining to the chief magistrates of Athens, the nine *arkhontes*. Given the many different statutes at issue in this chapter, I label hereafter this one law as Solon's Law on the Tamiai (or merely, the Law) for ease of reference:

> 8.1–2 τὰς δ ᾿ ἀρχὰς ἐποίησε κλ[η]ρωτὰς ἐκ προκρίτων, οὓς ἑκάστη προκρίνειε τῶν φυλῶν. προύκρινεν δ ᾿ εἰς τοὺς ἐννέα ἄρχοντας ἑκάστη δέκα, καὶ τούτους ἐ̣κλήρουν· ὅθεν ἔτι διαμένει ταῖς φυλαῖς τὸ δέκα κληρο[ῦ]ν ἑκάστην, εἶτ ᾿ ἐκ τούτων κυαμεύει[ν]. σημεῖον δ ᾿ ὅτι κληρωτὰς ἐποιήσεν ἐκ τῶν τιμημάτων ὁ περὶ τῶν ταμίων νόμος, ὧι χρώμενοι δια[τελ]οῦσιν ἔτι καὶ νῦν. κελεύει γὰρ κληροῦν τοὺς ταμίας ἐκ πεντακοσιομεδίμνων. (2) [Σόλ]ων μὲν οὖν οὕτως ἐνομοθέτησεν περὶ τῶν ἐννέα ἀρχόντων. τὸ δ̣ ᾿ ἀρχαῖον ἡ ἐν ᾿Αρ[εί]ω̣ι [πάγωι βου]λὴ ἀνακαλεσαμένη καὶ κρίνασα καθ ᾿ αὑτὴν τὸν ἐπιτήδειον ἐφ ᾿ ἑκάστηι τῶν ἀρχῶν ἐπ ᾿ [ἐ]νια[υτ]ὸν δ̣[ιατάξ]α̣σ̣α ἀπέστελλεν.
>
> [(1) He established the magistracies as allotted from a select group, whose members each of the tribes would select beforehand. Each of the tribes selected ten men (as candidates) for the magistracies of the nine *arkhontes*, and they allotted these men. From which time still (the law) distributes each (magistracy)

to the tribes for them to allot ten (men), then (for each magistracy itself) to allot (them by *kyamos*, "bean") from these (preselected) men. The proof is that the Law on the Tamiai, which they continue to use still even now, rendered (offices) as allotted from the census classes. For the Law directs that the *tamiai* be allotted from the *pentakosiomedimnoi*. (2) Solon thus established a law concerning the nine *arkhontes*. Formerly, the Areiopagos having summoned and judged by itself the man appropriate for each of the magistracies assigned them for a year and despatched them.]

A later, unconnected, citation pertains only to the *tamiai* themselves in the late 330s or early 320s when *Ath.Pol.* was written:

> 47.1 πρῶτον μὲν γὰρ οἱ ταμίαι τῆς 'Αθηνᾶς εἰσὶ μὲν δέκα, κλ[ηρο]ῦται δ ' εἷς ἐκ τῆς φυλῆς, ἐκ πεντακοσιομεδίμνων κατὰ τὸν Σόλωνος νόμον· ἔ̣τ̣ι γ[ὰρ ὁ] νόμος κύριός ἐστιν.
>
> [First, the *tamiai* of Athena are ten in number, and each is allotted from the tribe, from the *pentakosiomedimnoi* by dint of the law of Solon. For the Law is still valid.]

In neither passage does *Ath.Pol.* provide either a direct quotation of the Law in any part or state Solon's supposed intentions.[1] While these two passages constitute our most direct source for the Law, another passage in *Ath.Pol.* (22.5) notes a reform of 487/6, which stipulated that the nine *arkhontes* were to be chosen by lot from a pool advanced by the ten Kleisthenic tribes of the democracy:

> ἐπὶ Τελεσίνου ἄρχοντος ἐκυάμευσαν τοὺς ἐννέα ἄρχοντας κατὰ φυλὰς ἐκ τῶν προκριθέντων ὑπὸ τῶν δημοτῶν ἑκατὸν τότε μετὰ τὴν τυραννίδα πρῶτον.
>
> [When Telesinos was eponymous *arkhôn* (487/6) they chose for the first time after the tyranny the nine *arkhontes* by means of the lot (*kyamos*)—according to tribe—from those one hundred men who were preselected by the demesmen.]

It is this act that I label for convenience and clarity as the Reform, since in conjunction with the first passage (8.1–2) this notice appears to mean that the

1. F 150a and b Ruschenbusch, respectively.

Athenians only reestablished what they believed to be a law of Solon on this very subject, and therefore that the law of 487/6 was a reform, or return, to older legislation. As I shall show later, this was likely a new law and not Solonian, but for ease of reference I will refer to it only as *Ath.Pol.* understands it: a Reform (and duly capitalized hereafter, like the Law). Brief as they are, these passages together beget several interrelated problems, first among which is the relationship of the Law to the Reform, particularly with regard to the methods by which *Ath.Pol.* believes men were chosen to be *arkhontes* or *tamiai*. A second issue is the chronological and hence historiographic relationship between the two measures, and this impinges on whether the Law is in fact authentic or is something of a historiographic mirage.

It is the method of selection that offers the most promising route by which to untangle those connections. An obvious conundrum, nonetheless, arises from the fact that *Ath.Pol.* specifies that the method by which *arkhontes* and *tamiai* alike were to be chosen was a form of allotment, or sortition. The mechanics of the procedure need not have been very complex, but they certainly could be so if judged by other examples where sortition was used. As *Ath.Pol.* refers to the procedure (8.1; 22.5), the Athenians somehow either employed a number of beans (*kyamos*, in the singular) as counters or tokens, each one presumably standing in for a given candidate, or they utilized a method and objects that could easily be likened to such objects. A few Athenian inscriptions and other texts from the democracy suggest that in *Ath.Pol.*'s time the term might then have been completely generic and thus without particular significance, though that cannot be assured in the case of the Law if *Ath.Pol.* correctly reports this dimension of it.[2] While the physical and organizational dimensions of the procedure could be quite simple, their purpose is most intriguing. Described implicitly by the first line of *Ath.Pol.* (8.1) as *klêrôsis ek prokritôn* ("allotment from a select group"), the procedure must have encompassed at least two stages through which prospective *tamiai* would pass, resulting in fewer candidates at each stage before the final group was assembled as the next annual college of *tamiai*. The first stage, one might presume, will have consisted of choosing, by some means or another, one group of candidates first (thus reflected in the prepositional prefix *pro-* in *ek prokritôn*), and the second stage

2. E.g., *IG* I^3 41, *l.* 105; 258, *l.* 13; And. 1.96. The lexicographers (for which, see Oehler [1922] and Ehrenberg [1927], cols. 1485–86) regularly equate *kyamos* with allotment in general (*klêros*; *klêrousthai*), which suggests that the term "*kyamos*" here merely indicates a device that symbolized the whole process and need not indicate that the Law mandated the use of beans.

will have thus determined which of those men would proceed into the college itself. In principle, the process of allotment itself might have corresponded to several stages or even represent only a single act within a more extensive set of procedures. Therefore, since *Ath.Pol.* indicates allotment, but does not specify or imply that it was used in both stages, we should be careful not to assume that it was so used. For that reason, I will hereafter use the term "simple lot" to mean only a procedure that employs the lot on a single occasion to decide the matter of selection randomly and without either appeal or proviso, whereas a "complex lot" or "complex" procedure signifies the use of sortition in conjunction with election, a second round of sortition, or some other method altogether. The same distinctions ought to apply to any other method where either, on the one hand, its simplest, unencumbered, or "pure" form could stand alone or, alternatively, it could be combined with any other sort of process. Thus, this distinction applies equally to election, which ought by default to have been the only meaningful alternative method of selection available in an Athenian context.

Nothing might seem very strange about all of that except that the evidence for the Law (and just perhaps the Reform) also constitutes nearly the only evidence for the use of allotment in Athenian administration before the advent of the democracy, and perhaps even the reforms associated with Ephialtes in the late 460s at that. On the other hand, outside of the texts that I analyze throughout this chapter, positive evidence for any electoral procedure in archaic Athens is admittedly sparse. In the *Politics* (1274b41–a2), Aristotle states clearly that in his view election was likely the standard method used prior to Solon and that the lawgiver did not alter this.[3] Our sources, moreover, do indicate clearly that the Athenians popularly elected Solon as eponymous *arkhôn* in 594.[4] As a general rule, in any case, it seems to be only after the 460s that, in keeping with

3. Later in this paragraph (1274a15–16), Aristotle also pronounces his view that Solon probably granted to the Demos the power to choose magistrates. Wallace (1989), 33 and n. 119, holds that the two statements are contradictory, and prefers to take Aristotle's latter pronouncement as authoritative (and thus that Solon broke the monopoly on choosing magistrates that he believes the Eupatridai held). However, Aristotle may have had in mind either a reform to the electorate (i.e., broadening it) or a legal stipulation that citizens (of whatever class) retained the sole power to appoint magistrates, perhaps in conjunction with a reform to that method such as I argue for in this chapter. Either possibility seems reasonable and we need not assume that Aristotle was willing to contradict himself within a few lines.

4. On the popular election of Solon (apparently with elite acceptance): Hdt. 1.29 (the Athenians as a group); *Ath.Pol.* 5.2 (which does not say precisely who chose Solon, but does use the third person plural "they elected"): ἰσχυρᾶς δὲ τῆς στάσεως οὔσης καὶ πολὺν χρόνον ἀντικαθημένων ἀλλήλοις εἵλοντο κοινῆι καὶ ἄρχοντα Σόλωνα καὶ τὴν πολιτείαν ἐπέτρεψαν αὐτῶι . . . ; Plu. *Sol.* 14.2: δεξαμένων προθύμως αὐτὸν ὡς μὲν εὔπορον τῶν πλουσίων, ὡς δὲ χρηστὸν τῶν πενήτων.

democratic ideology, allotment and not election became the standard means by which the Athenians randomized many administrative procedures, including the selection of Athenians for most magistracies and of course for its jurors to various courtrooms and the like.[5] Thereafter, direct election of magistrates was confined to only a very few offices such as that of the generals that had great impact on the security of Athens. Insofar as one can identify the underlying purpose of such randomization, it appears to have been rooted in deep suspicion that some of those volunteering for office could, if situated together in the same college, collude either to defraud the *polis* or, in the worst case, to establish a tyranny.[6] But neither condition pertains in the same way to the early sixth century, and perhaps not even very much to the democracy before the reforms of Ephialtes. Also, it was not the case that allotment was *tout court* a democratic procedure. For example, the oligarchy of the Four Hundred also employed this procedure during its brief rule in 411.[7] Moreover, allotment of one kind or another was frequently used across the Hellenic world for all manner of decisions, and often found in communities that were certainly not democracies.[8] But for Solon to have employed the lot for something so important as a constitutional matter involving high office suggests that its use was political, and perhaps strongly political at that.

Before turning to explore what Solon might have intended to accomplish, we must probe just how the Reform and the Law relate to one another. Since *Ath.Pol.*'s discovery, scholarly thought on the Law has aimed not to clarify what *klêrôsis ek prokritôn* must have been so much to as to deny its historical validity. For one, C. Lehmann-Haupt thus rejected that *Ath.Pol.* meant to say that by virtue of the Law the *tamiai* must have been selected by *klêrôsis ek prokritôn*, and argued instead that the method of allotment was, in effect, an invention of post-Kleisthenic Athens applied only to the *arkhontes*; for the *tamiai*, the method must have been simple election without any *prokrisis* since they were

5. In the *Politics* (1273b40–41, 1294b7–9), Aristotle gives us a succinct idea of that ideology as it pertained to electoral procedure, namely, that direct elections had an undemocratic character since they favored those with proven ability as might result from education and other things that wealth, high birth, and connections entail.
6. On allotment as a weapon against tyranny and corruption, see, for example: Taylor (2007), 323; Hansen (1990), 58 and n. 15; Hignett (1952), 321–26; Ledl (1914), 339–78. Aristotle also gives voice to this idea at *Pol.* 1294b7–10: λέγω δ ' οἷον δοκεῖ δημοκρατικὸν μὲν εἶναι τὸ κληρωτὰς εἶναι τὰς ἀρχάς, τὸ δ ' αἱρετὰς ὀλιγαρχικόν, καὶ δημοκρατικὸν μὲν τὸ μὴ ἀπὸ τιμήματος, ὀλιγαρχικὸν δὲ τὸ ἀπὸ τιμήματος.
7. Thuc. 8.66.1, 69.4.
8. Glotz (1907), 1401–8, still provides the most comprehensive survey of allotment.

not as important as the *arkhontes*.[9] And so the Law would disappear as a real piece of legislation. In Lehmann-Haupt's estimation, *Ath.Pol.* was dependent on an antiquarian local history of Athens, an *Atthis*, for information about the early laws of Athens, and because its author could not find information about the census requirements for the *arkhontes* as mandated by a law of Solon for this reason he *alone* cited the Law on the Tamiai even though it was not a strict parallel. In short, for Lehmann-Haupt, the two laws only roughly paralleled each other and then only on the matter of census requirements, though he felt that it was still unclear just what Solon intended them to be for the *arkhontes*.[10] But at a minimum, on that interpretation and in concert with the evidence of Aristotle (which I will introduce shortly), the Solonian law that ostensibly underpinned the Reform concerning the *arkhontes* fell into abeyance during the tyranny of the Peisistratidai, and thus had to be renewed by the democracy in 487/6. In other words, according to Lehmann-Haupt *Ath.Pol.* would have cited the Law *only* in order to prove that Solon had in fact established the census laws as later formed a critical element in the Reform pertaining to the *arkhontes* in 487/6.[11] But that reading of *Ath.Pol.* fails to persuade since it requires one *not* to take the text's citation of the parallel at face value, it ignores the value of the passage at 47.1 that provides the same information but without relation to the *arkhontes*, and it does not provide adequate grounds for viewing *Ath. Pol.*'s citation of the Law as pertaining only to census requirements. Since *Ath.Pol.* (8.1) does not specify which of the two elements of the Law provided the parallel it was seeking to demonstrate, whether the use of *klêrôsis ek prokritôn* or the census, we should consider the possibility that both elements together provide the parallel for the law on the *arkhontes*.

Taking a different tack, C. Hignett nevertheless also felt compelled to argue against the authenticity of the Law. While his claims likewise fail on much the same grounds as Lehmann-Haupt's case, with which he otherwise disagreed,

9. Lehmann-Haupt (1906), with earlier bibliography, but mostly aimed at Blass' (1903) edition of Willamovitz (1893).

10. As Hignett (1952), 324, points out, other scholars pursued Lehmann-Haupt's ideas about the tyranny erroneously and, going so far as to think that the law on the *arkhontes* was observed without interruption, were unable to account for the reform of 487/6, which must have been significant enough of a change for *Ath.Pol.* to mention it as it does.

11. Lehmann-Haupt (1906), 306–07. Ledl (1914), 359–63, also suggested that the law pertaining to the *arkhontes* was a later development without real connection to Solon. Moreover, Ledl posited that the Law was a mirage and that prior to 487/6 there was no need for *prokrisis* for the *tamiai* since their number was simply fixed as that of the Ionian tribes and, therefore, that they were selected through simple allotment. But that notion misunderstands what *prokrisis* was and mistakenly presumes that it must have depended on tribal number.

certain points in his argument illuminate the question in a still more useful manner. That is to say that to explore his, Lehmann-Haupt's, and others' arguments against the law thoroughly can only aid us in evaluating the evidence with the aim of reconstructing the law's essential features. For his part, Hignett posited that *Ath.Pol.* (22.5) had in all likelihood mistakenly inferred the method of *klêrôsis ek prokritôn* for the *tamiai* from that later reform, in which the *arkhontes* were to be chosen by (either simple or complex) lot from a pool advanced by the ten tribes that Kleisthenes established in 508/7.[12] Hignett was probably not far off the mark when he averred that *Ath.Pol.* cited the law in order to show that *klêrôsis* was the method employed. Nonetheless, Hignett rejected the Law's authenticity. His reasons for doing so were grounded in his belief that *Ath.Pol.*'s author did not have access to the text of the original Law, and that its author inferred its stipulation of *klêrôsis ek prokritôn* from the later reform in a circular manner, perhaps not much differently than did Lehmann-Haupt.[13] This claim, in any event, denies the simple fact of the text as we have it, and does not explain why *Ath.Pol.* insists at both passages that the Law was still valid and thus that the Law's text ought still to have been available to *Ath. Pol.*'s author. In that case one need hardly postulate another antiquarian treatise on Athenian history, particularly an *Atthis*, as an intermediary source, even if Hignett felt that there was reason to suspect that *Ath.Pol.* might indeed have relied on an *Atthis* as he believed Plutarch did in the *Life of Solon* (which, however, seems to mention no such measure).[14] It is hardly clear, therefore, why Plutarch's apparent silence should ultimately be preferred, since a hypothetical *Atthis*, of course, remains an unknowable quantity, and the problem that Lehmann-Haupt deftly spotted in *Ath.Pol.* concerned its author's lack of information about the law on the *arkhontes*, in any event, and not the Law itself.

Hignett thought that *Ath.Pol.* was perhaps also misled by a statement of Isokrates (7.22) attributing the complex procedure of selection to the Athenians in the time of Solon:

> οὐκ ἐξ ἁπάντων τὰς ἀρχὰς κληροῦντες ἀλλὰ τοὺς βελτίστους καὶ τοὺς ἱκανωτάτους ἐφ ' ἕκαστον τῶν ἔργων προκρίνοντες.

12. Hignett (1952), 322–23; Hansen (1990), 57 n. 12 and 60 n. 29.
13. Hignett closely followed Wilamowitz-Moellendorff (1893) vol. 1, 260–90 (on Androtion), but suggests, 276–77, that *Ath.Pol.* could have consulted several *Atthides*, all democratic in orientation.
14. Hignett (1952), 322.

[(The Athenians) were allotting magistracies not from all citizens (that is, as in fourth-century Athens) but judging each man for his deeds aforehand they allotted the best and most appropriate.]

But in Hignett's view, Isokrates contradicted himself for having suggested later (12.145) that *klêrôsis ek prokritôn* existed well before Solon, even in the time of Theseus perhaps:[15]

περὶ δὲ τοὺς αὐτοὺς χρόνους καθίστασαν ἐπὶ τὰς ἀρχὰς τοὺς προκριθέντας ὑπὸ τῶν φυλετῶν καὶ δημοτῶν, οὐ περιμαχήτους αὐτὰς ποιήσαντες οὐδ ᾿ ἐπιθυμίας ἀξίας, ἀλλὰ πολὺ μᾶλλον λειτουργίαις ὁμοίας ταῖς ἐνοχλούσαις μὲν, οἷς ἂν προσταχθῶσι, τιμὴν δέ τινα περιτιθείσαις αὐτοῖς·

[At about this period (the Athenians) established candidates for office as preselected by tribesmen and demesmen, not having rendered the offices as the objects of battle, nor worthy of desire, but rather far more like burdensome liturgies to whomever they were assigned, and so like those posts that attach some honor to the men who hold them.]

Both passages support the notion that *klêrôsis ek prokritôn* was indeed established at an early time, and the second one further supports the testimony of *Ath.Pol.* (8.1; 47.1) that the initial stage of selection was handled at the level of the tribes. But Isokrates goes further in identifying the tribes' constituent parts as the relevant bodies, substituting of course the demes of his own time for the *naukrariai* that actually existed prior to Kleisthenes' democratizing reforms of 508/7. The second passage occurs in a lengthy section that relates the mixed constitution Isokrates believed had been achieved in early Athens. For Hignett to deny the validity of both passages because of the second passage's context demands perhaps too much of the fact that Isokrates' phrase "at about this period" (*peri de tous khronous*) is vague and, secondly, that Isokrates ascribes the measure to the Athenians generally and not to Theseus or to Solon.[16] That language would seem to open the possibility that it was Solon who was ultimately

15. Hignett (1952), 323; cf. Isoc. 12.130, 148.

16. Curiously, Pausanias (4.5.10) seems aware of this issue or perhaps of some degree of controversy in his time about just when allotment was introduced. In linking semimythical events in the Peloponnese to the chronology of (similarly mythical) Athenian *arkhontes*, Pausanias is keen to note that they were not allotted at that time (i.e., well before Solon on any interpretation).

responsible, since the same ascription to the Athenians is found in the first passage where it is, by context, more clearly related to Solon. While it may be too much to give any credit to Isokrates on the matter of precision, Hignett's objections are not compelling.

A similar problem emerges in the case of Demosthenes' evidence concerning the method by which the *arkhontes* were selected. Hignett, again, may also have been too ready to brush aside Demosthenes' (20.90) statement that Solon imposed what the orator terms a "double scrutiny" (*dis dokimasia*) for the *thesmothetai* as if this could have nothing to do with *klêrôsis ek prokritôn*, properly speaking:

> οὐ γὰρ ᾤετο δεῖν ὁ Σόλων, ὁ τούτον τὸν τρόπον προστάξας νομοθετεῖν, τοὺς μὲν θεσμοθέτας τοὺς ἐπὶ τοὺς νόμους κληρουμένους δὶς δοκιμασθέντας ἄρχειν, κτλ.
>
> [For Solon, having established this method for serving as a lawgiver, did not think it necessary that the *thesmothetai* allotted (to watch) over the laws should serve having undergone preliminary scrutiny twice (prior to service) . . .]

As has already been quite evident, Athenians of the fourth century regularly made some minor adjustment in how they spoke of archaic laws so that the force or implications of the laws would be made clear to their audience. What fact Hignett surely knew but whose implications he did not follow is that the six *thesmothetai* were none other than the nine *arkhontes* minus the *polemarkhos*, *arkhôn basileus*, and eponymous *arkhôn*.[17] Demosthenes cites these remaining six of the nine *arkhontes* in order to ground an argument that it is the laws, not those men establishing or administering them in the courts (as was the specific writ of the *thesmothetai* at this time, and perhaps earlier), that ought to be especially scrutinized.[18] That point would have been sabotaged had he cited the body of nine *arkhontes*, since the extra three did not administer the laws in the same manner as the *thesmothetai*. But there is no reason to think that the *thesmothetai* were selected by any other method, then or earlier, than that which applied to the other three *arkhontes*. Yet the *dokimasia* of the classical democ-

17. Concerning the number of *thesmothetai* in Athens following Solon, the matter is unclear although one would expect that the total number of magistrates serving in any college ought to have corresponded in some way (especially as a multiple) to the number of four Ionian tribes; cf. Figueira (1984) 449 n. 7.

18. On the duties of the *thesmothetai*, see Hansen (1991), 136, 190–91, 193, 197–99, 206, 215, 223–24, 229, 231, 248, 255, 263.

racy was of course not the same thing as a *klêrôsis ek prokritôn*, since the *dokimasia* determined not which men in a pool of qualified candidates could advance to take up office but whether candidates were qualified at all.[19] The classical procedure focused on questions of a broadly moral character that possessed some legal dimension, such as the care of one's parents and ancestral graves. In this there may be some parallel with the census classes that were so important to the Law, since at a minimum one's membership therein was a qualification for office and it would have required the approval of other parties, just as those facing *dokimasia* would have required the approval of either the Boule or the jurors sitting in court. I will return to this question later in the chapter. Thus, Demosthenes may offer some independent, but oblique, evidence for Solon as having established a law governing how the *arkhontes* were to be selected by a two-fold process. It does not follow as Hignett presumed, moreover, that this and the other sources communicate so exactly that their testimony must be rejected on this question if not adhering to the most precise framework of terminology. Thus, Demosthenes' claim of double scrutiny can be read as a reference to some kind of "complex" procedure by which these magistrates were selected.

Clearly, the Law mandated a procedure that must have encompassed at least two stages through which prospective *tamiai* would pass, and which resulted in fewer candidates at each stage before the final group was assembled as the final college. In other words, the first stage likely consisted of choosing one group of candidates in their tribes (*ek prokritôn*), and the second stage will have thus determined randomly (*klêrôsis*) which of those men would proceed into the college itself. While both Demosthenes' and Isokrates' testimonies support that interpretation, Demosthenes and *Ath.Pol.* muddy the waters since they point to Solon as the author of that or a similar two-fold procedure for the *arkhontes*. That quandary is best resolved by first examining a related disagreement between *Ath.Pol.* and Aristotle.

Aristotle on Procedures of Selection in Early Athens

A seemingly irresolvable conflict between *Ath.Pol.* and the historical reconstruction offered by Aristotle in the *Politics* concerns whether Solon could have

19. On the procedure generally, see Hansen (1991), 218–20.

established a law that used election, and not sortition, as a procedure by which to select magistrates. Aristotle aimed to refute the idea that Solon zealously undid a constitutionally "umixed" aristocracy so as to provide relief to an oppressed Demos by granting it "democratic" powers within a "mixed" constitution, and in the *Politics* (1273b39–1274a2) he focused largely on the matter of selection:

> εἶναι γὰρ τὴν μὲν ἐν ᾿Αρείῳ πάγῳ βουλὴν ὀλιγαρχικόν, τὸ δὲ τὰς ἀρχὰς αἱρετὰς ἀριστοκρατικόν, τὰ δε δικαστήρια δημοτικόν. ἔοικε δὲ Σόλων ἐκεῖνα μὲν ὑπάρχοντα πρότερον οὐ καταλῦσαι, τήν τε βουλὴν καὶ τὴν τῶν ἀρχῶν αἵρεσιν, τὸν δὲ δῆμον καταστῆσαι, τὰ δικαστήρια ποιήσας ἐκ πάντων.
>
> [(Some claim that) the Areiopagos was oligarchic, that the elected offices were aristocratic, and that the courts were democratic. It appears, however, that Solon did not undo (all of) the arrangements that had existed hitherto, but he (only) established the Boule and selection of (men for) offices, and rendered the Demos (as authoritative), having laid down that the courts would be drawn from all men.]

Aristotle later pursues the idea (1281b25–34) that Solon sought to dampen political danger arising from the number of poor in the *polis* by assigning to them the power to choose magistrates for office and to hold them accountable, since the Demos could exercise that authority within what Aristotle regarded as its natural or expected limits (I quote, for the sake of brevity, only 32–4):

> διόπερ καὶ Σόλων καὶ τῶν ἄλλων τινὲς νομοθετῶν τάττουσιν ἐπί τε τὰς ἀρχαιρεσίας καὶ τὰς εὐθύνας τῶν ἀρχόντων, ἄρχειν δὲ κατὰ μόνας οὐκ ἐῶσιν.
>
> [On account (of the limited capacity of the Demos to exercise justice and moderation) both Solon and some of the other lawgivers (of other *poleis*) assign to the Demos the selection of magistrates as well as the procedures of accountability, but they do not allow the Demos to serve in these offices alone.]

In much the same language, Aristotle echoes an earlier claim (1274a11–21) that the democratic institutions advanced by Ephialtes and others in the 460s were *not* in keeping with the *prohairesis* (a preselection, or even preelection) in Solon's procedures because they went too far in giving power to the Demos:

> φαίνεται δ ' οὐ κατὰ τὴν Σόλωνος γενέσθαι τοῦτο προαίρεσιν, ἀλλὰ μᾶλλον ἀπὸ συμπτώματος (τῆς ναυαρχίας γὰρ ἐν τοῖς Μηδικοῖς ὁ δῆμος αἴτιος γενόμενος ἐφρονηματίσθη καὶ δημαγωγοὺς ἔλαβε φαύλους ἀντιπολιτευομένων τῶν ἐπιεικῶν), ἐπεὶ Σόλων γε ἔοικε τὴν ἀναγκαιοτάτην ἀποδιδόναι τῷ δήμῳ δύναμιν, τὸ τὰς ἀρχὰς αἱρεῖσθαι καὶ εὐθύνειν (μηδὲ γὰρ τούτου κύριος ὢν ὁ δῆμος δοῦλος ἂν εἴη καὶ πολέμιος), κτλ.
>
> [It is apparent that this (rise of demagogues) did not happen on account of the *prohairesis* of Solon, but rather because of chance—for the Demos, being the cause of naval supremacy in the Persian Wars, was the object of political flattery and took base demagogues, although respectable men opposed them politically—since Solon seems to have granted (already) the most essential power to the Demos: to choose (men for) magistracies and to hold them accountable—for thus in control over this the Demos would not be a slave and an enemy (of the *polis*) . . .]

But, as cited above, *Ath.Pol.* (8.1–2 and 22.5) claims not only that Solon instituted *klêrôsis ek prokritôn* in place of election by the Areiopagos but that this system was also abandoned under the tyranny. *Ath.Pol.* might be taken to imply, too, that only with the Reform of 487/6 was that system revived.

The historical schema of the *Politics*, however, holds that after Solon granted to the Demos the right to select magistrates, the Peisistratidai made no constitutional change to this arrangement, and that it stood intact until at least the 460s. Moreover, that method is uniformly described as *hairesis*, and Solon's alleged grant of it to the Demos would be meaningless unless this were popular election, and certainly not allotment as the Law on the Tamiai used, according to *Ath.Pol.* Recently, L. Barucchi has suggested that both accounts form a coherent narrative in which the Reform was a genuinely Solonian law that had tribally based *klêrôsis ek prokritôn* combine election and sortition but from which the Peisistratidai effectively dropped sortition to render the process one of "simple" election.[20] That is a wholly salutary approach to reconstructing the Law's mechanics. But with respect to the Reform, her argument runs afoul of explaining why *Ath.Pol.* should have to resort to the Law on the Tamiai (which she does not discuss) as a source of information; if the democracy reestablished a neglected but genuinely Solonian measure at a time of significant political

20. Barucchi (2004–05).

upheaval, why should *Ath.Pol.*'s author have had so much trouble on that point?[21] Because *tamiai* and *arkhontes* were among the most senior magistrates of the *polis*, one cannot easily reconcile either the Law or the use of *klêrôsis ek prokritôn* for the Reform of 487/6 with Aristotle's historical framework in the *Politics*.

To reconcile *klêrôsis ek prokritôn* with the Areiopagos' role as Aristotle understands it also seems to pose great difficulties. But Barruchi's suggestion that the Areiopagos (as per *Ath.Pol.* 8.2) controlled the process of nominating candidates and then assigning them to office, but not the process of selection itself, may be especially useful.[22] While it is conceivable that such historical detail was merely ignored by Aristotle, that assumption does not, again, rescue us from the difficulty that the broadly incongruent historical outlines raise, especially in light of the evidence of *Ath.Pol.* and Demosthenes, namely, that Solon established "complex" procedures for two colleges of important magistrates: the *tamiai* and the *arkhontes*. This is all the more challenging given Aristotle's erstwhile attraction to an alternative hypothesis that Solon's constitutional changes were limited to a pair of powers—to hold magistrates accountable as well as to select them—to which *Ath.Pol.* pays no attention at all. At least as a pair, moreover, those two goals fit much better with the constitutional situation in Athens *after* the reforms of no less than Ephialtes, who likely deprived the Areiopagos of its powers, especially the capacity to hold magistrates accountable. Clearly, not all of the *Politics* should be taken at face value or treated a priori as the preferable account, at least not without specific justification. The detail of *Ath.Pol.* must also be treated with due circumspection, too, but the evidence for Solon having instituted a "complex" method of selection for at least one, and possibly

21. Perhaps in Barucchi's favor is that *Ath.Pol.* (22.5) does claim that the Reform constituted the "first time" since the end of the tyranny that the whole or part of the procedure was used. But since *Ath. Pol.* places the key phrase (τότε μετὰ τὴν τυραννίδα πρῶτον) at the end of the sentence, this phrase ought to modify not the use or reestablishement of the whole ostensibly Solonian law but merely the last provision mentioned, namely, that the *prokrisis* was to be determined by five hundred demesmen. The very next sentence (οἱ δὲ πρότεροι πάντες ἦσαν αἱρετοί) is not strongly explanatory in nature and so should not be read, as Barucchi (2004–05), 82, seems to have done, as clarifying the significance of the last phrase of that prior sentence. In other words, *Ath.Pol.* identifies the innovation not in the whole law (which it believes was Solonian, ultimately) nor in its reinstitution after the tyranny but in the fact that the pool of those performing the *prokrisis* was now made up of a limited group of demesmen, and hence that election at the tribal level was quite limited under this law.

22. Barruchi (2004–05), 71–72, points to the procedural distinctions implied by κρίνειν and διατάσσειν in *Ath.Pol.* 8.2, though we should be careful not to assume tacitly that the former verb must indicate the very same process as *klêrôsis ek prokritôn*. Barruchi, 75, defines that process rightly as "sceglire mediante elezione in una fase preliminare."

two, significant magistracies of the archaic Athenian state cannot be ignored.[23]

One can go much further, however, in establishing that indeed the Reform, and by extension the Law, employed a "complex" method of selection involving both election and allotment. As pointed out earlier, *Ath.Pol.* cites the Law in support of its contention regarding the census requirements and also allotment, but "simple" allotment does not fit with the evidence cited earlier pointing to election as the standard method by which all colleges, except that of the *tamiai*, were normally filled in archaic Athens even after Solon promulgated his Law. Likewise, the procedure involved must have had at least two stages, or else the phrase *klêrôsis ek prokritôn* would be meaningless, since the prefix *pro-* necessarily indicates an earlier stage of selection. How all of this might be reconciled is made clear by another passage of *Ath.Pol.* (26.2), which addresses the changes affected by Ephialtes, or in the aftermath of his murder, by those like Perikles who held him and his politics in high regard:

> τ[ὴν] δὲ τῶν ἐννέα ἀρχόντων αἵρεσιν οὐκ ἐκίνουν, ἀλλ ' ἕκτωι ἔτει μετὰ τὸν 'Εφιάλτου θάνατον ἔγνωσαν καὶ ἐκ ζευγιτῶν προκρίνεσθαι τοὺς κληρωσομένους τῶν ἐννέα ἀρχόντων, καὶ πρῶτος ἦρξεν ἐξ αὐτῶν Μνησθείδης.
>
> [(The Athenians) did not disturb the election of the nine *arkhontes*, but in the eighth year (458/7) following the death of Ephialtes they determined that those of the nine *arkhontes* to be allotted would be preselected from the Zeugite census class, and the first man who served from that class as eponymous *arkhôn* was Mnestheides.]

Unmistakably, *Ath.Pol.* thus states that even when the census class requirements were reduced (probably from that of the *hippeis*), the Athenians chose to keep a mixture of election (*hairesis*) and allotment (*klêrôsis*) from a preselected group.[24] That *Ath.Pol.* should situate this second reform so neatly with respect

23. Reacting to a customary preference for Aristotle's version among some scholars, Rhodes (1993), 60, argues that *Ath.Pol.* must always have been in conflict with the account of the *Politics* and that none of the offending passages (usally taken to be those of *Ath.Pol.* alone) were later insertions that garbled, in effect, a previously correct version of events.

24. Similarly agnostic about the pre-487/6 census requirements, Figueira (1984), 450–51, points to the year of ten *arkhontes* (579/8), and the inclusion of three Agroikoi ("Farmers") and two from the Demiourgoi ("Craftsmen") as all men of wealth, though not all of high status, as against the five Eupatridai. But Figueira may be going too far, 450–52, to see this unique college as representing a break with the census system itself since we do not know that these putatively non-Eupatrid groups do not in fact represent some element of, say, the *hippeis*. In the so-called Constitution of Drakon (*Ath.Pol.*

to the death of Ephialtes reveals that its author felt this measure to be remarkable for the very fact that the Athenians chose to retain a mode of selection that was not to be used by the democracy except in very limited circumstances, and that did not depend wholly on the simple lot; it was politically sufficient merely to lower the census requirement.[25] As Aristotle had suggested in a passage noted above (*Pol.* 1274a11–21), the democratic institutions advanced by Perikles and Ephialtes were *not* in keeping with the *prohairesis* that was typical of Solon's constitutional laws, for the sake of which the retention of a "complex" procedure must indeed have been striking in the democracy.

In addition, for the census requirement to be so prominent in this passage of *Ath.Pol.*, and the class of *zeugitai* to be the lowest body from which all prospective *arkhontes* were henceforth to be drawn through *prokrisis*, reminds us how *Ath.Pol.* (8.1–2) links the method of selection to the census class for both the *arkhontes* and the *tamiai* of Athena (also 47.1 for the *tamiai* alone). The import of this passage on the law pertaining to the *arkhontes* and by extension to the Law on the Tamiai has been wholly neglected. Even recent commentators on this period and its political developments have either ignored or, more rarely, attempted to explain away the transparent meaning of *hairesis* as if it could apply to any method of selection and need not be taken at face value as being nothing less nor more than election.[26] In sum, Aristotle's portrait of Solonian laws in the *Politics* goes too far in positing that election alone was the means by which magistrates were selected, even if it usefully illuminates the importance of election and some of its particular dynamics.

Barucchi may well be correct, then, that under the Law the Areiopagos did not itself select *tamiai* but merely oversaw the procedures by which candidates

---

4.2), by way of comparison, the *arkhontes* and the *tamiai* of Athena are to be drawn from the same class, which does not clearly correspond with any Solonian census class.

25. Confused about the nature of events in 458/7, Plutarch (*Per.* 9.4) resorts to personal animus as the most suitable explanation for Ephialtes' motives.

26. E.g., Hignett (1952), 227; L. Hall (1990), 323. In his commentary to this passage, Rhodes (1993), 329, remains unusually laconic. Rhodes' interpretation, 182, of *hairesis* as meaning nothing more specific than "appointment" depends on *Ath.Pol.* 13.2, which narrates the creation of an enlarged college of *arkhontes*, all of whom were elected in order to forestall the kind of political chaos that resulted from Damasias' illegal retention of the office of *arkhôn*. Rhodes' anticipatory objection to reading either instance of the verb (αἱρεθεὶς and ἑλέσθαι) as "to elect" is that "the word can mean no more than 'appoint' in contexts where the method of appointment is immaterial (cf. αἵρεσις in 26.ii), and the use of it here need have no implications for the method by which the archons were appointed." But isn't the method absolutely material to the passage in question? Damasias refused to abdicate his office and if elected, as I interpret it, he might well have done so on the grounds that he *was* elected and therefore had a mandate to govern, to which the Athenians responded first unsuccessfully by force and then by electing ten men to finish out Damasias' third (and illegal) year, thereby nullifying his claims politically. Cf. Figueira (1984), 450, 467.

advanced toward office. While Athenians likely continued to employ "simple" election at the tribal level for all colleges but that of the *arkhontes*, whom the Athenians perhaps elected *en masse*, the Law placed the *tamiai* in a new category for which the standard method of selection was no longer acceptable. Henceforth, prospective *tamiai* were subordinated to an unusual, and deliberately impersonal, second stage, over all of which the Areiopagos had authority. But there is more to work out with respect to chronology, for both the Reform and the Law used a similar "complex" method in which candidates had first to win election by their tribe before moving to a *polis*-wide competition that was determined randomly. The close connection between these two measures brings us to consider fully now a critical question that was apparent in Demosthenes' and *Ath.Pol.*'s testimonies, namely, whether the Law served as a direct prototype for the Reform, and if so, for what reason.

A Model Law

To return to the passages of *Ath.Pol.* quoted at the outset, *Ath.Pol.* (8.2) states in relation to the Law that prior to Solon the Areiopagos alone judged the fitness of prospective candidates and then assigned (*diatattein*) particular men to each of the available posts of *arkhontes*, but that Solon established a law concerning the *arkhontes*. While *Ath.Pol.* does not tell us what this law contained, its particle *oun* must indicate that *Ath.Pol.* thought it very similar to the Law, for tribally based allotment was a critical point of reference.[27] Second, on the Reform, *Ath.Pol.* (22.5) claims that the demes "preselected" (*prokrinein*) a large number of prospective *arkhontes*, of which only a few were then selected by lot according to tribe in order to serve as *arkhontes*; this is consistent with the less voluminous passage of 26.2, which indicates only that the men were drawn in accord with a certain census qualification.[28] Yet this second statement (22.5) contains two further claims that seem in contradiction with one another,

27. R. Buck (1965) argues that prior to the Reform of 487/6 the *arkhontes* were elected twice, first as a set of candidates (*prokritoi*) in the Ekklesia, and then those finally selected by the Areiopagos. Accordingly, the Reform would have replaced the role of the Areiopagos with sortition. Buck's argument is attractive to the extent that it does offer a means by which to resolve the seemingly contradictory statements in *Politics* and *Ath.Pol.*, but neglects to consider why *Ath.Pol.* stresses the evidentiary value of the Law on the Tamiai for the Reform, which I take to reflect the Law's likely role as the model.

28. Both the London and Berlin papyri of *Ath.Pol.* record the number of candidates as πεντακοσίων, which Kenyon and Chambers rejected in favor of ἑκατόν, concerning which, see Rhodes (1993), 273–74.

namely, that this reform *re-instated* what had been the case prior to the tyranny, and also that prior to this "all were elected" (*hairetoi*), which on its face should mean that *klêrôsis ek prokritôn* was Solonian, and that pure election was only Peisistratid (or even pre-Solonian).[29] As discussed earlier, Hignett was right to see a conflict between the two main statements. But instead of doubting the Law's authenticity as if it were merely an historiographic anachronism occasioned by the citation itself, it is most efficient to resolve the apparent conflict between these two statements by noting (as Hignett and the others have already done) that, again, *Ath.Pol.* uses the Law as the basis for its information about the selection of *arkhontes*. Furthermore, because *Ath.Pol.* gives much more detail about the Reform than about how Solon's Law applied to the *arkhontes*, on *a fortiori* grounds the more detailed information would likely be the starting point for *Ath.Pol.*'s immediate description.

I suggest that the problem is not with the Law, which *Ath.Pol.* cites as being still valid in its own time (and thus surely accessible as a genuine legal text), but rather with the other, ostensibly Solonian, law concerning the *arkhontes*. Presumably, that law is where *Ath.Pol.*'s dependency on an *Atthis* or other source led it afoul of early Athenian history; that source cannot have been the Law itself. The difficulty disappears, in fine, if one assumes that it was none other than Solon's Law that first used allotment, and it was how the Law employed the lot in conjunction with *klêrôsis ek prokritôn* that rendered it a model for the reform of 487/6. In other words, I argue that it was the Law that first established the procedure of *klêrôsis ek prokritôn*, but it did so, of course, for the *tamiai* of Athena alone. Moreover, I believe that this procedure was "complex" and involved a minimum census qualification, and that *Ath.Pol.*'s anachronism is not this Law but the one that it attributes to Solon concerning the *arkhontes* alone.

Despite their apparent disagreement, *Ath.Pol.* and the *Politics* appear to agree that the *arkhontes* were in fact always elected by a "simple" procedure until the Reform, such that *Ath.Pol.*'s characterization of the Reform's origins can be shown to be probably mistaken. If we assume at the outset that the *arkhontes* were elected through the sixth and early fifth century, there would be no conflict with Aristotle's statements in the *Politics* that Solon probably (*eoike*) did not alter the pure election (*haireisthai*) of *arkhontes*, as quoted earlier (and

29. Rhodes (1993), 146–48, 770, also treats at length the conflict between *Pol.* (1273b35–1274a3; 1274a16–17; 1281b25–34) and *Ath.Pol.* 8.1. Hansen (1990) also argues against *Ath.Pol.*'s claim of sortition in the time of Solon.

again, below).[30] That would also be in keeping with the implication of the second statement in *Ath.Pol.*, namely, that they were elected even under the tyranny.[31] Moreover, *Ath.Pol.* (13.1–2) elsewhere describes the chaotic tenure of the *arkhontes* in the years following Solon's legislation but fails to connect it with any law of Solon on these magistrates:

> Σόλωνος δ ' ἀποδημήσαντος, ἔτι τῆς πόλεως τεταραγμένης, ἐπὶ μὲν ἔτη τέτταρα διῆγον ἐν ἡσυχίαι, τῶι δὲ πέμπτωι μετὰ τὴν Σόλωνος ἀρχὴν οὐ κατέστησαν ἄρχοντα διὰ τὴν στ[άσ]ιν, καὶ πάλιν ἔτει πέμπτωι διὰ τὴν αὐτὴν αἰτίαν ἀναρχίαν ἐποίησαν. μετὰ δὲ ταῦτα διὰ τῶν αὐτῶν χρόνων Δ[α]μασία[ς] αἱρεθεὶς ἄρχων ἔτη δύο καὶ δύο μῆνας ἦρξεν, ἕως ἐξηλάθη βίαι τῆς ἀρχῆς. εἶτ ' ἔδοξ[εν] αὐτοῖς διὰ τὸ στασιάζειν ἄρχοντας ἑλέσθαι δέκα, πέντε μὲν εὐπατριδῶν, τρεῖς δὲ ἀγροίκων, δύο δὲ δημιουργῶν, καὶ οὗτοι τὸν μετὰ Δαμασίαν ἦρξαν ἐνιαυτόν.
>
> [When Solon (ended his tenure as lawgiver and) had left on his journey, even though the *polis* was still disturbed, the Athenians kept the peace for four years, but in the fifth year after Solon held office they created *anarkhia* [i.e., a period when there was no legitimate eponymous *arkhôn*] for the same reason (as that which occasioned Solon being made lawgiver). After this (period of peace), (but) in the same period (as the strife), having been elected as eponymous *arkhôn* Damasias governed for two years and two months, until he was driven from office by force. The Athenians then resolved, on account of being in a state of civic strife, to elect ten *arkhontes*, five from the Eupatridai, three from the Agroikoi and two from the Dêmiourgoi, and these men governed the year following Damasias.]

Even if for the sake of narrative coherence *Ath.Pol.* has simply omitted the detail of a "complex" procedure in the matter of these two elections, why would it omit any mention of a law of Solon's, established hardly more than a decade earlier, that bore on precisely who was to be considered worthy of selection as an *arkhôn*? Surely, there is no such omission whatsoever because Solon had

30. *Pol.* 1273b41–1274a3, 1274a15–21.
31. That claim would nevertheless still conflict with *Ath.Pol.* (8.2) on whether prior to Solon's reforms the Areiopagos chose the *arkhontes*, but as narrowly construed the issue is then irrelevant to the Law.

never established such a law.[32] If Solon did promulgate such a measure, after all, and Damasias for one refused to abide by it, why would *Ath.Pol.* not say so explicitly?[33] Thus, both *Ath.Pol.* and Demosthenes appear to be in error by attributing to Solon a law on the *arkhontes* that established a "complex" or twofold procedure of selection for them.

A critical incident involving one of the *arkhontes* at the battle of Marathon in 490, just three years prior to the Reform, assures us that there could not have been such a law before the year in which it was actually passed, 487/6. The issue involves whether the lot might have been used in the case of the one *arkhôn* serving as *polemarkhos* at the battle, for which our two sources, Pausanias and Herodotos, give conflicting accounts. For his part, Herodotos (6.109.2) claims that at this juncture the *polemarkhos* was chosen by lot (*kyamos*) and had a vote equal to that of the regular generals:

> ὡς δὲ δίχα τε ἐγίνοντο καὶ ἐνίκα ἡ χείρων τῶν γνωμέων, ἐνθαῦτα, ἦν γὰρ ἑνδέκατος ψηφιδοφόρος ὁ τῷ κυάμῳ λαχὼν Ἀθηναίων πολεμαρχέειν (τὸ παλαιὸν γὰρ Ἀθηναῖοι ὁμόψηφον τὸν πολέμαρχον ἐποιεῦντο τοῖσι στρατηγοῖσι), ἦν δὲ τότε πολέμαρχος Καλλίμαχος Ἀφιδναῖος, κτλ.

> [When the Athenians were both split and the opinion of the inferior men won the day, at that point, for he who obtained by lot the office of *polemarkhos* for the Athenians was the eleventh vote-holding man (because the Athenians of old had made the *polemarkhos* equal in vote to the generals), at that moment it was Kallimakhos of Aphidna who was the *polemarkhos* . . .]

Pausanias simply describes the man in question, Kallimakhos, as having been chosen by the Athenians to serve as *polemarkhos*, and the verb in question (*haireisthai*) is, again, the regular one used for election as opposed to allotment.[34] As M. H. Hansen notes, from 502/1 each member of the newly consti-

32. On the historical value of this passage in *Ath.Pol.*, and indeed the historiographic coherence and authenticity of the information that it contains, see Figueira (1984). Figueira, 449, proffers that *Ath. Pol.*'s repeated stipulation that these various *arkhontes* were elected was motivated precisely because a late fourth-century readership would otherwise assume that the *arkhontes* were chosen by sortition only and hence that their strife over the office was a historiographic error or politically unintelligble. Moreover, Figueira, 472, rejects attempts to see in the college of ten *arkhontes* the use of some form of *klêrôsis ek prokritôn*, though he is mainly troubled not with the general possibility of it then being used but the specific mechanics alleged for it in that one instance.
33. Figueira (1984), 448; cf. Wade-Gery (1958), 103–04.
34. Paus. 1.15.3: ὃς Ἀθηναίοις πολεμαρχεῖν ᾕρητο.

tuted democratic board of ten generals was likely chosen by mass vote in a "simple" procedure, and therefore the *polemarkhos* must have been chosen by another method altogether.[35] Since the *polemarkhos* was one of the nine *arkhontes*, I presume that the procedure can only have been that which was employed for all of the *arkhontes*. Hansen explains Herodotos' claim by suggesting that the body of nine *arkhontes* constituted the group from which this one magistrate was chosen, as each man drew at random a different office within the college.[36] Since the *arkhontes* were already elected for office, and a joint command of the *polemarkhos* and board of generals had also existed since 502/1, Hansen argues that the *polemarkhos* henceforth regularly obtained his position by a system of *klêrôsis ek prokritôn* very similar, if not identical, to that which I suggest was implemented by Solon with respect to the *tamiai* of Athena.[37] The Reform of 487/6 affecting the nine *arkhontes* also necessitated a reduction in the military role of the *polemarkhos*, the system of what we might call a joint command with the generals would likely have come to an end at that point. Afterward, the *polemarkhos* no longer held command with the generals, and for their part the generals were elected in a "simple" procedure that was no longer firmly based in tribal representation.[38] Curiously, those changes raised the political status of the generals to a higher level under the democracy. Despite all of the difficulties that generals and the Demos had with one another thereafter,

35. Creation of board of generals: *Ath.Pol.* 22.2. Fornara (1971), 6–10, suggests that prior to 502/1 the generals were hereditary officers drawn from each tribe, and that because the *polemarkhos* was the chief military officer of oligarchic Athens we need not assume that the others were elected. While we know very little about these Ionian tribes and their magistrates, it is worth noting that, as I discuss in later chapters, some tribal heads such as the *phylobasileis* do seem to have been hereditary.

36. Hansen (1990), 61; cf. Hamel (1998), 79–83.

37. Hansen (1990), 57. But Hansen doubts the authenticity of the Law itself and does not believe that it was possible for late fourth-century Athens to use a genuinely Solonian law. But Hansen does not see that *klêrôsis ek prokritôn* made use of sortition, which was integral to democratic practice, and he also errs in assuming that the *tamiai* of that time must have been subordinate to the "simple" use of sortition. But *Ath.Pol.* says only that Solon's Law was still being used and that it was the census requirements (8.1; 47.1), not the *prokrisis*, that were no longer observed. Hansen also objects, 57–58, that *Ath.Pol.* (8.1) states that one man each would be drawn from each tribe, but that is inconsistent with the mid-sixth-century bronze plaque (discussed in chapter 3) with names for eight, not four, treasurers. This is not a valid argument against the authenticity of the law per se, since the difference is both minor and does not pertain to the *system* of selection mandated by the law. The number of treasurers could easily have been increased at some point after Solon, or *Ath.Pol.* may have wrongly inferred the number of *tamiai*. Critically, nonetheless, both sources point to the tribal basis of selection.

38. College of generals without *polemarkhos*: Hdt. 6.109.2. Pointing to *Ath.Pol.* 61.1, Hammond (1969), 116, identifies the 470s as the period when the generals' success was now assured enough in public opinion that their office would remain elected, while the *arkhontes*' prestige had continued to wane after they were stripped of "simple" election. Without explanation, Hansen (1990), 61, posits the date of 487/6 for the reform affecting the generals; so, too, Hamel (1998), 79–83; Fornara (1971), 12 n. 4 and p. 19, sees it only as a *terminus post quem*.

the democracy maintained mass election as the sole method by which the Athenians chose their generals.[39]

Herodotos' evidence in support of *klêrôsis ek prokritôn* for the *arkhontes* before 487/6, and thus ostensibly for a Solonian law establishing that for the *arkhontes*, ought then to be rejected as a historiographic error. How the confusion about a law of Solon on the *arkhontes* germinated in the first instance is hardly knowable, but it is not out of the question that it arose first out of the immediately post-Marathon context. Since the Reform of 487/6 must have, on my reconstruction, made the *arkhontes* liable to sortition for the very first time and removed "simple" election, it likely aimed at democratizing the *arkhontes* and, by extension, the Areiopagos that would always be filled by former *arkhontes*. For that reason alone the Reform could survive a further, much more stringent, reform just thirty years later under Ephialtes. Since Marathon and the Reform of 487/6 were separated by only three years, one can easily imagine how Herodotos' source confused the order of events and associated a post-Marathon law with the very first instance known to him of the *polemarkhos* playing a significant role.[40] In short, Pausanias' far briefer text should be accepted as likely accurate.

Because the system of *klêrôsis ek prokritôn* had, on Hansen's reckoning, been instituted for the *polemarkhos* no earlier than 502/1, it is quite conceivable, if not probable, that Solon's Law on the Tamiai served as the model for this reform also. After all, given the importance of the generals, as Hansen's argument goes, the Athenians would not have followed into battle an incompetent man chosen at random, in which case election would be considered a political necessity. But there was even further precedent for the democracy to use *klêrôsis ek prokritôn*. As *Ath.Pol.* (21.6) reports, in 508/7 Kleisthenes employed something akin to that method when determining the eponymous heroes of the ten new tribes:

> ταῖς δὲ φυλαῖς ἐποίησεν ἐπωνύμους ἐκ τῶν προκριθέντων ἑκατον ἀρχηγετῶν, οὓς ἀνεῖλεν ἡ Πυθία δέκα.

39. For the procedures of selection used for generals after this reform, see Hansen (1991), 233–35, 238; Hamel (1998), 85–87; Fornara (1971), 19–27, 74–75. On the relations between the Demos and its generals, see, for example, Hamel (1998), 115–57; Roberts (1982).

40. In their commentary to Herodotos (6.109), How and Wells (1912), vol. 2 110, likewise spot the anachronism. Perhaps Herodotos might also have been misled by a source eager to invoke Solonian precedent.

> [Out of one hundred founders that were preselected, the Pythia chose ten, which (Kleisthenes) established as the eponymous heroes for the tribes.]

While *Ath.Pol.* is silent about the first step of the procedure, it in no way precludes that it was indeed the new tribes who "elected" ten heroes each, out of whose number only one might be chosen in the end by Apollo's Pythian oracle. Second, *Ath.Pol.* uses the verb *anairein* to describe the method by which Apollo's oracle made the final decision, and since this is a standard verb by which oracular responses are indicated, it would seem to eclipse any precise description of the method used to determine the initial round of candidates.[41] But it is the very submission of the question to the oracle that would surely have randomized the selection of eponymous heroes as far as the Athenians were concerned. While Kleisthenes initiated that process, *Ath.Pol.* offers no clue that he invented the procedure itself. Critically, since the heroes were mythical figures, Kleisthenes' procedure would not have offered itself as the best analogue for a law concerning magistrates, especially not those whose political impulses were to be checked. Put simply, to invoke the naming of heroes as the relevant paradigm would seem to elevate the *arkhontes* to a politically uncomfortable height just as the Reform checked the ability of elite Athenians to compete robustly for that office. But a law of Solon covering another college of senior magistrates would surely have good credentials, not only with respect to a measure affecting the *arkhontes* but even, perhaps, the eponymous heroes.

In sum, we should look to the Law as the likely paradigm not only for the Reform for the *arkhontes* in 487/6 but also for the *polemarkhos* in 502/1, and just perhaps also for the naming of tribes in 508/7. To be clear, it is my hypothesis that in 487/6, the young democracy passed a *new* law or decree that redefined the basis on which the *arkhontes* were to be selected henceforth, and there was no direct Solonian precedent with regard to the *arkhontes* except that Law. Any Solonian imprimatur alleged for the Reform by its proponents might certainly have helped with persuading Athenians, elite and Demos alike, to pass it, but we need not suppose that the law of 487/6 was in truth a *reform* of a genuinely Solonian law. Out of the historiographic confusion that arose concerning the relationship of these measures, Solon's Law emerges as a significant piece of legislation that was, ultimately if accidentally, compatible with the ideology of that new democracy.

---

41. E.g., Thuc. 1.25; Pl. *Lg.* 865d.

The Carrot: The New Class

What was it about the Law that rendered it so attractive a model for the early democracy, and all the more so that it could survive Ephialtes' reforms? Given the meager state of our knowledge for pre-Solonian Athens, that question occasions a necessarily speculative foray into post-Solonian political dynamics. Two assumptions are key. First, the Law was political in intent, notwithstanding its administrative repercussions. As per Aristotle's general outline of Solon's aims and his laws, discussed earlier in this chapter, the lawgiver aimed to stabilize Athens' strife-ridden political climate through limited concessions to otherwise opposed forces. Second, the Law did *not* alter Athenian politics and the sociology of elite power so much that the post-Solonian evidence is irrelevant. This assumption is a far greater leap, but I shall argue throughout the book that the Law was not a revolutionary measure that overturned the old order, but, to the contrary, it appealed to and ultimately affirmed elite expectations and values. Here, the core argument is that at its very origins the Law was simultaneously carrot and stick to that portion of the Athenian elite that had the greatest interest in serving as *tamiai* under its mandate.

While it was the matter of allotment that likely gave rise to suspicion in the fourth century that the Law was proto-democratic, the Law's census requirement points in a different direction, one in which the Law more securely established the dominance of the elite, or rather a section of it, over this office. Together, these two provisions entailed a very restricted pool of candidates whose prestige not only arose from that exclusivity but was also intrinsic to the enduring success of the Law itself. Accepting *Ath.Pol.*'s basic statements about *klêrôsis ek prokritôn* for the *tamiai* and the authenticity of the Law, Rhodes has argued that the "complex" process involving sortition and election (that is, at the level of the demes, or *naukrariai* before Kleisthenes) might have been part and parcel of removing the office of *tamias* from control of an aristocratic elite (the "Eupatridai").[42] Rhodes, I think, is right to identify the content and aim of the Law as political, but as I hope to show in the remainder of this chapter, the Law constituted a compromise with the elite that benefited them well. As noted in

42. Rhodes (1993), 148, points in particular to *klêrôsis ek prokritôn* as a device by which to open the office "both to the Eupatrids and to the non-aristocratic rich now for the first time made eligible." Stahl (1987), 176–77, expresses doubt about whether *klêrôsis ek prokritôn* was historically applied to the *arkhontes* (though on what basis is not clear), but does think that preselection handled by the tribes is plausible for archaic Athens and would not alter the political dynamics too greatly since it would still offer enough electoral maneuvrability to elite Athenians.

the Introduction (and again in the Appendix), we have no evidence to suggest that Solon disenfranchised the Eupatridai of any exclusive claims to serve as sacred treasurer, and so may tentatively dismiss them from the picture. What is of real consequence, nonetheless, is how Solon deployed a new census class to mollify an elite that would presumably challenge the Law if it hampered its power.

The significance of Solon's new class, that of the *pentakosiomedimnoi*, lies in it being a most exclusive club, and one that might have been created expressly for the *tamiai*. H. Van Wees has suggested that to produce five hundred measures (*medimnoi*) of barley—the typically Attic grain—as the notional minimum requirement for membership in the *pentakosiomedimnoi*, one would require something on the order of 40ha (c. 99 acres) of arable land, in addition to the team of oxen (and all other equipment) required of members of the *zeugitai* and even above the level nominally required to support the aristocratic pursuit of horse raising (by the *hippeis*, the next highest class).[43] Such wealth would have been impossible either to hide or to ignore. For his part, D. Roussel has argued convincingly that by virtue of the classes' nomenclature and their relative levels of wealth, Solon likely created anew the *pentakosiomedimnoi* as the highest class and thus added it onto an already existing system that had formerly been centered exclusively on the exercise of military power.[44] Although we cannot know just how many Athenians were *pentakosiomedimnoi*, and thus might be eligible for service as a *tamias*, even a rough calculation would suggest that so few Athenians fell into this category that a remarkably high proportion of them must have served as *tamiai* at some point in their adult life. For example, if we assume for the sake of argument that the *pentakosiomedimnoi* constituted no more than 1–2 percent of Athenian citizenry, and that the citizenry made up no more than, say, ten thousand people in 594, then the pool would be

43. Van Wees (2006), 358ff., argues also that even the *zeugitai*, as merely the lowest rung of the elite, would have needed some 16ha (c. 39.5 acres) of land.

44. Roussel (1976), 206 n. 24, however, identifies this preexisting structure as one consisting of Eupatridai (*hippeis*), Geomoroi (*zeugitai*), Demiourgoi (*thêtai*), which conflates two different categories that no source thus pairs: the Solonian census classes and the pseudo-constitutional divisions that Plutarch (*Thes.* 25; = *Ath.Pol.* fr. 3 Chambers) identifies. *Contra* de Ste. Croix (2004), 5–71, Raaflaub (2007), 130, argues that the census assessments, particularly that for the *tamiai*, were imposed only in the aftermath of the Areiopagos reforms of Ephialtes and Perikles (i.e., 462–50). But Raaflaub ignores the extensive evidence that shows by virtue of their *hiera* wealth that Athena Polias among other gods had long been greatly wealthy (so no *new* need for surety against temple theft), and he mistakenly infers from the influx of wealth in that later imperial period that the *tamiai* were in fact "financial officials." Van Wees (2006), 362ff., affirms the Solonian authenticity of the census.

no larger than approximately one hundred to two hundred men.[45] Of note is a mid-sixth-century bronze plaque that records what seems to have been a religious dedication offered to Athena by a whole college of *tamiai*, of whom the plaque lists five names of *tamiai*, and has space (where it is broken) for three more.[46] Just a generation or two after Solon, therefore, each of the four Ionian tribes must therefore have been represented, in a manner of speaking, by two *tamiai* for a total of eight in the college. If eight men were needed in any given year to complete a college, therefore, 4–8 percent of all eligible Athenians would have been actually serving as *tamiai* of Athena in any given year. Even if we assume that the *pentakosiomedimnoi* made up something as large as 5 percent of the citizenry, which seems far too large to be plausible, this one college would still contain nearly one out of every fifty eligible Athenians in any given year.[47] Of course, one should not forget that there were many other offices, including other sacred treasurers, which had to be filled such that the proportion of wealthy Athenians serving as magistrates was probably quite significant.[48] One could adjust the parameters of this calculation still further, but on any reason-

45. Even ten thousand may be too high, and it is offered as a guess that would concede some ground to those who might argue that there were plenty of wealthy Athenians available to become *tamiai* and to show nevertheless that such a premise is still untenable. In light of I. Morris' recent guess (2007), 219, that the *whole* population of Attica in 700 was only between five thousand and ten thousand people, the real figure for Athenian citizenry in Solon's time just a century later must have been truly miniscule. The number of citizens ought to have been no bigger than one quarter of that whole population (i.e., excluding women and children of both sexes), minus whatever slaves and resident foreigners contributed.

46. *IG* I^3 510. Focusing solely on the generals and their electoral procedures, Hammond (1969), 112 and 115–16, shows that *Ath.Pol.*'s phrase κατὰ φυλάς cannot mean tribal representation in the strict sense but rather that the number of offices corresponds to the number of tribes. Schwahn (1932), col. 1071, argued that the *tamiai* were only tribal officials, and not pan-Athenian, in Solonian Athens since *Ath.Pol.* (7.3) does not list them as such, but Hammond, 112 n. 3, points out that *Ath.Pol.* omits many things.

47. I borrow the upper limit from Van Wees (2006), 360, who estimates that the equivalent of the *pentakosiomedimnoi* in the late fourth century (which Van Wees takes to be slightly smaller than the liturgical class) constituted no more than 5 percent of the population, and that the top three classes together contained about 15 percent of the population (excluding slaves, an unmentioned variable). Given that the Athens of that era was far wealthier than that of Solon, the distribution of wealth was also markedly different between the two, and thus I posit that 1 percent is on the right order of magnitude for the early sixth-century *pentakosiomedimnoi*.

48. Some other colleges of sacred treasurers had fewer members than the number of tribes, such as the two *tamiai* created in the fourth century for the Two Goddesses (for which see chapter 4), and probably also the college of *neôkoroi* of Poseidon Hippios. Known only from a fragmentary inventory of dining equipment (*IG* I^3 405) from the late fifth century (413/2–412/1; 407/6–406/5), this latter board appears to have had no more than three members given the available space in the text (*ll.* 1–3, 25–27). Because the only identifiable man, Khaireleos of Kikkyna, is attested six years apart (*ll.* 2, 16, 26), the college might have served an extraordinarily long tenure. In any case, the Dekeleian War might also have been a factor in this unusual arrangment.

able estimate there would surely have been a very high proportion of the wealthiest Athenians serving as *tamiai* of Athena.

Several implications follow from even that rough sketch of possible numbers. While the pool of candidates from whom those eight were allotted must have been larger, and still more extensive was the number of men who won election in each tribe at the first stage of the procedure, how much larger? Solon's stipulation that the *tamiai* be drawn only from the highest census class, that of the *pentakosiomedimnoi*, must have been a radically limiting factor. On the lower figure suggested, each tribe ought to have had only a few dozen men eligible for this office at any one time, and it is difficult to believe that the richest men were evenly distributed, much less had enough peers, across the forty-eight *naukrariai* of Attica. Thus, the *naukrariai* and the smaller subdivisions of their *phratriai* would likely not have had a direct role in the actual elections held by the tribes, since in all likelihood many of them could not have consistently contained men who were both among the richest Athenians and also eager or willing to stand. The four tribes (or, potentially, some of their *trittyes* as groupings of four *naukrariai* each) must have been the smallest relevant field of political action for men hoping to serve as *tamiai* of Athena. There is no evidence regarding this or any other archaic Athenian law regarding restrictions on serving more than a single term, but any clause barring repeated tenure of an office would, clearly, restrict available numbers all the more and thus risk that colleges might often lack their full complement of men. Many of the wealthiest Athenians would, nevertheless, have stood against one another for this one post year after year, to say nothing of how frequently enough they would have won tribal election and been selected by the random allotment held at a pan-Athenian level. As *Ath.Pol.*'s repeated mention of census requirements strongly implies, the Law's stipulation on those requirements was therefore anything but an afterthought or *de riguer*. Why that was the case, and indeed what Solon might have intended the Law to accomplish, is a matter that bridges the formal characteristics of legal procedure and the more purely political aims of the lawgiver. That question likewise places the political sociology of these sacred treasurers, and by extension that of the rest of the Athenian elite, very much at the fore.

The stipulation that the *tamiai* of Athena belong to the very highest of the four census classes was a masterstroke of Solon's political efforts, for it aimed to balance the prestige of individual officeholders with the needs of the *polis* as a whole. Not only would the Law provide the Areiopagos with a tool by which to hold *tamiai* accountable for their actions in office, but it would concede to them a degree of freedom from having to compete or serve with those who might be merely prosperous yet lack sufficiently great wealth. In a passage of the *Politics* to which we will return (1309a9), Aristotle elucidates the logic underpinning aristocratic pretensions to rule: "the notables will not be governed by just anybody" (τοῖς δὲ γνωρίμοις μὴ ἄρχεσθαι ὑπὸ τῶν τυχόντων). Elsewhere in the *Politics*, Aristotle insists that the majority of citizens, whom he defines as those without wealth and as having no claim on virtue (*aretê*), should not hold senior magistracies since they are liable to commit crimes as well as to make serious errors of judgment.[49] In light of the probability that Solon retained election as the initial stage of the "complex" procedure, it is germane that in the *Politics* Aristotle regularly associates aristocratic "virtue" with elective offices.[50] Of special interest is how Aristotle states in an earlier passage (1309b4–8) that because of the common trust invested in those in charge of sacred property, those who serve as *tamiai* require a level of *aretê* that eclipses that which everyone else commonly has:[51]

> διὸ ἐν στρατηγίᾳ μὲν εἰς τὴν ἐμπειρίαν μᾶλλον τῆς ἀρετῆς (ἔλαττον γὰρ στρατηγίας μετέχουσι, τῆς δ ' ἐπιεικείας πλεῖον), ἐν δε φυλακῇ καὶ ταμιείᾳ (πλείονος γὰρ ἀρετῆς δεῖται ἢ ὅσην οἱ πολλοὶ ἔχουσιν, ἡ δὲ ἐπιστήμη κοινὴ πᾶσιν).
>
> [In serving as a general men have greater need of experience than virtue, for (naturally) they have less a share of command, but a greater share of fairness, but (the reverse is true) with regard to serving as a guard or *tamias*, for it requires a greater share of virtue than however much the general population possesses, since technical knowledge is available to all.]

Employing a similar vocabulary, *Ath.Pol.* (3.1) describes the basis for entering high office even before Drakon (thus, at least a generation before Solon) as

49. Arist. *Pol.* 1281b23–34. Aristotle goes so far as to advise that the most important magistracies be tied to liturgies in order to soften the fact that the poorer citizens are (optimally) excluded from holding office (1321a31–42). Underlining the connection between sacred finance and political power, Aristotle specifies (1321a35–39) public sacrifices, feasts, dedications, and buildings as what pleases the Demos.

50. E.g., *Pol.* 1273b35–1274a3; 1274a16–17; cf. Barucchi (2004–05), 69–70.

51. In the immediately preceding lines (1301b1–4), Aristotle further mixes the categories of virtue, power, and wealth, for which see Ober's comments (1991) and (1989), 249, on Aristotle's sociology and the role of *aretê*.

"virtue (or excellence) and wealth" (*aristindên kai ploutindên*), where the former term (modeled as it is on the superlative adjective *aristos*, "best") appears to have had no greater a formal basis than the sort of public approbation necessary for election:

> τὰς μὲν ἀρχὰς καθίστασαν ἀριστίνδην καὶ πλουτίνδην.
>
> [They established magistracies on the basis of excellence (*aristindên*) and wealth (*ploutindên*).]

In the *Politics* (1293b10–12), Aristotle also utilizes this pairing as a means by which to distinguish the "aristocratic" constitution from other forms of government:[52]

> ὅπου γὰρ μὴ μόνον πλουτίνδην ἀλλὰ καὶ ἀριστίνδην αἱροῦνται τὰς ἀρχάς, αὕτη ἡ πολιτεία διαφέρει τε ἀμφοῖν καὶ ἀριστοκρατικὴ καλεῖται.
>
> [For that government differs from both (oligarchies and the avowed "constitution") and is called aristocratic where they choose magistrates not only on the basis of wealth (*ploutindên*) but also on the basis of excellence (*aristindên*).]

The philosopher also claims Solon to have maintained as part of the mixed constitution a structure that retained election for the Boule and the (chief?) magistracies.[53] Clearly, for Aristotle as well as the author of *Ath.Pol.* (that is, if not Aristotle himself), Solonian Athens was characterized as having a constitution in which wealth, "virtue," and election went hand-in-hand.

Furthermore, "virtue" appears to have converged with a juridical authority that likewise reflected, or was perhaps dependent on, popular power. Plutarch states that the quality of "excellence" (*aristindên*) was also the basis on which a special court was chosen in Solon's time to judge those who had been responsible for slaughtering the Kylonian suppliants a generation earlier; the fragmentary opening of the *Ath.Pol.* seems to have employed much the same language in relating this very episode.[54] The term *aristindên* appears to have defined Ath-

52. Cf. *Pol.* 1272b35–37; 1273a23.
53. *Pol.* 1273b35-a4.
54. Plu. *Sol.* 12.3–4: ([Solon persuades those under the curse] καὶ κριθῆναι τριακοσίων ἀριστίνδην

ens' archaic legal standard for judicial competence. In the text of the reinscribed version of Drakon's law on homicide from the late fifth century, *aristindên* appears to be the criterion by which members of a murdered man's *phratria* are to be chosen in order to decide whether or not to allow the murderer's return to Athenian society.[55] In a lengthy prescription in the *Laws* on the proper punishments for temple-robbery, Plato defines *aristindên* as the quality by which the court of the ancient *arkhontes* (surely as a function of the Areiopagos) was selected in cases involving the death penalty (such as temple robbery).[56] Since that crime would clearly involve sacred treasurers, whether as accusers or defendants, Plato appears to suggest that the jurors ought to be equal in excellence to those standing watch over the temples. As already discussed earlier in this chapter, however, Aristotle goes so far as to claim that Solon shifted the courts to the Demos, which henceforth were to be selected on the basis of sortition alone. Although it is difficult to accept at face value since that reform "echoes" Ephialtes' later stripping from the Areiopagos most of its legal powers, Aristotle's assertion raises an interesting possibility. If there is some basis to that claim, Solon's main change in regard to requirements of service might then have been limited to the question of who had the right to pronounce sentence over others.[57] While high status would conceivably be necessary in capital cases in order to ensure a verdict that was not only legally binding but politically acceptable, especially in a case involving so heated an issue as the suppression of the Kylonian conspiracy, Solon conceivably shifted some element of that authority to the populace itself—if the event, of course, is historical.[58]

δικαζόντων). Rhodes (1993) reports that in their (third?) edition of *Ath.Pol.*, Kaibel and Wilamovitz-Moellendorf restored the first line as follows: ‹ἐδίκαζον δὲ τριακόσιοι ἄνδρες κατηγοροῦντος› Μύρωνος καθ ' ἱερῶν ὀμόσαντες ‹τελείων αἱρεθέντες› ἀριστίνδην [*non vidi*]. In the *Politics* (1272b35–37; 1273a23–24; 1293b10–11), Aristotle identifies this sense of aristocratic virtue as a criterion (along with wealth) for major offices in the Carthaginian *politeia*, but comes close to conflating the two insofar as they both allow the magistrate to govern free from distraction (e.g., 1273b5: διὸ δεῖ τοὺς δυναμένους ἄριστ ' ἀργεῖν, τούτους ἄρχειν, and the seeming definition of this quality at 1273a17–18: τὸ δὲ ἀμίσθους καὶ μὴ κληρωτὰς ἀριστοκρατικὸν θετέον).

55. *IG* I^3 104, *ll.* 18–19: [τούτος δ]ὲ τôι *ḥ*ọ-|ι πεντέκο[ν]τ[α καὶ] *h*ê͂ς ἀρ̣[ι]σ̣τ̣[ίνδεν *h*αιρέσθον], restored largely on the basis of [Dem.] 43.57: τούτους δὲ οἱ πεντήκοντα καὶ εἷς ἀριστίνδην αἱρείσθων.
56. Pl. *Leg.* 855c6-d1. The larger discussion on temple robbery (*hierosylia*) begins with the opening of Bk. 9 (853a1) shortly beforehand and occupies much of the dialogue's discussion thereafter.
57. Arist. *Pol.* 1273b41–1274a7.
58. Wolff (1946), 78ff., argues that the judicial authority of the *arkhontes*, against which Solon's putative grant of *ephêsis* was presumably aimed, was inherently social in character. As noted earlier, Plutarch and (probably) *Ath.Pol.* relate that the prosecution against Megakles and his comrades was decided by a court of three hundred men (before which Myron of Phlya lodged the accusation). However anachronistic Plutarch's version might be, *Ath.Pol.*'s claim that the jurors were selected on the basis of "virtue" seems difficult to reconcile with democratic ideology. Proof is impossible, but it seems

In any case, the principle that one should be judged by those of similar (if not higher) standing in at least certain cases was apparently so strong that even the democracy observed it when conducting examinations of those oligarchs who were part of the Thirty, to whom it conceded that their examiners would also be members of the upper census classes.[59] Otherwise, classical oligarchies frequently, if not always, employed criteria of wealth as the basis of political membership.[60] Solon's census, therefore, seems to have affirmed the obvious social power that those of the greatest wealth and status already enjoyed.

By detaching the wealthiest Athenians and apportioning to them alone a significant office, would it not have been dangerous insofar as it might also encourage these men to think of themselves as being above all others in the *polis*? Furthermore, we might wonder whether Solon was wise to promote great wealth as the criterion for this office since ambitious men might easily deploy it in the electoral politics of their tribes, which he left intact, and thus fan the flames of political instability within the elite and perhaps even between the elite and the rest of the citizenry. But it would be mistaken to view the census classes as positively and unproblematically instantiating the prestige of candidates without threat or pressure from the rest of the elite to conduct their task within acceptable limits. G. Anderson and others have recently argued that what might be called the "constitutional" structure of the archaic *polis* in general betokens what he terms "a supremely cautious negotiation transacted by a group of mutually suspicious, highly competitive political equals," given that early laws in many Greek states focused on first defining strictly the procedure under which magistrates enjoyed their power and then mandating heavy consequences for

plausible that this trial established the political basis for large-scale juries that the Solonian system evidently envisioned. Given that Aristotle believed control over the courts to be the most important power in a constitution (e.g., 1274a4–5 [on the Solonian courts]), Solon's reform would seem to justify Aristotle's other claims that Solon indeed had fundamentally altered the balance of power in the Athenian state but did not change the method by which chief magistrates were chosen.

59. *Ath.Pol.* 39.6; cf. Rhodes (1993), 470–71, on the somewhat unusual expression τοῖς τὰ τιμήματα παρεχομένοις, which is best paralleled in the late fifth-century oligarchic pamphlet that *Ath.Pol.* (4.1–4) preserves as the Constitution of Drakon. Apart from the constitution attributed to Drakon at *Ath.Pol.* 4.2, which almost all historians condemn as a later forgery, the earlier formula of "virtue and wealth" (3.1) suggests that some kind of census system had long been in place. Rhodes (1993), 113, suggests that in the constitution of Drakon at 4.2 the relative importance of the military commanders over *arkhontes* would be more in keeping with the late fifth century. However, Rhodes' objection that the use of weighed silver, in contrast to Solon's measures of produce, anachronistically forgets that *talents* are attested widely in Homer, for instance, and that silver bullion might well have served as money, for which see Kroll (1998).

60. On property requirements for oligarchies: Whibley (1896), 126ff.

failure to observe those limits.[61] For Athens, then, the Law would offer much the same benefit to the elite as a whole, for it would promise some measure of stable governance over magistrates. As discussed earlier in this chapter, disputes over the office of eponymous *arkhôn* were, according to *Ath.Pol.*, rife after Solon's tenure and point to the necessity of enforcing such laws in the broader interests of the elite as a whole.[62] With regard to the *tamiai*, the Law would provide a procedural means by which conflict over the possession of their office could also be formally resolved and controlled.[63] In other words, there could still be robust competition within a tribe but so long as the randomized process of sortition was carried out fairly at the next stage, there could be no justifiable basis for denying the validity of its results. Because so few Athenians could, under the Law, ever serve as *tamias*, that predictability can only have assured each candidate that if victorious he would be able to enjoy his office uncontested by his peers, much less by his inferiors.

The Stick: Indemnity

Whatever benefit the Law brought to individual members of the elite, especially the richest among them, it also ensured, I believe, that through the Areiopagos the elite as a whole could exercise firm control over those men who did serve as *tamiai*. This was possible because the new census class of the *pentakosiomedimnoi* that allowed the wealthiest Athenians to keep the office of *tamias* to themselves by necessity also required those men to declare their property in an official and necessarily binding manner. The principle behind each class, and indeed the whole system, was that it established that only those Athenians able to compensate the *polis* for certain fines or losses to property under their control would be allowed to hold a magistracy of a particular level. Each census class, then, corresponded to a certain threshold of financial indemnity that was keyed to a discrete set of offices. Men of lower census classes could not serve in

61. Anderson (2005), 180.

62. *Ath.Pol.* 13.1–3.

63. Foxhall (1997), 132, argues for a similar conclusion, but frames the issues within a more economically discrete perspective. Rosivach (2002), 39, suggests that because *Ath.Pol.* 7.4 notes that other ancient authorities used the evidence of votive dedications to determine how the Solonian class of *hippeis* was constituted, an authoritative copy of the law could not be found. But *Ath.Pol.* (13.2: φαίνονται γὰρ ἀεὶ στασιάζοντες περὶ ταύτης τῆς ἀρχῆς) seems incredulous at the strife over who could be *arkhôn* in the sixth century, and it is hard to imagine why a source would have invented a narrative of such conflict, much less a confusing one. The same is even more likely to be true for the office of *tamias* to which such narratives never became central to the historiography of early Athens.

a position above their class but, conversely, all offices at or below one's station were of course open, since one could obviously fulfill the financial requirements of those lower offices with ease. In short, the wealthier one was, the wider one's options and opportunities.

While it is one thing to see the possibilities inherent in a legal structure, there is evidence pointing directly to Solon as having established that magistrates must provide property as a kind of collateral should they commit an offense during their tenure. Attributing legal substance to the principal of indemnity, Aiskhines (3.21) credits Solon with a law prohibiting a man from disposing of his personal property until he had cleared his accounts with the *polis*:[64]

> ἐνεχυράζει τὰς οὐσίας ὁ νομοθέτης τὰς τῶν ὑπευθύνων ἕως ἂν λόγον ἀποδῶσι τῇ πόλει.
>
> [The lawgiver demands surety on property belonging to those yet to pass their *euthyna* until such time as they render accounts to the *polis*.]

There is no way to tell from this brief notice just which parts of the requirement might truly be Solonian and which are Aiskhines' reinterpretation of the law in terms that would have been valid or meaningful for the fourth century, although the notice about *euthyna*, a procedure of the democracy alone to the best of our knowledge, should not inspire unabashed confidence. What is certainly of interest in Aiskhines' claim is that Solon should have placed some kind of lien or restriction on the personal wealth of magistrates, and that this was subject to whatever authority rendered judgment as to whether a magistrate's performance was acceptable. In an extreme case, the census requirement would thus ensure that if there was, for instance, a very significant theft that could not be fully recovered, the estate of the condemned would be large enough to cover most, if not all, of the loss.

An intriguing but rather obscure passage in Pollux may shed further light on how the census indemnities worked. In providing a brief description of the census classes (8.129–31), Pollux correlates the Solonian census classes with the amount that members of each class spent on the public treasury in some regard that plausibly betokens indemnity:[65]

---

64. F101 Ruschenbusch.
65. *Ath.Pol.* 7.4 is the other essential source for the census requirements.

τιμήματα δ ' ἦν τέτταρα· πεντακοσιομεδίμνων, ἱππέων, ζευγιτῶν, θητῶν. οἱ μὲν ἐκ τοῦ πεντακόσια μέτρα ξηρὰ καὶ ὑγρὰ ποιεῖν κληθέντες· ἀνήλισκον δ ' εἰς τὸ δημόσιον τάλαντον· οἱ δὲ τὴν μέτρα τριακόσια, ἀνήλισκον δὲ ἡμιτάλαντον. οἱ δὲ τὸ ζευγήσιον τελοῦντες ἀπὸ διακοσίων μέτρων κατελέγοντο, ἀνήλισκον δὲ μνᾶς δέκα· οἱ δὲ τὸ θητικὸν οὐδεμίαν ἀρχὴν ἦρχον, οὐδὲ ἀνήλισκον οὐδέν.

[There were four classes (or *timêmata*): of the *pentakosiomedimnoi*, of the *hippeis*, of the *zeugitai*, of the *thêtes*. Those of the first category were so called by virtue of producing 500 measures, dry and wet; they spent a *talent* on the public treasury (*dêmosion*). Next, there were those of the 300 measures, and they spent a half-*talent*. Those paying the *zeugêsion* were registered from 200 measures, and they spent ten *mnai*; those in the *thêtic* class held no magistracy, and they spent nothing.]

But the monetary figures Pollux cites simply do not correlate arithmetically with the wealth required for membership in those classes; they are on two different scales and are not proportionate to one another. Going back ultimately to A. Böckh in the early nineteenth century, A. Moreno has revived the notion that sees the measures of foodstuffs required for each census class (thus, the 500 *medimnoi* for the *pentakosiomedimnoi*) as merely taxable capital that was a set proportion of what Pollux claims members of each class paid.[66] That argument has long been recognized as one predicated on a series of speculative inferences, the most difficult of which to accept is that the number of measures cited by Pollux and other sources as the benchmark for each class is not in point of fact any such benchmark at all. Pollux does not even claim that the payment was for tax, after all, much less for the war-tax (*eisphora*) as so often stated(!), but merely indicates what the members of these classes paid to the public treasury.[67] Pollux's statement is indeed puzzling.

66. That argument has been revived most recently, but unconvincingly, by Moreno (2007), 104–12, especially 105 n. 135. As per the text cited in the previous note, the ratio of values between the measures needed for membership in the classes—500 *medimnoi*; 300 *medimnoi*; 200 *medimnoi*—(5:3:2) simply does not correspond to the ratio of money that Pollux claims members of each class spent—one *talent* (i.e., 6,000 dr.; = 60 *mnai*); one-half *talent* (i.e., 3,000 dr.; = 30 *mnai*); 10 *mnai* (= 1,000 dr.): (6:3:1). Rosivach (2002), 36, likewise stretches an examination of the ratios among the measures themselves too far when he suggests that the difference between those required for the *hippeis* and *zeugitai* (thus, at the ratio of 3:2) entailed "not much difference between them," as if a 50 percent increase from the level required of *zeugitai* to that of the *hippeis* were neglible. Davies (1971), xxvi, already warns about trying to use this passage of Pollux as the basis of converting the Solonian requirements into terms relevant to the fourth century.

67. Notwithstanding his own argument that Pollux most likely refers to an *eisphora* collection of 428/7,

One might wonder, nonetheless, whether Pollux or his source has in mind the indemnity that I suggest the classes were set up to facilitate. Since Pollux states that the members of this class spent the money on the common good, or more preferably, the public treasury (*dêmosion*), the expenditures might be interpreted as referring not to donations or emergency measures, such as for war, but to the actual indemnity required of men serving as magistrates solely for the time that they were in service. Given that *Ath.Pol.* quotes (otherwise unidentifiable) Solonian laws that state how the *naukraroi* (the officers in charge of each of a tribe's twelve *naukrariai*) were to spend money from funds in their control, as discussed in later chapters, it is clear that Pollux cannot be communicating (at least not accurately) about the budgetary mechanisms of early Athens.[68] In other words, if this statement of Pollux has any authority—and that is far from certain—it might indicate the belief, at least, that the Solonian census classes originally entailed that men deposit with the treasury funds to be held in trust for the duration of their service, prorated to their class, and to be confiscated in part or in full if the magistrates committed certain crimes or fled prosecution.[69] As I shall argue in chapter 5, the lead sheet used by the treasurers of Nemesis at Rhamnous c. 500 also employs the same key term here for expenditure (*analiskein*) but in a way that indicates a kind of deposit made with a constitutionally authoritative entity such that the separation of possession from ownership has enough legal force to entail the idea of "expenditure" as a semantically appropriate expression. To read Pollux with that in mind might explain what he meant when he wrote that in conjunction with their census-appropriate offices men "spent" large sums of money on the treasury. Thus, to deposit such large sums as even ten *mnai* would not be so unworkable since magistrates who exited office without charge would receive their money back, and the deposit would not constitute anything like a tax, which is what Pollux has been taken to say.[70] No other explanation seems workable. If such sums were extracted as

---

Thomsen (1964), 14–23, provides a useful survey of the scholarship reaching back to Böckh that views this passage of Pollux as positive evidence for Solon's establishment of the classes as tied directly to payment of *eisphora*. To that list can now be added Moreno (2007), 104–12.

68. *Ath.Pol.* 8.3.

69. As to the authenticity of the passage, it may be germaine that [Dem.] 43.54 claims for the Solonian census classes another prorated set of financial obligations (pertaining to unwanted heiresses), but which van Wees (2006), 362 n. 17, thinks belongs only to the fourth century (*contra* Rosivach [2002]; cf. F77 Ruschenbusch.

70. Therefore, while the phrase οἱ δὲ τὸ ζευγήσιον τελοῦντες could be taken at face value to indicate those paying a tax identified as the *zeugêsion*, the participle τελοῦντες must be taken in the sense as belonging to a particular class (thus, *LSJ* s.v. τελέω II.3).

taxes, after all, how could any of the wealthy tolerate serving in such a state, for one thing? How the system could have possibly survived for as long as it did would be a mystery if Pollux is otherwise read to mean that wealthy Athenians had to spend significant resources on the state simply by virtue of their being so wealthy as to be members of one census class or another, since such heavy taxes would have caused the wealthy to fall out of the classes to which they were originally assigned.

But the matter at hand is not so much fiscal in character as it is political and religious. To return to a passage of Aristotle's *Politics* on the necessary qualities that a *tamias* and a general must possess, Aristotle presumes that the wealthiest are the least likely to steal from the gods. Yet Aristotle also leaves open the possibility that sacred treasurers might be called on to make up any accidental deficits or losses from their own funds, even though death was the standard punishment for temple-robbery (*hierosylia*) among the Greeks.[71] Immediately prior to his discussion of *hierosylia*, Aristotle makes this supposition clear (1309a4–14) when he delineates how a community with an aristocratic type of constitution ought to control embezzlement:

> οἱ γὰρ ἄποροι οὐ βουλήσονται ἄρχειν τῷ μηδὲν κερδαίνειν, ἀλλὰ πρὸς τοῖς ἰδίοις εἶναι μᾶλλον, οἱ δὲ εὔποροι δυνήσονται διὰ τὸ μηδενὸς προσδεῖσθαι τῶν κοινῶν· ὥστε συμβήσεται τοῖς μὲν ἀπόροις γίγνεσθαι εὐπόροις διὰ τὸ διατρίβειν πρὸς τοῖς ἔργοις, τοῖς δὲ γνωρίμοις μὴ ἄρχεσθαι ὑπὸ τῶν τυχόντων. τοῦ μὲν οὖν μὴ κλέπτεσθαι τὰ κοινὰ ἡ παράδοσις γιγνέσθω τῶν χρημάτων παρόντων πάντων τῶν πολιτῶν, καὶ ἀντίγραφα κατὰ φατρίας καὶ λόχους καὶ φυλὰς τιθέσωσαν· τοῦ δὲ ἀκερδῶς ἄρχειν τιμὰς εἶναι δεῖ νενομοθετημένας τοῖς εὐδοκιμοῦσιν.
>
> [The poor (will not serve in such a government) since they do not wish to serve as magistrates on account not being able to profit thereby, but all the more will wish to be fixed on their own affairs; but the wealthy are able to serve on account of not requiring any support to be drawn out of public property. The result will be that the poor will become wealthy by virtue of attending to their trades, and that the notables will not be governed by just anybody. With regard to the prevention of theft of public property, there should thus be a transfer of money (at the end of a magistrate's tenure) while all the citizens are assembled,

71. On temple robbery (*hierosylia*) as a capital offense: e.g., Plu. *Sol.* 17.1. See also n. 56 above.

and they should place copies (of the accounts) with the *phratriai*, military companies, and tribes. And with respect to serving without personal gain, one ought to have established honors for those in good repute.]

But in the face of loss or damage to sacred property, how would one proceed? Where such a crime occasioned fear of divine retribution, an indemnity would rescue the Athenians from possibly failing to appease the gods should a convicted *tamias* be found to have hidden his wealth, fled into exile, or simply refused to pay.[72]

Crimes of that nature, of course, also had a political character, as Aristotle makes clear when he states (1308b31-a4) that where magistrates were believed to be stealing such common property, the usual result was *stasis* (strife) between rich and poor:

μέγιστον δὲ ἐν πάσῃ πολιτείᾳ τὸ καὶ τοῖς νόμοις καὶ τῇ ἄλλῃ οἰκονομίᾳ οὕτω τετάχθαι ὥστε μὴ εἶναι τὰς ἀρχὰς κερδαίνειν. τοῦτο δὲ μάλιστα ἐν ταῖς ὀλιγαρχικαῖς δεῖ τηρεῖν. οὐ γὰρ οὕτως ἀγανακτοῦσιν εἰργόμενοι τοῦ ἄρχειν οἱ πολλοί, ἀλλὰ καὶ χαίρουσιν ἐάν τις ἐᾷ πρὸς τοῖς ἰδίοις σχολάζειν, ὥστ ' ἐὰν οἴωνται τὰ κοινὰ κλέπτειν τοὺς ἄρχοντας, τότε γ ' ἀμφότερα λυπεῖ, τό τε τῶν τιμῶν μὴ μετέχειν καὶ τὸ τῶν κερδῶν· μοναχῶς δὲ καὶ ἐνδέχεται ἅμα εἶναι δημοκρατίαν καὶ ἀριστοκρατίαν, γνωρίμους καὶ τὸ πλῆθος ἔχειν ἃ βούλονται ἀμφοτέρους. τὸ μὲν γὰρ ἐξεῖναι πᾶσιν ἄρχειν δημοκρατικόν, τὸ δὲ τοὺς γνωρίμους εἶναι ἐν ταῖς ἀρχαῖς ἀριστοκρατικόν, τοῦτο δ ' ἔσται ὅταν μὴ ᾖ κερδαίνειν ἀπὸ τῶν ἀρχῶν·

[In every constitution it is of the greatest significance that it is not allowed, by both the laws and the rest of the administration, for magistracies to profit. It

72. A set of early laws from Tiryns that are roughly contemporary with Solon offer an important point of comparison and suggest that this idea need not have been in any way unique to Solon. The laws in question impose on errant cult officers (apparently in charge of dispensing wine) a fine of thirty *medimnoi*. Foxhall (1997), 130, calculates that five hundred *medimnoi* of wheat alone could sustain about one hundred people in a year, or eighty-four if only measured in barley (as ought to be more typical of at least smaller farmers in Attica), as apparently Rosivach (2005), 600, assumes. On the data summarized there, the Tirynthian fine would thus correspond to full provisions for approximately six people on wheat for a year, or about five on barley; cf. Van Wees (2006), 358ff. But no such estimate makes sufficiently clear that the various members of the household would have had different caloric needs, and hence consumed different quantities (i.e., less than that of the active adult male presumed by such models). Moreover, all such calculations, it should be noted, do not subtract what would be necessary to feed slaves, a team of oxen, and any other animals (especially horses for luxury purposes); cf. Rosivach (2002), 37–38. For the text of the Tirynthian laws, see Verdeles, Jameson and Papakhristodoulou (1975).

is especially necessary for those in oligarchies to observe this. For thus the many who are deprived of serving as magistrates are not aggrieved, but take pleasure if someone should be at leisure in their private affairs, with the result that if they think that the magistrates are stealing public property, then it will grieve them on both counts: being deprived of honors and also of profits. A single situation pertains to both democracy and aristocracy, the notables and the mass possess what the other desires. It is possible for everyone to govern in a democracy, but the aristocratic government is one in which the notables are in power, and this will occur whenever it is not possible to profit from magistracies.]

With Aristotle's formulation in mind, perhaps it is not too far-fetched to suggest that one of Solon's goals was to establish by means of the Law a broad public confidence in the ability and willingness of those entrusted with power to hold themselves and one another accountable. In his fragmentary elegy on Eunomia ("Good Order"), after all, Solon claims that some Athenians, perhaps even the "leaders (*hêgemones*) of the Demos," were stealing public and sacred property alike and failing to guard the "holy foundations of Dike (Justice)."[73] Whomever Solon targeted, those responsible for the theft ought only to have been magistrates since public property in the strict sense of the term probably did not consist of moveable objects in the way that much sacred property did and thus was not subject to pilfering. I will describe those types of property in later chapters but merely point out here the prominence that this crime has in Solon's *Eunomia*: it is the first specific crime, rather than vague if profound wrongdoing, that Solon identifies. Moreover, it is this theft of public and sacred property about which the goddess Dike is said to be silent, and it is her silence that launches the poem into an expansive hymn on Dike's coming vengeance in which the city and its people will be utterly destroyed unless Eunomia checks the growth of injustice.[74] Solon's poem thus ties the fate of the *polis* to its leaders' behavior, in which case the security of the people would rest in no small part on its ability to choose its leaders well. If all or almost all magistrates were indeed elected, then the confidence of the electors would in all likelihood be a compelling issue in archaic Athens, especially if those electors constituted none other than the Demos.

73. 4 West, *ll.* 5–20.
74. Hymn: *ll.* 15–29; Eunomia: *ll.* 30–39.

But there is also the confidence of the elite at issue. As the sole pan-Athenian body entrusted with oversight of the *polis*, nothing but the Areiopagos could have been empowered to collect an indemnity from all incoming *tamiai*, to investigate, convict, and punish any errant magistrates, and then to transmute the indemnity into a fine should it be necessary. That supervisory function is also evident in Aeschylus' *Eumenides*, wherein it is the Areiopagos that displays a similar cast of "virtue" as Aristotle elucidated, in which "virtue" is indissolubly joined to wealth and the exercise of power. In the *Eumenides*, Athena characterizes the Areiopagos as the "saving force of the *polis*" (*poleôs sôtêrion*) and "untouched by profit" (*kerdôn athikton*).[75] Giving a positive form to Solon's lamentations in *Eunomia*, Aeschylus situates the Areiopagos as the *polis*' best guardian against crime by its magistrates. It is not surprising, therefore, that *Ath.Pol.* claims that Solon established that one of the principal functions of the Areiopagos was to conduct exit-procedures (*euthynai*) of magistrates and to punish those found to have transgressed the *polis*' laws.[76] Aristotle, of course, credits Solon with endowing the Demos with that very power, which cannot, strictly speaking, be reconciled with the authority of the Areiopagos prior to Ephialtes' reforms. It is worthwhile, nevertheless, to note how both Aristotle and *Ath.Pol.* wish to see Solon as having enlarged the capacity of the state to check its magistrates, even if they anachronistically identify the precise mechanism as an *euthyna*.

If Solon gave to the Areiopagos a tool with which to levy fines on *tamiai*, and indeed on all magistrates, through the census classes, he will have also had to ensure that the Areiopagos had the corresponding powers to undertake such action if it did not already have them. As R. Wallace has convincingly shown, prior to Solon the Areiopagos was almost surely an informal body without firm or extensive authority.[77] Moreover, Wallace makes a persuasive case that Solon not only formalized the membership of the Areiopagos as consisting of ex-*arkhontes* with lifelong tenure, but also granted to it oversight of the *polis* and its laws (*nomophylakia*) that by necessity placed it in power over any and all magistrates charged with carrying out those laws. Moreover, it is Solon, Wallace posits, who created the procedure of *eisangelia* by which citizens could denounce abusive or corrupt magistrates before the Areiopagos. In concert with

75. Aes. *Eum.* 701, 704.
76. Cf. Plu. *Sol.* 19.2. Wallace (1989), 57–64, argues persuasively that the broader ascription to Solon (of the Areiopagos as the *nomophylax* of the state) is historical, and not merely a fourth-century fiction.
77. Wallace (1989), 3–69.

those powers, indemnities required even of the wealthiest Athenians serving as magistrates makes excellent sense, for this would provide a critical means by which the Areiopagos could enforce its new writ.

In sum, for those Athenians who might have possessed the ambition to serve as *tamiai* of Athena, Solon's Law represented new opportunities as well as challenges. Electoral politics at the tribal level survived, but they were now subordinated to a random process; great wealth was required of them and over which a newly empowered Areiopagos had special authority, but in return that wealth and the exclusivity of their office set them apart from all others. Whatever the immediate reaction to the Law was, the long-term effects of the Law can hardly have been apparent, though the implications would provide far-reaching, as I will show in coming chapters.

CHAPTER 2

The Solonian Calendar and Solon's Other Laws

A significant legal monument in its own right, Solon's Law on the Tamiai poses an important question: was it Solon's only law that concerned a magistracy? As I will show in this chapter, the answer is surely "no." Solon appears to have mandated other laws that fixed what would henceforth be essential features of important magistracies, notwithstanding how customary many if not most of those duties had been. By legally committing an office to particular responsibilities in this manner, each measure established benchmarks to which the Areiopagos could hold magistrates accountable. These laws would also prove critical to the process by which Solon and his successors catalyzed the future growth of the *polis*' administrative apparatus, which I will explore in the next chapter. Property, as ever, lies at the heart of that development, for the laws likely spelled out what precisely a given magistrate's responsibility was for the financial and other resources of the *polis*.

The principle source of evidence for these laws is a sacrificial calendar for the whole *polis* that has often been associated with Solon himself but which appears only to have drawn on individual laws for its data. Inscribed on marble only in 399 after some eleven years of work, through both tyranny and war, by a special commission, this monument comprises two individual calendars. Given its complexity, hereafter I refer to the whole monument as the Calendar to avoid confusion with its subsidiary calendars and any comparanda. What preceded the Calendar remains a mystery. Neither any literary testimony nor any fragments of inscriptions have been identified as belonging to a *polis*-wide calendar antedating the Calendar. With the exception of a single text, Lysias 30

(*Against Nikomakhos*), no ancient source directly credits Solon with creating anything approaching a sacrificial calendar. That omission is telling. *Against Nikomakhos* details how the project of creating and inscribing the Calendar was part and parcel of a larger project, begun in 410, to restore Athens' political and moral wellbeing on the foundation of whatever Solonian laws could be discovered and published anew. But of course the process of discovery was politically freighted, and it may have been impossible at times to judge accurately just what was genuinely Solonian and what was merely ancient. In exploring that tortured political history, J. Shear has recently offered a detailed reconstruction of the Calendar's physical arrangement at the Stoa Basileios, particularly the complex relationship between the Calendar's Attic and Ionic calendars that likely represent two successive efforts at compilation (in which the Attic side was perhaps nullified or at least superseded).[1] But it is the general import of particular features of the Calendar's data that is most of interest here, for the Calendar expresses in monumental form Athens' commitment to observe its own financial and ritual obligations to conduct particular sacrifices. While the Calendar is a product of the democracy, its sources are those laws of Solon that specified the duties of magistrates responsible for meeting those obligations in an earlier time.

The Phylobasileis *and the Archaic Origins of the Calendar*

Like all sacrificial calendars, the Solonian Calendar presents a kind of raw data for whose interpretation there is no straightforward key. Such texts are often mined for their information on deities and sacrifices, but there is another dimension that is essential to their function but frequently neglected, and that dimension is public finance. Notwithstanding its great size and complexity, the Calendar is typologically like all other calendars in those respects. The purpose of the Calendar was to set out the financial obligations of the *polis* with respect not only to a whole schedule of sacrifices and offerings, all of which had to be specified for ritual purposes as well, but also to the various emoluments that the *polis* owed to certain priests and even magistrates who possessed ritual functions.

But the Calendar sets out those obligations in a very narrow framework. Its extant fragments indicate costs for those perquisites and sacrifices but other-

1. Shear (2011).

wise say very little about how those various perquisites and rituals were to be financed.[2] Without exception, the Calendar ignores those costs that might well accrue to the *polis* but lie outside of its most immediate purview, such as the very heavy expenses relating to processions for festivals, sacred embassies for festivals outside of Attica, the cost of Athenian support for religious affairs of many kinds at Delos, and so on, some of which I detail in chapters 4 through 6.[3] Nor does the Calendar detail even the costs of the fuel and equipment needed to butcher and prepare the sacrificial meat for consumption, and of course there are simply no instructions concerning how to arrange the sacrifices, whom to include and exclude, and the like.[4] Such concerns simply did not fall under the limited purview of the schedule nor, by extension, of whoever was charged with seeing that these obligations were met.

Where the Calendar identifies specific magistrates, it is solely in relation to their ritual capacity. The Calendar regularly stipulates the monetary equivalent for perquisites of two kinds—either *hierôsyna* owed to the *phylobasileis* (discussed below) or *apometra* owed to priestesses—usually in lieu of certain animal parts, the value of which typically exceeds that of the sacrificial offerings themselves.[5] Likewise, when stipulating the costs for sacrificial animals (usually specified as to type, occasionally with further detail on gender, age, and size), the Calendar offers no guidance as to the significance of these offerings or the rituals involved except, by virtue of the monument's own size and likely loca-

2. I suspect that there is more that the Calendar's prose texts (e.g., *IG* I[3] 237) can tell us about funding mechanisms, and I hope to return to this subject in another investigation. Hereafter, all references to fragments of the Calendar follow the system set out by Lambert "Calendar."
3. This celebration of the Delia appears to consist exclusively of rites performed in Attica, and not necessarily coordinated with the major celebration of the (quadrennial) Delia in which the Athenians dispatched sacred embassies to Delos itself (which the Athenians reinitiated only in 426), concerning all of which (and the festival's putative connection to Theseus), see now Chankowski (2008), 70–77, 86–106, 189. The Ionic Face does seem to preserve requirements that sacrifice for Apollo be offered on Delos, but the entries that follow are so modest that the major festivals such as the Delia must have occupied some other part of the Calendar, if at all. It is not clear whether the monument ever refers to the panhellenic festivals, Athenian embassies to oracular shrines (particularly Delphi), or even to the Athenian Amphiktyoneia over Delos.
4. The sole surviving reference to fuel only demonstrates the point, for F1B, col. 2 *ll.* 12–13 ([--] χσύλον *v.*| [--] *h*ιερôν *v.*) requires wood, *hiera* and (then, in the next line, sacrificial victims) to be given to some deity (or just possibly, the priestess whose *apometra* was valued in *l.* 10). Given this association of wood with offerings, and that the Calendar always omits the costs for the fuel necessary for cooking those sacrifices that its fragments fully or partially preserves, the wood here most likely served some ritual function. Alternatively, the wood was listed as an item due to the priestess, whose cash value she could receive in lieu of the wood itself.
5. The fragments explicitly attest ἱερώσυνα for the perquisite at F3A col. 1, *ll.* 4, 23, col. 2, *ll.* 39, 52; F6A, *l.* 6, and ἀπόμετρα at F1B, *l.* 10; F3A col. 3, *l.* 76; F6A, *l.* 3; F12A, *l.* 7.

tion, of their broad importance to the *polis*.[6] Therefore, to the extent that the Calendar is a budgetary document at least as much as it is a religious one, it is only concerned with those expenditures that are ritually demanded by an established schedule of sacrifices, which it duly provides, and not by any general, unscheduled, or otherwise undetermined obligations.

The corollary to its narrowly framed fiscal dimension is that the Calendar is inherently conservative, and where it did employ some or another innovation it did not disturb the precision of religious ritual. But the Calendar does show signs of important innovation that, in turn, illuminate its relationship to its sources. A little noticed but salient feature of the monument is that all of the costs stated for animals, food offerings, and perquisites owed to various parties reflect the economic conditions of the turn of the fourth century and not those of Solon's time. Plutarch states that in Solon's laws a single sheep or a *medimnos* of barley for sacrifice was valued at only a single *drakhma*, while the least valuable sheep in the Calendar cost twelve times that.[7] Admittedly, no values are known for these victims for most of the period intervening between Solon and the Calendar's completion.[8] But the Calendar's figures are in line with other Athenian sacred calendars of the late fifth and early fourth centuries and so clearly reflect contemporary financial costs.[9] Because costs were never ritually intrinsic to the offering itself, the Calendar's compilers could update what could

6. Robertson (1990), 44, rightfully expresses concern also about a tendency among modern scholars to consider the Calendar and laws as constituting a law-code and draws attention to how no ancient authors mention a coherent monument either available for consultation or as an emblem of justice.

7. In Lambert F3A col. 3, *l.* 60, the price or value of a single adult sheep, probably a ewe, is 12 dr. while that of a ram regularly lists at 17 dr. (F2A, *l.* 11; F3A, *l.* 64; F8A, *l.* 10); see Lambert "Calendar," 396, for different figures relating to age, gender (and for males, whether castrated or not), special quality. Even the price for a single sheep lacking age-teeth, and therefore of relatively little worth, has the price or value of 4 dr. (F3A, *ll.* 37–38; F6A, *ll.* 9–10).

Plutarch (*Sol.* 23.3): εἰς μέν γε τὰ τιμήματα τῶν θυσιῶν λογίζεται πρόβατον καὶ δραχμὴν ἀντὶ μεδίμνου. Another point of comparison is Plutarch's claim (*Sol.* 21.2) that Solon's law against defamation required a fine of 3 dr. payable to the insulted party with an additional 2 dr. payable to the public treasury (*dêmosion*); at Lysias 10.12 (of 384/3) and the approximately contemporary Isocrates 20.3 the fine cited for much the same offense is 500 dr., for which see Todd (2007), 633. For the evidence of other Attic calendars, see the tabular synopsis of Van Straten (1995), 175–79; cf. Lambert "Calendar," 397.

8. Too many scholars (e.g., Scafuro [2006], 190; Blok [2006], 218–22) treat the relation of Solonian fragments to the monetary values that some of those fragments mention in a cavalier, even circular, manner with regard to the texts' authenticity. Sacrificial values appear to be the most comparable figures over time, so long as there is no expectation that these must closely reflect market prices and they are not used to determine the authenticity of the fragments in question.

9. It is likely that the Calendar reflects the depressed economic conditions of Athens at the end of the fifth century, for which see Samons (2000), 275–91; Strauss (1986), 42–59. Van Straten (1995), 175–79, provides a convenient breakdown of the figures found in most surviving Attic calendar fragments.

be altered. To retain obsolete financial figures, after all, would likely impede the *polis* from carrying out the sacrifices precisely as mandated.

That principal, according to which the Calendar preserves information that might otherwise be lost through a wholesale updating, is also manifest in how the Calendar refers to the material that underlies its own arrangement of sacrifices. The Calendar merely indicates the source of authority for a particular sacrifice, signified persistently by the preposition *ek* ("from") and the general class of source, of which the certainly attested rubrics are as follows: "from those according to month" (*ek tôn kata mêna*), "from those according to unspecified (day)" (*ek tôn [hêmerai] mê rhêtêi*), "from those of the *phylobasileis*" (*ek tôn phylobasilikôn*).[10] Because none of the Calendar's fragments cite an individual law as a source, these rubrics can hardly reflect the manner in which the original sources for the document were organized if, following Lysias at least, they are ultimately Solonian in origin. Rather, it seems that these are general categories of sacrifice whose individual items are merely collated from the *kyrbeis* and rearranged.[11] The principle underlying these two former, temporally situated rubrics is, quite simply, the frequency with which the *polis* must provide specific sacrifices or perquisites; I will return to discuss the final rubric involving the *phylobasileis* shortly.

The general use of rubrics, critically, points to an assemblage of sources, not a single master calendar that had merely to be amended. S. Dow, for one, perceived that without dividing even a single calendar, let alone several, into their respective annual cycles and breakdown by month and day, it would have been very cumbersome and prone to error for the Athenians to ensure that they managed adequately the monies and other resources mandated by the Calendar, to say nothing of how the magistrates would manage their responsibilities therewith.[12] The very organization of the Calendar along these lines would therefore seem to offer another example of innovation by those responsible for producing the inscribed text.

The Calendar is, to put it bluntly, little more than a highly abbreviated set of

10. Lambert "Calendar," 371–72, is more doubtful than S. Dow "Greek Inscriptions" *Hesperia* 10 (1941), 35, that F2A might also indicate yet another rubric (Lambert only adds a question mark in the second bracket, hence: *l.* 3: [ἐκ?] νέων [-?]), and points out that omission of the definite article here would not accord with the firmly attested rubrics found among the fragments. If Dow's supposition is correct, then ἐκ νέων might indicate post-Solonian sources, but this remains only an awkward supposition at best; see n. 61 below.

11. Dow (1953–1957), 15–21; Stroud (1979), 9. Lambert "Calendar," 356–57, suggests that the former two categories may be subdivisions within the *kyrbeis*, that is, reflecting Solon's own divisions.

12. Dow (1960), 281.

instructions to one or more key magistrates concerning their fiscal obligations with regard to a limited schedule of sacrifices, each set of which might have been paired with a law establishing the general instruction to be followed. From the lengthiest fragment (F3A), covering not even two full days in the month of Hekatombaion on the Ionic Face—and then only in the category of sacrifices to be offered every other year[13]—a single column (col. 2) illustrates these features in an especially vivid manner:

τάδε τὸ ἕτερον ἔτος θύεται Α[-
῾Εκατομβαιῶνος
πέμπτηι ἐπὶ δέκα
ἐκ τῶν φυλο-
βασιλικῶν
Γλεόντων φυλῆι
Λευκοταινίων
τριττύι οἶν
⊢⊢⊢⊢ λειπογνώμονα
⊢⊢⊢⊢|| ἱερώ̣συνα
φυλοβ[α]σιλεῦσι
νῶτο
κήρυκι ὦμο
|||| ποδῶν κεφαλῆς
ἕκτηι ἐπὶ δέκα
ἐκ τῶν φυλο-
βασιλικῶν
Γλέοντων φυλῆι
Διὶ Φρατρίωι καὶ
᾿Αθηναίαι Φρα-
τρίαι βόε δύο
𐅄 [λ]ειπογνώμονε

13. Dow (1960) shows that almost surely this particular biennial sequence, one of two that the Calendar must have possessed (and which Lambert "Calendar" identifies tentatively on F2A), was performed in years starting in even-numbered Julian dates (i.e., 0/9, 8/7, 6/5, etc.), but Lambert "Calendar," 376, disagrees that the year 400/399 commenced this sequence altogether.

:ΔΓ⊢	ἱερώσυνα
	φυλοβασιλεῖ
	σκέλος
	κήρυ[κ]ι χέλυος
⊢⊢|||	ποδ[ῶ]ν κεφαλῆς
	τ. [.³.]ει κριθῶν
vac.	μ[έδιμ]ν̣ο̣.

[The other year these things . . . are sacrificed:

Hekatombaion:

On the 15th from that of the *phylobasileis*, to the tribe of Gleontes, to the *trittys* of the Leukotainioi: a sheep that possesses its underage teeth: 4 dr.

Privilege for the *phylobasileis*: 4 dr. 2 ob.

the chine: 1 dr.

For the Herald: meat of the feet, head: 4 dr.

On the 16th from that of the *phylobasileis*, to the tribe of Gleontes, for Zeus Phratrios and Athena Phratria: two kine that possess their underage teeth: 16 dr.

Privilege for the *phylobasileis*: the leg

For the Herald: a "*khelys*" of the feet, head: 2 dr. 3 ob.

. . . *medimnos* of barley]

The restrictive character of the monument did not preclude the *polis* from supplementing or offering much more than is listed here, but merely establishes the necessary minimums.

An illuminating case in point is the festival of the Synoikia, which this particular column covers on the 16th of Hekatombaion. An important event that ritually commemorates Theseus' unification of Attica with divine sanction, the Synoikia is relatively well attested in the heortological lore of antiquity, and its significance is underlined by the activities required on the previous day.[14] On the 15th of Hekatombaion, the Calendar specifies no deity as the recipient of sacrifice but merely demands that sacrificial animals be granted to certain groups and individuals for what is perhaps, in Dow's estimation, the prelimi-

14. On the Synoikia, see Parker (1996), 14, 112–14 (on this fragment), 169, 230; (2005), 207, 480–81.

nary sacrifice (*prothyma*) undertaken by those in charge of the Synoikia proper.[15] If in fact this is a *prothyma*, it is notable also for the relatively high value of the perquisites alone (14 dr. total), for the rite was one of minimal financial cost despite its ritual significance.[16] But the Ionic Face situates the festival within one of its two (alternating) biennial sequences, though few Athenian festivals are known to have been actually celebrated only in alternate years.[17] Moreover, the Calendar says nothing about what other bodies of the *polis*, or groups of citizens, might do for those very same festivals listed therein. By virtue of its own sacral regulations of c. 460, the deme of Skambonidai, for instance, is also known to have offered at the Synoikia a full-grown victim upon the akropolis that paralleled the offerings made by the *polis* at what was likely one and the same site.[18] If there was any doubt, the Calendar thus only commits the *polis* to funding the festival, and only in the very particular way that is listed above: every other year. Nothing precludes citizens or their demes from celebrating the festival every year, nor the *polis* even from providing other funds and resources—vastly greater than what is scheduled here—for the procession, ritual equipment, sacrifice, butchery, and so on in any year whatsoever. Although there does seem to be an annual sequence on the Calendar, the use of two lengthy biennial sequences (and probably cycles of still lesser frequency) show that on this monument the *polis* is interested in documenting only its most absolutely necessary obligations.[19] If it was ritually acceptable, so the logic must have been, to provide this specific funding for the Synoikia only every other year, then that is what the *polis* would do henceforth. It is this principal, I suggest, that the Calendar's compilers applied universally to the offerings listed thereupon.

---

15. *Prothyma*: Dow (1953–57), 22. It is not clear whether this *prothyma* was meant to presage a particular event, such as a contest, or served as an offering to one particular god before another god's sacrifice, for the distinction between which see Mikalson (1972).
16. For example, in the Teithras calendar (*Hesperia* 30 [1961], Face A, *l.* 9), Zeus is to receive a sheep as a *prothyma* whose worth does not even merit notation in terms of *oboloi* and likely consisted of a suckling pig, for which see Mikalson (1972), 583.
17. One biennial festival was that of Zeus Nemeios, which does appear in one of the biennial sequences (F2A; cf. Lambert "Nemean" [2002]), for which see Lambert "Calendar," 372–73 and 374, on a possible instance involving the Plynteria; cf. Parker "Polytheism" (2005), 468–69, on the problematic evidence for the Eleusinia also being biennial.
18. *IG* I³ 244 C, *ll.* 16–17. The duplication of the Synoikia may be an argument against Figueira's claim (1984), 465–66, that this festival was, even by the mid-sixth century, an oligarchic homologue to the Panathenaia as belonging to the Demos, and this is why the *phylobasileis* remained involved in it. That any oligarchic residue can justify the celebration held by the whole of the people of Skambonidai seems difficult to accept.
19. Annual cycle: F1A, both cols. 1–2. Lambert "Calendar," 357, raises the possibility that all of the Attic and Ionic script festivals listed on the thickest series of *stêlai* may have been annual or biennial.

The third example of editorial intervention in the Calendar concerns the nomenclature of key magistrates whose existence has universally been thought to indicate the fossilized nature of the contents, but whose presence points rather to the *polis'* continued commitment to fund those rituals that it deemed essential obligations of a recurring, fixed nature. At this juncture, it is best to turn more squarely to the role of the *phylobasileis* in the Calendar since it is their nomenclature that is at issue. Even after the radicalizing crises and political debacles of the late fifth century, it is clear that the restored democracy attributed ritual significance to the pre-Kleisthenic state's Ionian tribes, shorn nevertheless of the political roles they possessed prior to 508/7. For they appear on no less than the Ionic side of the Calendar, which was probably the last part of the monument that was inscribed and was considered authoritative. In the text cited above, on the 15th of Hekatombaion, (*ll.* 35–37), the *polis* must provide a young sheep for the Leukotainioi, a *trittys* of the Ionian tribe of the Gleontes, for both tribe and *trittys* to sacrifice.[20] On the same day, the *polis* grants to the *phylobasileis* the victims necessary for a preliminary sacrifice (here, a *prothyma*) before the Synoikia festival, which can only mean that the heads of as many as all four Ionian (that is, pre-Kleisthenic) tribes must still have held an active office. On the day of the Synoikia itself (the 16th of Hekatombaion), the Gleontes sacrifice to Zeus Phratrios and Athena Phratria, and their one *phylobasileus* is to receive a sacrificial perquisite (*hierôsyna*) consisting of various animal parts, or he is to receive the equivalent monetary value thereof.[21] These sacrifices were aimed at deities that protected, in effect, the *phratriai*, which served as essential quasi-familial associations of Athenians and thus were surely tied to one of the *phylobasileus'* core functions.[22] For whatever particular reason, Kleisthenes and his successors felt that those duties could not be transferred to the *arkhôn basileus* on the constitutional eclipse of the Ionic tribes in 508/7. Of note is the law of Drakon on

---

20. The age of the animal is assured by the term *leipognômôn*, which Lambert "Calendar," 396 n. 44, argues likely indicates a lack of age-teeth (and is commensurate with the relatively low financial value of the animal). Rosivach (1994), 148–53, esp. 151–53, points to the extensive lemmata in the lexicographers that *leipognômôn* was used for animals past their prime (i.e., having no more deciduous teeth to lose, and also being quite aged). While it is true that animals bearing this description are valued less than those that are *teleia* (i.e., adult with respect to their teeth), it does not make sense for the Solonian and other calendars to insist on the sacrifice of so many aged victims, and none that are young. It would thus seem that the lexicographers are at pains to explain a term that is no longer current and have drawn erroneous conclusions from whatever sources they had at their disposal.

21. Lambert "Calendar," 399, briefly lists the other officials that the Calendar identifies as recipients.

22. Lambert (1998), 206–09, suggests that Athenian worship of the gods of the *phratriai* (principally Zeus Phratrios and Athena Phratria, but Apollo Patroös also) was heavily bound up with Ionian identity, and further suggests, 210, that the Calendar's stipulations for Athena and Zeus' offerings at the Synoikia must have been carried out "in a central temple of the two deities" (but does not identify which shrine this ought to have been).

involuntary homicide (and the only of Drakon's laws that Solon retained as one of his own). As part of their republication of Solon's laws, the Athenians also undertook to inscribe this law anew and set it up at the Stoa Basileios, and thus at the headquarters of the *arkhôn basileus* himself.[23] Since the law names the *basileis* (sic) alone as responsible for judging certain cases, and invokes the *phratria* as a kin group responsible for pursuing the killer, the Calendar's sacrifices to the gods of the *phratriai* point to a ritual act in which the *phylobasileis* secure the good will of the divine over their jurisdiction as well as the harmony of the tribes and *phratriai* under their authority.[24] An obvious, fundamental principle in Greek religion is that just as one must sacrifice for oneself to acquire the good will of a deity, and thus to achieve one's wishes, so, too, do sacrifices conducted on behalf of groups or corporate bodies, ranging from a family to a whole *polis*, depend for success on the identity of the person responsible for, or actually committing, the sacrificial act and offering it to the deity.

For the *polis*' safety and benefit, it would appear, these old tribes and their subsidiary groups could in no way be swept away or allowed to die of neglect once they had been stripped of their constitutional functions by Kleisthenes' reforms. By such reasoning, the Geleontes (*sic*) and Leukotainioi were surely considered intrinsic to those rituals, such that no other person or body could conduct the ritual for it to be at all effective (or even acceptable to the gods).[25] N. Papazarkadas, too, has recently suggested that an enigmatic ritual group, the Epakreis, likewise constituted another pre-Kleisthenic *trittys* that held some ritual task on the akropolis until at least the early fourth century.[26] That the *phylobasileis* likewise possessed the exclusive authority to perform a function critical to the *polis* must surely have lain behind their continued participation, if not conduct, in an entangled array of legal and sacrificial duties. Indeed, the

23. *IG* I^3 105.
24. See n. 25 below; cf. Appendix n. 19.
25. For Lambert (1998), 210, the Geleontes "had for all practical purposes long since ceased to exist." Figueira (1984), 465–66, suggests that the Leukotainioi constituted not merely a *trittys* of the tribe, but rather that particular *trittys* which he believes must only have been made up of the Eupatridai, and it was on this basis that the Atthidographers and lexicographers could claim that the Eupatridai generally had an absolute privilege to conduct certain rituals (or, alternatively, to obtain the benefits therefrom). Of particular interest is Pollux's note (8.111) that the *phylobasileis* came from the Eupatridai (of which I quote only the immediately relevant section): οἱ φυλοβασιλεῖς· ἐξ εὐπατριδῶν δὲ ὄντες, μάλιστα τῶν ἱερῶν ἐπεμελοῦντο, συνεδρεύοντες ἐν τῷ βασιλείῳ τῷ παρὰ τὸ βουκολεῖον.
26. Papazarkadas (2011). Intriguingly, the best evidence for the Epakreis is a fragmentary lease (*IG* II^2 2490), which Papazarkadas re-edits and dates to the first quarter of the fourth century. Since leases of *hosia* land were used to fund sacrifices and other ritual ends, this particular text raises the question of whether the Epakreis appeared in the Calendar at all and thus required a special source of funding in the years following that document's completion.

phylobasileis maintained a key role in matters not only concerning involuntary homicide but also cases of manslaughter brought against animals and inanimate objects.[27] J. Carlier has even suggested that such authority would surely involve the *phylobasileis* in the *bouphonia* at the festival of the Dipolieia, in which the slaughterer flees and it is the ax that is taken to the Prytaneion (where the *phylobasileis* held court over these objects) and thence condemned (and perhaps even acquitted!) before being expelled physically from Attica.[28] Indeed, a fragment of the Calendar's Attic Face appears to indicate a key act of that ritual, the driving of oxen around a sacrificial table.[29] Both Pollux and Hesykhios claim that the *phylobasileis* were indeed the necessary officiants for a number of sacrifices, so widely in fact that we must imagine them involved in far more than the Synoikia, and possibly the Dipolieia as well.[30] In any event, the Calendar and Drakon's law would thus seem to be in concert, for they are both concerned only with the *phylobasileis*' responsibilities with regard to *phratriai* in a limited number of senses.

But because the republished homicide law identifies these magistrates only as *basileis* and quotes directly from Drakon's law, it is quite likely that the Calendar, whose extant fragments quote nothing at all, has actually coined the nomenclature of *phylobasileis* to avoid confusion with the *arkhôn basileus*. Later in that section of the Calendar dealing with the Dipolieia, by way of example, the text stipulates perquisites for the "*kêrykes* who . . . for the Dipolieia," which S. Lambert understands as phrasing that is intended to clarify that true heralds, and not members of the Eleusinian *genos* of the same name, were to receive the benefits in question.[31] In point of fact, the law is the earliest epi-

---

27. The legal reason behind these two areas of competency may lie in that these nonhuman agents could be thought of as having committed a kind of involuntary homicide or something akin to that category of action, since angry bulls, falling trees, and the like certainly could not be thought of as possessing human *intention* to commit an act resulting in the death of a person; see n. 28 below. On the legal authority of the *phylobasileis*, see also Carlier (1984), 353–59; MacDowell (1963), 86–89; Todd (1993), 275; Gagarin (1981), 46–47, 129.

28. Carlier (1984), 354–55. Sealey (2006) argues that the purpose of these trials held by the *phylobasileis* was not to assuage some feeling or another about ritual pollution but to seek vengeance against the object or animal. If so, it would be difficult, but not impossible, from a juridical point of view to reconcile acquittal with such an aim.

29. F1B, *ll.* 7–15, with further commentary by Lambert "Calendar," 386, in support of J. Oliver's (1935), 32, initial identification of the ritual in these lines.

30. Pollux 8.111 (see n. 25 above): μάλιστα τῶν ἱερῶν ἐπιμελοῦντο; Hesykhios s.v. φυλοβασιλεῖς· ἐκ τῶν φυλῶν αἱρετοί, οἱ τὰς θυσίας ἐπιτελοῦντες. Another fragment (F7A) consists of almost nothing more than the same rubric and designation of perquisites for the *phylobasileis*, but for which specific festival we are at a loss to know.

31. Lambert "Calendar," 387, discussing F1B, *l.* 14: κέρυχσιν *h*οι Διπολιεί[ο]ι[ς. . .].

graphic attestation of these magistrates' nomenclature, and one wonders whether it is from the Calendar that later citations among the Atthidographers, *Ath.Pol.*, and the lexicographers principally derive. But the reason for so altering the nomenclature was surely not one of banishing its obscurity to contemporary Athenians, as if they could not remember who or what these officers were, and since there was never more than one *arkhôn basileus* at a time, moreover, sheer numbers of *basileis* could not have been the relevant factor. The magistracy of the *phylobasileis* was no doubt intimately known to citizens, all of whom belonged to *phratriai* that logically would have come under the rules laid out by Drakon's law (and a nexus of other laws and customs, too). Moreover, unless the *phylobasileus* of any given tribe was restricted to a certain *phratria*, as the position of the Leukotainioi vis-à-vis the Geleontes might suggest, the mere fact that valuable perquisites and surely prestige were available would have been another incentive for various citizens to seek this office. Wherever there are comparable figures in the Calendar that enable one to check, the monetary value of the perquisites assigned to the *phylobasileis* compares well with that of the sacrifices they perform, a large portion of which they likely consumed as well.[32] (It is far more significant in the case of priestesses, to whom the Calendar regularly ascribes perquisites it labels as *apometra*, one of which reached fully 100 dr. in value).[33] It is difficult to imagine what Athenian would willingly pass up such an opportunity. But with the wording of the Calendar, emphasizing by its possible neologism that these kings belonged solely to the tribes, the *arkhôn basileus* was thus debarred from receiving the *hierôsyna* such as the mere plural "*basileis*" in the Calendar might allow.[34] With such choice of language, the text reminds us that the behavior of sacred treasurers and those wishing to attain such a position might well have played a role in shaping the laws that gave rise to the Calendar.

Otherwise, there are few obvious signs of change, and it is not impossible to

32. In the text cited above, at the Synoikia the lone *phylobasileus* of the Geleontes receives perquisites of an ox's leg worth fully 16 dr. (*l.* 52) when the oxen sacrificed were marked at only 50 dr. *in total*. This latter figure would seem to reflect an expectation that the depressed market conditions following the Peloponnesian War would hold good. For when the *hieropoioi* received in 410/9 a sum (5,114 dr.) with which to purchase cattle for a hekatomb sacrifice (*IG* I^3 375, *ll.* 6–7), the per capita amount available for that purchase (assuming fully one hundred head of cattle were to be bought) would of course be just over 51 dr.

33. Apometra: priestess of Demeter at Eleusis (F3A, *l.* 76), and for a survey of which in the Calendar see Lambert "Calendar," 398–99.

34. Conversely, the Drakonian law seems to open up that very possibility with regard to that law, after all, since the purely legal functions ought to have been taken up by the *arkhôn basileus*.

locate a few other instances where those responsible for the republication might have hewed as closely as possible to the original wording of their sources. Since, for example, the name of the relevant tribe is spelled here without an *epsilon* (thus, Gleontes) but is reasonably well attested elsewhere with it (thus, Geleontes), it is quite possible that Nikomakhos and his fellow magistrates stuck to the Solonian spelling wherever possible (in contrast to later sources on the tribe, interestingly enough).[35] In Euripides' *Ion* of c. 410, the tribal eponym is spelled with an *epsilon* as fits the meter.[36] Likewise, the possible appearance of the word *gylion* in F12, probably denoting a small pig, might also mark an instance where the monument clarifies the vocabulary found in Solon's laws since Athenians of the fifth century and beyond used words like *khoiros* and *delphax*, while *gylion* is otherwise unattested except for the lexicographers.[37] One must also consider the evidence of Lysias 10, which purports to quote sections from several laws of Solon in language quite different from contemporary Attic, all of which the prosecutor then proceeds to gloss for the jurors.[38] Another inscription closely related to the effort underlying the Calendar also evinces such a concern for the exact text of Solon's law, no matter the linguistic difficulties it caused for Athenians in the late fifth century.[39] One cannot omit mention of what may be the classic example of such loyalty to the text, the initial καί (*kai*) at the beginning of the republished text of Drakon's law on homicide, and which seems to link the law, supposed to be the first in a series, to a text that is completely absent from the inscription.[40] In tandem with its budgetary detail, the Calendar's no-

35. The name of this tribe is not otherwise attested epigraphically at Athens, but among the Ionian states (and frequently Roman in date and also of a funerary nature): mod. Casimcea: *IScM* V 132; Kolophon (or Ephesos?): *AJP* 1935, pp. 380–81, no. 6; Kyzikos: *CIG* 3664–65 and Lolling (1888); Odessos: *IGBulg* I 47bis; Teos: *CIG* 3078 121; Tomis: *IScM* II 300. The only known Athenian usage outside of the Calendar is that of an epithet for Zeus based on the stem of this name (in the grammatical singular): *IG* II² 1072, *l.* 6; like most of the Ionian texts, it too is Roman in date. The apocopated form is never attested in literary texts, and the tribe only appears in Plutarch (*Sol.* 23.5) and a few late texts listing the four Ionian tribes (e.g., St.Byz. s.v. 'Αιγικόρεως).

36. E. *Ion*, *l.* 1579: Γελέων μὲν ἔσται πρῶτος. Curiously, Euripides then switches in the succeeding lines (1580–81, in the 1979 Teubner ed. of W. Biehl) to name the tribes by their customary adjectival forms although they, too, would be named after the sons of Ion.

37. F12B = *IG* I³ 238. On the *gylion*, see Lambert "Calendar," 391, who rightly cautions, 390–91, that the text of Ross' transcription of this fragment (indeed, its only source) is problematic.

38. Stroud (1968), 24 n. 21, even cites Lysias 10.16–22 as a useful reflection of the difficulties that he believes slowed the project of the Calendar to a crawl over two periods, 410/9–405/4 and 403/2–399. Stroud also suggests that the *nomothetai* must not have modernized the language of those ordinances. Hillgruber (1988), 65–66, is less sanguine about the possibility that these passages reflect Solon's original law, but is ultimately unconvincing.

39. *IG* I³ 105, with Lewis (1967).

40. *IG* I³ 104, *l.* 11. As to other possible causes for this odd καί, see especially Stroud (1968).

menclature and vocabulary thus appear to reflect the very limited editorial intervention of its compilers and betoken a strict conservatism stipulating the exact requirements of the *polis* and nothing more.

Solonian Laws behind the Calendar?

Even if, aside from the particular issues identified so far, the commissioners responsible for the Calendar did not radically alter the often arcane data that constituted its subsidiary calendars but merely reshaped their arrangement and expression, a critical question remains. Whereas I have already had cause to suggest that the data did not derive from a single calendar of Solon's creation, the goal of this section is to determine still more concretely the degree to which that data might genuinely reach back to Solon through some other medium, and, correspondingly, whether it is possible to form a reasonably plausible idea of the lawgiver's intent. Irrespective of the answer to those two related problems, the result will open yet another window into how the various offices of sacred treasurer and their larger framework of state developed historically.

The immediate task at hand, nonetheless, is to examine more closely how the sources for the Calendar might match the known and probable content of Solon's laws, although the Calendar's fragments make no obvious reference to the laws, much less to the specific *kyrbeis* and *axones* on which the laws were inscribed originally. Notwithstanding how muddled ancient authorities on Solon and his laws could be, they do provide several intriguing clues about the distribution of sacral material among those laws. Perhaps following Eratosthenes' attempt to distinguish *kyrbeis* from *axones* on the basis of their physical characteristics, Aristophanes of Byzantion is known to have argued for a further distinction, namely, that a single *kyrbis* contained only (or all of the *kyrbeis*') sacral material and that the *axones* were exclusively associated with *nomoi*.[41] Both attempts at explanation, however, are likely in error, for the comic

41. Fr. 410 Slater, which I quote according to Slater's text, which in turn is based on Reitzenstein's (1897) edition of the manuscripts of the Etymologium Gudianum and Genuinum (EGud and EGen): Σελεύκου. Κύρβεις . . . ᾿Ασκληπιάδης δὲ ἐν τοῖς τῶν ἀξόνων ἐξηγητικοῖς (*FGrH* 339 F1) ἀπὸ Κύρβεως τοῦ τὰς †οὐσιας† (θυσίας Anecdota Graeca Oxoniensis 1, 221, 8) ὁρίσαντος ὥς (ἢ ὥς coni. Reitzenstein) φησι Φανίης ᾿Ερέσιος (fr. 22b Wehrli *Phain.*; cf. fr. 22a) ἀπὸ (ἢ ἀπὸ coni. Reitz.) τοῦ ταῦτα κυρωθῆναι τοῖς γράμμασιν. ᾿Ερατοσθένης δὲ (fr. 80 Strecker) τριγώνους αὐτάς φησιν εἶναι, οὐ τετραγώνους. ᾿Αριστοφάνης δέ φησιν ὁμοίας εἶναι τοῖς ἄξοσιν, πλὴν ὅτι οἱ μὲν ἄξονες νόμους, αἱ δὲ κύρβεις †οὐσιας† (θυσίας Anecdota Graeca Oxoniensis 1, 221, 11) ἔχουσιν. ἀμφοτέρων δὲ τετραγώνων (om. EGen.) τὸ κατασκεύασμα τοιοῦτον . . .

poets of the fifth century, who were in a position to know the devices at first hand before they eventually crumbled, made no such distinction whatsoever.[42] Moreover, a scholion to one of those sources, Aristophanes' *Birds*, identifies the *axones* explicitly as containing public religious matters pertaining to the state, but in addition to *nomoi*:[43]

> κατὰ δὲ ἐνίους ἄξονες τρίγωνοι ἐν οἷς ἦσαν οἱ τῶν πόλεων νόμοι γεγραμμένοι καὶ αἱ δημοσίαι ἱεροποιίαι.
>
> [According to some, the *axones* upon which the *nomoi* of the cities and the public acts of religion were inscribed were of three corners.]

While all other sources on Solon's laws suggest that both kinds of object contained *nomoi*, the scholion's distinction is worth noting for it would suggest, although it cannot be verified, that Solon established separate or distinct laws pertaining to religious festivals. Indeed, the scholion's use of the term ἱεροποιία (*hieropoiia*), which implies the activity of the class of sacred treasurers known as *hieropoioi*, thus points to those festivals that received explicit support from the *polis* such as to render them *dêmosiai*, that is, publicly funded and, by extension, under the supervision and support of *hieropoioi*, among others.[44] This connection would seem to agree with a citation in the so-called Antiatticist lexicon that Philokhoros along with Solon "in the *axones*" were a source for information on Solon's establishment of the publicly supported festival of the Genesia:[45]

> Γενέσια· οὔσης τε ἑορτῆς δημοτελοῦς 'Αθήναις, Βοηδρομιῶνος πέμπτῃ, Γενέσια καλουμένης, καθότι Φιλόχορος καὶ Σόλων ἐν τοῖς ἄξοσι.

On the obscure relationship of the *axones* and *kyrbeis* to one another, Stroud (1979) still offers the most comprehensive and judicious attempt at reconstructing the physical monuments, and argues that the two constituted distinct entities (where many scholars equate the two). Most recently, Davis (2011) posits that Solon's laws were originally inscribed on *kyrbeis* (which he takes to be a generic medium not specific to Athenian law) and then copied on *axones*, but his account is problematic and unpersuasive.

42. As T 26–28 Ruschenbusch cites Kratinos fr. 300 K-A, Σ Ar. *Av.* 1354 Holwerda (with 1353–57 = F55a Ruschenbusch), *Ath.Pol.* 7.1; Stroud (1979), 26–28.
43. Σ *Av.* 1354 Holwerda (= T 27 Ruschenbusch).
44. In published Athenian inscriptions, ἱεροποιία appears only once: *SEG* 2.8 (c. 330–325), *ll.* 8–9.
45. *Anecd.Bekk.* vol. 1, AntiAtt. p. 86 no. 20; *FGrH* 328 Philokhoros F168; Solon F84 Ruschenbusch. Also, note Hesykhios, s.v. γενέσια· ἑορτὴ πένθιμος 'Αθηναίοις. οἱ δὲ τὰ νεκύσια. καὶ ἐν ᾗ ἡμέρᾳ τῇ γῇ θύουσι.

> [Genesia: Since there is a festival paid for at public expense in Athens, on the fifth of Boedromion, called the Genesia, according to Philokhoros and Solon in the *axones*.]

The lemma thus makes the *polis*' financial support of the festival explicit through the term *dêmotelês*, a term that is almost exclusively associated with sacrifices and festivals as early as Herodotos and Thucydides.[46] Moreover, even though Philokhoros would seem to be the principle source, the lexicon's citation of Solon directly suggests that someone other than Philokhoros had access to the *axones* (or that Philokhoros quoted enough of the *axôn* or *axones* to give one the sense of accessing Solon directly). Or, the entry might suggest that even an intermediary source used the Calendar itself, since in his time Plutarch could see only fragments of the *axones* and *kyrbeis* housed in the Prytaneion.[47] No rubric identifying the *axones* is so far attested among the thirteen published fragments of the Calendar, but Lambert does suggest that the Genesia might be

46. Hdt. 6.57; Thuc. 2.15. The term remains consistently associated with sacrifices and festivals in the fourth century and afterward; cf. Aes. 1.183, 3.176; Dem. 21.53, 59.85–87; Din. XVIII fr. 3 Conomis *Din.* (= Harp. s.v. δημοτελῆ καὶ δημοτικὰ ἱερά); Pollux 9.10.3; Harp. s.v. οἰκέτην τῆς πόλεως; Paus. Gr. s.v. συστομώτερον σκάφης. The term, however, is not attested epigraphically in Attica until the late Hellenistic period: *IG* II^2 1035, *ll.* 14–15, 20; *Agora* XVI 336.

47. Plu. *Sol.* 25.1. No source gives us any more clear an idea than simply "wood" (*xylon*) for the medium of the *kyrbeis* and *axones*. A number of different genera and species might well have been used to good advantage depending on availability and the qualities of wood sought. One limiting factor was size. Stroud (1979), 8 and 45, estimates that, on the basis of the reinscribed first *axôn* of Drakon's law on homicide, that the original *axôn* contained a text of c. 2,250 letters, and posits, 45, that a text of that length could be comfortably carved on a four-sided log of 2.00m length (exclusive of the dowels pinning it into a frame), each of whose four sides had a height of 0.30m. Stroud bases those dimensions on a letter height (and, width + interlinear space) of 0.03m that he takes to be representative of archaic lettering in general. Of course, larger letters would require larger logs. In order to avoid warping and splitting, the logs ought to have been cut out of the heartwood of relatively straight trunks from trees of substantial size, particularly cedar, cypress, and boxwood. Each was available in the Aegean and possessed different qualities that might render them desirable for use in this fashion just as they were used in the sculpture of cult-statues and the like, for which see Meiggs (1982). While cypress and boxwood both exhibit relative freedom from knots, boxwood's dense grain might be best for being carved with so many small letters whose surrounding borders and voids could otherwise chip or flake off thereby rendering the remaining grooves of the letters less distinct. The difficulty that boxwood presents is that logs of the thickness that Stroud posits would have to come from the trees of the greatest size, whereas cypress and cedar could easily furnish such logs. Of course, Stroud's dimensions should only be taken as hypothetical.

As to whether any wood could remain intact enough for Plutarch to see remnants of the *axones* and *kyrbeis* some seven centuries later, without a protective varnish or plastering as well as shelter from sun and rain, no wooden beam would last perfectly intact even if cut from a relatively rot-resistant wood like cedar, cypress, or boxwood. Yet, the oak panel paintings of Polygnotos in Athens were said to have remained intact enough for (an unidentified) late Roman consul to abscond with them (i.e., when they were some eight centuries old): Synes. *Ep.* 54.135.

identifiable in one of the Calendar's fragments.[48] If that attribution is correct, it would mark one of the very few instances of correspondence between the Calendar and the other sources for Solon's laws. Tellingly, the mere presence of that festival in the Calendar would necessarily agree with the lexicon (and of course Philokhoros and Solon himself) that it was publicly supported.

Even so cursory a survey of those laws as our evidence permits reveals clearly that Solon's laws regarding such publicly funded festivals, along with the seemingly innumerable sacrifices of lower rank, were at once numerous and also spread across the whole of his legislation. In our only citation of sacred matters on a particular *axôn* or *kyrbis*, Plutarch specifies Solon's sixteenth *axôn* as the source for the values (*timêmata*) of sacrificial animals, discussed earlier.[49] Again, while the law(s) on that *axôn* would seem to be a locus of calendrical material, the *axôn* does not, however, appear to have been, or to have contained, a calendar. Plutarch moves immediately to other *timêmata*, of which the most striking is perhaps the bounty paid for wolves and their whelps to the four Ionian tribes, and while the connection of this bounty to sacrifice is obscure, the passage suggests that more is at issue. Curiously, Plutarch moves seamlessly from those bounties to the four Ionian tribes themselves, two of which (the Geleontes and Aigikoreis) he believes (on the basis of their names) were inevitably constituted from the farmers and shepherds, respectively, and thus, he must presume, intrinsically interested in the bounties. The etymology is easy to reject as a simplistic approach tried by many ancient commentators, but the quick transit from one subject to the other offers a useful reminder of the institutional significance of the tribes and their *phylobasileis* and might well reflect something of his source's interests.[50] If there was a single unifying reason behind those various *timêmata*, the most reasonable assumption would be that Solon stipulated the financial obligations of the *polis* and set down their value in absolute terms. Could the sixteenth *axôn*, after all, have directed the tribes or their chief magistrates such as the *phylobasileis* to make the bounty payments,

48. Lambert "Calendar," 367–68, follows an unpublished suggestion by S. Dow that the festival of the Genesia is attested on F1A col. 3, which records offerings on the day of that festival specified by our other sources, the 5th of Boedromion; cf. Lambert "Genesia" (2002).

49. Plu. *Sol.* 23.3 (F 77 Ruschenbusch): εἰς μέν γε τὰ τιμήματα τῶν θυσιῶν λογίζεται πρόβατον καὶ δραχμὴν ἀντὶ μεδίμνου. Plutarch also cites Demetrios of Phaleron (fr. 147 Wehrli *Dem.*) for the (market) value of an ox being 5 dr. in Solon's time, and states further that all of these values were established in Solon's sixteenth *axôn* for choice offerings (τιμὰς τῶν ἐκκρίτων ἱερείων), which were thus more costly than ordinary ones. It is not clear whether Demetrios was using the same source as Plutarch, or even that Plutarch had full access to that particular *axôn*.

50. See, for example, the alternative etymology for the Ionian tribes provided by Herodotos (5.66).

say, when serving their (rotating?) term in control of the Prytaneion? There is no easy answer to that problem, but the particular value of Plutarch's citation of the sixteenth *axôn* is the knowledge that Solon established a set value for sacrificial animals. A compelling reason for doing so would be that to fix the figure would be to provide iron-clad instruction to those magistrates in charge of procuring such animals, so that by purchasing animals only at the stated value, outright fraud on their part would be impossible.

Much the same appears to be true with regard to the *kyrbeis*, which like the *axones* maintained their authority well after the publication of the Calendar. An arbitrated settlement affecting the *genos* of the Salaminioi in 363/2, for instance, instructs that certain sacrifices which were to be paid for by the *polis* were mandated "from the *kyrbeis*" (*hê polis didôsin ek kyrbeô*[*n*]).[51] Because this prepositional phrase would seem to parallel the rubrics in the Calendar's fragments, where they seem to mean the source of authority for a particular sacrifice and the *polis*' obligations, it is likely that the arbitration text does not refer to the Calendar at all but back to the principal (if not exclusive) source for the Calendar. In other words, neither had the original *kyrbeis* lost their authority when the Calendar was created nor was the Calendar itself the proximate point of reference, even for another official act of the Athenian *polis* such as this arbitration was.[52] Nevertheless, that the reference point is general and does not specify, say, "the sixth law on the eighth *kyrbis*" is easily explicable in light of what is known of Athenian archival practices, all the more so since it is difficult to imagine how this particular emolument to the Salaminioi could have been recorded in several different places among the *kyrbeis*.[53] The arbitration text thus suggests all the more that the Calendar, too, had a more limited purview than sometimes assumed; it only applied, and in a strictly limited manner, to the obligations of one or more magistrates—it was in no way binding on the whole of the Athenian citizenry except as an object of their collective expenditure by magistrates acting on their behalf. Still later in the fourth century, moreover,

51. Rhodes/Osborne 37, *l.* 87: ἡ πόλις δίδωσιν ἐκ κύρβεω(ν). Stroud (1979), 15 n. 56, suggests that this rubric (i.e., ἐκ κύρβεω(ν)) nevertheless refers, in an archival sense, to the walls of the Royal Stoa on which many scholars believe the Solonian Calendar was inscribed, for which see Shear (2011), 86–95, 244–45.

52. Carlier (1984), 351 n. 157, is surely mistaken in thinking that the *axones* and *kyrbeis* lost their authority on completion of the project to republish.

53. Sickinger (1999), 87–91, points out that even decrees of the *polis* reflect that the Boule had a much more precise and regular system of reference for its laws than those decrees consistently employ. In other words, the inscribed decrees only imperfectly reflect what appears to have been an extensive and well-organized archive.

Lykourgos was able to cite or discuss the *kyrbeis* in an important trial involving a dispute between women claiming to be the rightful priestess for a certain cult.[54] But the *kyrbeis* themselves become a major topic of discussion for Hellenistic scholars interested in their religious content and origins (especially as it related to the difficult etymology of these objects as well as to their unusual physical appearance).[55] Insofar as it is preserved, the tenor of their debate presumes that sacral affairs were spread across the *kyrbeis*, not confined to some individual *kyrbeis*. Of course, in the case of either the *axones* or *kyrbeis*, the mere presence of religious content does not equate with material used for the Calendar per se, since religion permeated Athenian life and might be cited or clarified for any number of purposes. As to the distribution of sacral content, therefore, we are less well informed with respect to the *kyrbeis* than to the *axones*, but the overall picture looks much the same.

The language of these fragments affects a sense not only that Solon embedded his reforms concerning sacred affairs in all manner of legislation, and thus that they were far removed from any possible calendar as such, but also that the laws were not mere prose versions of a calendar's normally abbreviated data. This reading finds support in a note of Stephanus of Byzantium concerning a particular sacrifice as cited in the *axones*. The diction of the passage would fit only awkwardly within a typical calendar if Stephanus (or his source, by extension) quotes the relevant *axôn* accurately:[56]

> τὸ τοπικὸν ᾿Αγνουτόθεν, καὶ ἐν τόπῳ ᾿Αγνοῦντι· ἐν τοῖς ἄξοσιν ἐπειδὴ ᾿Αγνοῦντι θυσία ἐστὶ τῷ Λεῷ. εἰς τόπον ᾿Αγνουντάδε.
>
> [The toponym "from Agnous," and in the place: "Agnounti:" in the *axones*, since there is a sacrifice in Agnous for Leos. To the place is "Agnountade."]

Of obvious interest is Stephanus' use of *epeidê* ("since"), which must logically initiate the quotation itself and so be a part of it. No such causal conjunction appears in any of the inscribed fragments, and it is unlikely that they would

54. Lycurg. fr. 39 Conomis *Lyc.* (= Harp. s.v. κύρβεις; Apollodoros *FGrH* 244 F107a).
55. Theophrastos is the first of whom we know to have sought the origin of the *kyrbeis* in an etymology connecting them with the Korybantes and alleging that they thus contained Cretan rituals reflecting that origin (Porph. *Abst.* 2.20; Phot. 189.21; *PatmLex.* p. 150; Σ Ar. *Av.* 1354 Holwerda). Even more broadly, Hellenistic interest in the *kyrbeis* (conveniently assembled by Stroud [1979], 26–33) also evinces the opinion that they were strongly associated with sacrifices and festivals.
56. St.Byz. s.v. ᾿Αγνοῦς (= F83 Ruschenbusch).

since the language of the Calendar is one of sparse, laconic abbreviation that utilizes only those words and symbols that are required to meet its objectives. Furthermore, *epeidê* logically suggests (in tandem with the present indicative *esti* ["is"]) a longer sentence of which this is only the preamble: "whereas (or, since) there is a sacrifice for Leos at Agnous . . ." implying some or another injunction or order concerning that sacrifice (and presumably specifying the date, frequency, and specific offerings of the sacrifice, if not also the person responsible for carrying it out). Unable to cite either the Calendar's evidence for this sacrifice or another of Solon's laws employing *epeidê* for the use of a parallel, since both are the products of mere chance, we cannot complete that idea with any precision. A good case for an injunction involves Solon's prohibition of the sacrifice of an ox at a human grave in the manner (*enagizein*) typical of those offered to heroes, which J. Blok interprets as part and parcel of Solon's establishment of the Genesia as a public festival on a set day, such that the *polis* subsumed the ability of small ritual groups to determine the relations between the living and dead.[57] That view has much in common with Jacoby's problematic position, discussed in the introduction, but intriguingly articulates how that law ought to have had administrative repercussions, whatever Solon's intention. The Calendar's notice of the Genesia would thus reflect only a very small part of the original law and all of its other provisions.

One further clue is afforded by a fortuitous coincidence between the extant fragments of the Calendar and Athenaios, whose text contains the only other identified quotation of Solon's laws concerning religious affairs. Working ultimately from the Hellenistic antiquarian Polemon, Athenaios claims that Solon (in a law concerning the Deliastai) granted to the *genos* of Kerykes that two of their number thereafter possessed, in effect, the legal privilege of dining as *parasitoi* in the Delion on an annual basis:[58]

---

57. *Enagizein*: Plu. *Sol.* 21.5, with Ekroth (2002), 104–05, 228. With specific comments on *enagizein* at 236–237, Blok (2006) offers a reconstruction of Solon's legislation on funerals that conjures a much more substantial level of intervention than had been previously considered.

58. Ath. 6.234e (= Polemon F78 Preller; F88 Ruschenbusch). Noting that Harpokration (s.v. Δηλιασταί; = Lycurg. fr. 87 Conomis *Lyc.*) cites Lykourgos for the *datum* that the *arkhitheôroi* to the Delia were called Deliastai, Chankowski (2008), 95–96, rightly urges caution in assuming that the Deliastai of the Calendar must be *arkhitheôroi*, especially on the grounds that there was a Delion at Marathon (see n. 59 below). But the Marathonian location of a cult site need not undermine the authenticity of Athenaios and Polemon since the site is wholly Attic. Delos and Marathon did (ultimately?) have a strong connection with one another by virtue of Athenian command over Delos after 426, but it is safer to assume that the law in question pertains to local cult activities and so could be wholly Solonian if it cannot yet be shown that the Athenians dispatched regular sacred embassies to Delos at that time.

> ἐν δὲ τοῖς κύρβεσι τοῖς περὶ τῶν Δηλιαστῶν οὕτως γέγραπται "καὶ τὼ κήρυκε ἐκ τοῦ γένους τῶν Κηρύκων τοῦ τῆς μυστηριώτιδος· τούτους δὲ παρασιτεῖν ἐν τῷ Δηλίῳ ἐνιαυτόν."
>
> [In the *kyrbeis* concerning the Deliastai it is thus written "and the two *kêrykes* from the *genos* of the Kerykes for the Mysteries: these men dine as *parasitoi* in the shrine of Apollo Delios once a year."]

While R. Stroud posited that Polemon, and by extension Athenaios, used the Calendar as a source, Lambert suggests that this very ritual is extant on a fragment of the calendar that also mentions "two Kerykes from Eleusis" together in an otherwise uncertain epigraphical context.[59] A point in favor of that interpretation is that both the Calendar and Athenaios take pains to distinguish, in effect, the *genos* of the Kerykes from regular heralds (that is, mere *kêrykes*). Yet Athenaios' attempt at direct quotation from a *kyrbis* clearly does not accord with the few words preserved in the Calendar's text, switching between the nominative and dative(?) cases, while Athenaios' extensive elaboration of the Kerykes' identity (which I have omitted for sake of brevity) would clearly be excessive and unnecessary by the standard of typical Athenian inscriptions, too.

In light of the fact that none of those sources explicitly cite the Calendar per se as the source, and indeed some imply an independent check on or even use of *axones* or *kyrbeis*, the unavoidable issue is how much of the Calendar can be assumed to be genuinely Solonian in origin or is an amalgam of other, heterogeneous materials whose antiquity might well be dubious and surely confusing. There is still more compelling reason to suspect that Solon might indeed have been a major source now that a strong case can be made against the once universally accepted reading of Lysias' speech (30) against one Nikomakhos, one of the compilers (*anagrapheis*) responsible for the Calendar, claiming that *stêlai* were also a source for the monument. Since Solon is not known to have inscribed any of his laws on such objects, which are hardly typical until the early fifth century from an archaeological and epigraphic perspective, the sureness of

59. Stroud (1979), 25, on what is Lambert F12Λ (Group A or B), *ll.* 2–3: κηρύ[κ]οιν ⌊τοῖν ἀπ]- | ὁ 'Ελευσῖν[ος]. Lambert "Calendar," 384, suggests that the shrine which this fragment also mentions, noted only as a Delion, was located at Marathon (possibly known also as the Pythion) and connected with divination that was to be conducted prior to the launching of sacred embassies (such as to Delos or to the Pythia, at Delphi).

their presence in Lysias' speech would otherwise compel us to include all the regimes intervening between Solon and the Calendar as possible contributors, be they the normal Athenian oligarchy, the Peisistratid tyranny, or the early democracy. Even *Ath.Pol.*'s well-known statement that Kleisthenes did not disturb, in effect, the structure and personnel of Athenian religion would hardly offer an obstacle to that inference.[60] But M. Nelson (2006) has recently argued that Lysias 30 does not support the long-standing emendation (reprinted again in C. Carey's new Oxford text of 2007, which I reproduce below) of a critical passage (17) that would have *stêlai* as one of the two sources for the Calendar (parallel only to Solon's *kyrbeis*):

> θαυμάζω δὲ εἰ μὴ ἐνθυμεῖται, ὅταν ἐμὲ φάσκῃ ἀσεβεῖν λέγοντα ὡς χρὴ θύειν τὰς θυσίας τὰς ἐκ τῶν κύρβεων καὶ τῶν στηλῶν κατὰ τὰς συγγραφάς, ὅτι καὶ τῆς πόλεως κατηγορεῖ· ταῦτα γὰρ ὑμεῖς ἐψηφίσασθε.
>
> [I am amazed, unless considered thoughtfully, whenever he insists that I am acting impiously by saying that it is necessary to carry out the sacrifices from the *kyrbeis* and *stêlai* in accord with the instructions, that he lodges an accusation even against the *polis*, for in fact, you decreed them.]

Nelson's suggestion is that the passage reads merely χρὴ θύειν τὰς θυσίας τὰς ἐκ τῶν κύρβεων καὶ οὐ πλείω, κατὰ τὰς συγγραφάς (*khrê thyein tas thysias ek tôn kyrbeôn kai ou pleiô, kata tas syngraphas*), thus replacing καὶ τῶν στηλῶν (*tôn stêlôn*) and arriving at something closer to the mansucripts' καὶ τῶν εὔπλων (*tôn euplôn*) or καὶ τῶν ὅπλων (*tôn oplôn*) while meeting the rhetorical demands of the speaker's argument. In effect, *kyrbeis* would then be the sole source for the Calendar, at least as argued by the litigant of Lysias 30. The omission of *axones*, apparently not reflected in the manuscripts' garbled texts, poses an interesting problem for the reconstruction of Solon's original laws in their physical format but poses no difficulty with regard to their being a source for the Calendar, for the reasons discussed above.

The significance of Nelson's emendation for our understanding of the Calendar would be difficult to overestimate. One fragment (F3A, *l.* 77) had been thought to yield evidence of such a rubric for *stêlai* but that reading, pivoting on the fugitive remains of a single letter (thus, the under-dotted τ [letter *tau*] in ἐκ

60. *Ath.Pol.* 21.6: τὰ δὲ γένη καὶ τὰς φρατρίας καὶ τὰς ἱερωσύνας εἴασεν ἔχειν ἑκάστους κατὰ τὰ πατρία.

τῶν στ̣[ηλῶν]), was itself predicated on the text of Lysias and is, as Lambert shows, epigraphically ambiguous at best while other restorations are possible (even if none so far posited are any more likely).[61] One may look for comparison at the difficulty caused by Cicero's citation of one of Solon's laws on funerals as actually being *post aliquanto*, that is, "somewhat later" than Solon(?!) or Solon's other legislation (but still a product of the lawgiver?).[62] Cicero, sadly, offers no clarity as to which of the two he might have meant. To downgrade *stêlai* from being a *necessary* to being merely a *possible* source for the Calendar does not of course fully remove the possibility of additions to the sacral repertoire by all the regimes ruling after Solon, but it does provide further ground for thinking that the monument's fragments might indeed provide some genuine insight into Solon's legislation.

With that in mind, let us turn once again to the matter of certainly attested rubrics, and specifically to that of "from those of the *phylobasileis*" (*ek tôn phylobasilikôn*). From the outset, since the Calendar's presentation of these rubrics in its text lacks any accompanying language that would serve to explicate them, its overarching uniformity may inadvertently mask important differences among the rubrics. For that reason, the particular function of each of these *ek*-rubrics should be discerned carefully, and Dow's arguments that they commonly denote the authority behind a particular entry (rather than the source of funds) is not entirely convincing, in part for its failure to elucidate distinctions among the rubrics.[63] Unlike the other rubrics that are uniformly temporal, "from those of the *phylobasileis*" alone identifies a magistracy, and one critical for archaic Athens at that, as its point of reference. This rubric thus offers us a sort of mirror, albeit a cloudy one, into the laws of Solon if all of the previously argued points about our ability to access those laws through the Calendar are justified. If Nikomakhos and his colleagues shaped the material at their dis-

---

61. Lambert "Calendar" affirms, 378, the basic epigraphic reading of Dow, J. Oliver and others (i.e., ἐκ τῶν στ̣[ηλῶν] in F3A, *l.* 77, and perhaps F2A; cf. the possible [ἐκ] νέων of F2A, *l.* 3) but notes that the choice epigraphically is between T and Υ, and chooses to read *stêlai* avowedly on the basis of the emended text of Lysias (neither Lambert nor Nelson [2006] appear aware of each other's work). Robertson (1990), 68–71, had suggested συγγραφαί, and J. Oliver [1935], 28, had tentatively suggested σύμβολα), but as the Solonian laws quoted at Lysias 10.16–22 suggest (for which see n. 38 above), Solon's vocabulary could be rather obscure even by the early fourth century, so that if the Calendar's rubric identifies here a novel source, it might be impossible to identify it.

62. Cic. *De leg.* 2.64 (= F72a Ruschenbusch), with Blok (2006), 240–43.

63. Situating himself against the long-standing interpretation of these rubrics as indicating the various bodies from which funds were drawn and positively arguing that they were sources of archival or legal authority, Dow (1953–57), 15–22, falls short in depending very largely on negative evidence and the appearance of *stêlai* in the text of Lysias.

posal to be consistent and clear but not violate the wording or intent of Solon, then there is a good chance of a common rationale behind the rubrics that they chose, and so the difference between the temporal rubrics and this one would have to possess some purpose. If the rubrics were not of Solon's design, moreover, then we must imagine a stage at which the laws' particular stipulations on sacrifices and the like were first sorted into certain categories, and this raises an interesting problem: just what were the rubrics for?

The mere act of sorting ought to have produced all of the calendrical material itself, namely, that such and such offering of a sheep, say, was to be made every other year for Athena on a particular day. If that was successful, as it must have been ultimately since the Calendar was indeed completed as a whole monument, then what use would it have been to inscribe the rubric at all, for would it not be then superfluous? Since we are unable to correlate anything beyond a much later paraphrase of one of Solon's laws with the Calendar we cannot be sure that the rubrics were not his invention. Again, however, the weight of evidence points to a much more randomized distribution among his laws than the rubrics might outwardly suggest. But such rubrics would not be superfluous if they somehow keyed into what the monument's compilers determined were ongoing needs that affected the very present administration of the Calendar from 410 onward and therefore were worth the trouble and expense of inscribing.

The key would seem to lie in the rubric "from those of the *phylobasileis*" for, as discussed earlier in the chapter, it headed the very part of the Calendar mandating that at the Synoikia the *phylobasileis* and the *trittys* of the Leukotainioi were to receive certain sacrificial perquisites. Since the Calendar can easily be read as a document obsessed with maintaining tight financial control, it would hardly seem appropriate for the archival source behind those very privileges at the Synoikia to have been in the control of those able to receive those perquisites.[64] The number of such laws, too, need hardly have been few in number. After all, *Ath.Pol.* was able to cite from Solon's laws the ubiquitous use of "naukraric silver" for religious purposes, precisely over which we might expect the *phylobasileis* to have exercised authority.[65] But it would make sense for those administering those emoluments and the rest of the sacrifices to have control over, or merely access to, the information that lay behind the notice on the Calendar if there was need for either further clarity or appeal to the ultimate

64. Thus, Lambert "Calendar," 399: "These perquisites look to be part of the rather self-serving system specific to sacrifices on the authority of the tribe-kings."

65. *Ath.Pol.* 8.3.

authority (i.e., the Areiopagos) in case of dispute over the value of a privilege, and so on. Thus, magistrates other than the *phylobasileis* in this instance must have been the ones to need that information thereafter, and this was information that could reasonably be described by the plural "from those of the *phylobasileis*."

This source, I suggest, could well be *nomoi* of Solon on the *phylobasileis*. Thus, the fuller form of the rubric might have been ἐκ τῶν νόμων φυλοβασιλικῶν (*ek tôn nomôn phylobasilikôn*) as coming from a still fuller formula: ἐκ τῶν νόμων τοῦ Σόλωνος περὶ τῶν φυλοβασιλέων (*ek tôn nomôn tou Solônos peri tôn phylobasileōn*). An alternative would be to restore "sacrifices" in place of "laws" (thus, ἐκ τῶν θυσίων φυλοβασιλικῶν [(*ek tôn thysiôn phylobasilikôn*)]) as the immediate point of reference for the Calendar. This would be more sensible with respect to the Greek but would not alter the thrust of the argument advanced here, namely, that the rubrics refer ultimately to various statutes that have been regrouped around a single common feature.[66] After all, Solon might well have organized his laws according to the magistrates to which they pertained and not, say, according to procedure or crime, to judge both by the subjects of some laws identified as belonging to particular *axones* and also by *Ath. Pol.*'s citation (*Ath.Pol.* 8.1; cf. 47.1) of a "*nomos* concerning the *tamiai* of Athena" (*ho peri tôn tamiôn nomos*), which is none other than Solon's Law on the Tamiai.[67] In that case, Solon's laws concerning the *phylobasileis* would, one presumes, with relatively few additions or subtractions compromise the basis for the *ek*-rubric "from those of the *phylobasileis*."

What then of the temporal rubrics, especially if there is no other evidence that Solon created a calendar as such? Perhaps parallel to those relating to the *phylobasileis*, the laws in question must have provided key information to those magistrates who administered the sacrifices and, by extension, the privileges awarded to priestesses and other parties, such as the Kerykes, for example. In both cases, the rubrics point to a class of law rather than to any specific law on any particular *axôn* or *kyrbis*. The general reference of the arbitration decree for the Salaminioi to *kyrbeis* in the plural, where a singular would presumably be much more likely, points in the same direction. This interpretation would obvi-

66. Dow (1953–57), 20. Of course, by virtue of my earlier arguments on the nomenclature of this office, the use of *phylo-* in the rubrics as I tentatively reconstruct them should reflect the usage of late fifth-century Athens, not that of Solon.

67. Scafuro (2006), 179 n. 13; Sickinger (1999), 29; Stroud (1968), 32–33 and n. 11; cf. Ruschenbusch (1966; see Abbreviations), 28–30.

ously require or strongly suggest an intermediary collection of the relevant laws regrouped according to categories that only acquired meaning for the purpose of meeting the specific goals of the Calendar's compilers. The festivals and sacrifices were to be found originally in laws that cited only their month (thus, ἐκ τῶν [θυσίων] κατὰ μῆνα, or, *ek tôn* [*thysiôn*] *kata mêna*) or, worse, on an unspecified day that had (later) to be determined (thus, ἐκ τῶν [θυσίων ἐπὶ ἡμέραι] μὴ ῥητῆι, or, *ek tôn* [*thysiôn epi hêmerai*] *mê rhêti*), to take the two best preserved rubrics. But again, this need not imply anything more than the kind or level of sorting that produced the final distribution of material across the Calendar itself. So, the body of law that likely stands behind "from those of the *phylobasileis*" would seem to have concerned the sacrificial obligations and perquisites of the *phylobasileis* in all number of instances, not merely the Synoikia.

Thus, whatever other laws were available to the Calendar's *anagrapheis*, they drew heavily on laws that outlined the duties of key magistrates, for which Solon would be the most likely author. While some of those laws might have only outlined those duties relative to a particular religious festival that required the resources of the *polis*, Solon's Law on the Tamiai stands as a clear instance where the lawgiver set down essential features of the office. To establish, moreover, the new census class of the *pentakosiomedimnoi* and thereby to subordinate the office to the Areiopagos would dovetail seamlessly with a description of duties such as I posit for offices like the *phylobasileis* and others. An important point in this regard is that of the distinct annual tenure of the *tamiai* of Athena, which ran from Panathenaia to Panathenaia (*ek Panathênaiôn es Panathênaia*). This schedule was unique to them and no other magistrates operated on that schedule unless explicitly modeled upon the *tamiai*, like the *tamiai* of the Other Gods in the late fifth and fourth centuries.[68] Given that this tenure must inevitably tie in with the selection process that the Law mandated, it stands to reason that the Law also set down this tenure even if it only affirmed what had hitherto been customary. What is significant about the Panathenaic

68. This very schedule was also employed, as *Ath.Pol.* (43.1) tells us, in relation to those *tamiai* elected to serve in major financial posts that had nothing to do with sacred wealth, especially the *tamias* of the Stratiotic Fund. But Pritchett (1977) rejects as groundless Meritt's notion that the *hellenotamiai* came into office on the same day as the *tamiai*, which a number of other scholars accepted (including Ferguson [1932], 3 n. 1). The earliest epigraphic appearance of the phrase in question is that of the Kallias Decrees and the closely contemporary inventory *IG* I^3 290 (of 434/3); the last is *IG* II^2 1496 of 331/0, which is closely contemporary with *Ath.Pol.* Some scholars (e.g., Busolt/Swoboda [1926], 1135, followed by Schwahn [1932], col. 2112) had once thought the phrase signified tenure ending at the *beginning* of the festival (on or near the 20th of Hekatombaion), at least as it was carried out in the fifth century (before, erroneously, being converted to the *prytany* calendar). But if the college exited office at the beginning of the festival, how could they oversee the apogee of their efforts and how they could they also be held duly accountable for those efforts?

tenure is that it became the basis for a host of financial operations that depended on these officers and was tied to the staging of the Panathenaia itself (by far the most costly of Athens' religious events). While the expressly financial implications of this schedule are a much later development, what was likely to have been more relevant in Solon's time was to complete an inventory of Athena's property, just as the *tamiai* would do for centuries henceforth. Therefore, however special the *tamiai* were by virtue of Solon's Law, they appear to be only one office whose duties with respect to the property of the gods and the *polis* were stipulated by the lawgiver and hence rendered clearly subordinate to the Areiopagos.

The **Arkhôn Basileus, Naukraroi,** *and* **Kôlakretai**

That the Calendar should still at the turn of the fourth century crystallize the obligations and perquisites of some magistrates no longer playing anything but a narrowly framed role in Athenian religious life such as the *phylobasileis* cannot but prompt us to consider who else had the responsibility for carrying out the totality of the *polis*' obligations in Solon's time and beyond. Those obligations of course extended beyond mere ritual itself, for without property of some kind or another the *polis* could offer no sacrifice. We therefore turn to examine several key magistracies that were responsible for ensuring that the *polis* could meet the demands set out for it by the laws that underlay the Calendar, and all of whom might well have been subject to the kinds of laws that seem to have pertained to the *tamiai* and *phylobasileis*.

Many of the significant logistical duties likely fell to the *arkhôn basileus*. It is surely no accident that the Athenians erected the Calendar immediately in the vicinity of, if not actually a part of, the Stoa where this magistrate and his assistants were centered. In its lengthy description of the notable duties of the office in the late 330s or so, *Ath.Pol.* (57.1) says simply that:

> ὡς δ ' ἔπος εἰπεῖν καὶ τὰς πατρίους θυσίας διοικεῖ οὗτος πάσας.
>
> [In a word, this man manages quite all of the ancestral sacrifices.]

There could be perhaps no better or more succinct description of the Calendar and of the *basileus*' relation to it: not necessarily the conductor of sacrifices but the one who saw to their logistics. What *Ath.Pol.* does not provide is a sense of how difficult, involved, or onerous that task, or rather that nexus of tasks, really was, and the tract goes on to describe still other legal and ritual duties, ranging from the management of the procession and festival in honor of Lenaian Dionysos to the adjudication of disputes between rival claimants to priesthoods.[69] Many different colleges, of course, might well have played ancillary roles in ensuring that the money and other resources were available to meet these obligations, and then granted to the appropriate authority (that is, another college), who in turn acquired the animals and all of the sacrificial goods, equipment, and services necessary to meet the Calendar's requirements, and so on. Of course, not all of those ritual tasks can have been the same as in Solon's time; sacrifices and festivals change over time. Much of this managerial burden in the fourth century consisted of leasing out land and directing the monies to appropriate ends, as is clear not only from a welter of epigraphic evidence but from another section of *Ath.Pol.* as well.[70] How early such tasks fell to this one chief magistrate is a question central to the whole of this book's analysis, and I will explore it at length in coming chapters. But it is worth considering here N. Papazarkadas' recent suggestion that a "law on sacred precincts" (*nomos peri tôn temenôn*) must have governed the *basileus*' responsibilities for managing the leases of such property from a relatively early date, long before our earliest discrete evidence, namely, the decree of 418/7 mandating leases for the property of the shared *temenos* of Neleus, Basile, and Kodros, to which I will return.[71] That hypothesis is entirely in keeping with the thrust of my argument concerning the sources for the Calendar itself: very old, probably Solonian, laws that dictated to magistrates their responsibilities with regard to the *polis*' religious obligations. Moreover, Papazarkadas goes so far as to suggest that such a law was almost surely reedited or tinkered with at the very time when the Calendar was composed by its *anagrapheis*, though in no way does he suggest that this hypothetical law might otherwise be thought to have been Solonian, actually or putatively, in origin.

Still other magistrates, nonetheless, were required, to whom authority could be, and had to be, delegated, as is evident also in *Ath.Pol.*'s description of the duties taken up by the eponymous *arkhôn*. To this other high officer of the *polis* fell the responsibility in the fourth century at least of staging the whole of

69. *Ath.Pol.* 57.

70. *Ath.Pol.* 47.4–5. On the capacity and responsibility of the *arkhôn basileus* to lease sacred lands, see now the rather thorough reconstruction offered by Papazarkadas (2011), 51–75.

71. Papazarkadas (2011), 74–75.

the Thargelia and City (or Great) Dionysia religious festivals (complete with all of their theatrical, agonistic, and choral organization and wrangling with liturgists), the dispatch of the sacred procession and choruses to Delos, a special procession for Asklepios, and a festival for Zeus Soter, finally. None of these tasks could be completed without the use of assistants and the collegiate aid of various other magistrates. But this situation was hardly unusual, as even the *polemarkhos* had at the time of *Ath.Pol.*'s composition (that is, the late 330s or early 320s) the responsibility for conducting sacrifices to Artemis Agrotera and Enyalios, of putting on games for the Athenian war dead, and of providing special heroic rites for the erstwhile founders of the democracy, Harmodios and Aristogeiton.[72] The mere fact of such an aggregate of obligations had its echoes throughout the whole system of Athenian government, for the *dêmarkhoi* had many of the same tasks as well, always conditioned, obviously, to the more localized traditions and structures of Attica properly speaking.[73] Of course, we cannot forget that the *dêmarkhoi* replaced, in effect, the *naukraroi* of the Ionian tribes in a number of respects. Across such a broad array of sacrifices and duties, all of which involved still other magistrates to sort out the logistical headaches of providing victims, equipment, and material, whichever magistrate held this position would undoubtedly have been positioned atop a hierarchy of sacral offices. It is in this office of *arkhôn*, therefore, that we perhaps see the closest, most natural, amalgam of ritual power and political authority in the Athenian *polis* across the centuries. Nor can we ignore, too, that it was the office of the eponymous *arkhôn* that was the subject of severe electoral strife in the decade following Solon's reforms, as discussed in chapter 1. Whether a law on this magistracy like those I posit for many other offices was ever an issue in that strife, one could only speculate, but the office itself was clearly the object of desire among many powerful Athenians.

Of special note are the *paredroi* ("assistants") who served the three chief *arkhontes*, and whose own office long retained what seem to be archaic features. Through the fourth century, it remained the prerogative of those *arkhontes*—the eponymous, *basileus*, and *polemarkhos*—to choose for themselves, and without interference from any other party, two men to serve in so special a capacity as to suggest that they could function as surrogates for their *arkhontes* in a number of legal, administrative, and even ritual situations. It is that method

72. *Ath.Pol.* 58.1.
73. On the religious duties of the *dêmarkhoi*, both in the sacrificial as well as in the managerial sense, see Georgoudi (2007); Whitehead (1986), 127–28, 134–37; Papazarkadas (2011), 111–15.

of choice, and not some form, or even combination, of election or sortition in a "complex" procedure that betokens the personal power of the *arkhontes* (and, indeed, their *paredroi* who could operate with significant latitude), since the *arkhontes* could and did choose relatives in some known instances, the very act of which marks this office as distinct from all others of the classical period.[74] Moreover, even during that era, the *paredroi* could marshal religious processions as would their superiors, and Demosthenes tells of an instance in which a *paredros* had a man expelled from the theatre of Dionysos—apparently while serving an *arkhôn* who was his own son.[75] According to a note in Pollux, the *paredroi* of the *basileus* also had the ability to fine transgressors of the sacred area known as the Pelargikon, the amount of which seems so low at three *drakhmai* as surely to be a punishment of an earlier age.[76] A number of fourth-century and later inscriptions record honors for *paredroi* who had organized or overseen (*epimelesthai*) one or another major festival that fell to the *arkhontes*, and when it came to the Eleusinia they did so in conjunction with the *genê* of the Eumolpidai and Kerykes, too.[77] As powerful surrogates, therefore, the *paredroi* should be treated along with their *arkhontes* as a class of magistrate whose historical trajectory was closely tied to those festivals and the means by which they were funded and staged. While the *paredroi* exercised financial power that was significant in the fourth century at least, their guardianship or management of resources intended for communal religious life does not seem to have constituted the greater part of their function. But we must bear in mind that this distribution of tasks might not have been a simple trajectory of historical development, and we cannot be sure that the *paredroi* could never have undertaken tasks of a more expressly ritual nature. In other words, while some duties regarding, say, the maintenance of religious decorum (*kosmos*) might be age-

74. On these *paredroi*, whose nomenclature was also used for other assistants endowed with important responsibilities, see Kapparis (1998) and Rhodes (1993), 622, on *Ath.Pol.* 56.1 (indicating that the choice of *paredroi* still lay with the *arkhontes* in the late fourth century). Rhodes likewise points to the method of appointment as an archaic survival.

75. Dem. 21.178.

76. Poll. (8.101). On the fine, Judeich (1931), 119 n. 1, thus connects the nature of payment to ritual demands on the person obligated to pay for a transgression: "Die Festsetzungen der Strafe in Bargeld schränkt allerdings das Alter Fluches nach oben hin ein (6. Jahr.?)." On the Pelargikon, see now also Papazarkadas (2011), 33–34. Although Papazarkadas does not fully recognize the distinction between *hiera* and *hosia*, it should be pointed out that in keeping with Pollux's note and other evidence for the Pelargikon's inviolability (principally, Thuc. 2.17.1) *IG* I[3] 78, *ll.* 54–59, shows that this precinct constituted *hiera* land (esp. *ll.* 54–55, mandating that the incoming *basileus* mark off the *hiera* within it), for which the fine of violation was (now) fully 500 dr. (*ll.* 58–59).

77. E.g., *IG* II[2] 1230 (end of the fourth century); *Agora* XVI 181 (of 282/1).

old, the strictly financial powers of the *arkhontes* and their *paredroi* might have been a relatively late development, and one conditioned by changes in the relevant institutions, such as occasioned by Solon's laws.

My argument in this chapter has been that Solon laid down the duties for a number of important magistrates with a view to ensuring that officeholders carried out essential tasks on behalf of the *polis* in an acceptable manner. For all that we know, Solon's laws applied just as much to the chief *arkhontes* and *naukraroi* as to *tamiai*. But the very breadth of these magistrates' duties from the *paredroi* to the *naukraroi* and *kôlakretai* cannot but remind us of the problem they pose for the historical development of the whole apparatus that framed them. Even the grand scale of the Calendar alone seems analogous to the whole gamut of duties of these chief *arkhontes* and their *paredroi*, in which one senses not a single principle governing the distribution of tasks as a logical whole but rather the organic product of centuries of accident, of archaicism, of nostalgia, and of an accumulation of commitments and honors whose historical reason was not always so keenly remembered by the end of the fifth century. Such duties as they were could hardly have developed separately from the more abstract elements of the larger framework of institutions with which the *polis* served its religious needs. The duties of various sacred treasurers were enmeshed within particular as well as general historical developments affecting the structure of Athenian government, at the heart of which, as I shall show in this book's final chapters, lay the growth of particular kinds of property that greatly altered the administrative reality within which these magistrates operated. For that reason, with respect to the Calendar, if it is reasonable to suppose that indeed it came to be formed at a relatively late date out of what were originally a scatter of separate laws in the time of Solon (and perhaps beyond), then it is also appropriate, and indeed necessary, to consider how its formation out of those laws and duties might mesh with the creation of *new* forms of property itself.

CHAPTER 3

The Politics of Being a Sacred Treasurer in Archaic Athens

Even the most perceptive lawgiver cannot ensure that his laws will meet his original aims, and certainly not a generation or more later. Although we do not know what immediate reaction the Athenian elite had to the Law and to most of Solon's other laws concerning magistrates, this legislation appears to have survived by entrenching the privilege and power of the Athenian elite. Even under the democracy, Athenians offered large-scale banquets as a means of dispensing patronage in return for the prestige that was the life-blood of a successful political figure. Not only did Solon's *pentakosiomedimnoi* affirm the political utility of having great wealth of one's own, but where Solon stipulated the duties of magistrates and placed the *polis*' resources under their control he also transformed those resources into a prize all the more worthy of competition. Such was the vigor of that competition that sacred treasurers dedicated monuments to the gods that adopted the language of victorious athletes. However rich one might have been, to avail oneself of the *polis*' resources naturally put one in a still more advantageous position, since that sacrificial largesse could be dispensed at little or no cost to oneself. In short, the unintended consequence of these laws of Solon was that they offered strong incentives not merely to seek office but to develop its mandates and duties in such a manner as to enjoy greater resources that could, in turn, be put to political ends. The tyranny of the Peisistratidai embodied this dynamic of institutional growth, but the advent of democracy did little to change the fundamentals, which would have profound implications for Athens' future development.

A Sacred Competition: Athletics and the Sacred Treasurers

In an age from which so many religious dedications survive, those offered by sacred treasurers and *arkhontes* in the sixth century are remarkable as much for their self-identification as for adopting the contemporary language of athletic victors. Such appropriation reflects strenuous competition to enjoy prestige that went far beyond what the mere exercise of a limited, discrete administrative task might entail. In effect, their monuments announce a special authority over important religious cults, and therefore over how other Athenians, including athletes and other magistrates, participated in the ritual life of the community. Such a visible assertion of one's official role within the *polis* is already evident in the massive *trapeza*-type altar on the akropolis that Khairion dedicated to Athena while serving as her *tamias*, as first explored in the introduction to this book and detailed in the appendix. The physical monumentality of the altar betokens the kind of wealth required of *tamiai* as members of the highest census class.[1] But in point of fact, nothing so large as this altar survives from the early or mid-sixth-century akropolis that can be identified with a single dedicator. Of immediate significance is the dedicatory text and how it articulates the prestige of being a *tamias* of Athena. As noted in the introduction, the text (*IG* I[3] 590) was inscribed on the upper edge of the front surface, where its very large (and presumably painted) retrograde script would be clearly visible to anyone approaching the altar.[2] In this single line that I again quote, Khairion declares explicitly that he made the offering to Athena in his capacity as *tamias*, and does so by employing the present participle of the cognate verb (*tamieuôn*):

[------- ⋮ ἀνέθ]εκεν ⋮ ᾿Αθεναίαι ⋮ Χα[ι]ρίον ⋮ ταμιεύον ⋮ Κλε[δ]ị[ϙο ⋮ hυιός] ←.

[Khairion, while serving as *tamias*, the son of Kleidiqos, dedicated to Athena . . .]

Such language renders the altar unique among Athenian dedications, because *in officio* votives are rare within the Attic corpus and the precise phrase used here is also otherwise unattested.

---

1. Drawing on Snodgrass (1980) and I. Morris (1996) and (2000), 273–80, Anderson (2005), 184, identifies the expression of personal wealth within the context of a religious sanctuary as one of the chief characteristics of elite behavior in the archaic period, especially as a means of asserting one's primacy over erstwhile peers.
2. The height and size of the letters diminishes as the text progresses, but renders the name of Athena as the most conspicuous element of the text with the largest letters, and at the center of the inscription, too.

Contemporary athletic dedications from Athens and elsewhere, nonetheless, provide a comparative foil to Khairion's use of language and suggest that Khairion subscribed to the competitive ethos of elite athletics. From at least the early sixth century onward, when victors commissioned objects or monuments to be offered to the gods, their texts typically employed what would become a standard formula for such inscriptions, coordinating the aorist participle of the verb "to be victorious, conquer" (*nikan*) with the aorist indicative of the standard verb of dedication (*anatheinai*, thus *anethêke*).[3] Yet by the mid-sixth century, some victors commissioned inscriptions that altered the customary expression by substituting the present (*nikôn*) for the aorist participle (*nikêsas*), although still in conjunction with the customary aorist indicative verb (*anethêken*).[4] Whereas that latter combination signifies a coordinated action of two discretely defined steps that have a logical succession in time, the present participle elides the distinction and collapses the temporal aspect of the two actions (that is, of the participle and the conjugated verb) into a single moment.[5] The present tense thus marks a different notion altogether, for when a herald made the official proclamation announcing the entrance of a victorious athlete into his *polis*, he, too, appears to have used the present tense (*nika*) to describe an action that logically belongs to the past (that is, "he conquers" or "he is victorious," for "he conquered" or "he was victorious").[6] The present participle *nikôn* therefore reflects an ongoing status that the athlete would seem not to have relinquished even though the physical contest had long been concluded.[7] In effect, to replace one tense with another involves not merely a change in semantics but

3. The conjunction of the two verbs, but with an aorist participle, may be first attested by an athlete from Sybaris who, in the late seventh to early sixth century, dedicated a statue of himself to Athena as a tithe from the Olympic games: *EG* vol. I, 110ff. no. 3, fig. 14 (= Ebert [1972], addendum).
4. One possible example of this phenomenon comes from Eleusis in the mid-sixth century (*IG* I³ 992 = *I.Eleusis* 4), which might indicate that Athenian athletes adopted the convention at about the same time as it was first used anywhere else in the Greek world. The text of *IG* I³, however, removes the restorations that Hiller (*IG* I² 803) had previously offered: [--*h*αλλ]όμενος παῖ[δας νικôν] ἀνεθέκ[εν]. Cf. Raubitschek "Leagros" (1939), 155 n. 2.
5. On the temporal qualities of the aorist and present participles (apart from their aspectual implications), see also Cooper (1998) vol. 2, 844–46 (= no. 56.100.0).
6. On the religiously and politically freighted entrance of a (major) victor into his *polis*, see Sinos (1993) and Kurke (1993). A blackfigure amphora (c. 570) of Panathenaic shape (British Museum B144) shows a finely dressed man preceding a horse, announcing its entrance with the words ΔΥΝΕΙΚΕΤΥ ⁝ ΗΙΠΟΣ ⁝ ΝΙΚΑΙ (i.e., Δυν‹ν›εικέτ‹ο›υ ἵππος νικᾷ); following the horse a nude male (the owner?) extends a crown toward the animal and hoists a tripod. A fragment of Timotheos of Miletos (fr. 802 *PCG*) quotes a herald also using the present tense to announce a victory (μακάριος ἦσθα, Τιμόθε ', ὅτε κᾶρυξ | εἶπε· νικᾷ Τιμόθεος | Μιλήσιος τὸν Κάμνωνος τὸν ἰωνοκάμπταν); cf. D. L. 6.43.
7. Kurke (1993), 147–48, draws a similar conclusion about the use of the present tense νικῶ in a case where the honorand is made to speak with the knowledge that he has also been buried with public honors: Paus. 6.4.6 (with text of an inscription that is otherwise unknown).

rather allows the athlete—or the magistrate—to assert that he offers his gift to the gods in what seems to be an *ongoing* state of being victorious in some regard.

But did Khairion's altar also bear the same relation to his magistracy as athletes' offerings did to their performance in physical contests? Having triumphed in sport, some men dedicated the object or equipment with which they claimed victory in a particular contest: jumping-weights (*haltêres*) and *diskoi* are the clearest (and perhaps simply best preserved) examples.[8] Although such dedications are best attested at the Panhellenic sanctuaries, at least two Athenian athletes also engaged in this kind of practice at Eleusis in the sixth century.[9] To dedicate one's own equipment, however, has relatively few clear parallels in other ritual contexts and appears to be largely confined to athletics and war (magistrates having little equipment as such except insignia of their office, like a crown).[10] But in this case the very fact that the dedication could be used, unlike perhaps some spoils of war, might separate it from those other dedications and place it within a class unto itself.[11] The basic type of Khairion's altar seems not have been used for the act of a bloodletting sacrifice but rather for the presentation either of foodstuffs to a god or, conceivably, of the banqueting vessels that *tamiai* dispensed for select diners, as I will detail in the next chapter.[12] Whatever the ritual use of this particular altar, it is hard to imagine

8. No comprehensive collection of these inscriptions is available, but on the *diskoi*, see Jacobsthal (1933); Jüthner (1934). On an early(?) sixth-century bronze *diskos* from the shrine of Apollo at Amyklai (*SEG* 11.890), the inscription employs a dative of advantage that comes close to rendering the verb νικᾶν as a verb of dedication: Μέλας μ ' ἐνίκε Πυθαιεῖ.
9. Early sixth-century lead *haltêr* (one of a pair): *IG* I[3] 988 (= *I.Eleusis* 1); late sixth-century marble *diskos*: *IG* I[3] 989. (= *I.Eleusis* 6).
10. One partial exception is the dedication of clothing for Artemis Brauronia, for which see Linders (1972), 58–59. An Athenian example of the dedication of weapons not as spoils but as one's own equipment is that of Kimon's switching of a bridle (from his own horse, signaling the relative obsolescence of cavalry, to Plutarch's mind) for a shield (signaling his support for naval warfare) in Athena's temple: Plu. *Cim.* 5.
11. Where Snodgrass uses the language (1989–90) of offerings as either "raw" or "converted" from one's own wealth, Khairion's altar would constitute a compelling example of the latter kind. Snodgrass, 291ff., tellingly cites military spoils as prime examples of "raw" offerings, to which most athletic dedications could also be added.
12. Gill (1991) provides a rudimentary survey of the form and function of *trapeza* altars. Although he omits the altar from both catalogue and discussion, this monument clearly falls within the category of "tables with parallel slabs for legs" (= his nos. 12–21); cf. Dow and Gill (1965); Gill (1974); Dignas (2002), 248, 258ff. With respect to Athenian practices, other sets of (usually bloodless) offerings might also be due to a god such as at a *theoxenia*. As several sacrificial calendars indicate, these offerings were in fact to be placed on *trapezai* (though Athena does not appear to be among the gods usually worshipped in this fashion): e.g., *IG* I[3] 234 A, *ll.* 18–23 (calendar c. 480–60); *IG* II[2] 1358B col. B, *ll.* 4, 24–25, 53 (calendar of the Marathonian tetrapolis, of the early fourth century); cf. *IG* II[2] 1933 (late fourth-century catalogue of those who decorated the *trapeza* and set out the couches for a *theoxenia* in the Ploutoneion); *IG* II[2] 775, *ll.* 18–19 (247/6; honors for priest of Asklepios). On *theoxeniai* in general, see Jameson (1994), 37, 56.

that, by virtue of its size alone, it would not have served as a focal point for any and all sacred treasurers whose duties entailed provisioning sacrifices and other rites, to say nothing of the priests and the senior officers of the *polis* who performed those acts and enjoyed sacrificial meals in turn. If one assumes that by virtue of its monumental size the altar would have played a significant role on the akropolis, it would stand to reason that many of those who would henceforth serve as *tamiai*, *hieropoioi*, or priests would conceivably fulfill their own tasks or, as per the Calendar, receive their sacrificial payments (*hierôsyna*) using Khairion's altar, and perhaps none other. The altar must also have dominated a particular space, in any case, thereby pushing out even those *tamiai* who could afford similar gifts but who had the erstwhile misfortune of serving at some date after the altar came to occupy its spot on the akropolis. Very few Athenians could afford to commission such an object, and Khairion's explicit self-identification of himself as a *tamias* thus only underlines his special capacity as one of the *pentakosiomedimnoi* to afford this gift to Athena.

Several contemporary monuments offered by other sacred treasurers likewise express the power that these sacred treasurers could wield over others, including athletes. At least from the point when the Panathenaia was reorganized (probably 566/5), the *hieropoioi* of Athena discharged not only important sacrificial duties on the akropolis but also marshaled the Panathenaiac procession over which they held immediate judicial authority.[13] Among the many duties of the *hieropoioi*, whatever the cult, lay the responsibility to marshal processions and to discipline those acting without sufficient decorum (*kosmos*). Thus, a decree of the Athenian deme of Paiania (c. 450–430), for instance, establishes that this deme's *hieropoioi* and "whomever they instruct" are to "bear staves" (*rhabdoukhein*), perhaps in conjunction with a procession to an Eleusinion (whose location is obscure).[14] While the staves could be used to physically restrain worshippers who were out of hand, other decrees grant *hieropoioi* the power to fine those misbehaving at major festivals such as the Hephaisteia and the Lesser Panathenaia.[15] Contemporary with Khairion's altar (c. 565–50), several colleges of Athena's *hi-*

13. As to the date of the expanded festival, J. Shear (2001), 507–15, argues that the date for Hippokleides' tenure as eponymous *arkhôn* in 566/5 is more chronologically plausible than the alternatives frequently implied or claimed for the initial organization of the Greater Panathenaia that would award those honors to Peisistratos, *pace* Figueira [1984], 466–68.
14. *IG* I^3 250, *ll.* 9–11: ῥαβδοχε̃ν τὸς | ḥιεροποιὸς καὶ *h*ὸς ἄν κελ- | εύοσιν.
15. Hephaisteia: *IG* I^3 82, *ll.* 24–29; Lesser Panathenaia: *IG* II^2 334, *ll.* 6–7, 31–32 (= Rhodes/Osborne 81); 1496, *ll.* 98–99.

eropoioi dedicated on the akropolis a series of massive *poros* limestone *stêlai* (*IG* I^3 507–9), on which they identify themselves as those who not only first established the "contest" (*agôn*) but also prepared the *dromos* for Athena (here with the text of 507):[16]

> [---] τὸν δρόμοṿ [ἐποίεσαν ⁝---]
> [---⁝ Κρ]άτες [⁝ Θρασ]ύκλες ⁝ ʼΑ[ρ]ịσ-
> τόδ̣ιϙος ⁝ Βρ̣[ύσον ⁝] ʼΑντε[νορ ⁝---]
> [*h*ιροποιοί τὸν ἀ]γο[να ʼθέσ]αν πρôτο[ι] γλ-
> αυ[ϙ]όπιδι ⁝ ϙόρ[ει].

> (They made) the *dromos* . . . Krates(?), Thrasykles(?), Aristodiqos(?), Bryson(?), Antenor(?): They were the first (*hieropoioi*) to establish the *agôn* for the Gray-eyed (Glaukopis) Maiden.

While the *agôn* should be taken to mean the contests of the reorganized Panathenaia, the *dromos* likely signifies the Panathenaic Way, possibly including the mid-sixth-century ramp up to the Propylaia of the akropolis along which not only the sacrificial procession traveled but also those athletes who competed in the torch race to Athena's altar.[17] If the *stêlai* indeed marked the end of the *dromos* (their original locations are unknown), they, too, would have served a specific function for processions and perhaps the torch-race, such as marking the end of the course. In any case, their monumental size and lettering do suggest that the *hieropoioi* were concerned that, not just the goddess, but all Athenians—including the athletes—know that they were responsible for critical elements of the festival's procession and competition. Curiously, the *stêlai* make no mention of any other magistrate or figure such as might have been key to the initiative behind the project, like Peisistratos or especially Hippokleides, who was most likely the one responsible for the reorganization of the Panathenaia at this time.[18]

---

16. *IG* I^3 507–08 clearly preserve enough of the key term δρόμον. While 509 is fragmentary, it is clearly a similar dedication of magistrates since it records who served as *grammateus* and is also similar in size, material, and script to 507–08.
17. On the identity of the *dromos* and its architectural nature, see J. Shear (2001), 676–79. On the *dromos* for the Panathenaia, see Eiteljorg (1993), 9–11, 58–59, 63–66. Dismoor Jr. (1980), xvii, rightly emphasizes the theatral nature of the early Propylaia as an endpoint for this *dromos* and the whole of the Sacred Way.
18. Stahl (1987), 247–48. On Hippokleides, see n. 13 above.

The power and status of such magistrates is also manifest in a roughly contemporary blackfigure *lekythos* that depicts, and uniquely labels, two crowned and filleted *hieropoioi* as athletic judges(?) flanking the armed Athena that is typical of Panathenaic amphorae.[19] Such visible authority for the organization of religious festivals is also evident in a *stêlê* from Eleusis (c. 550) that provides unique insight into the electoral dimension of these monuments.[20] The text names an Alkiphron as the one who constructed "this lovely *dromos*" for Demeter and Kore, probably in his capacity as the eponymous *arkhôn* if not as the *arkhôn basileus*:[21]

δέμοι ᾽Αθεναίον ἄ[ρχον]
στέλ̣α̣ς καδέθεκεν ᾽Αλκίφρον
καὶ τόνδε δρόμον ποίεσεν
ἐραστὸν
Δέμετρός τε χάριν
[καὶ . . . τ]ανυπ̣έπλ̣ο.

As *arkhôn* for the Demos of the Athenians, Alkiphron fixed *stêlai* and made this lovely *dromos* for the sake of Demeter and finely-clothed [Kore].

Alkiphron's dedication draws an explicit connection between his office and the Demos, which must by default encompass the crowd of Athenian celebrants at the festival of the Eleusinia.[22] In concert with the argument advanced in chapter 1 that Solon retained popular "simple" election for the *arkhontes* and most other high offices, Alkiphron's acknowledgment of the Demos should be taken as decidedly electoral in nature.[23] Because the very prominence of the Demos—

19. Neils (1992), 18, 182–83 (no. 55), provides the most recent treatment of the vase per se, and Bieber (1944), 121ff., discusses the errant orthography of the inscription.
20. *IG* I³ 991 (= *I.Eleusis* 3, with Clinton's text there). Although the text was subsequently heavily damaged, it was already well recorded (for which, see notes in *IG* and *I.Eleusis*) and therefore largely secure.
21. On fragment a (cf. *I.Eleusis*, plate 2), it is clear that *l.* 1, which is the only retrograde line of the inscription, did not run so far as to square up with the first letters of the following lines. Therefore, the final word of *l.* 1 cannot be longer than is restored by Clinton. Wilhelm (1909), 28 (this inscription = no. 16), restores ἄ[ρξας], which also meets the requirements of space and meter. Raubitschek "Weihinschriften" (1939), col. 33, suggests that the *dromos* be understood as the processional way ("Festweg") on general grounds of probability.
22. Although Wallace (1989), 53–55, (1998) and (2007) argues for what is in effect a popular Solonian democracy, his work does not appear to make use of this text; cf. Donlan (1970). On the nature of the Demos in the early democracy, see n. 54 below.
23. Although these *stêlai* lack a secure archaeological context, one wonders whether the form of the

indeed, it is the first word of the text—points to a political connection between men such as Alkiphron or Khairion and the Demos, the substance of that connection must be explored next.

Electoral Patronage

It is impossible to imagine that those who erected votives on the akropolis, at Eleusis, or at any Attic sanctuary, can have neglected to consider who might see them and how they might react. Perhaps we need look no farther than the electoral bodies of the tribes, since the Law specifies that the *tamiai* were to be drawn from the tribes. It is the surprising strength of evidence for political feasting in classical Athens, when we might expect the democracy to have forbidden or made very uncomfortable such practices, that justifies consideration of whether such patronage must have played a correspondingly significant, if not much greater, role in archaic Athens.[24] The dynamic at work was one of patronage by wealthy men who sought influence and those offices with responsibility for religious events, especially those festivals and sacrifices from which their potential electors would benefit. In concert with such banquets, therefore, monuments like Khairion's altar and Alkiphron's *stêlê* would serve as a form of permanent electoral advertising, taking pains as they do to express the prestige and power of their dedicators to whom a wide audience will have owed its use or enjoyment of major sacrifices and festival competitions.

One intriguing touchstone by which we might explore the possible outlines of patronage in archaic Athens may be found in the benefactions that the fairly conservative political figure Kimon is said to have displayed in feeding citizens during the early fifth century. *Ath.Pol.* claims that Kimon provided ritual banquets for all the people of his deme (Lakiadai), which was a service that clearly

---

dedication itself might also be used to express a direct connection between the tenure of a magistrate and the service rendered to the *polis*. A *comparandum* is offered by Plutarch's claim (*Them.* 31.1) that Themistokles had dedicated a bronze statue of a female *hydrophoros* to commemorate his magistracy as an overseer of springs. Even though Plutarch does not record the object's inscription, the homology between the sculptural form and Themistokles' service would hardly seem to be accidental. The statue would seem to have been valuable or finely wrought enough not to be destroyed during the Persian sack of the akropolis but to be installed in a temple at Sardis.

24. Although the notion of patronage in pre-Roman Greece continues to be a major point of controversy, I use the term only in a general sense to describe the occasional relationship between a benefactor and a group of people, and without any of the connotations that the Roman institution of patronage might bring with regard to ongoing, legally defined obligations owed to the benefactor.

lay outside of formal liturgies (as *Ath.Pol.* stipulates, in fact).[25] Notably, his particular act of patronage was centered on a deme, and therefore on a part of the tribal system—yet Kimon is hardly known to have been a political innovator.[26] However these banquets factored into his electoral ambitions, his patronage speaks to the bonds between a benefactor and a particular community and suggests how those bonds might well have extended quite naturally into more formal shows of support, such as an election. Even within the liturgical system of the fourth century, for instance, the wealthiest members of the tribes were required to provide dinners for their fellow tribesmen at the major festivals, such as the Panathenaia and City Dionysia.[27] Demosthenes even placed his service as tribal *hestiator* ("banquet-provider," conceivably for a banquet to celebrate his tribe's victory in the Sounion boat races) in the same class as his other festival liturgy for the Panathenaia and boasted about both, but it is hard to believe that this entailed more than a few hundred men—as expensive as that must have been—rather than a sizeable proportion of the whole tribe.[28] Entirely outside of the liturgical system, the general Khares sent oxen back to Athens from the spoils of cities he plundered in 356/5 in order that these sacrificial victims be distributed among all of the tribes, and for expressly political purposes he also staged victory feasts (*epinikia*) in the agora for the Athenians in order to celebrate later successes.[29] Such patronage suggests (along with Demosthenes' boast) that the exceptionally wealthy and powerful were still able and eager to exercise and display their service as tribal patrons, and they were not shy about the political capital that they might enjoy as a result, even under the democracy.[30]

---

25. *Ath.Pol.* 27.3 (= Plu. *Cim.* 10.2); Whitehead (1986), 305–13. There is no direct evidence for a festival context, though it seems necessary on *a priori* grounds.
26. Wade-Gery (1958), 235–38, suggests that Kritias might have been the source for both Theopompos (*FGrH* 115 F89, 135) and *Ath.Pol.* (27.3), both of which label Kimon's wealth as τυραννικὴ οὐσία. On Kimon's politics and conservative position, see Strauss (2000).
27. Dem. 39.7, 20.21, 21.156; Σ Dem. 21.156; cf. Athen. 5.185c. Jones (1987), 48–51, collects much of the epigraphic evidence, but see also Davies (1967), 34 n. 14, for valuable discussion; cf. Parker (1996), 103–04.
28. Dem. 21.156: εἱστίακα τὴν φυλὴν ἐγὼ καὶ Παναθηναίοις κεχορήγηκα, οὗτος [scil. Μειδίας] δ᾽ οὐδέτερα. Although there is no direct evidence to tie the orator firmly to the boat races and their *hestiasis*, no other suitable occasion for tribal banquet within the Panathenaia is known, for which see Davies (1967), 36. The relevant text on the boat races is *IG* II^2 2311 (c. 400–350), *ll.* 79–81, which stipulates 300 dr. for three head of cattle(?) and 200 dr. for the *hestiasis* of the victorious tribe, while to the runner-up was granted merely another 200 dr. in cash.
29. Tribal feasts of 356 (for sacking Lampsakos and Sigeion): Σ Dem. 3.31 (Dilts 146). Feasts for victory over Philip's lieutenant Adaios: Theopompos *FGrH* 115 F 249 (= Ath. 532d-e). On Khares' political self-promotion, see Salmond (1996).
30. In a similar vein, Demosthenes is said to have provided 10,000 dr. of his own funds in order that spectators from every tribe might participate in sacrifices, according to the decree of ambiguous authenticity recorded at Dem. 18.118 and in a more confused form at Plu. *Mor.* 846a.

Given such naked largesse in the fourth century, it is difficult to imagine that earlier centuries did not witness a still more open system of patronage. Rightly skeptical of the degree of formal organization inherent in archaic Athenian institutions, G. Anderson thus suggests that in the early democracy the Kleisthenic tribes were largely dependent on the patronage of wealthy members before regular liturgies were established.[31] The implication, then, for the four Ionian tribes that held sway prior to Kleisthenes' reforms ought to be that they and their subdivisions of *trittyes* and *naukrariai* were all the more beholden to the patronage of their wealthiest members. Of course, even with a relatively small population the membership of these groups was not inconsiderable since as divisions of the citizenry each of the tribes alone notionally encompassed a quarter of the population, and each *trittys* fully one-twelfth of the population, too. If the whole tribe was the meaningful locus of major electoral activity in archaic Athens, after all, such patronage could only be exercised by the very wealthiest of Athenians, rendering the *pentakosiomedimnoi* and perhaps the *hippeis* as the only ones to participate in this level of activity with any regularity. Although we lack detail for Athens to establish the precise number of people attending sacrificial banquets for which we also know the cost, it stands to reason that to feed several hundred people on a single occasion would require a very significant outlay, perhaps roughly on the order of the choral liturgies of the classical period (just as Demosthenes seems to suggest).[32] The *polis*' own spending on such banquets in that era, however, could easily exceed a whole *talent* in cost for a hekatomb of cattle, whose financial impact alone would preclude all but the wealthiest from offering anything quite compara-

---

31. Anderson (2003), 130. Likewise, Parker (1996), 103–4, discusses the evidence for such "patronal banquets" in the context of the Kleisthenic tribes, but it is difficult to imagine why such festival liturgies should be the sole creation of the democracy, even if the particular means by which such needs were met were indeed new.

32. Two examples from Hellenistic Amorgos offer a useful comparandum. Minoa and Arkesine honored two different men for exceptional liturgical services as sacrificial benefactors, one of whom is said to have spent 2,500 dr. to feed 700 people for a six-day festival, while the other spent over 1,000 dr. to feed some 550 people on another occasion: *SIG*[3] 1045–46. Reger (1994), 85, suggests that each of these banquets served nearly the entire population of their respective *poleis*. Given such unusually precise detail, it seems reasonable to think that their actions represented the upper limit that such a patron could sustain there. Although the texts in question do not indicate how many animals (and of what species, age, and gender) were sacrificed, the sheer number of people fed raises the question of whether these benefactors had to purchase animals from other islands for, as Jameson (1988) shows, to strip Amorgos of its own herds and flocks would likely disrupt the economy to a significant extent. Festivals of such size would thus require patrons able to use considerable influence and wealth to manage such a wide-ranging operation. On the cost of choral liturgies in (fourth-century) Athens, see Wilson (2000), 87–95; Davies (1971), xxi.

ble.[33] In short, merely prosperous patrons could not easily afford to provide such meals for a large number of people on a regular basis, but they would be in a better position to host luxurious meals only for the officers or other elite members of one's tribe and not the wider spectrum of one's possible electors. Only those very few with the greatest resources could truly hope to engage at a level visible to the whole of their tribe, even when all others had a stake in the system and provided what largesse they could.

One instance from the early fourth century suggests how such electoral politics might have operated in conjunction with a sacrificial or festival occasion, at least at a level approaching that of a mere neighborhood in a deme. A plaintiff in an inheritance dispute, for whom Isaios composed a speech, claims that after his father "put on a banquet" (*hestiase*) to celebrate his own marriage, and then also offered a special wedding feast to his *phrateres* (*gamêlion eisênegke*), the wives of his fellow demesmen "elected" (*proukrinan*) his new bride (i.e., the plaintiff's mother) as one of the two female *arkhousai* ("governors") for the festival of the Thesmophoria.[34] The connection between her election and the feasts rests on the wider probability that these wives knew and approved of his mother's descent and that none of the *phrateres* objected to the introduction of the plaintiff and his siblings at a later date to their midst. The logical connection between these events consists in the approval of the *phrateres* and their (and others') wives from the first wedding feasts onward, or rather that his mother could not have been so elected without having received the approval garnered at those feasts.[35] If his father suspected her to be illegitimate, the speaker claims, his father would never have offered the feasts at all.[36]

33. For the purpose of comparison, the *tamiai* of Athena in 410/09 set aside the sum of 5,114 dr. for a hekatomb to be offered at the Greater Panathenaia (*IG* I^3 375, *l.* 7; = Meiggs/Lewis 84), while 4,100 dr. were set aside from the lease of sacred property for the sacrifice at the Lesser Panathenaia in 335/4: (*IG* II^2 334, *ll.* 16–25; = Rhodes/Osborne 81). In addition, the Athenian *amphiktyones* of Delos spent 7,724 dr. on a sacrifice for Apollo in 375/4: *IG* II^2 1635, *ll.* 35–36.

34. Is. 8.19–20. In this particular passage, the meaning of προκρίνειν is probably that of election (at least in the first stage of the process, as envisioned earlier in this book for the *tamiai* and then *arkhontes* of the *polis*) given that it is in the speaker's interest to portray her selection as both prestigious and one made with full knowledge of her legitimacy and birth, which cannot be the case if only a simple lot were used.

35. In the immediately preceding passages (Is. 15–16), the plaintiff emphasizes the strength of familial bonds created by jointly attending, watching, and conducting sacrifices with his grandfather, whose estate is at issue. That notion grounds the further claim that the *phrateres*, seemingly as a kind of distant relative, likewise acknowledged the plaintiff's mother at a moment of special ritual (i.e., the wedding feast to which her groom had invited them), for which see Lambert (1998), 72 n. 56, 182–83.

36. Is. 8.20.

Even if such prestigious ritual service in the Thesmophoria was not the avowed goal of the speaker's parents, the link between the two is implicit in the speaker's argument. What the speaker in that case also presumes is no significant difference of wealth or status between the relevant parties, but rather a high degree of familiarity. But another plaintiff in Isaios makes very much the opposite claim, namely, that a man would be obligated to put on just such a feast for the women (*hestian tas gynaikas*) if the bride was legitimate (as of course she must be, by law and convention) and obligated also to undertake other liturgies in the deme on "behalf of his wife" (*hyper tês gynaikos*).[37] Although this speaker makes no claim as to the Thesmophoria, he assumes that his jurors will accept that such feasts might benefit a woman and be very costly, and so implies the kind of large-scale sacrificial banquets that would be part and parcel of electoral politics more generally.[38] It is significant that two contemporaries could characterize so differently what appear to be the same kind of ritual banquets, held within the same context of *phrateres* and weddings, and in so doing suggest a very different set of social bonds and the reason for which one might cultivate them. One reasonable implication of such disagreement is that even where a particular ritual meal might be customary, it was quite possible to use the same occasion as a means of eliciting support from a variety of groups, sometimes for very different ends. Such politicking as this by means of a banquet was surely a survival of very old practices that pervaded and conditioned Athenian political and religious life, and not a novel creation of the fourth-century democracy.

What we can only guess at is whether it was customary for men who had already achieved office to use their access and authority over certain elements of a festival, say, as a means of rewarding those with whom they felt political bonds and the like. Could the *hieropoioi* of Athena, for example, have made sure to place the leading men of their tribes and *naukrariai* at especially honored points in the Panathenaic procession or have been especially lenient if they were found to have violated the decorum or *kosmos* of that event? It is difficult, after all, to imagine that power over the ritual and the resources necessary for its performance would not constitute the principle desideratum for any

37. Is. 3.80.
38. The plaintiff here also specifies that his opponent obtained a house worth three *talents*, which (with presumably other assets in his possession) puts him within the liturgical class (for which three *talents* was the minimum threshold, as defined by Davies [1981], 28ff.) and would rhetorically obviate any claim not to have thus provided a banquet.

and all sacred treasurers who could access them, and thus reward their supporters and allies in turn. If local Thesmophoriai, after all, were the object of electoral banqueting in the fourth century, then how can the great festivals and the extensive resources allocated to them not be an even greater object of pursuit in the sixth century?

A chief lesson of the evidence from the democratic centuries, nevertheless, is that although Solon's Law and his other reforms seems to have left tribal election in place as it had been practiced hitherto, its stipulation on allotment had no discernible dampening effect on the electoral drive of later generations of *tamiai*, and all the less on those magistrates whose election was unaffected by this or other laws. Moreover, for Solon to have created the *pentakosiomedimnoi* as the wealthiest of the census classes can have done nothing to quiet the electoral impulses of the Athenian elite. Whatever the typical dynamics between politically ambitious men and the relevant electors, there must also have been a very specific historical context that induced these men to act as they did, and I suggest that this was largely centered around the property and power that these offices wielded.

Tyranny and the Resources of the Polis

If we are justified in taking the classical evidence for political feasting as pointing to an even more robust practice prior to the democracy, then we must also suppose that such banqueting survived the tyranny of the Peisistratidai whose fall heralded the advent of the democracy. But the nearly total absence of magistrates' dedications offered by sacred treasurers in the decades following c. 550, and thus firmly within the period of the tyranny, calls for explanation. In brief, there are two dimensions of Peisistratid rule that together shaped how the *polis*' resources for religious life grew.

On the one hand, power was not exercised through a naked monopoly of force but rather through established offices and the traditional procedures of state. Thus, Herodotos claims that Peisistratos did not disturb existing magistracies (*oute timas tas eousas syntaraxas*) or alter the laws (*oute thesmia metallaxas*).[39] Because leading Athenians (including Kleisthenes and Miltia-

39. Hdt. 1.59.4: ἦρχε Ἀθηναίων οὔτε τιμὰς τὰς ἐούσας συνταράξας οὔτε θέσμια μεταλλάξας; cf. *Ath.Pol.* 16.1ff. and Rhodes (1993), 189ff. on the close relationship between the two texts. Sancisi-Weerdenburg (2000), 103, asserts that from a narratological perspective this information does not fit

des) are known to have held under Peisistratos the same office of eponymous *arkhôn* as did the younger Peisistratos in the 520s, one cannot avoid the suspicion that many if not all such men acted in collusion with, or were in some measure agreeable to, the Peisistratidai.[40] What authority Peisistratos and his allies did exert would rest on a network of men who were sufficiently loyal or cooperative, all the way through the *polis*' constitutional structure. Anyone who could reconcile himself to the Peisistratidai might avail himself of the same constitutional framework of Solonian laws that the Peisistratidai depended on in order to exert his own influence, albeit without challenging those more powerful than him.[41] Even Khairion, whose burial at Eretria in c. 540 has often been interpreted as the result of his (alleged) exile from Peisistratid Athens (but concerning which, see the appendix), might easily have been an ally of Peisistratos. In that light, it is easy to see why the language of electoral victory and the like for a dedication would have been out of keeping with that political environment. We need not assume that the Peisistratidai ignored or tampered with the Law itself, or even any of the other pieces of Solon's legislation concerning magistrates, so long as the Peisistratidai could be satisfied that the process of selecting *tamiai* or other magistrates posed no real threat to their predominance. And if the tyrants had done such a thing, their abuse of Solon's laws might only have ensured the laws' good reputation in the court of public opinion.

On the other hand, the Peisistratidai did not willingly brook opposition or any challenge to their preeminence. An intriguing example of their claims to power is that of the late archaic altar of the younger Peisistratos (the son of Hip-

---

with the oral traditions that form the basis of our sources about Peisistratos and his rule. Instead, Sancisi-Weerdenburg suggests that the various tales of coups by deceit, followed by exile, are in reality doublets of a traditional type and are unreliable. Although Sancisi-Weerdenburg's main concern is with the chronological implications of our evidence, it does not necessarily follow that the substance of such traditions are a priori unreliable even if their order (or number) can be shown to be false.

40. See n. 43 below. As preserved on a fragment of the list of eponymous *arkhontes* inscribed in the late fifth century (*IG* I[3] 1031a), these men held office in direct succession: Hippias, Kleisthenes, Miltiades, Kalliades and Peisistratos from 526/5 to 522/1. The dates are exactly inferred on the basis of Dionysios of Halikarnassos' testimony (7.3.1) that Miltiades was *arkhôn* in the 64th Olympiad (i.e., the first year of that quadrennium). Kleisthenes' name is not fully preserved, but Dillon (2006) does not persuade that Kleisthenes cannot have been named in this list and that the *arkhôn* for that year must have been named Pleisthenes. As Dillon, 94, concedes, the name Kleisthenes is statistically more probable than a Pleisthenes.

41. Stein-Hölkeskamp (1989), 146–47. Stahl (1987), 121–33, 185–87, also points to the same dynamic with respect to the judges that Peisistratos established to travel through the countryside, but surprisingly he excludes, 162, sacred treasurers without comment.

pias and grandson of the tyrant Peisistratos). Peisistratos' altar, which carries its epigraph in a conspicuous position very similar to that on Khairion's altar of about a generation earlier, explicitly identifies itself as a memorial (*mnêma*) for his magistracy (*arkhê*):[42]

> μνε͂μα τόδε *h*ε͂ς ἀρχε͂ς Πεισίστ̣[ρατος *h*ιππίο *h*]υιὸς | θε͂κεν ᾿Απόλλονος Πυθίο ἐν τεμένει̣.
>
> This memorial of his magistracy Peisistratos son of Hippias set in the temenos of Apollo Pythios.

The specific context of the altar remains unfortunately obscure because the style, and hence date, of the inscription is sometimes considered to be much later than the year in which Peisistratos is known to have been eponymous *arkhôn* (c. 525/4).[43] Because the eponymous *arkhôn* in Athens had special authority over the festival of Thargelia in honor of Apollo Pythios, Peisistratos perhaps offered his altar in a festival context like Alkiphron and the others, albeit within the context of his family's tyranny.[44] It is striking, nonetheless, that the altar's inscription neither makes use of competitive vocabulary, as does

---

42. *IG* I³ 948 (= Meiggs/Lewis 11). In May 2011, the Greek Epigraphical Society announced (http://www.greekepigraphicsociety.org.gr/newsletter_05-2011.aspx?menu=10) that a fragment of the altar's inscribed lip was recently (2009) recovered at what is most likely the findspot of the altar. The new fragment shows unequivocally (with photographs available on-line) that the epithet of Apollo can be fully restored (i.e., the standard text should now read Πυθίο, as I have rendered above). The altar is probably not of the *trapeza* type, although only the crown appears to have been (partially) preserved, and may be compared to the altar of Aphrodite Ourania in the agora (c. 500, on ceramic evidence), as Shear Jr. (1984), 27, suggests.
43. Arnush (1995) accepts the traditional date of Peisistratos' *arkhê* in 522/1 (against some earlier doubts about the identity of sixth-century *arkhontes* [see n. 40 above]) but argues that the altar's decoration and script (another long-standing point of contention) is commensurate with a date of c. 496, when Peisistratos may have been back in Athens to effect the return of his family. But Meritt (1939), 62–65, already showed that this Peisistratos was *arkhôn* in 497/6, which would thus allow the altar to be downdated, but admited that its epigraphic similarity with the dedication of Hipparkhos (d. 514) at the Ptoön is problematic. A remaining difficulty with Arnush's argument for an altar much later than the magistracy is the lack of parallels for *mnêma* being used to commemorate an event that occurred much earlier, as even Arnush's lone Athenian citation (that of the Athenian Kroisos, *IG* I³ 1240), 150, identifies itself as the memorial of the deceased, not of the fact of his death. Moreover, Arnush's argument, 151ff., for a direct and close relationship between the eponymous *arkhôn* and the Thargelia of Apollo Pythios does not sufficiently answer why Peisistratos should have commemorated his magistracy so much later, even if his nephew Hipparkhos was also eponymous *arkhôn* in 496/5. In her discussion of the altar's form, Ohnesorg (2005), 113 and 246, accepts a date of 520–10, without reference to the script's likely date or the historical issues involved. Keesling (2003), 52–55, argues against viewing the lettering as necessarily late, and therefore for the traditional date of the Pythian altar.
44. *Ath.Pol.* 56. Parker (1996), 95–96.

Khairion's altar, nor specifies what good thing Peisistratos did during his magistracy, as does Alkiphron's *stêlê*. Yet the altar's text appears to have long resonated among Athenians as an emblem of the tyranny, for Thucydides points to it as strong evidence in support of his argument that the Peisistratidai held these high offices "without opposition" (*anepiphthonôs*) in order to ensure the continued supremacy of their lineage.[45] In support of that claim, Thucydides not only cites the text verbatim (as confirmed by the actual altar), but also cites another altar (that of the Twelve Gods) dedicated by Peisistratos whose inscription was effaced, he claims, by the Demos at an early point in time.[46] Where Herodotos, for his part, details Peisistratid force against the most challenging of rivals, he specifies that those opponents were also known for their athletic victories (specifically in equestrian events, the preserve of the wealthy).[47] Political life, according to Herodotos, only worsened in the brief period between Hipparkhos' assassination in 514 at the Panathenaia and the overthrow of the whole tyranny in 510.[48] The overall picture, then, is of a regime that encouraged collusion and support and reserved force for those who could not be so convinced of the Peisistratid claim to dominance.

But for those Athenians whom the Peisistratidai brought into their regime, surely neither the rewards of office nor the legal cover afforded by Solon's laws can have been immaterial. After all, even if the electoral system was rigged through alliances and deals, it remained an electoral system, to the best of our knowledge; electors among the tribes still had to vote for their magistrates, and thus still had to be wooed with largesse, private and public alike. Furthermore, the stability of a regime such as this would depend to some extent not merely on quiet among the elite but on the satisfaction of those lower in the ranks to whom the largesse had to flow. Therefore, the Peisistratidai and their collaborators had

45. Thuc. 6.54.5: οὐδὲ γὰρ τὴν ἀρχὴν ἐπαχθὴς ἦν ἐς τοὺς πολλούς, ἀλλ ' ἀνεπιφθόνως κατεστήσατο.

46. Thuc. 6.54.6–55.3. On the Altar and Sanctuary of the Twelve Gods, see Gadbery (1992); Arnush (1995), 137; Keesling (2003), 52–55. The herms of Hipparkhos offer an important corollary, because they too were inscribed to declare themselves as monuments of Hipparkhos (i.e., μνῆμα τόδ ' Ἱππάρχου) and were likewise long remembered for their epigraphs ([Pl.] *Hipparch.* 229a-b); for the only extant example: *IG* I[3] 1023; see also Appendix, n. 11.

47. Herodotos claims (6.35) that even when Peisistratos held all of the real power in Athens, Kimon's son Miltiades nevertheless exercised significant enough influence (*edynasteue*)—in part because of the great wealth that allowed him to raise horses for his Olympic victory—for the Peisistratidai to send him on a colonial expedition although Herodotos claims (6.39) it was Miltiades' desire to avoid their rule. Furthermore, Kimon had allowed Peisistratos to be hailed as victor for his own three Olympic chariot victories, but Peisistratos' sons could not tolerate that Kimon had in fact won so consistently, and thus arranged for him to be murdered (6.103.2–3).

48. Hdt. 5.55.

a strong incentive to develop the administrative capacities of their offices in order to acquire still more of those resources and deploy them in a more public fashion. Likewise, there was little to prevent erstwhile patrons from availing themselves of whatever resources could be had to further their ambitions so long as they had the support of their betters. Of special importance is the refoundation or expansion of the Panathenaia as a major, even Panhellenic, festival at the outset of this period, as well as the construction of more grandiose shrines for a number of gods, even if it is true (as most now hold) that Peisistratos was not himself responsible, at least not solely, for the Panathenaia's transformation.[49]

Any expansion of a religious festival, of course, would require a corresponding improvement in the *polis*' revenue or a change to its fiscal arrangements. Yet such improvements are difficult to imagine in an atomized political environment such as that which existed between Solon's reforms and Peisistratos' ultimate success. However, if any laws provided a mechanism by which the *polis* would acquire its own resources to meet new and old obligations, it is but a short step to where the ambitious would naturally seek control of the *polis*' resources with which to further their own ends, all the more so where the *polis*' own apparatus offered a clear means by which to do so. After all, for the *polis* to stage and pay for a religious event such as a major sacrifice was to engage in much the same kind of activity as that which ambitious political leaders pursued. To someone enjoying such a sacrificial banquet was there much difference between what was offered by a man like Kimon out of his own funds and that offered by the *polis* but managed by a man like Kimon? One can only wonder if some Athenians could meaningfully distinguish between, say, those *hieropoioi* of Athena who first made the *dromos* for the Panathenaia and the *polis* that ought to have paid for it. For many Athenians, the power of a man might not always have been distinguishable from that of his office, and that very conflation fits the spirit of tyranny.

A central premise of this book is that once a major political figure like Solon or Peisistratos obligated the *polis* to certain religious commitments no successor or regime could easily untie those bonds. In general, even when some rituals were neglected and forgotten, the *polis*' financial and organizational commitments tended only to grow until a major reform effort could make sense out of the accumulated chaos. The Solonian Calendar, which was the subject of the previous chapter, provides a salient example of that phenomenon. For once the sheer num-

49. On the date when the Greater Panathenaia was thought to have been established (by the eponymous *arkhôn* Hippokleides, not Peisistratos), see n. 13 above. The ancient testimony in support of Peisistratos' role is a scholion to Aelius Aristides' *Panathenaikos*, for which see J. Shear (2001), 510.

ber and quality of sacrifices had risen under the Peisistratidai, Athenians as a whole would now have seen what was possible and, I presume, demanded of their *polis* no lesser (or cheaper) an expression of piety and celebration for their goddess than that which they knew was possible. The underlying sociology is well attested under the democracy, as I illustrated in the introduction.

While the manipulation of communal resources for political ends in archaic Athens might have been more pervasive than we can know, it might not have been enough to sate the appetite of the political elite. Since the evidence for Peisistratid support of artists at major festivals like the Panathenaia and Dionysia does not show unequivocally that Peisistratos and his family spent their own personal wealth, there is no good reason to think that they did not instead merely deploy the wealth of the state in accord with established law.[50] The power of the Peisistratidai lay partly in their ability to direct resources where it would advantage themselves and do so under the cloak of whatever laws there were that established the *polis*' formal obligations and the means to pay for them. But this may not have been enough, for Thucydides claims that the Peisistratidai employed a tax for the purpose of funding religion (6.54.5):

> καὶ ἐπετήδευσαν ἐπὶ πλεῖστον δὴ τύραννοι οὗτοι ἀρετὴν καὶ ξύνεσιν, καὶ Ἀθηναίους εἰκοστὴν μόνον πρασσόμενοι τῶν γιγνομένων τήν τε πόλιν αὐτῶν καλῶς διεκόσμησαν καὶ τοὺς πολέμους διέφερον καὶ ἐς τὰ ἱερὰ ἔθυον.
>
> [For the most part, these tyrants also pursued virtue and intelligence, and exacting only a twentieth of agricultural produce from the Athenians they ornamented their city well, distinguished themselves in wars and sacrificed appropriately.[51]]

The tax might certainly have been new, for we know of no precedent, and it would have given the Peisistratidai a tool that no one else could wield. We could only speculate on how the burden of that tax was spread across the population,

---

50. See Slings (2000) for a survey of this evidence. The hypothesis offered here would also have the advantage of explaining why so many poets and artists supported by the Peisistratidai in their later years (apparently by Hipparkhos most of all) would remain in Athens after the establishment of the democracy. If these individuals were paid with funds emanating from the public treasury, and not the Peisistratidai, they would not have been personally tied to them. Accordingly, once the Demos established sufficient control over the public treasury, there might be little objection to the continued presence of such persons provided that they took care to accommodate themselves to the new regime.

51. *Ath.Pol.* 16.4 and 6 echo the claim of taxation (as a tithe, not as a "twentieth") but make no claim as to what the proceeds were intended to purchase or achieve; cf. Hdt. 1.64. On the meaning of τῶν γιγνομένων as "agricultural products" in the context of taxation, see, for example, Pernin (2007), 372–74.

but as E. Stein-Hölkeskamp has argued, new or more rigorous taxation must have undercut the ability of wealthy Athenians other than the Peisistratidai to offer patronage and thereby to compete effectively.[52] To employ taxes for religious ends conjures a host of fiscal questions, but it is its effect on electoral politics that is most significant here. On the one hand, the money that it raised would have been directed to those magistrates who already had the responsibility for purchasing victims, paying the butchers, and the like, thus feeding an established electoral dynamic. Yet to increase the flow of money toward even established administrative ends can alter them in turn by requiring new magistracies to manage the tax, and so on, all of which would, of course, alter the political landscape itself.

That kind of change, moreover, conceivably weakened the traditional connection between a man's personal prestige and wealth, on the one hand, and the pursuit of office through electoral patronage, on the other. M. Stahl, for one, has suggested that to centralize taxes as well as the expenditure of that money for religious life might have also eroded the personal nature of many of these high offices, since this restructuring might have tended to disassociate the authority of an office from the man holding it.[53] To be fair, we do not know that, as Thucydides' brief notice would have it, the taxes collected by the Peisistratid state during this period were so centralized, especially in light of how much the tribes mattered to political life. Neither do we know that these taxes had the effect of punishing those members of the elite not especially attached to the Peisistratidai, even though that motive is plausible enough on its own. Nevertheless, to the extent that the power of a magistrate could be, in effect, more personal than institutional, then the agglomeration of resources by the *polis* under the Peisistratidai may have sown the seeds for a much more institutional vision of authority and law, even though the Peisistratidai themselves embodied personal power as did no other Athenians.

Democratic Rule and the Sacred Treasurers: The First Generation

On the expulsion of the tyrants in 510, and then Kleisthenes' reforms in 508, the principal impediments to competition for high office ought well, in principal,

52. Stein-Hölkeskamp (1989), 145–46.
53. Stahl (1987), 183–87.

to have abated. While the new political conditions would come to restrict elite competition, in this early period the democracy appears to have done nothing to restrict the electoral prerogatives of the elite inherited from the Solonian laws. Although there is much that we do not know about those first few years following Kleisthenes' reforms, and significant controversy remains concerning how politically autonomous the Demos was, there is no evidence for any move against the political aspirations and behaviors of the elite surrounding banquets and the like.[54] Since much of the story concerning sacred treasurers must be told through the proxy of their religious offerings, it is salutary to consider for a moment how readily the young democracy appropriated the forms and conventions of elite memorials. That athletic iconography still conveyed a strong sense of aristocratic power and legitimacy even in this period of the early democracy is fully evident in the bronze chariot group that the Athenian democracy dedicated to commemorate the defeat of the Boiotians (along with Khalkis and Sparta) in 506/5, whose assault had been aimed to restore the very short-lived oligarchy of 510–8.[55] Such was the ideological power of this monument

54. Herodotos' account (5.72; cf. *Ath.Pol.* 20.3) of the popular Athenian siege of Isagoras and the Spartans on the akropolis might suggest an action against elite authority as a whole (as argued by Ober [1993]; [1998]), but Kleisthenes' alliance with the Demos and the apparently belated use of ostracism (and even then as a limited instrument directed at particular members of the elite, in part orchestrated by rivals) arguably undercuts the notion of a "revolution" in this period. Anderson (2003) also credits Kleisthenes with a much greater impact, prior to whose reforms the Demos necessarily lacked a unified consciousness, given what Anderson sees as the atomization of archaic Attica, but which developed very quickly nevertheless. Even Ober (1989), 84ff., argues that early fifth-century elite political leaders might unabashedly display their ancestry and wealth as a means of acquiring popular support, presumably to ground their claims to certain kinds of expertise and the ability to provide critical aid to Athenians at home and abroad. However, the ostracisms may be taken to show that too great a success in some kinds of aristocratic symbolism and power might be seen as a danger to the balance of the whole system, for which also see Ober (1989), 75. Forsdyke (2005), 133–42, argues that the siege and the development of ostracism (in 487, ostensibly) represents the assertion of popular control over a form of struggle once confined to the elite, but ostracism does not obviously add up to anti-elite feeling per se.

The political history of the early democracy, it could fairly be argued, was marked largely by accident and unintended consequences of empire (after 479) that largely promoted the growth of mass power in a variety of institutional and ideological forms. Eder (1998) argues, too, that radical democracy only coalesced toward the end of the fifth century, and that the Kleisthenic and other institutional reforms moved Athenian society toward that state of affairs as a by-product of aristocratic political competition, which utilized mass popularity for certain ends but whose practitioners nevertheless supplied institutional expertise to the state. Furthermore, Eder also argues, 118ff., that ostracism is an expression of power that obstructs the kind of debate that is otherwise characteristic of democracy (contra Ober [1989], 156ff., where the *rhêtores* give expression to popular opinion, not dominate it). In an analysis of financial topics in fifth-century debates, Kallet-Marx (1994) similarly argues for the shaping and control of that opinion by political experts. In short, it is difficult to deny the continued dominance of the elite in many strands of Athenian political life, notwithstanding the show of force that could be mounted by the Demos and the more or less consistent pressure that it collectively might exert through one or another means.

55. *IG* I^3 501 A (= Meiggs/Lewis 15; *DAA* 168). Petrovic (2007), 209–22, offers a detailed textual and

that long after the Persians destroyed it in 480, the Athenians rebuilt it.[56] The date at which the monument was restored (c. 455) is all the more interesting since it fell after the reforms of Ephialtes, and shows how the radicalizing democracy of imperial Athens found in the dedication of 506 a potent sign of its own political lineage. Yet the equestrian imagery of that monument, so redolent as it is of elite athletics, suggests that the Demos was not yet eager to assert itself consistently, much less programmatically, against the elite. As for *tamiai* and other magistrates of the upper census classes, one could only presume that electoral patronage and competition could fairly flourish once more since the evidence for it in the later fifth and fourth centuries is relatively robust. Thus C. Keesling's recent downdating of several seated marble statues, which are often thought to represent *tamiai* or other sacred treasurers, to this very period would seem to have no obvious objection from the side of political history.[57] I will return to these statues in the appendix but make the point here that these statues, one of which may have a familial connection to none other than Khairion, do not represent simply a return to the kind of victorious advertisement from before c. 550. While the image of a seated magistrate may betoken the power of his office, the form itself bears no obvious relationship to the action of others, such as altars and *stêlai* marking an arena for athletic competition.[58] In its first decade or so the democracy, in short, appears to have done nothing to alter the essential dynamics that tied the pursuit of office to an enjoyment of its fruits.

But after Marathon the democracy did assert its privileges over magistrates of every stripe, even as it recognized many of its most august officers' privileges.

epigraphic commentary to this monument. Herodotos (5.77) explicitly draws attention to the ransom, noting that two *mnai* were demanded for each of seven hundred prisoners. In *DAA* (this is no. 168), Raubitschek, assumed that the monument was paid for by only a tithe of that ransom (thus amounting to only two *talents* and twenty *mnai*) and thus suggested that it would have taken time to collect the ransom and thus the monument might be better downdated to c. 505–500; *IG* suggests c. 505 without discussion.

56. See n. 51 above.

57. Keesling (2003), 182, dates the sculpture to c. 510–480, a period in which she argues, 36–62, that most akropolis votive sculptures were produced, but most others on the basis of sculptural style or letter-form seem to have preferred a date of c. 525–500 (e.g., Raubitschek in *DAA* 6, p. 11); cf. Shapiro (2001), 94.

58. A useful point of comparison lies in the epigrams that Kimon and other generals wished to affix to herms at the Stoa Poikile in celebration of their victory over the Persians at Eion in 476/5. But because the Demos insisted that the inscribed herms not name the men individually, it prohibited, in effect, all subsequent officeholders from suggesting that their service be commemorated in such a manner: Aeschin. 3.183; Dem. 20.112; Plut. *Cim.* 4, 7–8. I return to this event and its significance below.

The Hekatompedon Decrees of 485/4 not only reflect the changed political circumstances but also represent an effort by the democracy to establish the duties for the *tamiai* where it found Solon's Law wanting. The more fragmentary Decree A assigns authority to the *arkhontes* as well as to the *prytaneis* of the Boule for what seems to be the security of the akropolis, and Decree B mandates that the *tamiai* of Athena had to open certain buildings for inspection and to be present in the sanctuary no less often than three times every month.[59] On the other hand, the Demos did concede significant, and potentially problematic, authority to the *tamiai*, even as it established that this capacity was, in effect, delegated to them by the Demos. Decree B, for example, also stipulates that the *tamiai* of Athena had the power to collect fines from certain ritual attendants, and aimed to enforce that provision by stipulating that the *tamiai* themselves be subject to the same, quite heavy, penalty of 100 dr. if they failed to levy those fines.[60] Someone, after all, had to be responsible for ensuring that religious precincts, property, and rituals were duly respected. Even in the era of the radical democracy, it was of course customary for the *hieropoioi* of various cults to fine those who acted without *kosmos* or decorum in religious processions, for example.[61] But it is the appearance in Decree B of the procedures for the *euthyna*, a procedure of accountability to which I will return momentarily, and instructions that the *prytaneis* will make public any charges against the *tamiai* that reveals the precise mechanisms by which the Demos could make good on its threats.[62] The Decrees embody the sovereignty of the Demos and reflect its willingness to exercise its power over the *tamiai*, and therefore over all the sacred treasurers whose position and responsibilities fell far below those of the *tamiai*.

But the Decrees are significant also for being the second known measure enacted in a very short period of time during which the Demos was attuned to the matter of control over the *tamiai*, and the third known instance in which it was concerned more broadly with the behavior of elite Athenians. In 487/6, just two years prior to the enactment of the Decrees, the Athenians established or first used ostracism—it is not clear which—as a weapon against political leadership thought too influential to be safe for the *polis*' stability (or Demos' wel-

59. *IG* I³ 4 A, *ll.* 6–8, 16–17; B *ll.* 1–2, 13–14, 17–21.
60. *IG* I³ 4B, *ll.* 11–13.
61. Fines levied by *hieropoioi* of Hephaistos in festival: *IG* I³ 82, *ll.* 24–29; power of *hieropoioi* of Athena at Greater Panathenaia: *IG* I³ 82, *ll.* 24–26; Lesser Panathenaia: *IG* II² 334, *ll.* 6–7, 31–32 (= Rhodes/Osborne 81); 1496, *ll.* 98–99; cf. *IG* I³ 133, *ll.* 17–18, in conjunction with the Anakes.
62. *IG* I³ 4B, *ll.* 15–17, 24–25 (although the term is restored by *IG* at *l.* 17, the logic of the text renders it all but certain); *prytaneis*: *ll.* 24–25.

fare). In that same year, the Athenians also invoked Solon's Law on the Tamiai as a model for establishing on a new basis the selection of their most powerful magistrates, the nine *arkhontes*, as argued in chapter 1.[63] Unfortunately, we do not know the political relationship between the two measures—ostracism and the law on the *arkhontes*—and not even which of the two came first and under whose initiative. If the goal of this law was to render the *arkhontes* (and by extension the Areiopagos, perhaps) less a willful and aristocratic body that was indifferent or hostile to the Demos and its demands, one need hardly look further than the Law. J. Ober rightfully emphasizes that the imposition of *prokrisis* for the *arkhontes* likely constrained elite ambitions to gain and manipulate office to a significant degree, and it is telling that after this measure we never again encounter evidence of an *arkhôn* taking political initiative as Themistokles had in 493/2 when fortifying the Peiraieus.[64] On that interpretation, then, the Law was still working sufficiently well on both an administrative and political level for the Demos to be interested in adapting it for use with respect to the *arkhontes*. Otherwise, if the Law was not perceived as both a success and as a measure also friendly to the Demos and its interests, it is difficult to understand why the Athenians would have adopted that one archaic institution to alter another, both of which had the approval or authorship of Solon himself. In short, many Athenians might well have felt that the Law was truly working in *their* interests, though that had, in all likelihood, not been Solon's intention.

Likewise, it is in this period that we can see the Demos taking greater initiative in applying the resources of the *polis* to those essentials of Greek religious life—festivals, large sacrifices, and the like—in which it had a material stake. One need hardly rehearse, too, the extensive building program that commenced in the mid-fifth century and remade the akropolis with the Parthenon and Propylaia, to say nothing of the many expensive buildings erected in the agora and at key sites across Attica. As L. Kallet demonstrated, the institutional development that made such commitments possible, even amidst a surfeit of imperial wealth, depended on a political dialogue about the *polis*' finances that bound together the interests and views of both the Demos and its political leaders,

63. Forsdyke (2005), 146–77, 281–84, argues that ostracism was indeed Kleisthenic in origin, as many sources indicate (i.e., *Ath.Pol.* 22.1–4; Philokhoros *FGrH* 328 F 30; Ael. *VH* 13.24; Diod. Sic. 11.55.1), and that it was merely unused for some twenty years until first employed in 487/6, notwithstanding the contrary testimony of Androtion (*FGrH* 324 F 6) concerning its origins.

64. Following Carawan (1987), Ober (1989), 76–77, agrees with the idea that the law of 487/6 was meant originally to forestall intra-elite competition.

who regularly came from elite circles and wealth.[65] While it was they who set much of the agenda and possessed the financial expertise necessary to run the *polis* and Athens' newfound empire, it was the Demos that voted and it was the Demos that those leaders had to persuade. We ought therefore to think of Athens' ongoing and expanding financial commitments to religious life in the era after the first generation or so as arising primarily from the Demos.

These phenomena find early but ample testimony in regulations for a festival of Herakles at Marathon itself. The extant section of the regulations (c. 490–80) for the games of Herakles there (perhaps in commemoration of the battle) stipulate that the contests are to be overseen by thirty men, one from each of the ten new Kleisthenic tribes, and of not less than thirty years of age.[66] In addition, those magistrates (*epistatai*) are required to appear in the shrine and to swear a fearsome oath. These regulations represent, however, at least the second effort by the democracy to enforce some kind of behavior with regard to those involved with the Herakleia. A heavily damaged section from another side of the same *stêlê*, possibly inscribed a decade or so earlier (c. 500–490), appears to mandate particular forms of legal action against those who commit certain religious offences within the sanctuary (probably regarding lack of decorum), and to stipulate the fines that are to be paid.[67] Together, this pair of texts perhaps constitutes the earliest "sacred law" known from Athens, but it is their coupling that leads one to suspect that the Demos instituted the second text because the first one, whatever its scope, was no longer felt adequate to ensure proper celebration of the Herakleia (especially since the earlier text appears to predate Athens' victory at Marathon itself).[68]

With respect to the Demos' level of control over the Herakleia, there is a further point to consider. The large number of men involved, three from each of the tribes, marks a turning point. For the Kleisthenic reforms made possible the direct participation of a much larger number of citizens even if nothing whatsoever was altered with regard to census requirements (about which we

65. Kallet-Marx (1994).
66. *IG* I[3] 3. Where Vanderpool (1942), 337, was unsure about the correct interpretation of the last extant word at *l.* 12 (which he gives as unaccented ἐπιστατẹ[ν]), *IG* prints an infinitive followed by postpositive particle (*ll.* 12–13: ἐπιστατ῀ẹ[σαι δ]-| [ὲ]), which must take the board of thirty as its proper subject.
67. *IG* I[3] 2. Vanderpool (1942), 353, notes that this is apparently the earliest use of the term ἀσυρής "lewd" (*l.* 12: τἀσυρε̂). Its presence in this text implies that this section of the law is concerned with ensuring *kosmos*; the figures noted in the following lines are probably those of fines for various sorts of inappropriate behavior.
68. On the category of regulation and law usually termed "sacred law," see Introduction, n. 26.

cannot know given the poor state of the texts). Prior to the institution of the *epistatai*, however, the Athenian democracy appears to have established rules in the earlier of the two laws, and hence also established an authority in some or another body, for conduct at the sanctuary. Unmistakably, the regulations also reflect the concomitant growth in the state's number of sacred treasurers, due at a minimum to the increase in the number of tribes from what it had been prior to Kleisthenes if not also due to the Demos' commitment to fund what might have been a recently founded festival. Moreover, the *epistatai* might not have drawn men only from the higher census classes, or else it could have been difficult to ensure that such a large college would be fully manned. The effect of such service, nonetheless, will have been to open up to a larger section of the Athenian citizenry the possibility of enjoying for themselves—under the limits that they themselves imposed as members of the Demos—what it felt like to serve as a sacred treasurer.

With Athenian victory over the Persians, nonetheless, the Demos' approach toward the *polis'* sacred treasurers seems to have entailed no olive branch for those who might seek to become *hieropoioi* or *tamiai* rather than mere *epistatai*. Of relevance here is the Stoa Poikile and the manner in which the democracy is said to have placed significant limits on how several victorious generals commemorated their victory over the Persians at Eion in 476/5. As Aiskhines and later Plutarch claim, the Demos allowed Kimon the exceptional honor of having several epigrams inscribed on herms at the Stoa, a structure he is said to have commissioned, as thanks for his capture of Eion from the Persians.[69] Yet both Plutarch and Aiskhines emphasize that the epigrams did not mention Kimon by name (nor that of any of the other generals) and go so far as to provide the texts that support their assertion.[70] One and all, the honor granted to these generals was merely one of receiving any such epigraphic monument at all, and one of the epigrams states at the outset that the Athenians gave the monument as a kind of recompense (*misthos*) to the generals.[71] If the anecdote accurately reflects the historical event, the control exercised by the Demos in this instance

69. Aeschin. 3.183. It should be noted that in Plutarch's version (*Cim.* 4, 7–8) an Athenian demands in the Ekklesia that only those who won a victory individually (and thus not part of a larger college) should be rewarded with their own name on a monument also. On the authorship (Simonides?) and history of the epigrams, see Page (1981), 255–59, and n. 72 below.

70. In his telling of the event, however, Demosthenes (20.112) merely assumes that his jurors will know of the event so well as to not need any detail.

71. The second epigram, following Plutarch's (*Cim.* 4) text: ἠγεμόνεσσι δὲ μισθὸν 'Αθηναῖοι τάδ ' ἔδωκαν | ἀντ ' εὐεργεσίης καὶ μεγαλῶν ἀγαθῶν. | μᾶλλόν τις τάδ ' ἴδων κὰι ἐπεσσομένων ἐθελήσει | ἀμφὶ περὶ ξυνοῖς πράγμασι δῆριν ἔχειν. Aeschines (3.183) presents a very similar text, replacing only μεγαλῶν ἀγαθῶν with μεγάλης ἀρετῆς, and δῆριν with μόχθον.

might help to explain the paucity of even *ex officio* dedications during the ensuing era. While neither the anecdotes nor the epigrams themselves state explicitly why the Demos should have avoided naming the generals, the contemporary use of ostracism and the heavy fine only recently (479) levied on Kimon's father, Miltiades, for deceiving the Demos suggests that the Demos was eager to limit the personal aspirations and charismatic prestige of its most successful magistrates. Given that Kimon was the principal general responsible for the victory at Eion, and perhaps the preeminent political figure at home that could be associated with elite practices and views, the Stoa would seem to mark a significant shift from the political sociology of even the immediately preceding period between Kleisthenes' reforms and the Persian Wars, and well before the radicalization of the democracy usually associated with Ephialtes and Perikles from the late 460s onward.[72] Such limits on the celebration of leading figures are not hard to find.[73] What personal monuments could we imagine sacred treasurers now erecting upon the akropolis proclaiming their own service to the gods or *polis*, much less expressing that in the language of victory? The age when it was possible for an Alkiphron or Khairion to offer such memorials of their magisterial power had truly closed.

72. Identifying the Stoa of the Herms with that of the Poikile (on plans of the Agora excavations), di Cesare (2001) argues that the upper epigram (*IG* I³ 503/04) celebrates Themistokles at Salamis, but Kimon afterwards added the lower one to celebrate Marathon in competition with Themistokles; moreover, he speaks of "il legame intertestuale" between this second epigram and that of Eion celebrating Kimon directly. However, as summarized in the apparatus of *IG* to those texts, there is no basis for attributing them to the Stoa even if we cannot be sure of what monument originally bore them. For a detailed textual commentary and epigraphic reconstruction of these inscriptions, see now also Petrovic (2007), 158–77.

73. The Athenians, for example, also turned down the offer made by members of Perikles' own family to supply a number of public waterworks at their own expense: Plu. (*Per.* 14.1), with Kallet (2003), 129.

CHAPTER 4

The *Tamiai* of Athena and Their Duties

In the previous chapter, I argued that through the sixth century and into the early democracy sacred treasurers and other magistrates had both strong incentive and the means by which to exploit their offices for further electoral success. That dynamic catalyzed a process whereby at least some successful political figures, for which the Peisistratidai represent the high watermark, sought to enlarge the resources under their control as well as the opportunities in which to distribute that largesse. In turn, the *polis* came to develop new methods and administrative structures by which to meet its increasingly costly religious obligations. In turn, the democracy took up that same behavior, even as it asserted its own authority and initiative. Yet that development did not affect the administrative landscape uniformly. An unexpected consequence was that some sacred treasurers, none more so than the *tamiai* of Athena, held on to those privileges and duties that marked them off from the rest of the *polis*' magistrates. It was, as I shall show in the last two chapters of this book, to those other magistrates that management of those new resources was consigned. To understand what was at stake, the present chapter takes up a simple though critical problem: what were the duties of the *tamiai*?

Stewardship

In spite of our knowledge of Solon's Law on the Tamiai and the rest of his laws that governed sacred treasurers and other magistrates, to reconstruct the tasks of the *tamiai* as they were understood at that time or at any point in the sixth century would seem to be an impossible task. But the evidence from the classical centuries shows that the office retained tasks and privileges that only make sense within an archaic context and not a classical, much less a democratic, one. First, notwithstanding its rather obscure linguistic history, the term *tamias* is best interpreted as simply "one who dispenses (or distributes)," rather than "one who carves (sacrificial meat)" as it has often been translated.[1] As to what this might mean in the context of archaic, and indeed of classical, Athens, we must first plumb the description of the *tamiai* offered by *Ath. Pol.*:[2]

> παραλαμβάνου[σι δ]ὲ τό τε ἄγαλμα τῆς ᾿Αθηνᾶς καὶ τὰς Νίκας καὶ τὸν ἄλλον κόσμον καὶ τὰ χρ[ήματ]α ἐναντίον τῆς βουλῆς.
>
> [They receive the cult-statue of Athena, the Nikai, the rest of the ornament (*kosmos*), and the money in front of the Boule.]

Stationary objects like the cult-statue of Athena Polias and the golden Nikai, of course, could only be guarded and protected from damage or neglect that would arise from their only natural or customary use: to be the very object of worship. When constructed of valuable materials those statues were also subject to small acts of temple-robbery, by which gold ornaments and the like might be snatched. Both sources of loss figure in the inscribed inventories of the *tamiai* relative to the Nikai and the chryselephantine statue of Athena.[3] But

---

1. Chantraine (2009), Beekes (2010) s.v. ταμία; Sihler (1995), no. 454 A.4-B; Boisacq (1916), 939. *LSJ* s.v. offers the definition: "prop. one who carves and distributes, dispenser, steward." As Beekes points out, the etymological difficulty is that there is no parallel -ίας attested as a primary derivative, and thus one must posit an intermediary, which in this case is often construed most plausibly as the feminine. That quandary, however, also occasions an historical difficulty that is revealed by Buck and Petersen's (1945), 169–70, hypothesis that "ταμίας 'dispenser, steward' is clearly a masculinization of the fem. ταμίη 'house-wife, stewardess' . . . for it was she who dispensed the store of victuals in Homer." As with Busolt's claim about the derivation of the office from these (female and servile) posts (see the Introduction, n. 39), this idea ignores the other (male) *tamiai* in epic as well as the fact that contrary to their supposition of -ίας being feminine and demeaning, the feminine forms of such masculine terms as νεανίας or τραυματίας, or for common masculine names such as Καλλίας or Λυσίας, are unattested. If indeed the masculine form is a secondary formation from the feminine, one should approach with great caution any historicization of the forms and roles seen in early Greek epic.
2. *Ath.Pol.* 47.1 (= Harp. s.v. ταμίαι, in part; Souda s.vv. ταμίαι). On *Ath.Pol.*'s authorship and date of composition, see Rhodes (1993), 58–63 and 768, who doubts Aristotle's full or majority authorship. Keaney (1970) argues that Aristotle composed an unrevised text c. 330 and that this was revised early in the 320s, and Keaney [1980] provides further arguments on the relative order of *Ath.Pol.* and certain sections of the *Politics*; see also Day and Chambers (1962), 3–4 and 195–97.
3. The inventories, notably, record pieces lost by accident or recovered from attempted theft from the chryselephantine statue of Athena Polias, and thus reflect the degree to which the statue and its

since those statues and their materials were static and can hardly be said to be things that someone could dispense, we are left to consider whether it was the money or the *kosmos* that is at issue. Money and *kosmos* together represent not merely two distinct types of object or property but the two different kinds of sacred treasurer who tended to them, as first emerged in the sixth century. I will take up the question of money and its stewards in the following chapters but will delineate *kosmos* and its *tamiai* first.

In short, it was the *kosmos* that the *tamiai* of Athena dispensed, and they did so on a relatively active basis through the classical centuries. But, first, just what exactly was *kosmos*?[4] While the term *kosmos* was often applied to social decorum, such as was preferred in a religious context, it also embodied physical ornament such as jewelry. The *kosmos* of the gods was, however, something else. A fragmentary law of c. 335/4 (*IG* II[2] 333) shows that *kosmos* was indeed widespread among the gods and that it consisted of vessels, constructed of precious metals (often of large size), that were meant to be used in some fashion and not simply to be stored as inert treasure. This law appears to require that the Athenians melt decrepit gold and silver dedications on the akropolis in conjunction with an inspection (*exetasis*) and inventory of the contents in several treasuries.[5] As proposed expressly by Lykourgos, a lengthy rider (most of the preserved text of the law, in fact) stipulates that various sources of income be applied to perhaps one sacrifice, and more importantly here, to the creation of "sacred ornament," or *hieroi kosmoi* in the plural, for a number of major gods; not surprisingly, a variety of sacred treasurers are to carry out the necessary tasks (whose precise nature is opaque given the poor state of the inscription).[6]

constituent materials were considered *hiera* and thus under the guardianship of the *tamiai* of Athena, for which see H. Thompson (1940) and D. Thompson (1944).

4. Few scholars have attempted an even cursory examination of the subject. Rhodes (1993), 551, does offer that *kosmos* in *Ath.Pol.* "will include other items dedicated to the gods, and also the vessels and other equipment needed for religious ceremonies" but does not suggest why such material was so important for the *tamiai* to receive custody over it before the assembled Boule.

5. Exetasis: fr. a-b, *l.* 11; Greater Panathenaia: frs. c + e-f, *l.* 8.

6. The *nomos* ordains that *tamiai* for a number of cults (and some who are more strictly financial officers, along with the *epistatai* of some shrines) devote to this project what some might take to be *hiera* funds (frequently restored in this fragment, and not even surely attested at frs. c + e-f, *l.* 16: μετ]ὰ τοῦ ταμίου τοῦ δήμου ἱ[ερῶν χρηματῶν). But the *tamias* of the Demos is not otherwise known to have handled *hiera* funds so much as what were likely *hosia* (e.g., *IG* VII 4254, *ll.* 37–39). If it could be shown that indeed *hiera* funds were used to fund the project, this text would provide critical evidence that *hiera* funds were not totally sequestered. An interesting complication might be found at *l.* 18 (ἐκ τῆς ἀπαρχῆς τῆς ἀπὸ τῶν τ[εμενῶν), where the text indicates that income was also to be gathered from a tithe (*aparkhê*, due from *temenê*?); cf. *ll.* 15–16), which, as shown earlier in this chapter, customarily signifies *hiera*, not *hosia*, income and in any case is likely not the income due from a lease (i.e., μισθός).

The text does not spell out what precisely the *kosmos* of each god was, and thus whether Artemis Brauronia would have needed equipment quite different from that of, say, Zeus Soter. Thus, one might be justified in adopting Lykourgos' use of the plural "*kosmoi*" to indicate that each god's *kosmos* was, in principle, unique. But fragmentary references to equipment used by ritual figures known as *kanêphoroi* ("basket-bearers") and the presence of the word *pompe(i)a* ("processional") prior to the law's rider strongly suggest that at least part of the *kosmos* was to be used for religious processions.[7] The span of time envisioned by Lykourgos extended to at least four years since the sacred treasurers would produce *kosmos* each year for Dionysos in order to complete, the rider explicitly states, a quadrennial cycle.[8] One could only speculate whether that cycle was meant to coincide with that of the Panathenaia, but the clear inference is that the program of creating *kosmoi* and endowing the various cults with them, drawn variously from their own resources, was extensive in scale and costly.[9] This Lykourgan law shows, therefore, that *kosmos* was made of gold and silver, it was sacred, and that at a minimum it was to be used for the processions of (major) festivals.

What the *nomos* does not resolve is the degree to which the *kosmoi* were

---

7. "Processional": fr. a-b, *l.* 2: π̣ο̣μ̣πε̃α. *Kanêphorikon*: frs. c + e-f, *l.* 10; preceding the phrase]ν τὸν κανηφορικόν, *IG* restores the term as κόσμο]ν but χρυσοῦ]ν is preferable in light of the following evidence. At fr. a-b, *l.* 15, and thus in the first lines of Lykourgos' proposal, there is a further reference to the *kana* along with silver amphorae thus suggesting the importance of the processional equipment within the overall scheme, and that the *kana* are likely to have been of precious metal also. Humphries (2004), 92 (cf. her 119), quoting communication from D. M. Lewis, suggests that this law might also have entailed a great expansion in the number of girls serving as *kanêphoroi*, from thirty to one hundred, for which the pseudo-Plutarchean *VitaeXOrat.* on the life of Lykourgos (*Mor.* 852b) provides the critical evidence and also specifies that the equipment for the *kanêphoroi* be golden *kosmos*: παρασκευάσας τῇ θεῷ κόσμον, Νίκας τε ὁλοχρύσους πομπεῖά τε χρυσᾶ καὶ ἀργυρᾶ καὶ κόσμον χρυσοῦν εἰς ἑκατὸν κανηφόρους. Nonetheless, ps.-Plutarch's further specification that equipment be provided for one hundred *kanêphoroi* cannot be substantiated or rejected on the basis of the law's extant fragments.
8. frs. c + e-f, *ll.* 16–17 (as restored by *IG*): ποήσασθαι δὲ καὶ τ]ῶ[ι] Διονύσωι κόσμον | [ἑκάστου το]ῦ ἐνιαυτοῦ ἐν τῆι τετραετίαι ἐκ [τῶν ἱερῶν χρημάτων. The only other temporal marker is that of the Greater Panathenaia (*l.* 8), which was due to be held the next year, 334/3. Concerning the date of the inscription, of which the only sure indicator is that the rider of Lykourgos was passed on 6 Skirophorion and thus about a month and half before the Panathenaia, see Lambert (2005), 137–39. Note also that the two texts would seem to be a closely connected pair, each concerned with one of the Panathenaia festivals and even touching upon subjects common to each; in the other text, for example, the *kanêphoroi* are restored at B. *l.* 15, which, if correct, might further tie the two *nomoi* more closely together temporally.
9. A further indication of the cost's magnitude is that the rider employs προδεδανεισμένα twice (frs. c + e-f, *ll.* 7, 9), which is not only in keeping with the *daneisma* discussed earlier (though employed perhaps uniquely some seventy-five years before this law), but Migeotte (1980), shows that this term signifies lending through an intermediary (with specific comments on this text, 221–22).

homologous to the known treasure of the gods and thus whether a large portion of that treasure could find itself in processions of various kinds. In other words, was the *kosmos* none other than the vast repertoire of cups, incense burners, trays, wine strainers, and the like that occupy the bulk of all surviving inventories inscribed on marble *stêlai*? The most complete Attic inventories, those of Athena Polias, reveal that the Parthenon (divided into three separate areas: Parthenon, Hekatompedon, Opisthodomos) and the Erekhtheion (the Temple of Athena Polias) contained many hundreds of precious vessels and related objects, fashioned of gold and silver, and frequently endowed with elaborate, costly ornamentation in the fifth and fourth centuries.[10] The plurality of gods receiving *kosmoi* by virtue of the Lykourgan law, and the fragmentary inventories of treasure known for some of those gods as well as others not named therein, points to a widespread phenomenon in which the contents of those inventories served much the same function across many cults. A single quotidian example from the Hekatompedon treasury of Athena will illustrate the larger pattern, and incidentally the scale of wealth involved with respect to the goddess' *hiera* (sacred) property for use in procession. Beginning in 398/7 the *tamiai* recorded among many dozens of other entries merely "washbasin (of silver): weight 1050 dr.; washbasin (of silver); weight 940 dr." (that is, solid silver weighing a total of nearly 8.56kg [or, 18.9 lbs.], and perhaps equivalent to almost seven years' worth of gross pay for a skilled worker employed on the Erekhtheion but a decade earlier).[11] Although many items appear once (in our very fragmentary texts), these inscriptions are inherently conservative and assiduously record the same kind of material, and the very same items again and

10. Notwithstanding the terrible effects that financial crisis and the Peloponnesian War had upon the wealth of Athena, in the typology of objects recorded in the inventories there is little change evident between the fifth and fourth centuries. For the destructive effects upon the akropolis treasuries, see Hamilton (2000), 253 n. 40 and p. 259. Hamilton, 251, notes also that the Parthenon treasury was the least valuable (though mainly of gold) and also the last to be melted, such that a larger proportion of its treasures did survive into the fourth century. The pattern might well reflect a greater level of sanctity accorded to it and its treasures. Samons (2000), 28–54, 323–29, provides a basic overview of some critical elements in the operation of sacred treasuries during the fifth century.

11. The epigraphic evidence for these two objects is conveniently summarized by D. Harris (1995), 156 (V.231). For the calculation offered above, I add the assumption of a three hundred-day work-year (i.e., excluding festivals and bad weather) to the evidence of the accounts for the Erekhtheion in 409–07 (1 dr. per diem, without regard to the workers' legal status). The only other relevant body of data for Athenian wages, again in the field of temple construction, comes from that of the Eleusinian accounts in the 320s. These texts show that the wages paid then to the equivalent workers was in the range of 1.5 dr. per diem for unskilled and up to 2.5 dr. per diem for the most skilled (equivalent to those in the Erekhtheion accounts). On the problematic nature of the Erekhtheion and Eleusinian accounts, see Loomis (1998), 38–44, 105–07, 111–13, and Markle (1985), 293–94.

again over a lengthy period of time, with each year's inventory being a record produced by a unique board of *tamiai* with only slight variations.[12] The two washbasins continue to appear in the inventories until at least 341/0, for instance.[13] Other valuable and unusual votives are also recorded in the inventories, such as a gilded bridle in the Hekatompedon, for example, but they constitute a minority among the objects and are often composed of materials or in a fashion that would render them of very limited utility.[14]

Individual Athenians as well as their various civic bodies like the Boule had a strong preference for dedicating precious vessels over votives of similar expense but constructed in other forms. The fifth-century inventories of the Pronaos of the Parthenon, for instance, record a total of 202 different vessels of gold and silver and yet excluded all other kinds of object (except a gold wreath and two silver lamps).[15] Even in the mixed storage areas such as the Parthenon itself (as a distinct chamber of the homonymous temple), the combined inventories attest a total of 172 different vessels, while the next most common category is that of jewelry (at a minimum of 124 objects), followed by 97 weapons and pieces of armor (often bronze, but including gilt as well). These vessels typically fall into relatively few classes where type, metal, occasionally the dedicatory inscription, and weight are recorded, one after another seemingly without end and without much differentiation. These objects are accompanied only rarely by striking pieces whose individual histories could only occasion speculation, like the gilt bridle in the Hekatompedon. All of the extant treasury records thus

12. The consistency of these patterns may be grasped with only a glance at the tabular presentation, item for item, presented by D. Harris (1995) but checked against Hamilton (1996); cf. Kosmetatou (2001) and (2002). A grossly underappreciated fact is that the *tamiai* of Athena and other sacred treasurers are known to have used public slaves as aides in this period, which might explain the general cohesion of texts year over year and the consistency with which they record or describe items in a given sequence for each of the several akropolis treasuries. Without such help how would an incoming board know where to start? On public slaves and their financial expertise (e.g., *IG* II² 120, *l.* 12 [353/2]), see Lewis (1997), 69–71; Hunter (2006); and also the still very useful survey by Jacob (1926); cf. Rihll (2011); D. Harris (1995), 20–25.

13. *IG* II² 1444, *ll.* 27–29.

14. Bridle: *IG* II² 1433 (384/3–378/7), *l.* 11 (mostly restored); 1424a (371/0), *l.* 335; 1425 (368/7), *ll.* 267–68 (D. Harris [1995], 144 V.170). The recently discovered archaic shrine at Kythnos, which is surprisingly intact, and for which see Mazarakis-Ainian (2010), gives some perspective on what is surely missing from the (later) Attic inventories but nevertheless considered choice enough by the dedicants. Surviving materials range from bits of rock crystal to minor bronze or terracotta objects in large quantities, and even clam shells in the case of this particular shrine.

15. The counts for the Pronaos and the Parthenon are based upon D. Harris (1995), checked against Hamilton (1996); cf. Kosmetatou (2001) and (2002); Hamilton (2000). The lamps, moreover, are certainly appropriate for dining, but the gold wreath's purpose is harder to discern unless, one might suppose, it was meant for an especially honored guest such as an Olympic victor to wear during sacrificial meal.

present the same kind of proportion in which precious vessels are by far the most common item and represent the greatest proportion of the value secreted in each of the four treasuries of Athena for which we have epigraphic evidence. The same is broadly true also for the other Attic sanctuaries from which we have comparable evidence.[16] Clearly, it was these vessels and their associated objects that made up *kosmos* in a way that no other kind of votive could.

While we might never know the precise reasons and motives behind such dedications, we can hardly ignore how the common function that precious vessels and related equipment ought to have possessed was nothing less than service in sacrificial banquets. That these objects could also have been displayed publicly perhaps goes without saying, but given how the inventories insist on recording the weight and condition of these objects (and given how these often change over time), their use must have gone far beyond immobile display within the confines of a temple. While we cannot forget the processional demands on this *kosmos* as envisioned by Lykourgos' law, the overridingly common factor that unites these various pieces is that they were crafted for use either in the act of sacrifice, whose victims' flesh would be enjoyed in a feast, or at that feast itself; the great majority of vessels were meant for the consumption of wine at just such an event.

One cannot assume that these inventories offer a complete record of what the treasuries, much less all of the other storage spaces and structures of the akropolis, must have possessed; they record merely the objects valuable enough to deserve such permanent record. Alongside the precious vessels we should imagine a plethora of cheaper dining paraphernalia and sacrificial equipment that was to be used in concert with those more valuable, and hence more often catalogued, goods. The inventories, to put it another way, likely present a complete list of the valuable items alone and so exclude the necessary realia that had little monetary value, such as ceramic casseroles and the like. Only at the very end of the fifth century do such items as sacrificial knives (*makhairai*), bronze serving-trays (*skaphai*), and silver platters (*pinakes*) begin to appear in the inventories, whereas an abundance of elaborate and costly stools, thrones, baskets, and couches had long been recorded.[17] But sacrificial feasts could not be enjoyed without the full range of such items, so they must have been present.

16. An interesting exception to this pattern is Artemis Brauronia, whose published inventories reflect a preponderance of clothing as dedications, concerning which see Linders (1972).

17. Knives: D. Harris (1995), 151–52; trays: 155; platters: 178; brazier: 158. Harris inadvertently omits the two meathooks (κρεάγρα) from the Hekatompedon inventory for 368/7 (*IG* II^2 1425, *l.* 416).

Since the inventories record that some of those objects were the offerings of major civic donors such as the Boule itself, these, too, were probably much more valuable than any example that was used on a day-to-day basis and thus either worn quickly or was cheap to begin with.[18] While tables were presumably no less necessary for cultic meals, for instance, only a single example is attested, whose inherently valuable ivory inlay conceivably necessitated that it alone be recorded.[19] Such furniture, it stands to reason, would have little function without the rest of the dining equipment to complete the set. Given such uneven representation, therefore, it is not unreasonable to suppose that the actual repertoire of dining ware (especially in ceramic) on the akropolis must have been far greater than what the *tamiai* recorded in the possession of Athena. For all of the other Athenian gods who possessed their own *kosmos* it would seem almost certain that the same dynamic also applied. In sum, the *kosmos* of the gods consisted of precious vessels and related equipment that was designed for use in ritual settings and comprised a very significant, if not the greatest, part of their wealth. Accordingly, the *kosmos* was categorically unlike the static votives and cult-statues that had merely to be protected, however carefully.

Dispensing for Dignitaries

Having defined *kosmos*, we return to consider the problem of how the *tamiai* might have dispensed it, for what purpose, and to whom. Given its extraordinary value, we should not assume that the *kosmos* of the gods would ever be handled by more than a few individuals, and then only by those with the greatest authority to do so. Within the *polis*, who could lay claim to such privileges on any regular basis except those who served as its highest magistrates, its Olympic victors, those crowned with special honors, and the like? Thus, the *kosmos* was in all probability only to be used by a very few people who had the ability, or even the ritual obligation, of using it, and so could be more easily managed by the treasurers while maintaining a sense of decorum and dignity, that is, a sense of *kosmos*. Other, cheaper materials and less refined spaces will have had to suffice for any larger group of Athenians still included within those

18. For example, the Hekatompedon inventories, from as early as c. 405 but extending to 368/7, record a sacrificial knife with ivory sheath that the Boule dedicated in 407/6, concerning which see the epigraphic summary in D. Harris (1995), 151–52 V.207.
19. D. Harris (1995), 93.

attending the sacrifice and able to consume its bounty afterward, but the precious *kosmos* of the greatest cults was a thing apart.

A speech against Alkibiades, which cites his behavior at the Olympics of 420/19, provides compelling evidence that the *kosmos* was indeed restricted to senior magistrates and that the use of it could be a highly charged political matter as well. Alkibiades' accuser specifies that he outrageously held onto and misused an assemblage of *pompeia*, including gold *khernibeia* and *thymiatêria*, which are objects of ritual purification (through lustration and incense, respectively) and thus betoken the sacrificial ritual itself.[20] Although Alkibiades was famous as being one of the very richest of Athenians, even in his capacity as an Olympic victor in the notoriously expensive chariot races he evidently still required ritual vessels for his celebration, and, according to his accuser, he persuaded the Athenians leading the official delegation to provide them to him.[21] Given that those men were sacred ambassadors (*arkhitheôroi*), the *pompeia* can only have come from one or more gods' shrines in Athens. Since there is good evidence that private persons owned the same kinds of *kosmos* that the gods possessed, what was important in this instance was that Alkibiades displayed that of the gods, and thus presented tangible evidence of his ability to do so, and his accuser goes so far as to say that he held onto the *pompeia* too long, and thus gave all the other Greeks the mistaken impression that the sacred embassy had taken them out on loan from *him*.[22] One conclusion to be drawn is that without the approval of the *tamiai* and their peers even very powerful Athenians would not have had access to the gods' sacral dining equipment, and the episode reminds us that these treasurers were charged with ensuring that the vessels were treated in an appropriate manner within or beyond the sanctuary in a suitably sacralized place.[23] Whether or not the accusations were truthful, the charge

---

20. [And.] 4.29: ἵνα δὲ μὴ μόνον Διομήδην, ἀλλὰ καὶ τὴν πόλιν ὅλην ὑβρίζων ἐπιδείξεια, τὰ πομπεῖα παρὰ τῶν ἀρχιθεώρων αἰτησάμενος, ὡς εἰς τἀπινίκια τῇ προτεραίᾳ τῆς θυσίας χρήσασθαι τοῖς χρυσοῖς χερνιβίοις καὶ θυμιατηρίοις.
21. On Alkibiades' wealth and connections, see Ostwald (1986), 291ff. and *passim*.
22. Personal ownership of precious metal vessels, even if politically controversial, is fairly well attested in Athens: e.g., Dem. 27.10; [Dem.] 53.8–9; Thphr. *Char.* 18.7; Plu. *Mor.* 828a-b; Lys. 19.25 with Vickers (1984). On the fifth-century epigraphic evidence (mainly the so-called Attic Stelai: *IG* I^3 421–30): Amyx (1958), epecially 206–08; Lewis (1966), 183 with his n. 37; cf. Pritchett (1953); Pritchett and Pippin (1956); Amyx and Pritchett (1958); Walbank (1982).
23. Although we do not possess evidence for penalties assessed upon Athenian magistrates for mishandling dining equipment in their care, a sixth-century Argive law does allow the Argive *tamiai* of Athena and other sacred treasurers to punish those who damage the objects: text of Vollgraff (1929), *ll.* 9–11: δαμόσ-| ιον δὲ χ[ρ]όνσθο προ[τὶ τὰ] | [ἰαρά]. The Argive law thus explicitly allows a public entity (*damosion*) to use the vessels.

would be absurd if it were not regular practice for a Panhellenic victor or other influential citizen to receive (and hand back) some ritual vessels that belonged to the gods, even if handled or provided by a sacred embassy in the interim. By that token, then, the case of Alkibiades at the Olympics might well provide a useful touchstone for some of the contemporary parameters governing the use of *kosmos* by magistrates on other religious occasions within Athens proper.

Beyond the festivals and occasions such as a *theôria* to Olympia or another major shrine, so wide an array of magistrates seems to have consumed ritual meals when engaged in their duties that a fairly strong, positive case can be made for them to have been the principal users of the *kosmos*. To be sure, most of these meals were probably of humble fare and consumed with the aid of the most quotidian of equipment, but it is the ubiquitous nature of the meals that is of relevance here and the broad correlation between the rank of magistrates and the *kosmos* that they were allowed to enjoy. Speaking mainly of the regular meals enjoyed by the *prytaneis* of the Boule, Demosthenes states unambiguously that the object of such occasions, though operating on a level below a festival sacrifice, was nevertheless to bind the members of a board into a common purpose.[24] Although Demosthenes did not feel compelled to say so, the sacral importance of such meals, through which such bonds might conceivably be strengthened, should not be underestimated. Demosthenes goes so far as to emphasize that the generals likewise dined together as well as "nearly all magistrates" (*skhedon hôs eipein hai arkhai pasai*). While Demosthenes' claim only implies and does not openly assert that these collegiate meals might have a religious basis to them, it is difficult to imagine that this was not the case for all concerned.[25] Yet such a broad claim, namely, that the purpose of such meals was to effect a sense of unity and cooperation among magistrates, would seem to apply to most if not all boards of officers.

This is not to say that the status of magistrates, relative to their political and judicial power, might not also condition how and where such meals were enjoyed, of course. Even some senior magistrates ate in places other than the Pry-

24. Demosthenes (19.190) emphasizes the point with the prefix συν- and the stem κοιν-: ἡ βουλὴ ταὐτὰ ταῦτα, εἰσιτητήρι ' ἔθυσε, συνειστιάθη, σπονδῶν, ἱερῶν ἐκοινώνησεν· οἱ στρατηγοί, σχεδὸν ὡς εἰπεῖν αἱ ἀρχαὶ πᾶσαι.

25. Meals held separately at the Prytaneion clearly did possess an important religious and political component, as the frequent awards of *sitêsis* there to especially honored guests of the *polis*, victorious athletes or the like is well documented. For a fuller discussion of meals at the Prytaneion, their connection to other rituals involving food like the *theoxeniai*, and their potential significance for still other meals served by some sacred treasurers, see Dow (1937) and Bubelis (2007), 140–61.

taneion, as the *prytaneis* themselves ate together in the *tholos* while most of the *arkhontes* (as *thesmothetai*) dined as a college in the Thesmotheteion, perhaps on conclusion of their daily tasks.[26] Other important colleges might also dine together at an elite level, as *Ath.Pol.* claims that while managing the Panathenaia, the *athlothetai* received their dinners in the Prytaneion and rightly suggests that this was a form of compensation since meals there were customarily reserved for only the most important magistrates and honored guests of the *polis*.[27] Given how much responsibility the *athlothetai* bore for the religious as well as athletic dimensions of the festival, their dinners would seem to derive their importance from both spheres of activity, though they need not have been meals of the highest rank. Curiously, the *prytaneis* of which Demosthenes speaks appears to have instituted as standard practice, at least no later than 341/0, having one of its own members serve also as *tamias* for the group, probably in conjunction with the cult of the Hero Strategos (to whom the Boule had given some plate as *kosmos*).[28] One might easily imagine the practice of such dining, which must have surely proceeded with much poorer equipment than Athena, or even the Hero, could offer, at the various headquarters of much lesser Athenian authorities.[29]

But across a wide range of contexts there is evidence for precisely this activity. K. Clinton has adduced such a building at Eleusis as the *epistasion*, a structure with several dining rooms that served as the *locus* for the *epistatai* there, and for which a singular magistrate (whose precise authority remains unfortunately obscure) inscribed an inventory of dining equipment in 357/6.[30] On Ai-

26. Arkhontes: Σ Plat. *Phaedr.* 235d. According to *Ath.Pol.* 3.5, in the time of Solon all three (major) *arkhontes* met at the Thesmotheteion, but the Souda (s.v. ἄρχων) claims that prior to Solon the various *arkhontes* had not been allowed to sit in judgment at the same building. Rather, on *Ath.Pol.*'s interpretation, each of these magistrates was required to conduct his legal tasks at the specific structure associated with his office. Aside from the three major *arkhontes* (eponymous, *basileus*, *polemarkhos*) the rest were known simply as *thesmothetai* in the classical period (cf. *Ath.Pol.* 56–59), which suggests both that the college dined at the building that housed these general *arkhontes* and that *Ath.Pol.* either records, in effect, a shift in appellation over time or is simply mistaken about Solonian nomenclature.

27. *Ath.Pol.* 62.2. On the religious and political significance of the *athlothetai*, see Nagy (1978); Schmitt-Pantel (1992), 364ff. On the privilege, and religious significance, of dining at public expense in Athens (especially at the Prytaneion), see Bubelis (2007), 159–73.

28. Tamias of *prytaneis* (first attested): *IG* II^2 1749. Dow (1937) remains an essential survey and commentary upon the epigraphic evidence for the longstanding practices of the Boule and its *tamiai*; see also Bubelis (2007), 37–38 and 160–61. On the Hero Strategos, see Lewis (1979); Rotroff (1978), 207, tentatively suggests the eponymous tribal hero Leos as an alternative identification of the divinity.

29. On the locations at which magistrates conducted their business, see Haensch (2003).

30. In his discussion of *I.Eleusis* 140 (*IG* II^2 1541), Clinton, 124–26, also identifies those using the dining rooms as officials and priests in a generic sense, but does not intimate that this would have included

gina in the fifth century, and then Samos during the mid-fourth century, the Athenian settlers (*klêroukhoi*) also practiced very much the same kind of magisterial dining with temple treasures, although independent of expressly Athenian administration per se.[31] The relevant text from Samos also goes so far as to stipulate that it is the *kosmos* of Hera that it lists, all of which bears a thoroughgoing similarity to that catalogued for the various Athenian shrines, and the *tamiai* responsible for that *kosmos* state very clearly that the Boule of these *klêroukhoi* had some of that *kosmos* in its possession at the time of inventory (346/5).[32] Even under the democracy, therefore, when serving as magistrates many Athenians could expect to enjoy official meals at public expense and to do so with the treasure of their gods. While it is clear that *tamiai* of various kinds were intrinsic to that privilege, how did the *tamiai* of Athena dispense what was incomparably more valuable *kosmos* and on what occasions?

Kosmos *and Its Spaces*

How the *tamiai* of Athena completed their tasks, especially in the archaic period, is best understood by considering the legal authority that the early democracy conceded to them. As protectors of Athena's property, the *tamiai* enjoyed wide powers over the ritual space of the akropolis as a whole, and were not merely confined to oversight of the treasuries, though that was a major responsibility. As noted in the previous chapter, Hekatompedon Decree B (485/4) mandates that the *tamiai* impose heavy fines of 100 dr. on priestesses and female ritual attendants (*zakoroi*) caught lighting certain fires (probably for cooking with braziers).[33] The decree further establishes that the *tamiai* also have the authority to fine (though at far lesser rates) other violators of the sanctuary, including whichever butchers release the offal of sacrificial victims within

---

the *epistatai* themselves. Clinton, 126, further suggests that the magistrate in question, Leptines (likely the target of Demosthenes' speech [20]), was a sort of volunteer for a task that no one wanted and so should not be identified as a magistrate. But the mere fact of inscription argues for sufficient authority within the state to have a public body pay for the inventory to be inscribed at all.

31. Aigina: *IG* I³ 1455–56 (= *IG* IV 39 + add. p. 378, 1588); Samos: see n. 32 below. The *klêroukhoi* and their inventories deserve more thorough treatment than can be offered here, but see Bubelis (2007), 40–43; note also the third-century decree and *exetasmos* inventory of the *klêroukhoi* on Imbros (*IG* XII (8) 51 = *Nouveau choix* 21), for which see Tréheux (1956) and (1991), 143–47.

32. *IG* XII (6) 261. Kosmos: *l.* 12 (κόσμος τῆς θεοῦ); claim: *ll.* 54–55 (τὴν βουλὴν τούτων | ἔφασαν ἔχειν). In the latter passage, the *tamiai* enumerate the items in the possession of the Boule as being four of twelve bronze *prokhoi* along with a bronze *kyklos*. On this text, see Bubelis (2007), 42–43.

33. *IG* I³ 4 B, *ll.* 13–14.

the precincts of Kekrops and the Hekatompedon.[34] While regulations concerning the proper uses of fire might naturally fall to the *tamiai* for enforcement, so as to keep the treasuries and their contents safe, their control over butchers cannot be justified on precisely the same grounds since offal does not pose an outright danger, however offensive it may be.[35] That degree of control speaks instead to a general authority over those involved even customarily with the akropolis. What we do not know is how their authority might have related to that of the priestess of Athena and others whose priestly claim to perform particular rites and to enjoy presumably an unchecked freedom of access (and surely freedom from the presence of offending figures, acts, or substances) might well have trumped any legal power of a magistrate but conceivably required magistrates to enforce those claims on a daily basis. For example, Plutarch claims that dogs were forbidden from entering the akropolis, so to whom would the priestess of Athena turn if she spotted such a creature or felt that some other person was negligent in removing the beast?[36] Although there are no ready answers to these issues, the Hekatompedon Decrees do not appear to have restricted the authority of the *tamiai* in this regard to any single part of the sanctuary, and they provide no grounds on which to suspect justifiably that these magistrates did not already enjoy significant authority well before 485/4.

Such legal control also finds a natural complement in the architecture and spaces of the early akropolis itself, and it suggests that the authority exercised by the *tamiai* over sacred equipment extended naturally to the spaces in which objects were stored and used ritually. In particular, the Pinakotheke, located in

---

34. *ll.* 10–13; in *ll.* 8–10, the overall content is unclear but it is clear that the issue concerns how the (otherwise unspecified) *hierourgountes* act with regard to the altar and temple. Offal: Németh (1994).

35. Fire was a common hazard, and Xenophon notes (*HG* 1.6.1) that the Old Temple of Athena on the akropolis burnt in 406. It is largely on the basis of the tasks outlined in the Hekatompedon decrees, moreover, that Jordan (1979), 23–28, labels the *tamiai* "precinct governors."

36. Dogs: Plu. *Mor.* 290a-d; Parker (1983), 357–58. Evidence for other Athenians with enforcement powers upon the akropolis is thin but intriguing. One text (*IG* I^3 45) goes so far as to mandate that for some emergency (perhaps involving slaves making their way onto the akropolis through some breach in the construction, and thus gaining access to the altars as suppliants too easily), archers are to be posted upon the akropolis, but only three in number and from the tribe then in *prytany*, until some structure could be finished and thus seal illicit entry to the shrines. However great the threat, the restrictions upon the archers' number and tribe might well indicate fear of armed Athenians taking possession of the rock and effecting a coup. If so, the *tamiai* and *hieropoioi* must then have exercised their powers at once with little more than a few public slaves and yet answered directly to the Boule, and especially to the *prytaneis* in session. Thus *Ath. Pol.* (44.1) states that the *epistatês* of the *prytaneis* took possession of the keys to the temples as well as the state seal every night which were surrendered, presumably, by those same sacred treasurers; cf. Rhodes (1993), 532–33; Hansen (1991), 140–41, 250. The *hyp.* ii.7 to Dem. 22 also specifies the threat of tyranny posed by the possession of such items.

the northwest wing of the (Mnesiklean) Propylaia at the entrance to the akropolis, has long been interpreted exclusively as either a dining space (*hestiatorion*) or a treasury (*thêsauros*). J. Travlos proposed the former interpretation on the basis that the Pinakotheke has an off-center doorway, which is typical of classical *hestiatoria*, and could accommodate the sizeable number of seventeen dining couches (*klinai*).[37] It is perhaps not a coincidence that the Parthenon (and later, the Hekatompedon) inventories also record a group of seventeen *klinai*, specifying seven of them as products of Khios and ten as coming from Miletos, well known for producing premium grades of such furniture.[38] Although P. Hellström objected to the dimensions inherent in Travlos' restoration of the Pinakotheke for this use, he did suggest that Travlos' proposal could be accommodated if enough space (0.1 m) was left on the (south interior face of the) North Wall.[39] Yet, as J. de Waele has argued, the Pinakotheke also seems to have had some functions as a treasury (*thêsauros*), notably as the place where the paintings of Polygnotos were hung.[40] An interesting and unavoidable difficulty is that while the Pinakotheke was fitted with doors, its two windows flanking the doorway appear to have never been fitted with grills, though their sills are so high (2.4 m) above the floor level of the entranceway as to make illicit

37. Travlos (1971), 482 figs. 618–19.

38. Andrianou (2009), 107–22 and Appendices I-III, collects and surveys the evidence for furniture epigraphically recorded (and sometimes archaeologically attested) in Greek sanctuaries and suggests, 113, that the large number of (usually bronze) couch parts recorded in the inventories might reflect the use of couches that could be disassembled systematically when not in use and hence would conserve space. Contemporary with the earliest surviving inventories, Kritias speaks of Chian and Milesian couches together (fr. 35 D-K [= Ath. 11.486c]; B2 West [= Ath. 1.28b]), and Milesian couches also appeared in the auctioned property of the Hermokopidai, for which see Pritchett and Pippin (1956), 227–29.

39. Dinsmoor and Dinsmoor Jr. (2004), 384, argue that the design reflects how the architect attempted to accommodate to Doric aesthetic canons the practical demands of stable wall-joints. Hellström (1975), 87–89, does note the solution to the space's asymmetry discussed here but still prefers a solution based upon how to reconcile aesthetically the architecture of the Propylaia to the entrance wall of the Pinakotheke. While there is no evidence for direct attachment of paintings to the walls, the space available between the North Wall and the couches on that side of the space (0.1m) might be enough for some kind of free-standing apparatus. Since we do know the format or size of the paintings that is only a guess. Andrianou (2009), 114–15, details the evidence for wooden tableaux inventoried among the sanctuaries, but none of our information provides a useful point of departure for thinking about the physical format of Polygnotos's paintings at the Pinakotheke.

40. De Waele (1990), 30–31. For tapestries or paintings as a staple in fifth-century images of lavish dining, note Ar. *V.* 1208–15, and Eur. *Ion* 1132–65 (within a larger description of a feast, 1122–95, to which I return in chapter 4); cf. Men. *Dysk.*, *ll.* 393ff. Andrianou (2009), 115 and 151, notes the meager evidence for the inventorying of pillows, covers, carpets, and similar textiles, for which the fullest record happens to be that of the treasure belonging to the Hero Strategos, for which see n. 28 above.

access difficult.[41] It would be easier to imagine that such objects were transferred to the space from their permanent home for use on special occasions, but as R. Tomlinson has suggested, a number of other *hestiatoria* appear to have been endowed with such paintings, such as the Knidian Leskhe at Delphi.[42] Instead of an exclusive interpretation of the space as *either* treasury or *hestiatorion*, there does not appear to be any a priori reason why honored diners could not also use the space on special occasions (such as the Panathenaia or Synoikia), dining on luxurious couches brought out from the Parthenon and owned by Athena herself.[43] If Polygnotos' paintings were hung or stood along the North Wall, perhaps above the couches, all three proposals concerning use and the requirements of architectural dimension could, it seems, be satisfied. The paintings might well have been brought out from a treasury. The Athenians built still other significant facilities for dining rooms throughout Athens in the late fifth century alone—often next to the entrance of a sanctuary—and afford a clear topographic parallel for the use of the Pinakotheke as a *hestiatorion*.[44] Although none of those other spaces are known to have housed paintings, perhaps we need not envision only a binary set of options—*hestiatorion* or *thêsauros*—but rather a space that could be used more flexibly to serve ritual diners without compromising the safety of fine furnishings.

But the practice was hardly confined to the democracy, much less to its later decades. In the sixth and early fifth centuries, such dining may have been accommodated within a number of other structures, some of which might also point toward the storage of sacral dining equipment within or immediately adjacent to the *hestiatorion* proper. Near the entrance of the akropolis was situated one edifice (the so-called Northwest Building) that despite its apparently incomplete porch consisted of two rooms capable of holding fifteen and twenty-one dining couches respectively.[45] Although this building may have stood only briefly between the Persian Wars and the construction of the Mnesiklean Pro-

41. For the relevant architecture details and plans, see Dinsmoor and Dinsmoor Jr. (2004), 382–84.
42. Tomlinson (1980), 224–28.
43. Departing from some of his earlier work, Hellström (1997), 120, later accepted the arguments of Tomlinson (1980) that the Pinakotheke was intended for sacrificial banquets in honor of Athena Nike.
44. Börker (1983). Other Athenian examples from the late fifth century include the sanctuary of Artemis at Brauron, the West Building of the Asklepieion, the Pompeion at the Dipylon Gate, and South Stoa I.
45. On the so-called Northwest Building as a double *hestiatorion*, see Hellström (1997), 120. This structure has architectural parallels at Aliki on Thasos, for which see Bergquist (1973) and Tomlinson (1981), and at Perakhora, for which see Tomlinson (1969), 164–72.

pylaia, a large apsidal structure (Building B) appears also to have been erected close by during the late sixth century, for which a very large cistern (suitable for supplying fresh drinking water as well as for cleaning the refuse of banquets) may originally have been constructed.[46] In addition, prior to the Persian Wars a group of relatively large temple-like structures were erected in the mid-sixth century on the akropolis and were adorned with elaborately sculpted pediments. Often assumed to be treasuries (thus frequently termed "Schatzhäuser" in modern parlance) that elite families donated, these buildings possess an architecture that is broadly suggestive of other, mostly archaic treasuries of other Greek, usually Panhellenic, shrines.[47] Even so, these edifices have no obvious Athenian successors and their attribution to elite Athenians rests on nothing other than the feeling, however attractive it might be, that the Athenian state was simply too weak and decentralized at that juncture to effect such a project.[48] Without further evidence, moreover, the political implications of such an attribution of patronage can scarcely be explored, although we may speculate as to whether the Schatzhäuser were also *in officio* memorials erected to advertise

46. Tanoulas (1992) has argued that the apsidal Building B might have occupied the site of the Pinakotheke prior to the Persian Wars and also served as a *hestiatorion*, but as Hellström (1997), 120, points out there is no direct evidence for its precise location (as it is known only from spoliated blocks and fragments).

47. On the description and identity of these buildings and their architectural sculpture, see Heberdey (1919); Rups (1986); cf. Hurwitt (1999) and Camp (2001). Hölscher (2001), 151, notes that these structures appear to deviate completely from the pattern of treasuries situated in the Panhellenic sanctuaries, but he neglects to consider the much earlier yet similar structures oriented around the altar at the Samian Heraion, which have also been called "Schatzhäuser," for which see Buschor (1930), Buschor and Schleiff (1933), Floren (1987), and Furtwängler and Kienast (1989). In any case, Hölscher points out that the earliest temple of Athena, for which see now Korres (1997), is roughly contemporary with these buildings and thus raises the difficulty of understanding why there was a particular need for such buildings, but this neglects his earlier opinion, 144ff., that a treasury might be built merely to provide cover or a framework for a spectacular but vulnerable offering, in which case it, too, would also function as a dedication and should not be viewed from a narrowly functional perspective. Finally, Hölscher thinks it implausible that such buildings could either be communal or familial dedications because that (somehow, in his belief) would have been impossible under the tyranny and so opts for their identification as small temples on analogy with the later "Erekhtheion" (actually the Temple of Athena Polias), or somewhat less likely (in his opinion) as *hestiatoria* for the ruling elite. Kolb (1977) argues for disassociating these and other buildings, such as the early Athena temple, from the Peisistratidai as patrons. Such hypotheses in aggregate point also to another view, namely, that the Peisistratidai should not be assumed a priori to have intervened in or obstructed such dedications as a matter of policy; cf. Boersma (2000).

48. Anderson's recent argument (2003), that Attica was unified politically only at a very late date toward the end of the sixth century, would provide some ground to the notion that great families donated the structures in place of a weak and uncentralized state. An alternative would be to posit that each of the four Ionian tribes maintained a separate structure of its own upon the akropolis, namely, as a *hestiatorion* and treasury for exclusive use by its own members in conjunction with rituals that the tribe was obligated to perform.

one's power as a magistrate just like Khairion's altar and the *stêlê* of Alkiphron.

Nevertheless, the immediate issue is what function the Schatzhäuser might have served. Although their architectural plans are hardly knowable below the pediments, there is no compelling reason that these structures must have functioned only as treasuries, or rather, only as treasuries for *kosmos*.[49] Other reasons for the existence of these and still other structures are not hard to find. As B. Nagy has shown, for example, the Peplotheke is attested only epigraphically in the late fourth century and has also defied archaeological detection, though it must have been large enough to accommodate a long series of enormous *peploi* woven periodically for the Greater Panathenaia; perhaps it was managed in conjunction with the treasury-like Khalkotheke.[50] Therefore, while the Schatzhäuser could have fulfilled this or any number of purposes in the sixth century, we cannot exclude the possibility that at least one of these structures also served to accommodate ritual dining, even if it also operated as a treasury of sorts.[51] The Pinakotheke, after all, might suggest that a treasury and *hestiatorion* were functionally as well as ritually compatible with one another given that dining equipment and fine furnishings must be stored somewhere, preferably quite secure. A single structure, even if not very large, might in principle accommodate a dining room as well as some of the sacred vessels, couches, and other equipment, the whole of which could be locked behind strong grills or doors when not in use. Perhaps this kind of unified collocation of functions is what lies behind one of the instructions that Hekatompedon Decree B (485/4) mandates. The decree requires the *tamiai* to inspect certain *oikêmata*—not *neôi*, temples—every ten days.[52] Although the decree does not state the purpose, its stipulation does imply that the contents or at least the interiors of those

49. Judeich (1929), 398 and 400, identified the Schatzhäuser with the *oikêmata* as known from Decree B and went so far as to suggest that they served as predecessors to the Opisthodomos because of his judgment that they served as a kind of vestibule for the priests and their helpers.

50. Nagy (1984).

51. Hölscher (2001) provides the most recent treatment of the question and notes that the various uses ascribed to such buildings (as *hestiatoria*, cultic depositories, storage for vulnerable votive gifts, and in their earliest architectural phases sometimes even shrines) are all potentially commensurate with one another, but also, 144, that the erection of such a building for storage must also conceptually be linked with (contemporary) development of inventories. Intriguingly, Hölscher, 144ff., points toward the possibility that the earliest "treasuries" (i.e., after c. 550) were already erected without being meant to fulfill an immediate need of storage, but merely to serve as very public votive monuments in their own right that display fragile and costly votives created specifically for such a space. Yet Hölscher, 146, only nods obliquely to the difficult problem of who possessed sovereign authority over such buildings in a sanctuary belonging to a *polis* or *ethnos* if dedicated by a private entity having no (or no substantial) authority within the state.

52. *IG* I^3 4 B, *ll.* 2, 13–14, 17–21.

buildings were valuable or important enough to warrant such inspection. Moreover, for such frequent inspection to be meaningful, the *oikêmata* must have been frequented enough by some party that the *prytaneis* could expect the contents or interior to have been disturbed somehow within the space of any ten days. Yet, curiously, no such problem concerning access is known for the later treasuries maintained by the *tamiai* entirely within the Parthenon and Erekhtheion, such as the Opisthodomos and Hekatompedon.

The decree, furthermore, also indicates that on the akropolis there was a building specific to the *tamiai*, and expressly indicates, at that, that it would come under their responsibility exclusively. Amid fragmentary lines whose sense is not entirely clear, the decree stipulates that the *oikêma tamieion* was, as it seems according to a plausible restoration of the key verb, henceforth off-limits not only to *zakoroi* but also to priestesses (*ll.* 13–14):[53]

τὰς] ḥιερέα[ς] ṭὰς ἐμ πόλει ⁝ καὶ τ-
ὰς ζακόρος [μὲ *hέχεν* οἴ]κεμα ṭαμεῖον ⁝ ἐμ πόλει

[The priestesses on the akropolis and the *zakoroi* are (not to possess) an *oikêma tamieion* on the akropolis.]

Of course, the *tamieion* might have fallen outside the scope of *oikêmata* that the *tamiai* were to open as the decree mandates, for the *tamiai* were to gain even greater control over this structure if the *zakoroi* and priestesses were to be excluded.[54] By virtue of the manner in which the decree specifies the structure's identity, the *tamieion* must then have served as some kind of structure that

---

53. *IG* I³ thus accepts the restoration proposed by Dittenberger (1891), 473, who admits that his restoration depends upon a spelling of the proposed infinitive that is unusual (i.e., ἔχειν in fully regularized Attic), but for which the limited space provides for very few alternatives. With regard to the aspiration of the initial vowel, several examples (mostly dipinti) have now come to light, for which see Threatte (1980–96) vol. 2, 750–51. Dittenberger terms the structure from which the women would be prohibited a "Vorrathskammer" and thus plausibly connected to the prohibition of the following lines against kindling any cooking fires. Upon that hypothesis ἔχειν would mean here "to have control over" and thus imply that the *oikêma tamieion* was indeed the *tamieion* and that over this structure henceforth the *zakoroi* had no rights.

54. In canvassing some of the problematic attempts to locate the *oikêmata* and even to identify one or more of them with the *tamieion* itself in spite of the decree's description (thus, Dörpfeld), Dinsmoor (1947), 124–25, terms the *oikêmata* "compartments for the storage of treasure under the supervision of the treasurers of Athena" (124) based upon the existence of other buildings at Delos and the Panhellenic sanctuaries that are called *oikoi* and commonly believed to be treasuries (only clearly justified in the case of Delos, however). On the nomenclature of such buildings, see also Arafat (2009), 581–82, 585.

would now be unique to the *tamiai* but was not in their exclusive control prior to passage of the law. Of interest is the fact that the term is not attested in other Athenian inscriptions prior to the end of the Hellenistic period.[55] Thus, while direct comparison with other epigraphic usage of the term "*tamieion*" is not possible, it would seem that the structure was not rebuilt after the Persian sack of the akropolis. Or, the rarity of the term could suggest that as an institution the *tamieion* was not reestablished either, or at least not on the same basis as it had existed prior to the Persian Wars. Among Athenian literary sources, the term first appears in Thucydides, whose usage in two passages suggests that *tamieion* signified merely a secure place where valuable objects where stored, whatever their nature.[56] Neither his text nor others indicate that a *tamieion* had to function more narrowly as only a place where votive treasures, *kosmos*, or even money could be safeguarded, and thus in need of particular architectural features and the like. Since in Athens the *-eion* termination regularly signifies the place where a particular college of magistrates conducted its business, the simplest interpretation might be that the *tamieion* served as a place where the *tamiai* kept whatever equipment it was that they would use most frequently in the pursuit of their regular duties (including dining together), but not necessarily as a treasury of anything more valuable.[57] This hypothesis, then, leaves the other *oikêmata* as possible treasuries housing those objects worthy of a higher grade of protection than the *tamieion* might have offered. A decree of the 350s, employing phrasing quite suggestive of Decree B, stipulates that the *prytaneis* of

55. *SEG* 21.469 (of 129/8) would be the earliest text known but the reference is fugitive and requires restoration (C, *l.* 30); otherwise the earliest certain reference is *IG* II^2 3504, *l.* 5 (end of the first century BC).

56. By virtue of Thucydides' usage, the issue also hearkens back to the portentous move of the Delian League's treasury to Athens in 454/3: Thuc. 7.24.2 (the Athenians are said to have used their siege cross-walls at Syracuse as a *tamieion* in which they stored money and grain); 1.96.2 (Delos is likened to a *tamieion* for the Athenians in their capacity as hegemons of the Delian League). Chankowksi (2008), 38–39, accepts the long neglected emendation of a passage in Plutarch (*Arist.* 25.2: καὶ γὰρ τά χρήματά φησιν ἐκ Δήλου βουλευομένων ᾽Αθήναζε κομίσαι παρὰ τὰς συνθήκας, καὶ Σαμίων εἰσηγουμένων) offered by J. N. Madvig *Adversaria Critica ad Scriptores Graecos* (Hauniae: 1871), 150, (and advanced further by Huxley [1990]) that the text should read ταμίων instead of Σαμίων, thus making the *hellenotamiai* the movers of the idea (though these officers are never attested as merely *tamiai*). If that interpretation is correct, however, it would support reading Thucydides as meaning *hellenotamiai* by *tamieion*, but the idea falters since the emendation would render the καί before the key word useless and thus undercut the concessive nature of the genitive absolute that is so vital to Aristides' claim that the move was not just, *even though* the Samians had proposed it; Huxley opts for deleting καί but without explanation. Instead, Thucydides' use of *tamieion* in 1.96.2 appears to be merely metaphorical.

57. Haensch (2003), 175, makes this point with regard to a number of other Athenian magistrates and their places of official business, such as the *hipparkheion* for the cavalry commanders (*hipparkhoi*).

the Boule inspect the Khalkotheke in conjunction with the *tamiai* whenever they (or, more precisely, the public slave) opens the structure, which that decree also calls nothing less than an *oikêma*.[58] Since the Khalkotheke was not a temple and did not contain one of the treasuries known for its precious *kosmos*, this later decree suggests that the earlier *oikêmata* were also treasuries of some sort. But unlike the Khalkotheke, the earlier structures might have had more in the way of valuable objects, hence the regulations of Hekatompedon Decree B.

The fourth-century text, nevertheless, invokes these orders so that a thorough inspection of the objects stored therein could take place within a discrete frame of time, and thus be concluded, but Decree B mandates an ongoing, open-ended, commitment that betokens greater interest in ensuring the security and condition of the building's contents. Moreover, Decree B also declares that *tamiai* who fail to show for this duty must pay fines to none other than the *prytaneis* or else undergo a procedure (*euthyna*) by which the (later) democracy regularly held its magistrates up for scrutiny.[59] Such penalties and control speak first and foremost to the early point at which the *tamiai* were clearly under the authority of the *prytaneis* and thus also to the importance of this issue for the governance that the *polis* exercised over its magistrates. That the Athenians were so concerned with the presence of the *tamiai* and the frequency with which they opened the structures might suggest that the *oikêmata* were something more than mere treasuries whose contents were rarely touched. Nothing in the logic of the decree would seem to exclude or prohibit the possibility that the *oikêmata* were spaces that were customarily used for banqueting or as erstwhile treasuries, perhaps simultaneously, and that Decree B sought to keep these spaces in as fine an order as possible by insisting that the *tamiai* maintain especially close control over them and their contents. We may only wonder, therefore, whether these structures did not function as both *hestiatoria* and treasuries of the *kosmos* along with the Northwest Building prior to the Persian Wars.

Such architecture and the treasury practices that lie behind it might also explain a curious episode involving a crime committed by a number of sacred

58. *IG* II[2] 120 + add. p. 658 (of 358/7 or 354/3), *ll.* 13–15 (καὶ ἐπειδὰν τὸ οἴκημα ἄ- | [νοι]χθεῖ ἐξετάζεν κατὰ ἔθνος ἕκαστα καὶ ἐπιγράφεν τ- | [ὸν] ἀριθμόν), with Rhodes (1972), 139. On these decrees and the *exetasmos* procedure, see Tréheux (1956). The decree requires (*ll.* 9–13) a herald to announce to a certain Eukles (an important public slave, for which see Hunter [2006], 8–12) whenever the *prytaneis* decide to make the inspection; see ns. 12, 36 above. Cf. *IG* I[3] 4 B, *ll.* 17–21: τὰ ọἰκήματα | [. . . . τõι *h*εκατ]ομπέδοι ⁝ ἀνοίγεν ⁝ [τὸς] ṭαμίας ⁝ μὲ ὄ- | [λειζον τρὶς τ]õ μενὸ[ς] θ̣εάσθαι ⁝ τὰ[ς *h*έν]ạς ⁝ ἐμέρας | [τὰς πρὸ τε̃ς νο]μενία[ς καὶ τ]ε̣̃ι̣ [δεκάτει κα]ὶ τε̃ι εἰ- | [κάδι *h*υπὲρ *h*έμ]ịσυ ⁝ πα[ρ]ọ́ντα[ς].

59. *IG* I[3] 4 B, *ll.* 21–25.

treasurers at some point early in the fourth century. On that occasion, according to the relatively lengthy accounts provided by two scholia to Demosthenes' speech against Timokrates, *tamiai* of Athena as well as those of the Other Gods apparently used divine treasure from the Opisthodomos as collateral in order to secure their own personal loans from which, they believed, they could profit immensely. The scholia do not state explicitly, to be sure, that the treasure was in the form of vessels and the like, and their use of the term *khrêmata* ought to point to cash, but the removal of very large amounts of coin from the akropolis would surely have raised suspicion immediately if I am correct (as I argue in chapter 6, especially) that the *tamiai* did not have responsibility for making purchases on behalf of the cult and the like, and the scholiasts or their sources might well have gotten this detail wrong. Alternatively, it was the *tamiai* of the Other Gods who were the main conspirators and removed the cash, since, strictly speaking, we are not well enough informed about the *tamiai* of the Other Gods to be sure that they operated in a manner exactly parallel to the *tamiai* of Athena, whose handling of money appears to have been minimal. When those loans fell through, nevertheless, the creditors must have demanded the treasure, some or all of which the *tamiai* duly supplied, and so the *tamiai* then burnt the Opisthodomos in an effort to conceal their embezzlement, which would surely be revealed ultimately at the time of the annual *paradosis* inventories (that is, prior to transferring the treasure to an incoming board before the Boule).[60] The theft is thus difficult to imagine if the *tamiai* were not in a position to remove from the akropolis items like silver or gold *phialai* on a more or less customary basis without raising suspicion, and at this time the Opisthodomos is not known to have contained anything but cultic equipment and small items in containers, and not large amounts of coin.[61] The theft, more-

60. Σ Dem. 24.136 (Dilts 272a-b). Σ a suggests that the *tamiai* of Athena were particularly responsible, but that the *tamiai* of the Other Gods were also arrested although they were not, in fact, complicit. On the controversial date and circumstances of this theft, see Cohen (1992), 114–15, 203–4, 221–24, who suggests that the date cannot be determined any more precisely than falling between 386/5 (when the two boards of *tamiai* were formally separated) and 354/3 (the date of Dem. 24). Cohen's interpretation of the wealth as cash depends, in an immediate sense at least, upon Σ a's statement that it was χρήματα τῆς πόλεως that was stored in the Opisthodomos, but this may not be correct for we have no evidence that the public treasury or the *hosia* money for Athena's cult was housed there at that time, much less that any *tamiai* had access to it (see D. Harris [1995] for the inventories of treasure stored there in this very period). Could the scholiast's error stem ultimately from the rhetorical exaggeration of its source, such as another speech of the fourth century that is now lost to us?

61. Hamilton (2000), 255–56. Hamilton notes further, 251 and 417–18, that the inventories for the Opisthodomos only begin after 405, that is, after the *tamiai* of Athena and those of the Other Gods had been amalgamated. Previously, the Opisthodomos had likely contained the coin as well as the *kosmos* in the custody of the *tamiai* of the Other Gods, just as Kallias Decree A (*IG* I^3 52A, *ll.* 15–18) directs.

over, must have been grandiose in scale, since all of the *tamiai* were then still in all likelihood drawn from the wealthiest census class of Athenians, as per Solon's Law on the Tamiai. Yet, the treasurers still felt it worth the risk of execution for temple-robbery in order to employ the treasure for collateral far beyond the capacity of their personal wealth. Regular use of divine property—namely, *kosmos* along with related equipment—at festivals or other ritual meals, however, would provide just such an opportunity for the theft to have occurred without immediate notice or alarm.

That episode and its evidence for the circulation of *kosmos* off of the akropolis bring us to consider the processional use of *kosmos* once again. Just how these vessels were used in a procession, especially when too heavy to carry without risk of damage, remains unclear since our sources do not give us much of a visual impression about what such an event might look like, though one might imagine that on the grandest of occasions the *kosmos* was attended by any number of other magistrates in the course of its time outside of the treasuries.[62] The cycle of festivals that was encoded in the Calendar, discussed in chapter 2, would likely have been the focus of the processional *kosmos* (i.e., as *pompeia*).[63] The Athenians undertook such refurbishment of that part of the *kosmos* that consisted of processional vessels (*pompeia*) as to suggest that these objects were indeed used frequently enough to be worn and damaged. A fragmentary catalogue from 420/19 explicitly identifies a wealth of *pompeia* that perhaps was consigned to the melting pot. The text records that the *tamiai* of Athena removed a number of precious metal objects, which are not itemized in the extant part of the inscription but described collectively as *pompeion*, and that they turned this material over to yet another board (perhaps of *epistatai*).[64] The high value of these objects (clearly preserved on the stone as 5,163 dr.) indi-

62. Of special interest is Thucydides' description (6.32.1) of the prayers offered at the embarkation of the Sicilian expedition, for which gold and silver cups were used. By far the most famous description of a religious procession is that of Ptolemy II's at Alexandria c. 279/8, an event that need not have very much to do with those of classical, much less archaic, Athens. In any case, as detailed by Kallixenos of Rhodes (*FGrH* 627 F 2 = Ath. 5.201b-f, 202e-203f), we know little about the display of *pompeia* in the procession except that one of the carriages did display gold cups alongside a gold *kratêr* (202E).

63. Kavoulaki (2000), 145, suggests that *pompeia* were, by definition, limited to those festivals that had a definite place within the schedule of religious events, for which she cites the number of relevant Athenian festivals as more than thirty. Nonetheless, there is no reason to believe that such processions could not be conducted for any number of gods during even very minor festivals.

64. Among Attic inscriptions, the term "*pompeia*" is first attested clearly in *IG* I^3 473 (420/19). The board of *epistatai* is heavily restored at *ll.* 7–8: ἐ̣[πιστ]-| [άτα]ις. D. Harris (1995), 28ff., omits this inscription from her discussion and otherwise credits the earliest attestation of recycling to 410/09 (*IG* I^3 314–16).

cates, along with the presence of the *tamiai*, that the *pompeia* was some part of Athena's *kosmos*, just as the newly commissioned *kosmos* of Lykourgos' *nomos* of a century later was probably to be made and used in conjunction with processions.[65] As P. Butz has shown, the mid-sixth-century bronze plaque that names a group of *tamiai* probably documents a collegiate dedication of new bronze *pompeia* to Athena that likely originated from recycled dedications.[66] Some things, clearly, never really changed with respect to the *tamiai* of Athena.

It is hard to discount the social and religious role that display of the vessels and equipment might have had for all those variously involved in the procession directly or as spectators, all moving (one presumes) toward the site of sacrifice and consumption where the *kosmos* would be set down and handled during and after the sacrificial act itself, depending, of course, on the precise nature of the ritual involved.[67] What, too, did the sacred treasurers do when very large

---

65. See 7–8 above.

66. Butz (2002), 154–56. While the verb συλλέγειν ought to mean "to assemble" and would seem to have nothing obvious to do with commissioning votives (for which we might expect merely προσποιεῖσθαι), in a fragmentary account (*IG* I³ 376) of c. 409/08 the *tamiai* of Athena regularly use this verb to indicate that they (or, on one occasion, the allies: *l.* 15) had assembled so much coined silver or gold. The object of their efforts is labeled only with the adjective ἐπέτειον "annual," and while in this case it clearly refers to coined money in others it refers to dedications offered in a given year and inventoried thereafter under that year, for which see chapter 5, n. 50. Those later texts, therefore, raise the possibility that with regard to the mid-sixth-century plaque the *tamiai* collected new *kosmos* to dedicate, not that they commissioned it from recycling old vessels as Butz suggests. No clear interpretation is at hand, however, and the text may offer us an instance where we are simply unable to appreciate fully the technical vocabulary of the mid-sixth century.

Otherwise, *epeteia* appear to have served as a means by which a board could make up some inexplicable (but relatively small) loss to the (*hiera*) property of a god within their year of service: Cavanaugh (1996), xviii–xix. Although D. Harris (1995) does not list or discuss the *epeteioi* dedications in general, one should note the dedication (a small wreath) offered by the *syllogeis* of the Demos in 369/8 as an *epeteios* (V.461; possibly 460 and 462). However, there are numerous texts in which *epeteia* (to use the usual neuter plural term) alone were entered or objects were declared to be such, as, for example: *IG* II² 1400 (of 390/89), *l.* 58; 1422 (of c. 371/0), *l.* 11. In addition, public wealth (whether *dêmosia* or *hosia*) might on occasion be directed into the treasuries, being thus converted to *hiera* wealth, to judge by the spectacular example afforded by a *tamias* of the Stratiotic Fund in the 340s, Nikeratos of Kydantidai. Under his direction, the Hekatompedon possessed in 344/3 silver ingots (amounting to over twenty-seven *talents*) that had somehow been set aside for the fund but never used. So, too, with regard to a collection of small votives, including a silver owl from the priestess of Athena, which the *tamiai* in 341/0 recorded as additional contributions made during their year of office (D. Harris VI.18a); the entry for this set of offerings reflects an administrative adjustment to the inventory that they had already completed, and thus, although unusual, nothing more than an effort to be exactly correct.

67. Thus, Parker "Polytheism" (2005), 180, for one states "processional vessels (πομπεῖα) were symbols of wealth put to good use in the service of the gods" but does not elaborate on just what "service" that might be and how it worked into the complicated, manifold experiences that characterized Athenian festivals, for which see 155–91 (with specific remarks on processions: 162–63, 170, 179–80). See also the collection of evidence in True et al. (2004). On the capacity of processions to articulate the social identity of a group, particularly in Athens, see Connor (1987); Kavoulaki (1999) and (2000), Hedreen (2004).

crowds at significant events were on hand, and whose size would far outstrip the number of couches and other paraphernalia available, to say nothing of risking the very survival of such objects? Could one rule out the use of the *kosmos* by large groups of Athenians dining together after a sacrifice in some important festival? The great weight and size of many vessels might argue for the answer of a qualified "yes" in response, but it is by no means certain. And central to that activity were always the *tamiai* of Athena and their peers in serving other gods.

Of special interest is whether the *tamiai* themselves ever enjoyed the *kosmos* that they dispensed. By means of a special law (*nomos*), the Athenians in the 330s reorganized certain aspects of the Lesser Panathenaia and provided for the distribution of special cuts of sacrificial meat to the most important magistrates of the *polis*, along with the priestess of Athena and particular ritual helpers.[68] After settling the matter of how the Athenians were to pay for the sacrifices in honor of Athena Polias and Athena Hygieia (namely, through the lease of newly acquired *hosia* land, to which I devote the next three chapters), the law stipulates that upon the akropolis the *hieropoioi* grant first to the *prytaneis* five portions of sacrificial meat, to the *arkhontes* three such portions, to the *tamiai* of Athena one such cut, one other to the *hieropoioi* themselves, and finally three to the generals and *taxiarkhoi*.[69] All of those officers took their perquisites well apart even from the only other Athenian citizens allowed to receive meat, and then probably in another location, at that.[70] This text assures us, then, that the *tamiai* were indeed situated at the apex of Athenian sacral administration, close to the most important magistrates of all, the *prytaneis* and generals, and it seems likely that in the company of such important men the *tamiai* also enjoyed Athena's *kosmos*.

Dignity and Prestige: The Hieropoioi *of the Semnai*

Such prestige as the *tamiai* and *hieropoioi* of Athena enjoyed was not confined to them alone but was characteristic of the whole class of sacred treasurers of which they are perhaps the best-known members. Whereas the duties of each college were particular to the cults in which they served, even under the democracy of the fourth century these other magistrates enjoyed a politically con-

68. *IG* II^2 334, *l.* 12 (= Rhodes/Osborne 81).
69. *ll.* 10–16.
70. *ll.* 24–25.

spicuous place in the cult's affairs, proximity to the divine, and freedom from managerial burdens. The *hieropoioi* of the Semnai (or Furies) provide a revealing example of this pattern. Despite the relatively abundant evidence for certain elements of the cult, especially its procession, the goddesses' *hieropoioi*—her sole known officers—are not known to have administered any sacred property, precious vessels, or even a shrine as such.[71] Nevertheless, the annual(?) procession over which these particular *hieropoioi* probably served as marshals seems to have been a major undertaking in its own right.[72] The importance of the event, and thus the duty of the *hieropoioi* in it, derives in no small part from these deities' interest in the safety of the Athenian *polis* and the legitimacy of its legal institutions. The final lines of Aeschylus' *Eumenides*, for one, underscore the security that Athena and (as propitiated by her) the Semnai bestowed upon the *polis*, and while the tragedian brings to life a version of the first procession by which Athenians are said to have undertaken to install the Semnai, he does not clearly identify any of its participants with historical magistracies.[73]

For all of its dramatic potential, Aeschylus' procession nevertheless touches upon the very real desire of Athenians to seek from certain gods the safety (*sôtêria*) of the *polis*. This task fell to senior magistrates as well as the highest ranking sacred treasurers, as the *hieropoioi* or other officers, including *tamiai* among at least some demes, were also called up to provide prayers for the *sôtêria* of the *polis* or the democracy, or on behalf of the *polis*' women and children, the demesmen, and so on.[74] In most instances known to us, such tasks could be carried out in the sanctuaries of the gods involved and thus not require anything but the regular administrative apparatus (even if the cost for sacrifices was high). Such service was anything but pro forma, and its dynamics are visible in the case of the oracular cult of Amphiaraos at Oropos, which came

71. Parker (1996), 298–99, provides a basic overview of the evidence.

72. Most of the direct evidence for the procession is Hellenistic or Roman in date: Philo *Quod omnis probus liber sit*, 140; *SEG* 26.98; *Hesperia* 15 (1946), p. 199 no. 40; *Hesperia* 24 (1955), p. 228 no. 26; *Agora* XVI 218, with Lambert "Genesia" (2002), 81–82. Parker (1996), 298, infers that the *hieropoioi* did indeed have charge over the procession in these later eras.

73. A. *Eu.* 1021–47. Although it may not be possible to clearly identify the *hieropoioi* here, Sommerstein (1989), 275–86, sees a number of other ritual officers in addition to the ritual attendants of Athena that are especially prominent in this passage.

74. E.g., *IG* I^3 258, *ll.* 22–27 (local *tamiai* on behalf of the deme of Plotheia); *tamias* of Boule sacrifices and distributes the meat (*apothyein*, for which see *LSJ* Suppl. s.v. ἀποθυσία) on behalf of *prytaneis*: *Agora* XV 38 (341/0), *ll.* 74–78; cf. *Agora* XV 45 (331/0 or 330/29) records honors given by the demesmen of Teithras to their councilors (*bouleutai*), in part for seeing to the sacrifices that the demesmen had indicated (*ll.* 9–11, restored *exempli gratia*); Dem. 21.114–15 (*hieropoioi* of Semnai on behalf of Boule); *Ath.Pol.* 54.6–7 (regular duties of a class of *hieropoioi*); *IG* II^2 403, *ll.* 16–20 (priestess of Athena Nike must offer *arestêrion* on behalf of the Demos).

under Athenian control in 335/4. Athenian magistrates and the citizenry at large paid such assiduous attention to this important cult that when gifts to Amphiaraos from a foreign power—namely, Olympias, the Macedonian queen and mother of Alexander the Great—were not intercepted, there were severe repercussions for those involved.[75] On the positive side, an ex officio group of *epimelêtai* consisting of the most important Athenian military, political, and financial officers organized and oversaw Amphiaraos' festival in 329/8.[76] If such occasions entailed anything in the way of sacrifice and banqueting they must also have required money and *kosmos*, and therefore the personnel to handle that might well have extended beyond those august personalities.

But one duty did regularly come under the purview of these officers that links them to the rest of those magistrates who shared the nomenclature of *hieropoioi*. The task at issue was overseeing, and perhaps even preparing, the ritual processions that were intrinsic to the celebration of many religious festivals. Demosthenes, for one, boasted that he was chosen "from among all Athenians" three times as *hieropoios* to conduct those "rituals of commencement" (*eisitêtêria*) for the Semnai, without which the procession could not even have set off.[77] How preeminent *hieropoioi* were over such ritual parades finds an interesting echo in the decree of Paiania discussed earlier, in which the deme grants powers to its *hieropoioi* and "whomever they instruct" as helpers. The democracy, clearly, abided this kind of hierarchy. Demosthenes, moreover, brags that he was specially chosen to perform the sacrifices in question. The

---

75. Hypereides defended one Euxenippos (3.19–21) on the charge that he subverted the democracy by allowing Olympias to offer a dedication (by proxy) to Hygieia in the shrine of Amphiaraos. Following Oikonomides, Mitchell (1970), 24 n. 99, argues that Euxenippos must have been an official of the cult (i.e., a sacred treasurer?) to have been capable of such an act. It may be significant that the shrine would continue to attract dedications by such powerful figures as Lysimakhos, one of the Ptolemaic queens, as well as L. Mummius and Sulla, for which see *I.Oropou* nos. 383, 427, 434, 443 respectively, while its priests, *agônothetai*, and *epimelêtai* also made their own dedications (mainly in the late Hellenistic period): nos. 349–50, 405, 430, 435, 437, 439, 502–10.

76. Festival organization and Athenian elite: Humphreys (2004), 95–96. Intriguingly, some of these sacred treasurers also contributed privately to a collegiate dedication of *prytaneis* thankful for being crowned victorious by the Demos: *Agora* XV 49 (329/8), *ll.* 45, 55–57 (a copy of the *stêlê* itself to be erected in the shrine also). The text records private contributions made by only twenty-one *bouleutai* with the precise purpose of funding this statue, which the Boule as a whole evidently dedicated in the sanctuary of Amphiaraos.

77. Dem. 21.114–15. Photios, s.v. ἱεροποιοί, distinguishes between ten regular *hieropoioi* chosen by lot and those of the Semnai "who are unlimited in number" (εἰσὶ δὲ καὶ ἄλλοι ἱεροποιοὶ τῶν σεμνῶν θεῶν οἵ τὸν ἀριθμόν εἰσιν ἀόριστοι). As Demosthenes' citation of his achievement would seem to show, the election for the post was an honor that reflected one's political standing. Lykourgos is also said to have served in this capacity (at least) ten times: Din. VIII fr. 2 Conomis *Din.* (= Etym. Magn. s.v. ἱεροποιοί).

orator assumes that his audience will know what precisely is meant by the process of being "selected" (*haireisthai*) from all of the Athenians. A scholion to this speech adds that it was the Areiopagos that chose him and draws attention to Demosthenes' language, noting that the orator used "selection" or even "election" and not the term for sortition, which was customarily used for all but a few Athenian magistracies.[78] If indeed the Areiopagos selected the *hieropoioi*, it would befit the institutional functions that it retained following the reforms of Ephialtes in the late 460s and the close relationship it maintained with the cult of the Semnai.[79] In keeping with selection by so prestigious a body as the Areiopagos, Demosthenes' claim to prestigious service is not without merit. His declaration also prompts us to ask what criteria might have been so restrictive and so prestigious that to acknowledge this particular office could assure fellow citizens of his significance and standing.

Notwithstanding Demosthenes' self-aggrandizement, the evidence shows that such *hieropoioi* were likely chosen according to criteria that would have excluded all but a very restricted group of citizens distinguished by political prominence and wealth. Even though the orator claims that he was selected "from all of the Athenians," his rhetorical stance raises doubt about the accuracy of such a claim, and the Areiopagos' involvement suggests that the pool of possible candidates may have been formed from those who had already held a prominent magistracy involved with religious affairs.[80] To claim that one has proven victorious in competition with all other Athenians ought not be taken at face value and should invite suspicion that the relevant pool of competitors was in fact very small.[81] Although neither Demosthenes nor the scholion de-

78. Σ Dem. 21.115 (Dilts 407, *ll.*16–18). With regard to the information concerning the Areiopagos, the scholiast quotes what appears to be another version of the speech, if it is not merely an elaborate paraphrase of sorts (*ll.* 13–16): τί γάρ, φησίν, ἔθυσα ταῖς σεμναῖς θεαῖς· εἰ δὲ ἔφοροι καὶ τιμωροὶ τῶν φόνων αὖται, πῶς ἂν ἠνέγκαντο τὴν θυσίαν; ἀλλὰ καὶ ἡ ἐξ ᾿Αρείου πάγου βουλὴ εἵλετό με ἱεροποιόν, ἥτις μάλιστα τὰς φονικὰς δίκας ἀκριβῶς δικάζειν πεπίστευεται. Wallace (1989), 109–110, 177 (cf. 196), also accepts the accuracy of the scholiast to Demosthenes 21.115. Although he does provide clear details, Philo's language concerning those chosen to participate in the procession (140: καὶ οὐχ οἵων ἄν τυχῇ) suggests that the lot was not used even for a procedure of *prokrisis*.

79. On the relationship of the Areiopagos to the Semnai: Wallace (1989), 9ff., 218.

80. Dem. 21.115: περιεῖδε δὲ ταῖς σεμναῖς θεαῖς ἱεροποιὸν αἱρεθέντ ᾿ ἐξ ᾿Αθηναίων ἁπάντων τρίτον αὐτὸν καὶ καταρξάμενον τῶν ἱερῶν.

81. An interesting parallel is that of the epitaph (*IG* I³ 1330) of Myrrhine, the first priestess of Athena Nike, who claims that she, too, was chosen from among all of the Athenians. On Myrrhine, the circumstances and date of her selection, and the significance of her epitaph, see now Lougovaya-Ast (2006). There is reason to doubt, however, that Myrrhine was first chosen by lot (c. 450–45) to serve as a mere attendant and only later became priestess, as Lougovaya-Ast, 218, argues. After all, the text uses one and the same verb (ἀμφιπολεύειν) to describe what she considers two distinct roles.

scribes the process (and hence the criteria) of selection, Philo states that the pertinent requirement consisted of moral excellence. Yet such a quality was contingent upon social approval, as Philo describes those honored with serving in the rituals as "well-regarded" (*nenomismenôn*) and "striving for a blameless existence" (*bion ezêlôkotôn anepilêpton*).[82] Given the highly contentious nature of Athenian politics and society, Philo's statement urges us to consider whether it was possible for anyone to meet such subjective standards and also come to the attention of the Areiopagos without substantial political support. In rhetorical anticipation of recounting his service as *hieropoios* for the Semnai, moreover, Demosthenes first states that he had been chosen to conduct sacrifices on behalf of the Boule as its *hieropoios* and also that he served as an *arkhetheôros* to the Isthmian games.[83] The approval necessary for such magistracies points immediately toward Demosthenes' political standing and suggests that to be selected as a *hieropoios* of the Semnai was a significant achievement, and not merely another magistracy. The *hieropoioi* of the Semnai, therefore, do appear to have constituted another instance where other Athenians served alongside members of the *genos* and conducted specific rituals of importance but were drawn from an even more restricted pool of politically prominent candidates than their peers in other cults.

In sum, the very act of dispensing *kosmos* for the meals of other magistrates inevitably reminds us of the electoral banquets that I argued in the previous chapter were an essential part of political life. Competing successfully as private patrons, the richest of Athenians could then obtain the service of using none other than Athena's wealth to serve once more as patrons of a kind, this time at the most august intersection of politics and religion. That these practices are documented amply in the classical democracy is neither accidental nor insignificant. Numerous official as well as festival meals in evidence for the fourth century alone would have afforded ample occasion for the use of at least some of the treasure in the shrines and temples across Attica and beyond. What these practices reveal is how extensively the Athenians used the treasure of the gods in their celebrations, and therefore that this *kosmos* was meant to be seen and,

82. Philo *Quod omnis probus liber sit*, 140: ἀλλὰ δι ᾿ ἐλευθέρων ἕκαστα τῶν νενομισμένων ἀνδρῶν τε καὶ γυναικῶν ἐπιτελεῖν, καὶ οὐχ οἵων ἄν τυχῇ, ἀλλὰ βίον ἐζηλωκότων ἀνεπίληπτον. Likewise, Philo adds that the ephebes who provide cakes for the sacred meal were the "most esteemed": ἐπεὶ καὶ τὰ πρὸς τὴν ἑορτὴν πέμματα τῶν ἐφήβων οἱ δοκιμώτατοι σιτοπονοῦσι, πρὸς εὐδοξίας καὶ τιμῆς, ὅπερ ἐστί, τὴν ὑπηρεσίαν τιθέμενοι.

83. *Arkhetheôros*: Dem. 21.115. The *hieropoioi* of the Semnai were likely chosen from among the ranks of the Boule, as Rhodes (1972), 130, implies.

in a very tangible sense, enjoyed, even as it was under guard. An important concomitant to that conclusion is that the sacred treasurers handling the treasure would have been readily seen by those witnessing the display or procession of sacred vessels as *kosmos*. Likewise, these men would surely be known to the chief magistrates, priests, and other ritual figures with whom they carried out their service. Given the lengthy history of such behaviors and indeed of *kosmos* itself, perhaps the most pressing question to arise is whether visibility and rank were considered so intrinsic to the various offices of sacred treasurer as to render them far more political than administrative.

CHAPTER 5

Athena's Property and *Hiera* Wealth

While Solon's laws, as I argued earlier, created strong incentives for the elite of Athens to develop the resources and responsibilities of the *polis* that they could deploy through their own offices, it was not a trend eagerly taken up by everyone. For the richest of Athenians who served as the *tamiai* of Athena, prestige lay in stewarding the goddess' statues, sanctuary, and *kosmos*, perhaps as they had always done, as I detailed in the previous chapter. But there was another sort of sacred property that *Ath.Pol.* claims rested under the authority of the *tamiai*, one that poses special problems precisely because it could be used in so many different ways: money. In order to understand precisely what that money was historically, we must disentangle it from the development of imperial finance with which it and the *tamiai* of Athena are too often associated in modern accounts of Athenian fiscal habits and religion. As I will show in this chapter, the *tamiai* were not customarily responsible for money even when it was devoted to sacrifice and the like, and whenever it did come under their purview it possessed a sanctity that separated it from all other kinds of property and rendered it fiscally immobile. The sanctity and static character of that wealth closely paralleled the privilege and exclusivity of the *tamiai* above all, who enjoyed freedom from the logistical and other difficulties imposed by the need to fund an increasingly robust religious life adequately. For that there were other sacred treasurers.

Sanctity and the Tamiai

To return to the definition of the *tamiai* offered by *Ath.Pol.* and quoted in chapter 4, the final item over which they had custody was money. While that description of the *tamiai* may seem straightforward at first, its succinct character leaves much in doubt:[1]

> παραλαμβάνου[σι δ]ὲ τό τε ἄγαλμα τῆς ᾿Αθηνᾶς καὶ τὰς Νίκας καὶ τὸν ἄλλον κόσμον καὶ τὰ χρ[ήματ]α ἐναντίον τῆς βουλῆς.
>
> [They receive the cult-statue of Athena, the Nikai, the rest of the ornament, and the money in front of the Boule.]

But was the money as sacred as the cult-statues and *kosmos*, and if so, how? And how would sacred money be handled? Was this also something that the *tamiai* dispensed? What the Athenians termed as sacred, however, has not always been properly understood. As the epigraphic and literary evidence shows from at least the early fifth century, the Athenians did not endow funds or other property with a unitary, singular quality of sanctity (or even its opposite), but rather employed a graded set of terms by which to distinguish that which was truly sacred from lesser categories of property.

In order to chart properly the historical origins and significance of this system, we must first untangle it from the financial structures that the Athenians developed in the fifth century in conjunction with Athens' imperial power and which has often confused matters. Beginning in the 440s, a number of inscribed financial accounts style the *tamiai* as none other than "the *tamiai* of the sacred money (*hiera khrêmata*) of Athena Polias." This appellation occurs in its fullest form in those documents that the *tamiai* themselves published, but even there it is frequently abbreviated such that the term *hiera* is usually omitted.[2] The

1. *Ath.Pol.* 47.1 (= Harp. s.v. ταμίαι, in part; Souda s.vv. ταμίαι).
2. E.g., *IG* I³ 297, *l.* 13: *h*οι ταμίαι τõν *h*ιερõν χρεμάτον τε̃ς ᾿Αθεναίας. Given that the fullest expression is found in inventories such as *IG* I³ 297 that the *tamiai* of Athena created, it has the best claim to being their appropriate nomenclature. *Pace* Samons (2000), 30 n. 17, it is not helpful to speak of "titles" for these treasurers so much as a nomenclature that was largely fluid and dependent on changing circumstances. To some extent, the appellation of the *tamiai* appears to be contextual. While the *tamiai* themselves tend to display great consistency in their own documents, laws and decrees exhibit greater variation since these were promulgated by political leaders and edited by *grammateis* who were not *tamiai*. Those other parties had reason to designate these *tamiai* in such a way as not to engender confusion with the various other *tamiai* attached to other gods, or even with those whose

nomenclature persists (though most frequently in an abbreviated form) throughout the documents of the fifth century and beyond, even when for a brief period the *tamiai* of Athena were combined with the board of *tamiai* of the Other Gods, itself only a creation of 433/2.[3] No other term is applied to these magistrates. But this nomenclature reveals a problem, for if the sacral status of the money was never in doubt, why would the money, and by extension the *tamiai*, be so described at all? To call the treasure *hiera* so consistently points to the existence of *other* property—maybe even under still other *tamiai* if we carry the logic far enough—that was not *hiera*. Otherwise, the term would be superfluous and out of place in the many dozens of surviving documents in which great brevity is a commonplace.

One other category, that of *hosia khrêmata*, did exist, and its role in the financial life of Athens with respect to the gods stands in need of both clarification and magnification. Because it was easily understood by Athenians and does not commonly appear in any literature or documents, what was meant by *hosia* and what its legal status as a category of property might have been vis-à-vis *hiera* and *dêmosia* has remained especially obscure. Even in the stock phrase "*hiera kai hosia*" its translation has often posed problems to modern scholars, and it is sometimes ignored as if it were merely a formality or a doubling of the obvious quality of sanctity implicit in the word *hiera*.[4] All the more so, the fre-

---

writ had little to do with divine affairs, such as had begun to emerge perhaps in the late fifth century. Although we do not have inventories and accounts from before the 440s, the fuller nomenclature, therefore, might well have emerged so as to dispel such confusion. For the earliest texts of all (*IG* I^3 510 and 590) are dedications of the early to mid-sixth century, as I shall discuss below, and the other early (fifth-century) texts in which *tamiai* are identified are decrees (using merely *em polei* as the only restrictive); cf. Cavanaugh (1996), 4; Ferguson (1932), 164 n. 1.

3. Full nomenclature: e.g., *IG* II^2 1400 (inventory of the Opisthodomos, 390/89), *l.* 2. Abbreviated: e.g., *IG* II^2 1436 (inventory of the Hekatompedon, 350/49), *l.* 1.

4. Although Migeotte (2006), for one, argues that the (mainly late classical and Hellenistic) sources distinguish firmly between "public" and "sacred" in financial matters, he does not identify the Athenian evidence for *hosia* as constituting an intermediary category in its own right. Moreover, Migeotte does not see that *hosia* would explicate the seemingly binary opposition of the former categories for most other Greek states (which I take to be partly illusory since, as I will show below, "public" can easily cover that which is "*hosia*"); cf. Jacquemin (1998).

Given such obscurity even in the work of Migeotte, noteworthy instances of the difficulty of translating *hosion* or *hosia* in other realms are not hard to locate elsewhere. For instance, regarding the final sentence of a law (from 403) regarding the limited rights of illegitimate children quoted at Dem. 43.51 (νόθῳ δὲ μηδὲ νόθῃ μὴ εἶναι ἀγχιστείαν μήθ ' ἱερῶν μήθ ' ὁσίων ἀπ ' Εὐκλείδου ἄρχοντος), Lape (2002–03), 123, translates the law's prohibition of illegitimate children from that which is *hiera* and *hosia* (treating the issue in the most neutral manner possible) as barring them from "religious rites or civic privileges." Carey (1998), 102, even translates the phrase as "right of proximity" with no reference to religious sanction whatsoever. Connor (1988), 169, translates it as "civic privileges." Parker (1996), 123 n. 9, goes so far as to translate *hosia* as "things which may be freely discussed or disposed of without offence to the gods." Although Blok (2010), 62–65, provides a general literature

quent translation of *hosia* as "profane" or something approximating that misleads by suggesting too great an opposition to that which is *hiera*.[5] Likewise, there is the danger of subsuming into a single category all that is in some sense sacred and so ignoring the web of distinctions that the Athenians made.[6] Recent discussion, especially by J. Rudhardt, has elucidated that *hosia* represents not merely a lesser grade or degree of sanctity than *hiera* but rather signifies that which is normative in the social order.[7] With respect to the nexus of financial relationships between the *polis* and its gods, texts that employ *hiera* would therefore privilege those materials, actions, funds, or assets that partake the highest quality of sanctity, whereas the much less frequently encountered *hosia* must signify a lesser grade, whose objects of description cannot be deemed fully *hiera* for some reason.[8] But W. R. Connor's (1988) formulation of *hosia* as "those [things] of great importance to the order of society but not specifically sacral" perhaps comes closest to the sense that I argue the Athenians understood when applying it to matters of finance and property, and for which I offer "sanctioned" as a close abbreviation.[9] By "sanctioned," too, I mean that it is the Athenians who must have declared that something was *hosia*, and neither *hiera* nor even *dêmosia* (public) or *idia* (private). In short, *hosia* must reflect a particular choice.

Also on the basis of the nomenclature for the *tamiai*, W. S. Ferguson had in point of fact already advanced the hypothesis that non-*hiera* property must have existed but developed neither the argument nor the implications. Al-

review of the question, she does not propose a succinct translation of the term *hosia* so much as a contextualized reading of it as it appears in financial accounts, and thus, 88, suggests that this is "a specification for *dêmosios*, namely the commonly owned money to be spent in a way *pleasing to the gods*" (my emphasis). So too Ismard (2010), 179–80, 184–85, 284, struggles with the concepts of *dêmosia* (and *dêmosion* for the public treasury) and while unaware of *hosia* defines *hiera*, 184, as merely denoting a quality of extra-patrimoniality in property (i.e., not easily alienated) beyond the level implicit in *dêmosia*.

5. Papazarkadas (2011), 1–15, concludes that *hiera* and *hosia* were distinct, but sees too great an opposition between these categories though he hews, 76 n. 256, to the position articulated in this book as well as that of Samons (2000), 325–29, that *hosia* denoted that which was sanctioned.
6. Fouchard (1998), 61, goes so far as to collapse all that is *hosia* into merely another form of *hiera*, and thus treats it as being opposed somehow to the sphere of civic and personal life when commenting on a remark of Plato (*Rep.* 344a7-b1) that tyranny takes complete control of all areas of life: ἔστιν δὲ τοῦτο τυραννίς, ἣ οὐ κατὰ σμικρὸν τἀλλότρια καὶ λάθρα καὶ βίᾳ ἀφαιρεῖται, καὶ ἱερὰ καὶ ὅσια καὶ ἴδια καὶ δημόσια, ἀλλὰ συλλήβδην.
7. Rudhardt (1992), 22–36; cf. Maffi (1982); Connor (1988); Samons (2000), 325–29.
8. Connor (1988), 164, suggests that the distinction might well have originated in matters of public finance (and further citing Solon 4 West in support of the an early date for that development). Swoboda (1888), 289–90, already points to the functional differences between *tamiai* and *hieropoioi* in Athenian administration of Delos alone.
9. Quotation at Connor (1988), 162.

though neither *hiera* nor *hosia* is well attested in surviving documents, Ferguson suggested that in the realm of state finance these adjectives only came to be applied together on the eve of the Peloponnesian War, and that from that juncture they were henceforth treated as separate funds (thus, occasioning the appearance of the *hiera* element in the nomenclature of the *tamiai* first in the so-called Kallias Decrees, both of which he dated to 434/3).[10] In addition, Ferguson maintained that all of the *hosia* funds rested under control of the one and only board of the *tamiai* of Athena and that they simply did not produce permanent documentation of their control over *hosia* funds.[11] Ferguson also argued that after 417 the *hellenotamiai* alone handled the state's *hosia* funds while the *tamiai* held control over those which were *hiera* and belonged to Athena (that is, when he supposed that they took over duties from the *kôlakretai*).[12] The latter magistrates, to whom I will return at length in the next chapter, were an archaic institution in charge of dispensing public funds for a variety of religious and other purposes, but whose office the Athenians terminated in 411 or shortly thereafter. Thus, for Ferguson, *hosia* was a relatively late development and one that was not strongly tied to the *tamiai* of Athena.

More recently, Samons has offered a thoroughly different reconstruction of Athenian finance in this era, which is convincing in many respects. Yet, Samons has averred that the Athenians never designated money as *hosia*, although his objection applies necessarily only to the *tamiai* of Athena's *sacred* money (that is, *hiera*).[13] Samons' argument, nevertheless, appears lodged in the circular assumption regarding evidence produced by the *tamiai* of Athena, since it cannot meet Ferguson's hypothesis that the *hosia* funds were simply not inscribed on documentation that survives to our time. Moreover, Samons' reading of the nomenclature as merely emphasizing the sacred nature of *all* the money that

---

10. Samons (2000), 158–63 and 215–28, offers strong arguments in favor of dating Decree A to 433/2 and Decree B to 422/1.

11. With regard to the working material of a treasury archive as opposed to the documents inscribed on stone *stêlai*, the available evidence shows no discernible difference in the typology of materials and in many of the principles of organization, such that most scholars interested in archival practices make no distinction between treasuries and other kinds or places of record-keeping: e.g., Faraguna (2005); Rhodes (2001 and 2001); Sickinger (1999). The recent discovery, to be published by Ch. Kritzas (see *SEG* 51.410), of c. 120–150 bronze plaques from a classical Argive treasury archive (that of Pallas Athena) might well alter that perception once details of the plaques become clear. It seems quite possible a priori that some other large Greek *poleis* like Argos did not make the kinds of categorical distinction between kinds of wealth and treasuries that the Athenians developed.

12. Ferguson (1932), 3, 163 n. 1; cf. Connor (1988), 165–66. Ferguson, unfortunately, does not explain why he invoked *hosia* as an adjective with which to describe funds that were neither *hiera* nor *dêmosia*.

13. Samons (2000), 29 n. 11; cf. his pp. 325–29.

entered Athena's treasury, or rather that *all* money entering Athena's treasury must ipso facto have been *hiera*, fails to persuade that *hosia* cannot have been part of the fiscal picture even if Ferguson's reconstruction of the act of amalgamation is problematic in other regards. This is not to argue that Ferguson must have been correct regarding any point concerning the relationship of *hiera* to *hosia* and whether they were under the control of the *tamiai*. The objection should be lodged that the nomenclature does not easily support Ferguson's reading, for if all of the money were under the control of the one board surely there would have been no need to make any titular reference whatsoever to merely one of those monies and not both simultaneously. Rather, what is required is a much closer examination, first and foremost, of the documents produced by the *tamiai* themselves as measured against other texts so as to pursue the possibility raised by Ferguson that the non-*hiera* money might well have been *hosia*.

Unfortunately, neither Ferguson nor Samons exploited the roughly contemporary account (*IG* I[3] 253; c. 450–425) for Dionysos at Ikarion that does appear to distinquish between *hiera* and *hosia*. The text provides annual accounts for the "silver of Dionysos," in opposition to that money which it appears to identify as *hosia* (and for whom no deity is named), as well as that belonging to the Ikarians, as in the following portion covering the third of six consecutive years:[14]

[----10–12----] δημραχο͂ν παρέδοκε[ν]
[ἀργυρίο *h*οσί]ọ ⁝ κεφάλαιον ⁝ TTTTXX
[Διονύσο ἀργ]υρίο ⁝ κεφάλαιον ⁝ XXX[.]
[---c. 6--- ᾿Ικα]ρίο ⁝ ἀργυρίο ⁝ κεφάλαιο[ν]
— — — — *vacat*

. . . acting as *dêmarkhos*, . . . transmitted
Sum total of (*hosia* silver): 4 *talents*, 2,000 dr.
Sum total of (Dionysos') silver: 3,000+ dr.
Sum total of Ikarian silver: (--)

We may assume that Dionysos' money must be *hiera* by virtue of it belonging to the god. Although none of the figures for Dionysos' *hiera* money is entirely

14. The inscription is an opisthographic *stêlê*, but the other text (254), which is a roughly contemporary decree of the Ikarians on the responsibilities of festival liturgists, seems to have only a broadly topical link with the text discussed here. For a significantly improved edition of both texts, see now Makres (2004) (with texts reprinted in *SEG* 54.57–58), which I employ for the rendition above.

preserved, it appears to have increased very little, and then only by a single addition, over the time covered by the whole document. In contrast to the *hiera* funds of Dionysos, the two other funds do show considerable change but the inscription does not reveal by virtue of what sort of financial operation either of them grew as they did. The common restoration of the text's *l.* 23, reprinted above, is that it must record *hosia* money (here in the grammatical genitive singular *hosiou*), but no great weight ought to be placed on a single letter that cannot be read clearly on the stone. The other fund appears to be money that either belongs to the deme's eponymous hero Ikarios (as many scholars assume) or to the deme of Ikarion itself. The identity of *Ikarian* is key. While my translation above reflects the grammatical ambiguity, there is no sufficient reason to see in this text a reference to a hero that is otherwise so poorly in evidence.[15] Since it does not stand to reason that a mere hero was more important than Dionysos and so deserved more income, the fund in question is likely to have been categorically different from that of Dionysos. Hence, I suggest that the money cannot belong to a god (since that is what Dionysos was) but rather to the deme of Ikarion itself, which might very well have applied the money to Dionysios' cult anyway. On that reading of the evidence, it would also be more likely that the fund in *l.* 23 is different yet again because it would be superfluous to have two funds of public money listed if in fact they were categorically of the same type. In short, it is quite possible that the text records three separate funds under the control of the deme: *hosia* money, Dionysos' *hiera* money, and, finally, its own *dêmosia*. If so, then the text might stand as evidence that *hosia* and *dêmosia* constituted two separate categories of public money or else the text would have combined them in a single entry.

But what about the property of Athena Polias? Circumstantial evidence for this other non-*hiera* treasury of Athena is more extensive and earlier in date than both Ferguson and Samons were aware, thereby allowing us to escape somewhat the trap of documents dating only to the late fifth century and its necessarily imperial context. Already the Hekatompedon Decrees of 485/4 em-

15. Whitehead (1986), 43 n. 20, follows Lewis (1963), 26 n. 45, and Lewis' editorial comments to *IG* I^3 253, in thinking that the account's 'Ικαρίο must reflect funds in the possession of an eponymous hero (Ikarios) of the deme, Ikarion; cf. Lewis (1956). Kearns (1989), 172, notes the very limited evidence for an Ikarios as the hero (namely, St. Byz. s.v. 'Ικαρία), and also accepts Lewis' interpretation of *IG* I^3 253. Georgoudi (2007), 98; Makres (2004), 126; Blok (2010), 66–69; Ismard (2010), 292–93, also follow Lewis without comment. A simpler explanation for 'Ικαρίο in that text is that this word is merely an adjective pertaining to the funds (as C. Buck [1888], 306, initially suggested, *pace* his own explicit claim, 313, that it belonged to a *genos*), and hence a more succinct expression than something like δημοσίο τô 'Ικαρίο which would aid one in distinguishing the deme's public treasury from that of the pan-Attic public treasury.

ploy a telling phrase—"on the akropolis" (*em polei*)—in order to describe not only the *tamiai* but also bronze objects (*khalkia*), priestesses, and a structure called the *tamieion*, which, as noted in the previous chapter, must have been the headquarters and archival storehouse of the *tamiai* themselves.[16] Likewise, a fragmentary decree from the 460s instructs the *hieropoioi* of the Eleusinian Mysteries to manage *hiera* money "as a *tamias* does" (*tamieuesthai*) concerning the treasure of Athena on the akropolis, which it also marks as being "*em polei*":[17]

> τ̣õ δὲ *h*ιερõ ἀργυρί[ο . . . 7 . . .]-
> [.]ΣΚ[. . . .]ιναι ᾿Αθεν[αίοισι..]-
> [.]σθαι *ḥ*ọ́[τι] ᾄ̣ν̣ β̣ọ́λọ[νται καθά]-
> περ τõ τε̃ς ᾿Αθεναία[ς ἀργυρίο]
> τõ ἐμ πόλει· τὸ δὲ ἀρ[γυρίον τὸ]-
> ς *h*ιεροποιὸς τ̣[ὸ] το[ῖν Θεοῖν ἐ]-
> [μ] πόλ̣ẹι ταμιεύεσθ[αι . . . 6 . . .]

> [Whatever they wish to do, the Athenians have the power to . . . the *hiera* silver . . . , just as they do the *hiera* silver of Athena on the akropolis (*em polei*). The *hieropoioi* are to *tamieuesthai* the silver of the Two Goddesses . . .]

Even though articulated through a denominative verb ("to do what *tamiai* do"), it is clear that the text invokes the *tamiai* of Athena as a model for whatever their counterparts at Eleusis are to do henceforth, and thus constitutes a particularly compelling version of the scholastic texts quoted earlier, for which the *tamiai* were also the paradigmatic point of reference.[18] Both documents there-

---

16. Hekatompedon: *IG* I^3 4 A, *ll.* 11–12 (*tamiai*); B *ll.* 1 (*khalkia*), 13 (priestesses—and not the attendants, the *zakoroi*), 14 (*tamieion*). Eleusis: *IG* I^3 6 A, *ll.* 33–34; C, *ll.* 36–37 (discussed later in this chapter). Other fifth-century decrees of relevance are: *IG* I^3 32, *l.* 12 (referring to *epistatai* for construction on the akropolis); the Kallias Decrees *IG* I^3 52 A, *ll.* 15, 21, 30 and B, *l.* 13 (restored) (again, referring to *tamiai*); 234, *l.* 10 and 240, *l.* 10 (location of a shrine or altar, perhaps for Kourotrophos); 244 C, *l.* 17 (location of sacrifices of deme of Skambonidai for the Synoikia); 386, *l.* 5 and 387, *l.* 4 (Eleusinian treasure held by the *epistatai*); 474 A, *l.* 1 (*epistatai* for the shrine of Athena Polias). On the date of the Hekatompedon Decrees, see now Stroud (2004).
17. *IG* I^3 6 C (= *I.Eleusis* 19), with text and discussion of Pafford (2011) for *ll.* 32–33. In addition, I forebear to restore the verb in *ll.* 33–34. On Clinton's readings and restoration in *I.Eleusis*, the text would have in part read τọ̃ δὲ *h*ιερõ ἀργυρί[ο τε̃ς ἀπαρ]-| χε̣̃ς ἐ̣χ[σ]εῖναι ᾿Αθεν[αίοισι χρ]-| [ε̃]σθαι.
18. Following this passage, the (damaged) text might be interpreted as mandating the Eleusinian *hieropoioi* to act in concert with the *tamiai* of Athena. In the Kallias Decrees (*IG* I^3 52 A-B, for whose dates

fore suggest that another treasury had existed well before imperial finance would shape the other documents on which Samons, Ferguson, and others have relied. Ferguson, also, may well have been correct to infer that the nomenclature arose at the juncture when the Athenians amalgamated Athena's (sacred) treasury with that of other, imperial monies, even if the chronology must be adjusted. After all, the texts cited so far suggest strongly that this other treasury, or at least the kind of funds that it ought notionally to have contained, originated long before that imperial amalgamation and thus reflects a different historical genesis than Ferguson supposed.

From Sacred Finance to Imperial Reserve

Since those early texts do not resolve whether the *tamiai* in the 480s and 460s also controlled only *hiera* wealth as seems to be the case later (for the other treasury could, in principle, have been under their custody but merely located elsewhere), a fruitful approach is to ferret out the financial tasks attested for the *tamiai*, especially with regard to the income and expenditures documented for the cult of Athena. For at this point in the investigation, it still remains unclear whether the nomenclature of the *tamiai* is necessarily meaningful, especially after the imperial era passed with Athens' defeat in 404. If *hosia* funds or other property can be identified, however, there would be more reason to think that the *tamiai* occupied only a limited, though abundantly documented, position with respect to the financial structures at issue and also that other magistrates played a correspondingly important role.

Several different sources of income for Athena can be easily identified in the fifth and fourth centuries, and while none connect those funds directly to the *tamiai* they do suggest that this money both obtained status as *hiera* on receipt and that it was not regular or sizeable enough to pay for the regular expenditures needed for Athena's cult. No source provides a sum for the total cost of Athena's worship in a given year, or even for a single festival on any one occasion. One cannot ignore, however, two texts from the late fifth century which

see n. 13 above), the Athenians give extensive instructions to the newly created board of the *tamiai* of the Other Gods, whose duties were both explicitly modeled on the *tamiai* of Athena in many respects and ordered to act in conjunction with them. Among their provisions, the decrees seem to stipulate that both colleges *tamieusesthai* (?) the money of their respective deities within the Opisthodomos (and the *tamiai* of Athena were to retain the esteemed position on the right of the chamber), but the key verb is largely restored: B, *l.* 23: τα[μιευέσθο.

suggest that the aggregate cost for the Greater Panathenaia might well run into the range of nine *talents* or so, and perhaps higher on some occasions.[19] Although those figures reflect the level of expenditure that the Athenians were willing and able to sustain before the financial exhaustion of the last years of the Peloponnesian War, at all other times the quantity of money needed cannot have been anything but very sizeable. To that must be added the costs for other festivals like the Synoikia as well as any number of more quotidian sacrifices along with the expense of maintaining the sanctuary and its shrines, which in the late fifth century might have mounted to an additional *talent* per annum.[20] The crux, then, is whether the Athenians customarily used *hiera* funds even in part to pay for regular foreseeable costs.

With respect to the money that was certainly or probably *hiera*, the various modes by which it was acquired were not motivated by financial efficiency and might not have always resulted in sufficient funds for staging the Panathenaia and other festivals, and so on. As I have argued in earlier chapters, what administrative structure did develop was intended, first and foremost, to serve deeply rooted political and social needs on the part of the *polis* as well as the political careers of those striving to gain office, irrespective of the economic and administrative consequences. But *hiera* wealth met still more fundamental needs.

To judge from a variety of epigraphic and literary sources, moreover, Athena's *hiera* wealth represented for the Athenians something like a potent talisman of their power over the enemies of the *polis*, foreign and domestic alike, but it did so administratively as the junior partner, if you will, of the public treasury. On the one hand, special tithes from the auctioned property of defeated military foes were regularly granted to Athena, with the bulk of the proceeds directed into the public treasury (*dêmosion*).[21] Of special note are the "first-fruits" (*aparkhai*) that the special magistrates known as *hellenotamiai* ex-

19. With the exception of the Lykourgan *nomos* on the Lesser Panathenia, which I discuss later in this chapter, there appear to be no other texts that state or address the cost of these festivals directly. Problems with the funding of those festivals do emerge in the Hellenistic era as a persistent concern (thus rendering actual costs more visible in the relevant texts); cf. Shear (2001), 86–91, 496–500; G. Oliver (2007), 193–227.

20. It is often challenging to estimate the quotidian expenses of any cult, or even a particular festival, unless we have some key information about them at a detailed operational level, namely, which person(s) completed what task and required what resources to complete their task(s). The evidence from the accounts of independent Delos are relatively rich in this regard and point to an array of relatively minor costs whose aggregate sums were nonetheless quite sizeable, for which see Jacquemin (1988).

21. The typically Athenian literary sources, for which see especially Pritchett (1971–91), vol. 1, 193–200, customarily refer to this tithe merely as a *dekatê*; cf. (1979) vol. 3, 240–95, and (1991) vol. 5, 68–203.

tracted as 1/60 from the tribute paid to Athens by its erstwhile allies and paid over to Athena herself (between 454 and 404). The *polis* also surrendered a particular tithe (an *epidekaton*) to the goddess from property confiscated (and granted first to the public treasury) from those Athenians who had been condemned for having transgressed the community's fundamental religious and social norms. [22] The quantity of income for the *polis*, and thus Athena, from such procedures could be enormous. For example, D. Lewis has suggested that the (gross) auction proceeds for properties confiscated from those condemned for profaning the Mysteries in 415 might have reached close to one thousand *talents*.[23] Other texts such as the Phaselis Decree (c. 469–450) stipulate that fines, some of which were crushing financial burdens for all but the very richest, were owed to Athena alone, not to the public treasury, and that the money was *hiera*.[24] Although none of the texts state just which magistrates would receive such fines on behalf of Athena, the logic implicit in such penalties and in Athena's position as the sole divine recipient of such property suggests that the money (or whatever form it might take) was indeed *hiera*, surely representing as severe a punishment as could be properly applied.[25]

To interfere with that which was *hiera* would, one presumes, risk accusation of having tampered with the possessions of the goddess. In extreme cases, such

---

22. E.g., *Agora* XVI 73 (of 337/6), *l.* 22; mostly restored in fifth-century decrees, such as *IG* I[3] 46, *ll.* 28–29; cf. Σ A. *Lys.* 313 (= Photios o352); And. *De Mysteriis* 96; Plu. *Mor.* 834a, e. As these texts show, the *epidekaton* was extracted secondarily out of the proceeds that went to the *polis* first, that is, in what appears to have been a standard formula: καὶ τὰ χρήματα αὐτοῦ δημόσια ἔστω, καὶ τῆς θεοῦ τὸ ἐπιδέκατον).
23. Lewis (1966), 188. On the epigraphic evidence for these sales, the so-called Attic Stelai, see chapter 4, n. 22.
24. Phaselis Decree: *IG* I[3] 10, *ll.* 19–22: ἐ-| [ὰν δέ τις παραβ]α[ί]νηι τὰ ἐψη- | [φισμένα, ὀφ]ε[λέτ]ω μυρίας δ[ρ]- | [αχμὰς ἱερ]ὰς τῆι ᾿Αθηναίαι; see also Samons (2000), 33 n. 32. Samons' (2000), 55 n. 126, claim that certain decrees provide evidence of fines payable to Athena or to the public treasury, is somewhat misleading as it might suggest that the decrees provided an option to those enforcing the laws. Neither would such ambiguity be ever tolerable in Athenian law nor do the few decrees cited by Samons bear it out. *IG* I[3] 63, *ll.* 4–5, and 71, *ll.* 29–31, provide (as partially restored) for fines payable only to Athena (thus becoming *hiera khrêmata*), cf. 59, *ll.* 47–50.
25. The logic is manifest in the imposition of an *epidekaton* in the Khalkis Decree (of 446/5) regarding Athens' troublesome neighbor and erstwhile ally Khalkis (*IG* I[3] 40). In this case, the Athenians earmarked the proceeds for Olympian Zeus at Khalkis (*ll.* 33–36). Little is known about the pantheon of Khalkis, but this decree suggests that Olympian Zeus was the *polis*' preeminent god and thus a close parallel to Athena Polias in Athens. The principle that I assume the Athenians to have followed is that the *epidekaton* would go only to a *polis*' paramount god. The penalty therein is mandated merely for those citizens of Khalkis that swear falsely, in which case no citizen of Khalkis would fail to ensure that Olympian Zeus would receive full payment. It was in Zeus' sanctuary that a copy of the decree was to be erected (*ll.* 61–63), and so it would not be surprising if it were by this god that the Khalkidians swore their oaths. On the transformation of private property into *hiera*, see also Jacquemin (1998).

corruption might conceivably approach the capital crime of temple-robbery itself.[26] Such reasoning would easily explain *Ath.Pol.*'s claim that the early Areiopagos carried up to the akropolis the fines levied on magistrates under its supervision (and, in accord with my arguments in chapter 1, which the Areiopagos extracted from indemnities).[27] Even in the fourth century, long after the Areiopagos had been stripped of its authority over magistrates, the nine incoming *arkhontes*, so *Ath.Pol.* states, of each year swore that they would offer a gold statuette if found to have transgressed their oaths of office, a practice not without parallel elsewhere, and perhaps one of the kinds of punishment that *Ath. Pol.* thought the Areiopagos had once levied.[28] Under such a regime, in any case, even the highest magistrates of the state could not easily escape their obligations if punished, whereas fines owed to the public treasury were conceivably under much greater threat of politically inspired manipulation, corruption, and interference. Perhaps it was the case that by rendering the fines to Athena the *polis* removed any hope even for a legally determined judgment nullifying or reducing payment of the fine: in principle, *hiera* could never be removed, granted, surrendered, or sold.[29] In any case, how much income such penalties might have generated for Athena's treasury one can only guess, but the use of Athena's *hiera* wealth as a kind of penal instrument does not suggest that acquisition of income for such things as sacrifices was at all a primary goal or even a tolerable consideration.

26. The procedures by which Athenians must have paid their fines are not clear, but it stands to reason that those owed to the public treasury would constitute a kind of public debt and so would conform to the normal procedures applying thereto, including a set schedule for payments to be paid on that debt, for which see Hansen (1991), 257–58, 261; Langdon in *Agora* XIX pp. 58–60. Allen (2000), 220 and n. 21, appears to have no foundation for her claims that Athens collected fines by means of magistrates called *kolastai*, for which I can find no evidence (cf. Lys. 27.3, for instance). With regard to fines owed to Athena, however, was it the case that the fines were to be paid immediately under the supervision of some magistrate who could then confirm that the sum had duly been paid and then order any sanction against the condemned to be lifted?

27. *Ath.Pol.* 8.4; cf. 7.1. Concerning this passage, Rhodes (1993), 155–56, suggests that the *Ath.Pol.* or its source might well have made use of a much older document (as the abbreviated reference to the *akropolis* as *polis* indicates) listing penalties but not the crimes.

28. *Ath.Pol.* 7.1, 55.5. Whereas one might assume that the statuettes were to be dedicated on the Athenian akropolis, a robust tradition holds that the statuettes were to be dedicated at Delphi: Pl. *Phdr.* 235d; Plu. *Sol.* 25; Poll. 8.85; Souda s.v. χρυσῆ εἰκών. The purpose of these objects would seem to be two-fold, namely, to proclaim the power and honor of Athena (but in some conjunction with Apollo?) along with the shame of the magistrate. Such goals are manifest in the bronze *zanes* statues at Olympia, which athletes caught cheating paid for through their fines and had crafted in the image of Zeus: Paus. 5.21.2–7 (cf. 21.8–17); Hyp. frs. 111–12 Jensen; (Plu.) *Mor.* 850b. A number of stone bases for individual *zanes* survive along the route into the stadium below the so-called treasuries and thus advertise conspicuously the conviction of the athletes in question, concerning all of which see Hermann (1974).

29. On the evidence for such (limited) judgments involving confiscated property that the *polis* had auctioned off already, see Langdon in *Agora* XIX p. 59.

Expenditure, too, appears to have been similarly constrained where the *tamiai* were concerned. Regardless of the quantity of money involved, the *tamiai* appear to have had only very limited duties with regard to disbursing any of Athena's *hiera*. The sole early text evincing such duties is the so-called Praxiergidai Decree (*IG* I^3 7; c. 460–50), a document that has long figured in attempts to chart the secularization of Athenian religion through the *polis*' perceived takeover of administrative matters once the exclusive domain of the *genê* since the decree can be read to indict the *genos*' maladministration of their role in Athena's cult.[30] The decree is commonly restored and accepted to read that the *tamiai* and *kôlakretai* made a joint payment to the *genos* of the Praxiergidai (*ll.* 6–9):

[*h*οι δὲ πολεταὶ ἀπομισθο]-
[σάν]τον· ^{v} τὸ δὲ ἀργύριο[ν ἐς τὲν ἀναγραφὲν ἒναι ἀπὸ]
[τôν] τε̃ς θεῶ κατὰ τὰ πάτρι[α· *h*οι δὲ ταμίαι τε̃ς θεô καὶ]
[*h*οι] κολακρέται διδόντον [αὐτοῖς τὸ ἀργύριον. ^{v}]

[(The *pôlêtai* are to lease out property); the silver (for the inscription[?] is to come from the monies) of the Goddess, according to ancestral custom. (Let the *tamiai* of the Goddess and) the *kôlakretai* give (them the silver).]

For what precise purpose the *genos* needed the funds, and a decree of the Boule and Demos to secure them, remains unknown, but a case might be made that the payment was intimately connected to the *genos*' annual ritual of cleansing Athena's gigantic robe.[31] Because the text also stipulates the contribution from

30. E.g., Davies (1993), 57–58; Burkert (1992), 263; cf. Rhodes (1972), 93–96. See further the discussion in chapter 1.

31. Lewis' (1954), 19, restoration (repeated of course in *IG*) of τὲν ἀναγραφέν in *l.* 7 does not fit the context, for he supposed that this decree, as was standard in later Athenian decrees, required provision for the publication of the text on a *stêlê*. But it is not at all clear that we are right to retroject that practice to a relatively early date; most early Athenian decrees do not preserve such a provision. The Phaselis Decree of c. 469–50 (*IG* I^3 10, *ll.* 22–27) is the lone exception. Moreover, Lewis does not explain why money for an *angraphê* would require completion "according to ancestral custom" or have anything to do with the *tamiai*; cf. Parker (1996), 307. The term is never used in the inventories of the *tamiai* or decrees related thereto, and its first sure appearance in a fifth-century text associated with any sacred treasurers (i.e., Kallias Decree A: *IG* I^3 52A, *ll.* 22–30), refers to a one-off registration of a massive repayment to be made by the Demos into Athena's sacred treasury. (But see the earlier *IG* I^3 139, *l.* 3, for the term possibly appearing in a different sort of religious context.) The job of publishing an account or list simply fell to other magistrates, and there is no reason to attribute that to the *tamiai* in this case. A spare reading of the text suggests that whatever object or act that the expenditures owed to the Praxiergidai were to facilitate is to be found in *l.* 7. Thus, a restoration such as τὸ δὲ ἀργύριο[ν ἐς τὲν πλυντερίαν ἒναι ἀπὸ] | [τõν] τε̃ς θεῶ κατὰ τὰ πάτρι[α· seems distinctly preferable to Lewis' and occupies exactly the same number of letters in this *stoikhêdon* inscription.

Athena's treasury as being made in accord with ancestral custom (*kata ta patria*), it seems to imply that this specific payment was categorically unique and hence required some reference to its legitimacy. That the decree would invoke ancestral custom concerning payment from Athena's *hiera* must indicate that the *tamai* did in fact customarily handle this payment. A straightforward reading must indicate that these officers are to assist the *tamiai* in rendering the payment to the Praxiergidai, since it does not appear to instruct the *kôlakretai* to add any supplement from the public treasury or to conduct any other financial act.[32] In other words, the decree presumes that there is only one source of money, but the act of paying the *genos* nevertheless requires the joint action of the two boards. Since the text does not mandate any supervisory control for the money once in the hands of the Praxiergidai, it appears to be concerned only with facilitating payment, and so the immediate issue with which the Athenians were concerned must have lain with the *tamiai* who customarily handled that payment, not the *genos* or the *kôlakretai*. While the specifics escape further clarity, the decree does not encourage the view that the *tamiai* conducted any but the most basic financial operations with expertise, and even less so with respect to significant festivals and the like.

The evidence from the era in which imperial wealth was amalgamated with that of Athena's sacred treasury, the second half of the fifth century, suggests that little had changed in this regard, and all changes effected were highly circumscribed. Where the *tamiai* are known to have spent from Athena's *hiera* money, the common purpose was broadly religious, but the projects were on a different order and confined also to a relatively short period of time. Construction of temples in the 440s especially, like the Parthenon and other major projects on the akropolis such as the chryselephantine cult-statue of Athena herself, are all documented as projects to which the *tamiai* transferred money alongside those contributed by other boards of magistrates with access to very large sums and yet possessing no tangible connection to cult.[33] But these disbursements, sizeable as they are, do not obviously constitute expenditures as such since the

---

32. The other epigraphic evidence shows consistently that the *kôlakretai* were solely in charge of *spending* money in the possession of the public treasury; they had no known functions with regard to receipt of funds and no responsibility for funds that were *hiera*. Harding (1994), 91–94 and 134–38; Rhodes (1992), 99 n. 4 (cf. 102 n. 5); and Samons (2000), *passim*, are especially clear on this point, but see also Jordan (1979), 159–60; Meritt, Wade-Gery, and McGregor in *ATL* vol. 3, 359–66; Blamire (2001), 106.

33. The evidence is distributed across a number of overlapping accounts: Parthenon: *IG* I^3 436–51; Propylaia: 462–66; cult-statue of Athena Parthenos: 453–60.

tamiai merely transferred money to another authority (usually, the *epistatai*) who had the responsibility for spending the money on a wide array of labor, objects, materials, and services in accord with the public contracts that had been let out.

Two accounts from the late fifth century reveal that with respect to festivals and other regular needs of the cult, such transfers were the closest the *tamiai* of Athena came to being directly involved in the management of the cult's day-to-day financial affairs, and then only on a historically circumscribed basis. The money at issue, moreover, might not have been *hiera* but rather could have emanated from a different source altogether, and it bespeaks the result of experimentation, not of longstanding duties. Covering several years during the Peace of Nikias (418/7–415/4), the first account (*IG* I^3 370) is somewhat fragmentary but appears to state that the *tamiai* (*ll.* 66–67) loaned (that is, made a *daneisma* of) a sum of nine *talents* to the *hellenotamiai* and their financial assistants (or assessors: *paredroi*). In turn, the *hellenotamiai* and the *paredroi* then gave (*edosan*) the money to the *athlothetai* in preparation for what was likely the Greater Panathenaia of 414 (thus, almost a year after the loan, made in the second *prytany* (i.e., civic month) of 415/4).[34] The text, however, is damaged at the crucial juncture following the verb that denotes the initial transfer, after which there is a relatively lengthy lacuna that defies easy restoration (thus, *l.* 66: ἐδανείσαμ[εν . . . 15 . . .]), since no other Athenian text ever shows that the *tamiai* made a *daneisma*.[35] The difficulty with that term is that it should appear at all, since it is known almost exclusively as a common term for interest bearing loans in commercial contexts.[36] Can we imagine a board of magistrates ex-

34. Lewis (1959), 246: the Lesser Panathenaia of 415; Davison (1958), 32 (followed by Pritchett [1970], 106): the Greater Panathenaia of 414. On these *paredroi*, Kapparis (1998), 391–92, notes that we have no evidence for them outside of a few inscriptions but surely errs when separating them from the *paredroi* that appear in this very text (*IG* I^3 370, *l.* 50) as if they were "Paredroi of the Strategoi," which I take to be a phantom magistracy.

35. In Kallias Decree B (*IG* I^3 52B), Lewis restored the text of *ll.* 13–14 to prohibit the Athenians from taking out *daneismata* from the "other moneys of Athena" (*l.* 12), thus: μὲ χρε͂σ[θ]α[ι μεδὲ δαν]-[είζεσθαι ἀ]π ' αὐτο͂ν, replacing Kirchhoff's (*IG* I^2 92) ἀπαναλίσκειν. To my knowledge, however, there is no cogent basis for either restoration, and the space of eleven letters that δανείζεσθαι occupies could be filled equally well by the standard verb used for such transfers (παραδιδόναι), here in the present tense rather than the usual aorist such that the prohibition would extend indefinitely into the future. Despite the attention given to Decree B, the proper identity of the verb at issue has occasioned almost no comment. But Samons (2000), 236 n. 90, does acknowledge the "anomalous" usage in *IG* I^3 370 (though he accepts, 222, Decree B's restoration); cf. Meiggs/Lewis 58; Linders (1975); Lewis (1959), 246; Meritt (1934); Wade-Gery (1931).

36. Chantraine (2009), Beekes (2010) s.v. *danos*; Millett (1991), 28–30; Cohen (1992), 115; see also n. 37 below.

tracting interest ex officio from another board?[37] The ambiguous nature of that account's terminology accords with the much more numerous texts that have long portrayed the *tamiai* as financial experts, namely, with regard to the loans that funded the earliest stage of the Peloponnesian War.

With regard to those loans, the role of the *tamiai* consisted in handing over to the generals or *hellenotamiai* (and very occasionally, still other boards) an amount of treasure whose precise value they had already determined and entered into the records along with exact date of transfer, the identities of the principal magistrates involved, and the simple annual interest calculated on each transfer. The detail with which each transfer was recorded is strikingly exact and fairly regular over decades' worth of such transfers.[38] One mundane example will suffice, such as this entry from accounts dating to early in 425/4 (*IG* I³ 369), which is a text produced by the magistrates (*logistai*) in charge of accounts. The entry gives the fairly well-preserved formula for one such transfer, one of two such acts executed by a single board of *tamiai* that year (in contrast to no less than six transfers made in the prior year) (*ll.* 16–20):

τάδε παρέδοσαν *h*οι τα[μίαι Φοκιάδες ἐ-]
χς Οἴ]ο καὶ χσυνάρχοντες, ἐπὶ Σ[τρα]τοκλέος ἄρχοντος καὶ ἐπὶ τε̃ς βολε̃ς *h*ε̃ι Πλ[ειστίας πρõτος ᵛ]
[ἐγραμμ]άτευε, στρατεγοῖς περ[ὶ Πε]λοπόννεσον Δε[μο]σθένει ᾿Αλικσθένος ᾿Αφιδ[ναίοι, ἐπι τε̃ς Οἰν]-
| [είδος] πρυτανείας τετ‹ά›ρτες [πρυτα]νευόσες, τρίτει ἑ[μέ]ραι τε̃ς πρυτανείας ἐσ[ελελυθυίας, ἐχς] | [
᾿Οπισθ]οδόμο ΤΤΤ·τόκος τούτο[ις ἐγέ]νετο 𐅇𐅆ΗΗΗΗΔ

[The *tamiai*, [for whom] Phokiades from Oion was secretary, handed over, while Stratokles was eponymous *arkhôn*, this money to the generals for the Peloponnese: to Demosthenes the son of Alkisthenes of Aphidna, when the tribe of Oineis presided in the fourth *prytany*, on the third day

37. While no such instance of a demand for interest is attested for Athens, Migeotte (1984), 302–03, does point out an instance of such in his commentary to a Hellenistic text from Miletos (his no. 96) in relation to the term προδανείζειν (also found in some fourth-century Athenian texts); see n. 44 below, and chapter 4, n. 9.

38. The earliest text that might give some trace of the formula, albeit in a simpler and less precise form, is the fragmentary account associated with the expedition to put down the rebellion of Samos in 441/0 (*IG* I³ 363).

of the *prytany* already completed: 30 *talents* from the Opisthodomos; the interest was 5,910 dr.]

However, the Athenians never described these financial acts as loans, even though the *tamiai* did calculate and state in the inscribed accounts the simple annual interest (*tokos*) that they levied. In the account with the *daneisma*, however, the *tamiai* do not state the interest calculated on the nine *talents* or anything pertaining to repayment, and it is not easy to see how they could have done so within the lacuna.[39] It is as if these documents indicate one or another element of the transaction as being like those of commercial loans, but never go so far as to signify that these disbursements were loans in the fullest sense possible. Whereas those other loans and accounts record transfers of *hiera* funds to other boards of magistrates, the *daneisma* is not labeled as such and so ought to represent a transfer involving some other category of money.

With terse and formulaic language, the inscriptions show that the *tamiai* completed loans and other disbursements as discrete acts in which absolute custody of the funds was the most relevant issue. As can be seen in the case immediately above, the inventories of Athena's sacred treasure employ the same language by which annual boards announce their surrender of custody (*paradonai*) over all of Athena's relevant treasure to another annual, incoming board. Likewise, each incoming board employs in the beginning of its inventory the complementary antonym *paralabein* to denote its acceptance thereof.[40] The language must reflect an actual procedure. As quoted at the beginning of this chapter, *Ath.Pol.* states that the assembled Boule witnessed this two-part trans-

39. The gap of fifteen letters would easily satisfy the indication of interest as usually given in the texts, discussed below, in which the *tamiai* "loan" money to the generals and other major officers of the state. In their commentary to this inscription, Meiggs/Lewis, 234 (at their no. 77), note that the payment is an anomaly but fail to distinguish this from the other transactions since they would all seem to be loans from a purely functional standpoint (as Ed. Meyer [1899] vol. 2, 135 n. 1, overstated originally). Samons (2000), 236 n. 90, offers that the transaction could have been a short-term loan, perhaps because (he speculates) the *athlothetai* needed the payment but had not yet received official approval for using the funds already under their control (cf. Lewis [1959], 246]). That option likewise fails to satisfy for why would the *tamiai* call this transfer a *daneisma* (see n. 44 below, and chapter 4, n. 9) but not charge interest on it, and could they have done so without running afoul of the Boule, whose vote, Samons justifiably imagines, was necessary anyway?

40. Both Woodward (1956), 114, and Tréheux (1956), 472, aptly describe the procedure of *paradosis* as a process in which outgoing and incoming boards cooperate in both the inspection (the *exetasmos*, which Tréheux explores at length) and inventory. With regard to the "loans," we possess only documents indicating the act of transfer, not of receipt for any boards of *tamiai* that received even partial repayment of a "loan." For basic description of categories of inventory, see Tréheux (1956); Aleshire (1989), 103–10; cf. Cavanaugh (1996), xix-xxii.

fer (that is, surrender—acceptance) of custody by *tamiai* in relation to Athena's cult-statue, the Nikai, the rest of the ornament (*kosmos*), and the money belonging to the goddess. And Kallias Decree A, too, stipulates that the Boule and its *prytaneis* witness the counting out and transfer of moneys and other treasure into the Opisthodomos by Athena's *tamiai* and the newly created *tamiai* of the Other Gods.[41] This same language is what *Ath.Pol.* also uses to indicate how, in the 330s at least, the *athlothetai* transferred olive oil to the custody of the *tamiai* on the akropolis prior to its being distributed as athletic prizes for the Panathenaia.[42] That the language of these transfers should be homologous with that of finite tenure shows that the loans, such as they were, also represented a similarly clean, irrevocable end to the custody that any board had over the treasure so consigned.[43] In a commercial context, however, repayment of a loan might well extend, even when default is not at issue, across lengthier periods of time than is represented by the annual tenure of these *tamiai*. But the texts reveal no concern with managing such transactions spanning a number of different boards' tenure. In other words, it is not at all certain that the *tamiai* even collected the money due to Athena's sacred (*hiera*) treasury though it seems plausible enough; their attested authority was merely to disburse the payment and calculate the simple annual interest due on it. It seems quite possible, therefore, that the Athenians did not, at least officially, consider the money that they received from Athena as a loan per se but as treasure occupying some other notional category that merely conformed to some of the basic accounting procedures applied to loans.[44]

---

41. *IG* I³ 52A, *ll.* 9–11, 20–21.
42. *Ath.Pol.* 60.3.
43. Notably, it is in the accounts of the *logistai* (*IG* I³ 369), covering 426/5–423/2, that we find both language suitable for commerce (i.e., debts as [*khrêmata*] *ôphelomena*; interest as *tokos*) as well as what is the most truncated form of the nomenclature for Athena's *tamiai* of sacred property (i.e., merely, *tamiai*).
44. Among the few non-epigraphic texts that in some fashion cover the finances and political thinking of this period, the evidence suggests that the similarity between these transfers and commercial loans was familiar, if slightly uncomfortable. Herodotos (5.36.3), for example, claims that (in 499/8) Hekataios suggested that the wealth of Apollo's shrine at Didyma should be "razed" (καταιρεθείη) by the Ionian states then in revolt from Persia; cf. the use of this verb in legal and accounting contexts: *LSJ* s.v. καθαιρέω II.4–5. But for their speech to the congress of the Peloponnesians in 432/1, Thucydides (1.121.3; cf. but 143.1) has the Corinthians propose to take out the treasure of Apollo at Delphi and Zeus at Olympia as an interest-bearing loan (*daneisma*) in order to fund a navy capable of competing with the Athenians. One presumes that Thucydides would not have planted such a proposal within his narrative if he did not think that it would have seemed credible enough to his audience in the late fifth century, even if his point was to incite incredulity about the feasibility of such plans. Yet, Thucydides never has Perikles speak of the great treasure in such terms (Perikles, who in his retort to the congress at 1.140–44, at 143.1 derides the Corinthian plan not as a loan but as a "disturbance"

With regard to the payment of a *daneisma* in 415 for the upcoming Greater Panathenaia, and why the *tamiai* should have handled this financial act at all, Athenian innovation is a likely cause and would explain the only other attested instance of the *tamiai* having disbursed funds for a festival. Since that text uniquely attests a *daneisma*, the matter of who would normally have made such payments to the *athlothetai* is in question. As W. K. Pritchett suggested, it might be reasonable to assume that the *kôlakretai* would have provided the money at all other junctures. But Pritchett conceded that because the office of the *kôlakretai* likely still existed at this time (that is, before being terminated in 411 or shortly thereafter in favor of an expanded office of *hellenotamias*), it would be difficult to account for the *athlothetai* while the *kôlakretai* were still available to handle the duties in question.[45] In turn, Samons has suggested that by 415 the Athenians had consolidated the public treasury with that of the *hellenotamiai*, thus occasioning a process by which the Athenians pared down the duties of the *kôlakretai* over several years before abolishing their post finally by 411.[46] On that hypothesis, the payments to the *athlothetai* prior to the consolidation may very well have been the province of the *kôlakretai*, easily in keeping with a scholiast's contention that these officers were *tamiai* with respect to "expenditures for the gods."[47] Moreover, it would have been the process of financial experimentation and adjustment that necessitated the *tamiai* to make the payment of 415 to the *hellenotamiai*, that is, in lieu of another board that would henceforth make those payments from the public treasury. Whatever that arrangement was initially, it evidently proved unsatisfactory and occasioned the second known instance of the *tamiai* making such a payment, and likely handling other financial duties also for a very brief time. The second text at issue, known commonly as the Choiseul Marble, is an annual account of 410/9 for Athena Polias and Athena Nike, whose separate cults then shared common management by Athena Polias' *tamiai*. The text shows that the *tamiai* did in fact dis-

[*kinêsis*; cf. 6.70, where it is used of Syracusan fears that the Athenians will disturb the treasure at their shrine of Olympian Zeus]). Rather, Perikles speaks of this operation only in terms of Athenian "use" and eventual "return" as if this treasure were merely like any other tool or weapon (e.g., 2.13.5: χρησαμένους τε ἐπὶ σωτηρίᾳ ἔφη χρῆναι μὴ ἐλάσσω ἀντικαταστῆσαι πάλιν). Likewise, with regard to repayment of the loans, Andokides (3.8–9) speaks only of the sums being "brought up" (*anapherein*) to the akropolis. This physical language seems much more likely to have been the standard phrasing, for it appears also in Kallias Decree A's mandate on repaying Athena, for whom three thousand *talents* of Attic coin were to be brought up and counted out in repayment to the deity: *IG* I[3] 52A, *l.* 4: ἀνενένεγκται.

45. Pritchett (1970), 111–12.
46. Samons (2000), 236–42.
47. Σ Ar. *Av.* 1541bα Holwerda.

burse (*paradonai*) the significant sum of 32,000 dr. to the *athlothetai* for use in the upcoming Greater Panathenaia of 406 and an additional large sum (5,114 dr.) to the *hieropoioi* of Athena, specifically to mount a hekatomb sacrifice.[48] Clearly, such a transfer requires further explanation.

Since the payment to the *athlothetai* alone is roughly comparable to that of the earlier account, and by virtue of the fact that it was also made in the second *prytany* toward an upcoming Greater Panathenaia, the two accounts bear obvious comparison. In contrast to the earlier text, nevertheless, this later account uses the normal language for transfers of sacred money for military purposes (that is, *paradonai*), showing further that the *daneisma* of 415 must not have been a regular or long-lived procedure. But it also declares, uniquely again, that this and all other expenditures so listed therein are made from what is usually taken by modern scholars to be *annual income* (*ek tôn epeteiôn*) of some sort.[49] While the term *epeteia* could stand for dedications received in the course of a year, and then melted, the size of the funds involved here appears to be too great to sustain such an interpretation, and there is no demonstrable connection between annual dedications and melted treasure in this text.[50] Furthermore, this source of wealth has no necessary connection with any of the other financial operations conducted by the *tamiai*, certainly not the *daneisma* since we know of no schedule for its repayment. Since the *tamiai* are never attested elsewhere

---

48. *IG* I³ 375, *ll.* 6–7. (= Meiggs/Lewis 84).

49. *IG* I³ 375, *ll.* 3–4: ταμίαι *h*ιερο͂γ χρεμάτον τε͂ς ᾿Αθεναίας Καλλίστρατος Μαραθόνιος καὶ χσυνάρχο[ν]- | τες παρέδοσαν ἐκ το͂ν ἐπετείον φσεφισαμένο το͂ δέμο ἐπὶ τε͂ς Αἰαντίδος πρότες πρυτανευόσες.

50. The term *epeteia* can be troublesome, for its use here and in other inventories suggests that the Athenians employed it to indicate two different categories of property: annual monetary income (as also in the Epistatai Decree *IG* I³ 32, *ll.* 20–21, concerning Demeter and Kore) and votives catalogued as having (once) been annual in some or another respect. Samons (2000), 275 n. 105 and 277–78, acknowledges that the term is also used for the first time in the Hekatompedon inventories for 409/08 (*IG* I³ 339, *ll.* 17–18; = not listed in D. Harris) to denote votives added after the regular inventory had been inscribed, but, 274, suggests that in the case of *IG* I³ 375 it might indicate income that somehow replaced diminished levels of tributary "first-fruits" owed to Athena. But that hypothesis, it would appear, is in danger of collapsing the distinction between Athenian usages. With respect to votives, it is clear that the Athenians were not very exact, or we are very much confused, about what it meant to be "annual" in this way. As West and Woodward (1938), 72–73, first showed, the term *epeteia* was used in the Hekatompedon inventories from 398/7 onward not, in point of fact, to denote new annual additions to that treasury but rather objects (belonging to the Other Gods) that had come into the treasury at one point and then, more or less, stayed together as a group thereafter. That usage would imply that "annual" indicates not so much the time of entry into the treasury but rather some element concerning who gave it, or under what circumstances. The term also appears in Delian inventories in the 360s (e.g., Chankowski 27 [= *ID* 104–12], *ll.* 84–88), but in this instance appears to signal supplementary objects not included with the previous year's inventory (and thus best translated as "supplement"). As Tréheux (1955–56), 138, notes, the Delian colleges add a paragraph denoting the verbal process (thus, of παραδιδόναι and παραλαμβάνειν) of transmitting the objects before Athens when indicating the *epeteia*, which is not true in the purely Athenian case.

as having handled income, this inscription seems to attest the *tamiai* performing the role of some other board on a stopgap basis, that is, as intermediaries.[51] By way of parallel, a decree of 407/6 demands that to build new ships the generals borrow (that is, take out as a *daneisma*) the necessary money from the *apodektai*, and that they would later be compensated by the board in charge of trireme construction, whose budgetary account had presumably already been exhausted but would be replenished in due course by the Ekklesia.[52] While that decree is itself a product of those years in the Ionian or Dekeleian phase of the Peloponnesian War that saw Athens' financial wherewithal severely restricted, and thus cannot be taken to reflect normal protocol, the accounts of 410/9 were produced by the democracy in the immediate aftermath of the oligarchy of the Four Hundred. Indeed, perhaps the unusual responsibility entrusted to the *tamiai* for handling money destined for the Panathenaia reflects the special trust that the Demos placed in them, particularly if other parts of the state had been functioning so haphazardly on restoration as to occasion a financial debacle that, in turn, precipitated this unusual move. Since this account also postdates the consolidation of the public treasury with that of the *hellenotamiai* and is very closely contemporary with the abolition of the *kôlakretai,* there can be little doubt that it bears witness not to any of the longstanding duties of the *tamiai* as merely revealed by chance in a few texts. Rather, the account arose out of the unique circumstances of this specific moment in Athenian financial history, and it was one that was highly strained by renewed warfare against Sparta on several fronts and by the terrible crisis that afflicted Athenian internal politics.

51. Meiggs/Lewis (1988), 258, take the payments from annual income to reflect an exhausted treasury. On that interpretation, it would make sense if the *tamiai* of the sacred treasure then assumed control over what I shall argue later in this chapter must have been entirely unrelated funds and sources of income, over which they usually had no control, in order to meet their own obligations in a streamlined fashion, as well as those normally met by those other funds and their treasurers (i.e., for purposes of funding sacrifices and related, ongoing religious expenses). Flament (2006) argues that this text is even evidence for the short-lived adoption of some of the financial proposals of the Four Hundred, in which case the transaction ought to be accorded even less weight with respect to the longterm historical development of these magistrates.

52. *IG* I³ 117, *ll.* 4–9; cf. Faraguna (1992), 183. Other examples of this kind of action can be located without difficulty. When the Demos voted in 329/8 to establish new sacrifices for Amphiaraos, for example, the money had to be lent by the *tamias* of the Demos until the next Ekklesia could convene and set matters aright: *IG* VII 4254 (= *I.Oropou* 298), *ll.* 37–45. Likewise, when the Demos voted to grant a pension to an exiled Delian c. 344/3, it stipulated that the *tamias* of the Demos pay the first installment out of its own operational cash fund and that the *nomothetai* must promulgate at their next meeting a *nomos* establishing regular payment henceforth, and thus included in the budget, as dispensed by the *tamias* of the Demos: *IG* II² 222, *ll.* 35–46.

The fundamental lesson to draw from the immediately preceding analysis is that the Athenians had ample cause to resort to the *tamiai* of Athena to ensure certain key payments were made for the Greater Panathenaia only when other elements of their fiscal structure at the end of the fifth century could not adequately perform that function. The two cases discussed here illustrate well the principle that during the second half of the fifth century only the *tamiai* are known to have conducted those financial tasks that either grew out of the amalgamation of Athena's sacred treasury with imperial monies or were occasioned by the empire's fortunes. The evidence does not reveal a more quotidian set of financial tasks that would signal that they might also have undertaken such tasks in the era of Solon. Thus, as sacred treasurers the *tamiai* can now be shown to have had little to do with finance even when the circumstances of imperial power must have favored or demanded it. This is in and of itself an important conclusion, for the *tamiai* constituted a remarkably conservative institution not just in matters concerning *kosmos* and cult-statues but also with regard to money that could be deemed fungible and which, in this case alone, was accorded the same degree of sanctity as those other religious objects.

Nevertheless, significant questions remain, though thrown into much sharper relief through this analysis. Having laid to rest a number of problems, the immediate issue now concerns the nature of the money that the *tamiai* only handled very briefly on those two occasions, since it was used for the Greater Panathenaia but connected somehow to the public treasury. It is this money, one suspects, that occasioned the Athenians to stipulate that the *tamiai* of Athena were in charge of her *hiera* property, which was hardly directed to regular financial use even during the era of imperial consolidation. To determine the nature of the money in question will also help us establish what the usual parameters of financial competency were for the *tamiai* and indeed all other sacred treasurers, and how that system came to be.

CHAPTER 6

Hosia Property and the Public Treasury

While the political origins of financial innovation are now clear enough, and it is manifest also that the wealth handled by the *tamiai* of Athena and sacred treasurers of that type was not part of that innovation, it is now time to consider the fiscal origins of that other type of property by which the Athenians came to fund their religious life. Prior to the democracy, Athenian fiscal operations were structured around the tribes in what may have been a largely decentralized apparatus. Within the established framework of archaic Athens' constitution, one might presume that whatever innovation there was would likely arise through slight modification of established fiscal protocols and the like. But there is some reason to think that Solon and the Peisistratidai also had a direct impact on those fiscal institutions. And, in light of the political calculus of the period, which I explored in chapter 3, the system may have been more open to innovation than we might expect. The key to this dynamic lies in the tribes, for they and their constituent units (especially the *naukrariai*) were the locus not only of electoral politics but also of the fiscal apparatus itself, and thus they provided ample room for competitively minded Athenians to deploy the resources of the *polis* in new ways.

By the advent of the democracy, the Athenians seem to have developed the institutional methods by which they could create *hosia* wealth from ordinary public wealth (*dêmosia*) merely by fiat. This invention allowed them to steward public money more effectively, but it also required further fiscal and budgetary innovations as well as new magistracies that were cateogrically unlike the traditional office of the *tamiai* of Athena and others of that ilk.

Some Features of the Archaic Budget of Athens

Whereas Solon shaped the fiscal institutions of Athens only incidentally through laws that laid down essential duties for magistrates involved with sacred affairs, he may have molded others more directly. As with the Law on the Tamiai, it is especially difficult to plumb what might have gone before, and in response to which particular problems Solon might have framed a law. Nonetheless, Solon at least affirmed, if he did not grant for the first time, control over income and expenditures to the heads of forty-eight regional units, twelve each to the four Ionian tribes, the *naukraroi*. Underlining their importance to the management of the early Athenian state, *Ath.Pol.* (8.3) goes so far as to quote conventional phrases from the financial clauses in some of Solon's laws, without, unfortunately, specifying just which laws those were:[1]

> [ἦ]ν [δ ' ἐπὶ] τῶν ναυκραριῶν ἀρχὴ καθεστηκυῖα ναύκραροι, τεταγμένη πρός τε τὰς εἰ[σ]φορὰς καὶ δαπ[άνας] τὰς γιγνομένας· διὸ καὶ ἐν τοῖς νόμοις τοῖς Σόλωνος οἷς οὐκέτι χρῶνται πολλαχο[ῦ γ]έγραπται 'τοὺς ναυκράρους εἰσπράττειν' καὶ 'ἀναλίσκειν ἐκ τοῦ ναυκραρικοῦ ἀργυρ[ίο]υ'.

> [The magistracy of the *naukraroi* was set over the *naukrariai*, having been assigned to deal with income and expenditures. For that reason, even in the laws of Solon that they no longer use it is frequently written "the *naukraroi* must exact" and "spend from the silver in the possession of the *naukraroi*."]

We cannot be sure that the laws in question were not of the same type as I argued existed for all other important magistrates who had responsibilities for public or sacred property of one sort or another, namely, that they fixed duties that had largely been customary with relatively few additions or alterations. Even so, the structure implicit in these duties bespeaks a decentralized system of financial control where each *naukraria* might have had, in effect, its own treasury and somehow in aggregate they made up, presumably, parts of a larger one for the whole tribe. That this could have been an unwieldy system, or at least one prone to paralysis when confronted with difficulties, seems likely given *Ath.Pol.*'s own insistence that the *naukraroi* had complete charge of both income and expenditures. Unless we assume that *Ath.Pol.* has assigned inadver-

1. *Ath.Pol.* 8.3 (quotations); 21.5; Kleidemos *FGrH* 323 F 8; cf. Pollux 8.108.

tently too much responsibility to the whole of the forty-eight *naukraroi* where at least some of the relevant authority must have been delegated to others, the Solonian treasury would have been unusually ponderous.

How plausible is such a system, however? While we have no evidence that the *naukraroi* acted as a single college, much less one that oversaw a central treasury, the *naukraroi* must have delegated authority to an executive board of their number as well as to other magistrates who operated at their collective instructions. The *phylobasileis*, as examined in prior chapters, held only ritual and judicial power with respect to the tribe that paralleled the service of an *arkhôn basileus* on behalf of the whole of the *polis*. But the *naukraroi* certainly did have an executive of some sort in their own *prytaneis*, who loom so prominently in Herodotos' account (5.71) of the Kylonian conspiracy as magistrates with some unspecified sovereign capacity within the *polis*.[2] To be clear, however, we have no evidence that the *prytaneis* held financial authority above the regular *naukraroi*, even if this is a reasonable assumption. It is quite possible that Solon left the treasury structure decentralized, or, rather, that he left it in the hands of the tribes to decide how to operate their share of fiscal authority, such as it was.

An essential point to consider is how primitive the treasury might have been from a purely fiscal point of view. If truly decentralized, then one could hardly speak of a budget and of planning expenditures relative to income over a period of time, at least not on a *polis*-wide level. Moreover, before Solon we know of no ongoing expenditures that were significant enough to occasion problems for which some kind of a budgetary process might provide relief. In principle, the *polis* might well have had a long tradition of directing certain resources to magistrates on a more or less customary basis for the staging of particular sacrifices and the like before Solon determined which responsibilities were fixed to which particular officers. His laws concerning the *naukraroi*, then, ought to have given some institutional rigidity and clarity to those practices, and done so in a manner that strengthened the power of the Areiopagos and

2. The bibliography on these *prytaneis* of the *naukraroi* is at once extensive and tangled, but it is worth pointing out that most scholarship upon them has concentrated not on any financial power but upon how they might have shared political control with the *arkhontes* (so prominent in Thucydides' account of Kylon: 1.126). Notwithstanding his intriguing attempt to situate the *prytaneis* as the "tax-collectors" of archaic Athens, Jordan (1970) fails to convince on a critical point, namely, that the *prytaneis* were the predecessors of the *tamiai* of Athena and thus acted in their capacity as guardians of the akropolis and its shrines. Without that supposition—and there is no evidence that Solon created the *tamiai*—as well as a mistaken conflation of *tamiai* with "tax-collectors," there is no reason to suppose that as "tax-collectors" the *prytaneis* had any authority to do what they did.

not just the tribes over them. But so long as the costs were relatively small the *polis* could rely on a combination of private patronage and benefaction, on the one hand, and, on the other, the same kinds of episodic income that are characteristic not only of *hiera* wealth but also of any rudimentary public income derived by force of some kind: fines, confiscations, war booty, spoils of piracy, and so on. Stahl, too, has pointed out usefully that private benefactions ought to have played a significant role in the financial life of the *polis*, or rather that of the tribes where electoral patronage was also, and not coincidentally, concentrated.[3] The decentralized nature of the *naukraroi*, moreover, might reduce the overall level of income from any source that required a *polis*-wide approach.

But with the laws of Solon and ultimately the Peisistratidai came an increased pressure to deploy public resources for religious life that initially must have outstripped the ability of the *polis* to pay for it all out of the treasure on hand. Once a major festival like the Greater Panathenaia had been instituted on as formal and grand a basis as it was from 566/5, I take it as axiomatic that there had to be in place a more regular and dependable means by which to fund those events, even if private parties still played a nominally important and simultaneously autonomous role. For with the construction of temples and the repeated staging of great festivals, an episodic income would be drained and not easily or readily replenished from such intrinsically uncertain sources as war, fines, piracy, diplomatic gifts, and so on. With that supposition in mind, therefore, Thucydides' claim (6.54.5) that the Peisistratidai employed a tax of some sort appears still more plausible (as I quote again from chapter 3):[4]

> καὶ ἐπετήδευσαν ἐπὶ πλεῖστον δὴ τύραννοι οὗτοι ἀρετὴν καὶ ξύνεσιν, καὶ Ἀθηναίους εἰκοστὴν μόνον πρασσόμενοι τῶν γιγνομένων τήν τε πόλιν αὐτῶν καλῶς διεκόσμησαν καὶ τοὺς πολέμους διέφερον καὶ ἐς τὰ ἱερὰ ἔθυον.

3. Stahl (1987), 250 n. 85. But Stahl does not make enough allowance for the development of rather sophisticated fiscal mechanisms in the sixth century in Athens and elsewhere; cf. Lewis "Property" (1997). For instance, perhaps as early as the mid-sixth century the cult of Artemis at Ephesos, on at least the same order of significance as that of Athena Polias at Athens, derived a portion of its income from leases of property or from taxes and duties upon a wide range of goods, such as salt and timber, and possibly the lease of sacred land in the form of a "garden" (*kêpos*): *IvEphesos* 1 (Jeffery [1990], 339, argues for a date of c. 550). Upon a conservative reading of the text, the totals are fifty *mnai* in gold and 284 *mnai* in silver, which at a traditional ratio of gold to silver at approximately 13:1 provide a sum total equivalent to nearly seventeen *talents* of silver.
4. Gallo (2000), 21–22, notes that this is one of the few instances where the sources attribute direct taxation to a tyrant (though regularly assumed by many scholars to be much more common), and, 24, that the taxation imposed by the Peisistratidai fed into a larger claim that they ruled in a moderate manner. A more doubtful, or at least more negative, case is the claim in [Arist.] *Oec.* (1347a14–17) that Hippias instituted a tax upon all births and deaths, by virtue of which Athena received various measures of wheat and barley.

[For the most part, these tyrants also pursued "virtue" and intelligence, and exacting only a twentieth of agricultural produce from the Athenians they ornamented their city well, distinguished themselves in wars and sacrificed appropriately.]

It is natural to suppose that this income would have gone solely to a public treasury, but is it plausible that this could have gone into anything but a central treasury? Can the Solonian system of *naukrariai* have competently redirected the receipts in an efficient manner to fund a central effort like the Greater Panathenaia? The answer might well be "yes" insofar as funds were needed for those efforts that were still organized around and through the tribes' own institutions. But for any single outlay, especially on a large scale, the answer is doubtful.

It is conceivable, therefore, that while the political ambitions of elite Athenians prior to the Peisistratidai might have spurred efforts to come up with greater amounts of money and other resources, for which the *naukrariai* are the obvious locus of interest, it was only on the eve of the Peisistratid tyranny and under their further direction that the Athenians had cause to reform their financial institutions on a more fundamental level. That innovation does not appear to have come at the expense of the *naukraroi*, who seem to have maintained their key position without alteration. Rather, insofar as the Athenians did create a newly centralized treasury, they did so by placing over it a single college of magistrates known as the *kôlakretai*, who were ultimately subject to the *naukraroi*. Most of our information, however, concerns their duties in the period between Kleisthenes' reforms and the abolition of the *kôlakretai* in or immediately after 411 when the Athenians shifted at least some of their functions to the *hellenotamiai*.[5] In a lengthy passage (quoted here in full), a scholiast

5. The principal source for this change comes in a mistaken or poorly transmitted note of Androtion. Despite both his own extensive first-hand knowledge of Athenian finances in the early fourth century and his expertise in Athenian history, Androtion is reported as having claimed that it was Kleisthenes who replaced the *kôlakretai* with the *apodektai* (Harp. s.v. ἀποδέκται = *FGrH* 324 F 5 [cf. *Ath. Pol.* 48.1], with Harding [1994], 91–94; Rhodes [1993], 557–58, and [1972], 99). That statement obviously cannot be true, not least because the *apodektai* performed the *opposite* tasks of the *kôlakretai*, namely, as receivers of public income once created, perhaps in 418/7 (*IG* I³ 84). It is surely a coincidence that this inscription, which decrees instructions for leasing sacred land, also contains the last known appearance of the *kôlakretai*.

For the argument that the abolition was occasioned by the amalgamation of the public treasury with the imperial one of the *hellenotamiai*, see Samons (2000), 237–42, 259–60; cf. Harding (1994), 92–94 (see n. 7 below); Rhodes (1993), 391–92, and (1972), 99 n. 4; Sealey (1975), 286; Pritchett (1964), 474 n. 3; Pritchett (1970), 111–12; Meritt, Wade-Gery, and McGregor in *ATL* vol. 3, 364–65, with Samons (2000), 260 n. 46.

on Aristophanes' *Birds* (of 414) defines the *kôlakretai* by invoking *tamiai* but complicates the comparison by articulating a number of tasks that befell both sets of magistrates:[6]

> τὸν κωλακρέτην· τὸν ταμίαν τῶν πολιτικῶν χρημάτων. 'Αριστοφάνης ὁ γραμματικὸς τούτους ταμίας εἶναί φησι τοῦ δικαστικοῦ μισθοῦ. οὐ μόνον δὲ τούτου τὴν ἐπιμέλειαν ἐποιοῦντο, ὥς φησιν, ἀλλὰ καὶ τὰ εἰς θεοὺς ἀναλισκόμενα διὰ τούτων ἀνηλίσκετο ὡς 'Ανδροτίων γράφει οὕτως· τοῖς δε ἰοῦσι Πυθῶδε θεωροῖς κωλακρέτας διδόναι ἐκ τῶν ναυκληρικῶν εἰς ἐφόδια ἀργύριον καὶ ἐς ἄλλο ὅ τι ἂν δέῃ ἀναλῶσαι. ταμίαι δὲ ἦσαν καὶ προεστῶτες τῆς δημοσίας σιτήσεως.
>
> [The *kôlakretês*: the *tamias* of political monies. Aristophanes the Grammarian (of Byzantion; fr. 395 Slater) claims that these were the *tamiai* of pay for jurors. Not only did they have the responsibility for this, as he states, but also the monies expended with regard to the gods were spent through these [magistrates], as Androtion (*FGrH* 324 F36) writes thus: the *kôlakretai* give to those journeying to Delphi money for travel expenses from the funds of the *naukraroi*, and for whatever else there is a need to spend. They were *tamiai* and the patrons of public dining.]

Until their abolition, the *kôlakretai* did have charge of many public payments that were important to the religious and political life of Athens. These magistrates are well attested epigraphically in the fifth century as being in charge of payments made from the public treasury for a variety of one-time projects as

---

6. Σ Ar. *Av.* 1541bα Holwerda. Several other lexical items appear to be intimately related to this scholion: Hesykhios s.v. κωλακρέται· ἀργυρικοὶ ταμίαι, οὕς τινες οἴονται μόνου τοῦ δικαστικοῦ προΐσασθαι, and two items in the *Lexica Segueriana* of Bekker's *Anecdota Graeca* p. 275, *l.* 22: κωλακρέται· οἱ τῶν ἀργυρίων ταμίαι, οἱ τὸ δικαστικὸν ἐταμιεύοντο τριώβολον καὶ τὰ εἰς τὰς θεούς ἀναλισκόμενα χρήματα; p. 190, *l.* 15: κωλακρέται· οἱ κρατοῦντες δικαστικὴν ζημίαν. Just what the second entry means by specifying goddesses alone as the beneficiaries, or the last entry by a penalty or damage having to do with the courts, however, is a mystery; cf. Σ Ar. *V.* 724b, 788b Koster-Holwerda. A passage in the Souda concerning the *kôlakretai* very closely echoes part of the scholiast's quotation (or paraphrase) of Androtion but does not attribute the information, and it is impossible to tell how the Souda relates to the scholiast: s.v. κωλακρέται [= Arist. *V.* 695; cf. s.v. χασμᾷ; Paus. Gr. s.v. κωλακρέται; Phot. s.v. κωλακρέται; *Lex.Rhet.Cant.* s.v. κωλακρέται]): κωλακρέται· οἱ ταμίαι τοῦ δικαστικοῦ μισθοῦ καὶ τῶν εἰς θεοὺς ἀναλωμάτων. 'Αριστοφάνης· σὺ δὲ χασκάζεις τὸν κωλακρέτην, τὸ δὲ πραττόμενόν σε λέληθεν. Jacoby (*FGrH* IIIb Suppl. 1, 147) raised doubts concerning the extent to which the scholiast accurately reports the words of Androtion, suggesting instead that it is at best Aristophanes the Grammarian's paraphrase that we read in the scholion; cf. Harding (1994), 134.

As for the common reinterpretation of *nauklêria* (as per the Greek text) for *naukraria*, see Chantraine (2009), Beekes (2010) *s.v.* ναύκληρος (736–37); Beekes (2010) *s.v.* ναύκληρος.

well as continual outlays. For instance, other sources show that the *kôlakretai* were responsible for the jury-pay since it was instituted in the late 460s as well as the compensation owed to regular magistrates and even some priests.[7] Likewise, the *kôlakretai* even paid for the colossal statue of Athena Promakhos on the akropolis.[8] Clearly, for the *kôlakretai* to be called *tamiai* and patrons of public dining must signify not that they dispensed anything to senior magistrates, for this was the task of the *tamiai*, but rather that they were the ones who paid for the great sacrificial banquets at which the Demos dined, which constituted the public in its broadest sense.

But how do we square duties such as these, even when they are known only from the democratic era, with those of the predemocratic *naukraroi*? Clearly, the *kôlakretai* were centralized and flexible enough that the Athenians maintained their magistracy through almost all of the period of radical democracy and imperial finance, which together drastically increased the revenues under their control as well as the complexity of their disbursements. Therefore, even if we are to suppose that the Athenians altered their duties, which is quite possible, we should look to the latter part of the sixth century as having determined the essential reasons for their longevity under the democracy.[9] The principal cause, I suggest, is that the imposition of large-scale taxes across the *polis*, such as those Thucydides claims Peisistratos imposed, would have been best handled by a sufficiently central authority in control of a single treasury, even if it was subordinated to the tribal authorities.

While such a singular treasury and college of magistrates would represent an

7. *V.* 724 (and Σ *Av.* 1541bα Holwerda [= Androtion *FGrH* 324 F36], quoted above) with Samons (2000), 241 n. 111; Harding (1994), 135. It is likely in connection with such payments that another scholiast to Aristophanes (Σ *V.* 788 Koster-Holwerda) reports that the *kôlakretai* also handled moneychangers' fees, which is to say that it likely fell to these magistrates to turn large amounts of coin into the small denominations that jurors and others expected. After all, these magistrates were the ones who paid other magistrates' wages: e.g., c. 420, a mixed pool of jurors, *bouleutai*, and sitting *hieropoioi* chosen to be *hieropoioi* for a festival of Hephaistos: *IG* I[3] 82, *l.* 21.

    But Harding (1994), 93, is surely mistaken when interpreting the nomenclature of the *kôlakretai* as indicating that they "were once receivers of revenue" for the cognate verb *ageirein* indicates an active process of procurement (e.g., *Od.* 3.301; Alc. 119–10 L-P; Ar. *Fr.* 168), not the passive sense implicit in "to receive." Within even a rudimentary monetized economy, to procure something requires expenditure unless it is simply taken by force, which is not the case here. Thus, the historical shift that he wishes to see, 93–94, in these magistrates as being one from receiving revenue to disbursing revenue is mistaken; cf. Chaintraine (2009) s.v. ἀγείρω.
8. *IG* I[3] 435, *ll.* 6, 37, 65, 96, 122.
9. Such an alteration may lie behind Harpokration's statement (s.v. ἀποδέκται; = *FGrH* 324 F 5) that Androtion claimed that Kleisthenes instituted the *apodektai* in place of the *kôlakretai*, which obviously cannot be true insofar as the whole boards are concerned. It would be a sensible mistake if Kleisthenes created the *apodektai* to take over particular duties, namely, the handling of receipts. On the *apodektai* in the democratic budget process, see chapter 7 n. 44.

important step in and of itself, it need not have squelched the ability or drive among other parts of the *polis* to develop further institutionally in different directions. Because the *naukraroi* were instrumental to the staging of religious festivals it is reasonable to think that the *naukrariai* also competed against one another, just as did tribe against tribe, for splendor and prestige. In turn, such institutionalized competition dovetailed with that of ambitious Athenians, such that the *naukrariai* might well have served as a locus for financial innovation. A note in the Souda claims that *dêmarkhoi*, whom it explicitly glosses as *naukraroi*, were responsible for providing order (*diakosmoun*) at the Panathenaia, just as various *hieropoioi* did in the classical centuries, as discussed mainly in chapter 3.[10] Just what the *dêmarkhoi* did in this regard is rather difficult to say, but it is the alignment of such duties between these magistracies across the Kleisthenic divide of 508/7 that may be significant.[11] A little noticed passage of Photios does claim that the *naukraroi* did lease out *dêmosia* property of some sort:[12]

> ναύκραροι· τὸ παλαιὸν ᾿Αθήνησιν οἱ νῦν δήμαρχοι· καὶ οἱ ἐκμισθοῦντες τὰ δημόσια.
>
> [*Naukraroi*: the present *dêmarkhoi* in Athens used to be these, and they were the ones to lease out public lands.]

Yet the *dêmarkhoi* were also responsible for collecting some of the few cultic taxes required of all Athenians.[13] The extensive financial control of the *naukraroi* implies that at their basic level, the tribes and their parts served to organize much of, if not all, the finances of the *polis* before Kleisthenes' reforms.[14] For

10. Souda s.v. δήμαρχοι (only the final lines of which are quoted here): οὗτοι δὲ διεκόσμουν τὴν ἑορτὴν τῶν Παναθηναίων. Thucydides (1.20.1), it should be noted, also uses this term in relation to the procession at that Panathenaia in which Harmodios and Aristogeiton slew Hipparkhos, who was then engaged in this same activity: τῷ ῾Ιππάρχῳ περιτυχόντες περὶ τὸ Λεωκόρειον καλούμενον τὴν Παναθηναϊκὴν πομπὴν διακοσμοῦντι ἀπέκτειναν. Nonetheless, Thucydides leaves open the question of whether Hipparkhos acted as a *naukraros*.
11. Whitehead (1986), 136–37.
12. Photios s.v. ναύκραροι· τὸ παλαιὸν ᾿Αθήνησιν οἱ νῦν δήμαρχοι· καὶ οἱ ἐκμισθοῦντες τὰ δημόσια. The earliest epigraphic attestation for the (or, a) public treasury, apart from the tablet of Nemesis discussed below, is a decree concerning Salamis (*IG* I³ 1, *l.* 7) that also likely belongs to the democracy, is therefore post-Kleisthenic, and would reveal nothing about the *naukraroi* even if the text were completely preserved.
13. For some examples of these various imposts and the burden upon *dêmarkhoi* for their collection and management, see Whitehead (1986), 135–36.
14. *Ath.Pol.* 21.5; Kleidemos *FGrH* 323 F 8; cf. Pollux 8.108. A possible parallel for management of the budget by the tribes of a *polis* is that of Epizephyrian Lokroi in the third century. Migeotte (1988),

that reason, one can imagine that the *kôlakretai* became much more important to the operation of the Athenian treasury, and that it, too, became much more centralized, once those reforms had abolished the Ionian tribes and their *naukraroi* in favor of a new system that did not wholly carry over their duties as being distributed among so many *ex officio* stakeholders. In other words, these officers likely had as one among many duties the obligation to ensure that religious processions were conducted in a particular fashion, and they possessed the financial capacity to ensure that some participants thereof (or whole embassies) were duly paid for by the state, presumably so that they would attain a sufficient level of pomp and respectability. The *naukraroi* also had a high degree of organizational control over tribal military units, including those of the nascent Athenian fleet, for which their ability to secure revenue was likely critical.[15] Since the *naukraroi* also had control over income to the public treasury, they possessed the capacity and responsibility to organize the manpower necessary for the processions themselves, just as did their successors in the post-Kleisthenic *dêmarkhoi* (and of course the *hieropoioi* for the whole *polis*). The *naukraroi* would have been especially well suited to judge and, thereby, to assemble all of the different elements necessary for the proper functioning of the community in its religious, military, and financial dimensions.

In sum, the tribes and their officers, especially the *naukraroi*, were the organs of government that mattered to all fiscal affairs prior to Kleisthenes' democratizing reforms. At their direction, it was the *kôlakretai* who dispensed money to whichever other magistrates were in charge of putting on, say, the Panathenaia or instructed to conduct a sacred embassy to Delphi, and so on. Notwithstanding the dispersed character of the *naukraroi*, the *kôlakretai* appear to have been centralized enough to control a single public treasury and efficiently enough that the democracy retained their college even as it gave new and important tasks, like payment for jurors, for them to manage. Since these tribes, as I argued in chapter 3, also constituted the principal electoral units

197–99, emphasizes the unusual extent to which the *polis* overtly managed the cult of Olympian Zeus (which loaned funds for much of the *polis*' military and civic expenses), and follows Musti (1979), 211, in seeing what seems to be a distinct fund (the *phatarkhion*) as the public treasury, administered in turn by each of the twelve *phatarkhoi* of a given year. If so, then the treasury and its officers might well have been organized along tribal lines, since the *phatarkhoi* seem to be nothing more that officers in charge of *phatarai* (i.e., the Attic *phratriai*, which were essential to the enrollment of citizens in tribes).

15. On the close connection between the financial and military responsibilities of the *naukraroi*, long a vexed tangle, see now the reconstruction of Schubert (2008), who points especially to their responsibility for funding the Athenian fleet such as was also transferred to the *dêmarkhoi* after Kleisthenes.

themselves, their fiscal power under the *naukraroi* make all the more sense why they would have been the locus of electoral patronage and political life. To win election at the tribal level alone would have conceivably put one in an advantageous position from which to influence how much money was dispensed, to whom, and under what conditions. Therefore, it is plausible that it was the tribes and their *naukrariai* rather than the central institutions of the *polis* that would have been most ready to engage in fiscal innovation of one sort or another even as a central treasury had begun to take shape.

Creating Hosia *in Archaic Athens: The Case of Nemesis at Rhamnous, c. 500*

While the Kleisthenic reforms of 508/7 did not immediately squelch the competitive political spirit of the elite that motivated fiscal changes, it did alter the fiscal landscape by elevating certain central institutions while broadening the basic structures that served as the arena in which financial experiments could be undertaken. Not only did the reforms create an expanded Boule (now with five hundred members) to serve as a central organization of Athenians without regard to census class, but the Boule also drew its members from 139 demes in place of the forty-eight *naukrariai* of the old system. Likewise, the number of tribes expanded from four to ten. Simply put, there were far more opportunities for Athenians to serve as magistrates, and the units of tribes and demes now represented, each in their own way, smaller portions of the citizenry. To that mixture, one must obviously add the fact that the tribes were made up of demes from across the Attic landscape in patterns that had little geographic cohesion. As J. Ober, for one, has recently argued, such arrangements were vital to redirecting information about governance in new ways and along new routes between citizens who may formerly have had little substantive contact with each other outside of the old, essentially regional structures of tribes and *naukrariai*.[16] Such conditions look especially favorable to fiscal innovation, and I will deal with them at greater length in the next chapter, but my caveat here is that we should not dismiss a priori the decades leading up to those reforms under the oligarchy and then the tyranny of the Peisistratidai. After all, Solon's laws provided an essential ingredient for this development.

16. Ober (2008).

Can we be at all precise about how and when the Athenians first created *hosia* wealth? Even if the democracy alone could be proven as the exclusive inventor of *hosia*, the relevant locus of innovation appears to have been among the new demes and thus commensurate with longstanding practices under the *naukrariai*. Several scholars have also identified the demes and not the Boule as the locus of experimentation in financial matters during the classical era, but I think that this innovation goes back to the sixth century.[17] Of special interest are the recent arguments of J. Blok. She maintains that from perhaps the mid-fifth century onward Athenian demes developed a new financial mechanism by which they designated a portion of public (*dêmosia*) money as *hosia* in order to serve as a reserve fund for unanticipated expenses relating to their major religious festivals.[18] This hypothesis usefully focuses our attention on how early and autonomous the development of religious finance in the demes was, even very small ones, and all the more so for elucidating the essential fact that *dêmosia* money was turned into other kinds of money—whether *hiera* or *hosia*—by nothing other than the decision of the relevant authority. Yet one must be careful to note that except for a few unique cases discussed in the next chapter, the Athenians long endowed *hiera* wealth as religiously or juridicially august and so correspondingly untouchable from a financial point of view.[19] As a result, the fuller implications of that operation for the three categories thus created or deployed remain unclear from Blok's account, particularly where it comes to how the structural or systemic relationships between these categories might have meshed with the larger institutional framework in which the sacred treasurers or other magistrates managed these various assets.

Going further than Blok on some points in my interpretation and dissenting on others, I propose a rather different reconstruction. As with Blok, a useful starting point is that the Athenians used an accounting mechanism as they earmarked public assets to serve religious life in various ways, and so (as with Blok) by fiat created *hosia* money out of *dêmosia* money. But I would go further in arguing that perhaps in this way the Athenians also designated certain real properties such as quarries or arable land as *hosia* or at least capable of producing *hosia* income in turn. In ultimate point of origin as well as ownership, all

17. Blok (2010); Ismard (2010), 297; Chankowski (2007), 105.
18. Blok (2010).
19. Thus, Blok (2010), 81, writes of "*hieros* rentals," but the two terms are never found together. Blok also assumes that the Eleusinian "first-fruits" (*aparkhai*) are *dêmosia*, when the relevant text (*IG* I^3 78; = *I.Eleusis* 28a-b) never indicates that.

hosia wealth remained a kind of public wealth, even though some *hosia* assets could in turn generate more of the same (such as through loans of *hosia* money, whose interest would of course be of the very same category, that is, *hosia*). Although used to benefit the gods in one or another manner, *hosia* wealth did not belong to any divinity and so should not be spoken of as if it were *hiera*. From the time *hosia* was first developed it also acquired a separate and somewhat more august identity than that which remained expressly public, although it was less sacred, of course, than that which was *hiera*. It is for that reason that *hosia* wealth could best be described as "sanctioned," for its purpose was to serve religious ends but it was not to be confused with that property that belonged expressly to the gods: *hiera*.

It is the earliest surviving Athenian treasury account of any kind that points to the development of *hosia* wealth as a distinct category. Not only does the text belong to the first decade or so of the Athenian democracy but it also suggests that the public treasury played a significant role in the creation of *hosia* wealth. The text in question is a small opisthographic lead sheet from Nemesis' shrine at Rhamnous (c. 500), which names a college of magistrates, the *epistatai*, on one side, and on the other lists a series of monetary transfers that a college of *hieropoioi* made on behalf of the cult:[20]

A ἐπιστατôν
B τὸ χρêμα
ἀνέλοται
τὸς *h*ιεροποιὸς
τὸ ἐν τôι μολυβδίοι
*h*ιγραμμένο

20. Petrakos Ὁ Δῆμος τοῦ Ραμνοῦντος 181; as to the date, Petrakos correctly offers "Τέλους 6ου-άρχῶν 5ου αἰ." I have amended the text from Petrakos' version in order to correct certain minor errors of transcription (e.g., the numeral in *l.* 7 is probably 162, with the final mark for a single *drakhma* off the now ragged edge of the sheet, which might explain also the figure of 100 dr. in *l.* 8, which I restore as 162 also; the upper-left angle of the akrophonic sign for *pente* at the right edge of *l.* 11 is also evident in the drawing). The very precise drawing of the lead sheet published by Petrakos shows that the second to last name covers (or, is covered by) another name or phrase, which Petrakos suggests reads ATOPA ⁝ ΠΟΝΔ. Based upon the drawing, the section after the colon might also be read as HONΔO (i.e., ὧν δο-, or ὧν Δ O if a numeral is indicated such as δέκα ὀκτώ in case the O is not merely superfluous). In her discussion of this text, Blok (2010), 77–79, does not attempt any restoration of the numerals or discussion of their relationship, nor of the partially legible line noted here. Faraguna (2005), 68, also cites this document (which goes so far as to identify itself as such: *l.* 5) as important evidence for the beginnings of archival practice in Greek *poleis*, usually as a function of developing financial administration.

Νεοκλέει ⁝ ΗΠΔ|–|–
Πυθοδόροι ⁝ ΗΠΔ|–[|–]
Τεισαμεν[ô]ι ⁝ Η[ΠΔ|–|–]
Στράτον(ι) ⁝ΗΠΔ|–|–
[δε]μόσιον : *hέ*χ[οσι]
[παρ]ὰ Δίονος ⁝ Η [--]
[παρ]ὰ Στράτονο[ς ⁝--]
[πα]ρὰ Τεισαμεν̣[ô ⁝--]
vacat

[(A) Of the *epistatai*
(B) The money "expended" to the *hieropoioi* (as has been) written upon the lead sheet:
Nikokles: 162 dr.
Pythodoros: 16(2) dr.
Teisamenos: 1(62) dr.
Straton: 162 dr.
Of public (money): they possess—
From Dion: (100+ dr.)
From Straton: (--dr.)
From Teisamenos: (--dr.)]

Three problems that confront us are, first, what is the nature of the transactions the sheet records; second, what is the nature of the money involved; and, third, what is the position of the various men and colleges listed thereupon. Since no similar working document survives from Athens, one can only resolve these issues by examining the text very closely. On side B, the sheet declares what appear to be (total) (current) expenditures that one party—which I presume to be the *epistatai*—made to four different men and amounting to what is very likely a total of 648 dr., divided into four equal amounts. (For the moment, I will take the text at face value and so use the language of expenditure but will soon show why that interpretation must be modified.) Below that data, the sheet lists first the public money (*dêmosion*) that the same *epistatai* possess currently and secondly the names of three men from whom money was received (that is, to judge by the traces of the preposition *para* in several successive lines). Between the lists, two of the names are identical (Straton and Teisamenos), and while each of those is relatively common over the length of Athenian history their doubling here is very unlikely to be coincidence; the presence of another man shows, however, that the groups themselves cannot be identical.[21] Moreover, neither group can be the same as the *epistatai*, who paid out or received money but remain unidentified as individuals, in contrast to the two named groups of men with whom they conducted their transactions.

Why such parceled distribution or receipt of public money would be utilized, especially where the *hieropoioi* appear to be acting as subordinates of the *epistatai*, is puzzling. If the sheet merely ended on side B with the names of the four men who received money, we would readily infer that the *epistatai* simply made a record of the money that they distributed individually to four *hieropoioi*. Yet the following statement that the *epistatai* received public money (*dêmosion*) from what are likely three *hieropoioi* complicates that view and requires us to interpret the seemingly straightforward vocabulary of *analiskein* and *ekhein* as meaning something other than "expend" and "possess," respectively, as they appear on the sheet. While the sums received from the second grouping are not preserved, enough remains of the figure in *l.* 12 to suggest that perhaps these were in the same range as those that were spent. One should not assume that the two transactions concern precisely the same bundle of cash, since the sheet could well note transfers involving two batches of money given that the expenditure appears above (*ll.* 1–10), and therefore chronologically prior to the receipt of money at the bottom of the sheet (*ll.* 12–14). Moreover, even the figure partially preserved for Dion (150 dr.) falls well short of the sum he would have had to handle if the 648 dr. were broken into three equal parts (that is, 216 dr.); a different set of akrophonic figures would have been required to signify the sum of 216. Between the two transactions is some entity, presumably the *epistatai*, which, at the time of the text's inscription, currently possesses public money. Assuming a logical flow to the order in which the sheet presents its data, it first appears that the *epistatai* paid out equal sums of money to four men and then received (as currently in their position) another batch of public money brought by three men, two of whom are likely the same as those to whom the *epistatai* made their payments.

The payments are puzzling, since they are likely all equal in size and the sheet does not list for what goods or services such large sums were expended, or at least what the four men were supposed to purchase, lease, contract, and so on. Could this be, in effect, a sort of accounting rubric, in which "expenditure"

21. Without incorporating the names upon this sheet, *LGPN Attica* lists 188 individuals known under the name of Straton (only one in Rhamnous) and 30 for Teisamenos (none in Rhamnous) across the span of Athenian history.

is used, even if awkwardly, merely to signify the transfer of money from one group of officials to another and has nothing to do with spending cash to purchase goods or services? Without doubt, the verb *analiskein* is not commonly known to possess such a technical meaning as proposed here, which I suggest might best be translated in this sense as "to surrender possession of an object to another party" and not "to expend, to spend" here.[22] The standard formulae for the transfers of *hiera* wealth, discussed in the previous chapter, would provide a different means by which to express this kind of financial act, even though those terms (that is, *paralabein* and *paradonai*) first appear many decades later than the lead account of Nemesis and also occur in texts that do not necessarily involve the transfer of money at all.[23] But as noted in the previous chapter, even the accounts of the *tamiai* resorted on occasion to using the language of loans by which to express what seems merely to have been a transfer of money between boards of magistrates. Given, too, that the amounts are at once large and likely equal in size, one might fairly doubt that these are really expenditures in the strict sense. In the other transaction, in which the *epistatai* appear to have received public money, the text merely uses *ekhein* "to possess" and not *dekhesthai* "to receive," although they must have received that money in order to possess it. Conceivably, the difficulty with using *dekhesthai* would be that to receive the money does not perforce indicate any degree of legally sanctioned possession such as would be appropriate for magistrates who are to be held responsible for the money in question. This choice of vocabulary thus appears to mark off each stage of a serial process in which the money was transferred from one party to another through an intermediary, but whichever party was in possession of the money had to take full legal control of it, and that this is what the sheet documents. In other words, I suggest that "*ekhein*" actually signifies receipt here just as "*analiskein*" signifies deposition or a grant of money, and thus that the sheet records two different transactions, each being one-half of the process of transfer (but with different batches of money).[24]

22. Cf. Chantraine (2009) s.v. ἁλίσκομαι; Beekes (2010) s.v. ἀναλίσκω. Blok (2010), 77, translates this line of the text as "is taken off" without further explanation.

23. Blok (2010), 78, suggests a much more direct connection between the use of *para* here and *paralabein* and *paradonai* in those later texts, but we have, unfortunately, other than this text no evidence that such language of surrender and transfer was used for non-*hiera* wealth.

24. E. Harris (2006), 235, offers much the same interpretation of *ekhein* (i.e., denoting possession and not ownership) as it appears in fourth-century legal contexts; cf. Beekes (2010) s.v. ἔχω; Chantraine (2009), s.v. 1 ἔχω. While Blok (2010), 78, assumes that the three men are not only *hieropoioi* but also, that by virtue of the preposition *para*, they are paying back to the treasury the money in their possession she does not fully explore that possibility and its implications.

The significance of this reading of the text lies not only in the degree of legal culpability that the individual *hieropoioi* had for their own parcels but also for connecting the *hieropoioi* to a larger fiscal structure, and thus for tracking the flow of money through the hands of various sacred treasurers. The key question is the source of the money, which I take to be the public treasury of Athens itself under the *kôlakretai* since there would be no need for such extensive use of couriers if it was the deme's own money, located as it was so close to the shrine of Nemesis. If the *epistatai* received large sums of public money in roughly equal batches from several individuals and also paid it out or granted it to another set thereof, it stands to reason that these individual *hieropoioi* merely acted as the couriers. Likewise, the four men to whom another batch was paid out in similar fashion might also be couriers, ferrying the cash to whichever college was to receive it in the end. Parceled distribution would also make sense wherever two colleges of magistrates and their treasuries were not located immediately next to one another, and also whenever final payment or expenditure was to be made to someone located at some distance from the treasury. It could well be the case, therefore, that the public treasury supplying money in this case was not that of Rhamnous but rather that serving the whole *polis* of the Athenians, and the men physically ferried the money in the form of coin from the *asty* of Athens itself. Once it was collected and counted at Rhamnous, the *epistatai* (or even the *hieropoioi*) could then break that sum again into smaller amounts so as to facilitate expenditure in a more or less timely and efficient manner by handing the parcels to several men who would then spend the money to procure whatever was needed, such as sacrificial animals, or to fulfil building contracts. The appearance of two men in both transactions would thus be easily explained as representing two individual magistrates who carried out two different tasks at separate times as members of a larger college of *hieropoioi* (as both Blok and I presume they all were).

Given that the sheet records individual names rather than that of their college, it bears amplifying that these men were *personally* responsible in the legal sense for the cash that they brought from one location to another. In this sense, then, the use of *analiskein* (and *ekhein*) is less difficult to understand, for it could easily signify that indeed a payment was made at one location (first, at the public treasury) to each man who then had to make a corresponding payment at the other end (that is, at Rhamnous), and until he made that payment he was fully liable for the cash and did not serve with any protective indemnity in case of accident or robbery, alleged or real.[25] The degree of personal liability evinced in this document finds a striking echo in the Solonian census classes. As I argued in chapter 1, Solon established the *pentakosiomedimnoi* as a superclass that, while feeding the prestige of the wealthiest Athenians, enabled the Areiopagos to demand a heavy indemnity from *tamiai* should they be found at fault or condemned for an act committed in their tenure. The whole of the census classes likely made similar demands down through the ranks, to which system these *hieropoioi* and *epistatai* ought also to have been subject, hence the record of names here. Even the fifth-century loans involving *tamiai*, discussed in chapter 5, seem to reflect the presence of that system, whereby a single board had absolute custody over property and hence bore full culpability should something have gone wrong. One important effect of this was to set up a clear chain of transfers and thence to document that chain at every step. Accordingly, the administrative process by which men handed physical custody of property over to others ought to have been easily repeated so that all such transfers of coin operated the same way where it was not possible or desirable to reconcile account-books of different boards of magistrates with one another. On that reading, then, the sheet details parts of two different transfers, one from the public treasury to the *epistatai* at Rhamnous through the shrine's *hieropoioi* and the other from the same *epistatai* to another group of *hieropoioi* for some other purpose altogether.

Turning to the nature of the money involved, the first point to be made is that the sheet appears to be the product of a regular administrative protocol

25. The procedure and its legal form as I envision it shares something of the spirit if not the substance of the commercial principle of "cash sale." While Pringsheim's (1950) thesis on cash sale does hold that the Greek "law of sale" required the absoute cession of title and ownership with the simultaneous transfer (or rather, exchange) of object and cash payment that thesis, nevertheless, has no direct relevance to the argument that I advance since I do not think that the transfers in question ever could have been confused with a commercial transaction (i.e., no goods or services were exchanged). The "expenditure" was a convenient enough and correct means by which to designate the abandonment or assumption of legal authority for money that the state either owned outright (*dêmosia* or *hosia*) or held in its custody (*hiera*). That the vocabulary used for these transfers should be found mainly in later commercial contexts should not mislead us to assume that they could only have been commercial. In other words, the pattern might just as well bespeak the lack of surviving early documentation and the relative flexibility of this vocabularly, not wholly the relatively primitive nature of the institutions using it. Rather, we may see here an instance of shared vocabulary between what we would think of as distinct spheres, namely, commerce and the state. Thus, I suggest that these two verbs (i.e., *analiskein* and *ekhein*) merely anticipate the vocabulary employed by inventories and related inscriptions of the late fifth century and beyond (i.e., *paradosis* and *paralêpsis*), as discussed earlier in this chapter (cf. Pringsheim, 219–32, on [commercial] *paradosis*), and thus in a separate manner the vocabulary also anticipates the use of "loans" also to effect emergency intrastate transfers of money.

and not an experiment or idiosyncratic attempt at keeping records of unusual transactions. By all appearances, the sheet was merely one of a series produced and kept by the *epistatai* with some frequency and according to a more or less standard method. Furthermore, as I have suggested above, the vocabulary of transfer implies the presence of an administrative framework that could hold magistrates to account at a level lower than, or at least preliminary to, any judgments rendered by the Areiopagos or, after c. 462, by the courts. If such a system undertook audits of those magistrates entrusted with cash and other property, as was the case with the *euthyna*, it would make sense for the various magistrates to submit official documents bearing the same kind of information that the Rhamnousian lead sheet carries. However such procedures might have been carried out among the demes, wherever the central institutions of Athens were concerned that framework would, I presume, have applied across demes just as it applied to Athens and its pan-Athenian magistrates. Moreover, such a system need not have been centralized beyond the *kôlakretai* except where, and to the extent that, the recently constituted democratic Boule made decisions regarding how public money was to be distributed. Why the Boule and that larger framework are important lies in how the lead sheet appears to document one, and very likely two, instances where public money was transferred by *hieropoios*-courier to the *epistatai* of Nemesis at Rhamnous. The sheet would thus record the distribution of money from the pan-Athenian public treasury to sacred treasurers serving, in effect, a local cult, and though unique as a document, it seems to reflect a much broader and well-established set of protocols and institutions in place to handle that kind of transfer already by the end of the sixth century.

There remains the question of why the sheet should specify that the money was public (*dêmosia*). Just as the later accounts of Athena also imply the existence of something that is not *hiera*, the sheet points to a category of money that was closely related to *dêmosia* but not the same as *dêmosia*. As brief as it is, that declaration would be pointless if it were not necessary for the board to designate this batch of money as public so as not to confuse it with other money that was not public but might reasonably be confused for such. Since the text nowhere mentions or implies the presence of *hiera* or private money (*idia*), which would presumably require explicit notation, the most likely foil for the money in question would be at once very closely related to the public money but not in and of itself public strictly speaking. Even if the pan-Athenian public treasury transferred money through the *hieropoioi* to the *epistatai* at Rhamnous, that money need not have remained public in the strict sense of the term, even if, say, the *hieropoioi* were magistrates attached to the public treasury. Just as legal custody of the money changed at the point of transfer, it is conceivable that the money in question could likewise acquire a different status at each juncture, hence the declaration of the *epistatai* that they possessed *dêmosia*. By default, I suggest that the other category must have been *hosia* rather than *dêmosia* and that this *hosia* originated, by that very act of declaration, in *dêmosia* funds.[26] In sum, the lead sheet suggests that already in c. 500, and thus before the Persian Wars and the growth of imperial finance, the Athenians simply, but nevertheless with profound implications, created *hosia* funds as a kind of accounting rubric for funds that they earmarked for religious expenditures.

In sum, the fiscal arrangements sketched in this chapter likely had no single piece of legislation as its genesis but rather resulted from experimentation that was carried out in the spirit of competition and required slight adjustments as well as far-reaching innovations. But alongside a nascent central treasury, what is most worthy of note is how extensively the tribal system shaped financial matters, so much so that the *naukrariai* (and then, the demes) seem to have been the greatest incubators of new financial techniques, including the creation of an entirely new kind of property in *hosia*. Aside from the impetus of figures like Peisistratos, the evidence does not betoken any general overhaul or a single overarching principle of administration. Even at the cusp of the fifth century, when Athenian administration should not have been very large or complex, the sacred treasurers of Nemesis remind us that many different men might already be required to manage funds and business on behalf of a deity. Notwithstanding the weight of their responsibilities, however, these treasurers need not have enjoyed any of the prestige or visibility that the *tamiai* of Athena enjoyed, and in them we see a new course of development.

26. Blok (2010), 77–79, argues only that the sheet shows that public money could be used for religious purposes but labels all such ends as *hieros* [*sic*] and thus commits what I take to be an error of categories, for that adjective should properly pertain only to ritual (*hiera*) but would not apply to the building, say, of temples, for which the use of public money in the strict sense (*dêmosia*) might be more expected (though still unproven).

CHAPTER 7

Sacred Property in the Democracy

Inevitably, the question must then be why it was necessary or advantageous for the sacred treasurers of Nemesis to mark out a distinction between these two categories of money (*dêmosia* and *hosia*) when both appear to have remained fully under the control and ownership of the state. In some sense, that is also a question concerning the origins of the whole system, but the matter cannot be approached directly since it is first necessary to lay out what we can know about the fundamentals of *hosia* wealth. But much more remains to be done in the rest of this chapter to mark out the way in which *hosia* funds and other property were developed, and thus to show which sacred treasurers were involved with its management, which were not, and why. Looking ahead, it is clear that from at least the mid-fifth century onward Athenian texts document a diversity of methods and a multiplicity of properties that sacred treasurers employed in order to raise income for the cults to which they were attached. Heralding the growth of *hosia* funds as a useful administrative tool in that period, the relevant documents thus shed the necessary light on this vital aspect of Athenian sacral administration in some of its earlier incarnations as well. Yet the Athenians also maintained a different system for funding Athena's cult that did not rely on *hosia* wealth but on the Boule's direct allocation of public income, which appears to have been the essential mechanism used in the archaic age and which gave rise to *hosia* wealth ultimately.

Generator of New Wealth for the Gods

Seemingly unrelated to the transfers and designations exhibited by the earlier lead sheet, another document from Nemesis' cult, this one from c. 450, shows that later colleges of *hieropoioi* at Rhamnous made extensive interest-bearing loans to private parties as a means of raising income without recourse to the public treasury, and that this income was likely *hosia*. Of far greater significance is how the one surviving account of those loans differs from those produced by the contemporary *tamiai* of Athena, which do not reflect any concern with *hosia* money whatsoever.[1] The accounts, which cover several years running, express themselves differently year-to-year, but an adequate feel for the text and its contents can be had from just a single year (whose modern calendar date remains unknown) (*ll.* 20–26):

> ἐπὶ Ναυσιμένος ἄρχον-
> τος κεφάλαιον τô ἱ-
> ερô ἀργυρίο τô πα-
> ρὰ τοῖς τὰς διακοσίας ἔχοσι ⁝ ΜΜΜ𐅆ΧΧ
> τô δ ’ ἄλλο ⁝ ΜΧ𐅅ΗΗΔΔ𐅂𐅂𐅂
> ||

> When Nausimenes was *arkhôn* (of Rhamnous) the sum total of *hiera* silver from those holding "two-hundreds": 37,000 dr.; the sum total of the other silver: 11,723 dr. 2 ob.

There can be no doubt that the operation reflected here, though it involves the *hiera* money of Nemesis, represents a mode of administering a god's property that bears little obvious resemblance to that known for Athena and her *tamiai*. This is the only instance known to me of Athenians employing *hiera* wealth as a means of creating further wealth of any category. Moreover, for all of the complicated series of transactions implicit in loaning out such substantial sums in packets of two hundred and three hundred *drakhmai* at a time, the account is especially succinct, even for ancient standards, and certainly by those of Athena

1. *IG* I^3 248 (= Meiggs/Lewis 53; Petrakos Ὁ Δῆμος τοῦ Ραμνοῦντος 182). Whitehead (1986), 160, assumes that the cult's magistrates (*pace* his phrasing of "state, not deme, control" in his n. 76) belong to the deme of Rhamnous, presumably because the account dates its years by virtue of the *dêmarkhos* not the eponymous *arkhôn* whose name would seemingly signify only *polis*-wide matters of governance. It does not strictly matter to the issue discussed here, but others have thought that the magistrates are indeed those of the *polis*, properly speaking: Boersma (1970), 78; Linders (1975), 13 and n. 38.

as drawn up by her *tamiai* for *hiera* wealth.[2] One year of Nemesis' account, for example, also uses a standard commercial verb for indebtedness (*ôphelein*), which is never found in the *tamiai*'s own accounts for Athena as a term with which to describe the Demos' indebtedness to her and for which the only possible point of comparison would be the unique *daneisma* of 415/4.[3] Unlike Athena's accounts, furthermore, those of Nemesis never explicitly identify the parties involved or otherwise describe the acts that they record, or add other details that would help us in clarifying their nature. But this text does, as shown in the passage quoted here, reveal that the *hieropoioi* were able and willing to lend the *hiera* money of Nemesis and therefore could raise income directly for the goddess herself without benefit or need of an intermediary. Yet, as shown in chapters 4 and 5, there is no evidence that any of Athena's treasurers, whether *tamiai*, *hieropoioi*, or still others, conducted a similar operation.

Why Nemesis' *hiera* should have been treated in this manner, and Athena's or any other god's not, may be better framed as a question regarding the relationship of all three categories of money or property to one another, whether with respect to any specific cult or to the larger financial framework utilized by the Athenians. Differing considerably from Nemesis at Rhamnous' accounts, though perhaps contemporary with them, is the inscribed account (*IG* I^3 253) of the deme of Ikarion, c. 450–425. This text shows that the deme likely did manage *hosia* money side by side with money that must be *hiera*, as discussed in the previous chapter. Apparently, the *dêmarkhos*, acting as a sacred treasurer, did not engage in anything like Nemesis' treasurers with regard to loans and the like but did work to increase the *hosia* funds under his control.

The precise nature of the relationship between *dêmosia* and *hosia*, however, is not one of two parallel categories of public money or property but rather, as suggested in previous chapters, a structural one in which *hosia* may be *derived* secondarily from that which is, by default, *dêmosia*. That understanding, at least, is what emerges from a rather later text than that of the Ikarians, namely, Demosthenes' speech against Timokrates. According to Demosthenes, his opponent proposed a law granting relief to debtors of the *public* treasury (that is, the *dêmosion* itself). The law, on Demosthenes' argument, would deprive the

2. Whitehead (1986), 160 and 166–69, and Millett (1991), 175–76, both subscribe to the suggestion of Pouilloux (1954), 148–49 (this text = his no. 35), that individuals might have taken out packs of loans, bundled in 200 or 300 dr. amounts, rather than the dozens of individuals that the sums involved would require if the ratio of borrower to bundle was one-to-one, as objected by Finley (1985 [1951]), 285.

3. *ôphelein*: *l.* 8, indicating those who hold debts of 200 dr., or bundles thereof.

gods of *hiera* money, and the *polis* of its *hosia* money, by eliminating, in effect, the penalties accruing to unpaid debts owed to the public treasury:[4]

> Τιμοκράτης οὑτοσὶ τοσοῦθ ' ὑπερεῖδεν ἅπαντα τὰ πράγματα, ὥστε τίθησι τουτονὶ τὸν νόμον, δι ' οὗ τῶν ἱερῶν μὲν χρημάτων τοὺς θεούς, τῶν ὁσίων δὲ τὴν πόλιν ἀποστερεῖ κτλ.
>
> [This Timokrates overlooked all affairs to the extent that he proposes this very law by which he would deprive the gods of their *hiera* money, and the *polis* of its *hosia* money . . .]

Tellingly, Demosthenes does not claim that the gods will be deprived of any *hosia* money, even though their worship would presumably benefit from it (as the Ikarian account's likely pairing of *hiera* and *hosia* naturally would suggest), and so he appears to be making a claim that is strictly correct insofar as the matter of legal ownership of the funds involved goes: the gods own that which is *hiera*, but the *polis* owns that which is *hosia*, even if *hosia* funds benefit the gods.[5] It is a distinction that Demosthenes maintains throughout the speech, the only surviving piece of classical literature to raise the issue, and amplifies the difference between the two categories by claiming that unpaid debts of *hiera*

4. Dem. 24.9.
5. Extracted from a slightly longer sentence, the portion quoted above also served as a convenient expression of the relationship of *hiera* and *hosia* in at least one strain of a later lexicographic tradition: Herrenius Philo *De Diversis Verborum Significationibus* s.v. ὅσια; [Ammonius] *De Adfinum Vocabulorum Differentia* no. 358; Rhetorica Anonyma περὶ τῶν σχημάτων τοῦ λόγου vol. 3 of L. Spengel *Rhetores Graeci* (Leipzig: 1856), p. 120, *ll.* 26–31. Harpokration (s.v. ὅσιον; = Photios o352; Souda s.v. ὅσιον) explicitly acknowledges the value of Demosthenes' speech on this issue but quotes another passage (24.120) in illustration.

Within the anonymous late antique commentaries to one of the rhetorical works of Hermogenes (C. Walz *Rhetores Graeci* vol. 3 [Stuttgart and Tübingen: 1834]), *De Figuris in Libris*, a scholiast penned κατ ' ἄθροισιν εἰς μερισμόν· τῶν μὲν ἱερῶν χρημάτων τοὺς θεούς, τῶν ὁσίων δὲ τοὺς οἰχομένους ἀποστερεῖ. The passage bears some resemblance to that of Demosthenes 24.9, but it is very difficult to imagine that τὴν πόλιν has simply been replaced by the far more restrictive τοὺς οἰχομένους. Since this entry follows immediately after comments on Thucydides, the obvious question is whether the scholiast or his source has hit on another classical passage that has not yet (for us) been identified. If so, one of the orators might be a good candidate. The entry makes very good sense on its own since the verb οἴχεσθαι can be used to describe men on an embassy (e.g., *IG* I[3] 61, *l.* 51). Other orators certainly drew the distinction, as Harpokration (s.v. ὅσιον) quotes Isocrates (7.66), Hypereides (fr. 32 Jensen), and others (secondarily through Didymos of Alexandria) in this regard. As quoted earlier in this chapter, a scholiast to Aristophanes (Σ Ar. *Av.* 1541bα Holwerda) states that the *naukraroi* funded sacred embassies to Delphi. On the possible equation between *hosia* funds and the earlier "naukraric silver," see chapter 6.

incurred a ten-fold penalty while those of *hosia* were only doubled.[6] That *hiera* funds should at all be an issue must only reflect the collection of debts or levy of penalties for severe crimes, which, as shown in the previous chapter, required the public treasury to collect the debt and then turn over a special tithe (*epidekaton*) to Athena as the goddess' *hiera* money. But those owing such funds would be the magistrates responsible for auctioning off the property of the condemned, not the condemned themselves who would likely be in exile or sentenced to death. Unless we are to imagine that even in the mid-fourth century the Athenians imposed fines like that in the fifth-century Phaselis Decree noted earlier, whose only penalty was a monumental fine accruing to Athena wholly, Demosthenes would appear to exaggerate his case greatly by intimating that Timokrates' law would benefit those punished with paying such fines (but for which there is precious little other evidence in this later period).

While his treatment of *hiera* wealth may reflect some rhetorical excess, Demosthenes treats the matter of *hosia* funds in an apparently different manner. Demosthenes consistently labels funds owed to the public treasury not as *dêmosia* (he never employs the term in this way) but as *hosia*, even though he claims that the *polis*, bereft of those *hosia* funds, would be unable to meet its most basic functions of payment to jurors and the like.[7] Each of those outlays should naturally have been paid with *dêmosia* funds since they have nothing to do with the gods. While it might serve his case to exaggerate the effects of the proposal by collapsing some distinctions and making it appear as if funds for the gods were especially threatened (or that certain quotidian functions of government were more sanctioned than they were in truth, as the use of the term *hosia* would imply), Demosthenes would likely not go so far in his examples as

6. Dem. 24.11; 82; 111; 112; 130; 137. Penalties: 82–83, 111–12, 130; cf. 120, 128–30. Papazarkadas (2011), 67, objects that it would be wrong to take Demosthenes at face value on a ten-fold penalty since the evidence for most leases points only to the two-fold penalty and such a high fine would surely dissuade any potential lessor from taking up a lease. Papazarkadas, however, fails to recognize the difference between *hosia* and *hiera* wealth (as noted earlier in this chapter) and so misapplies the evidence for *hosia* to the category of *hiera*, which, exactly as he senses, was not to be leased given the very severe penalty for those who insisted on doing so but failed to make due payment. A much more cogent objection even on that basis, however, would seem implicit in his having identified *Agora* XIX P26, *ll.* 506–11, as an instance where a man was fined only a two-fold penalty for having failed to return *hiera* money to the tribe that entrusted it to him. But here it is clearly a case of a tribe and not the *polis* as it is in Demosthenes' attack on Timokrates. Moreover, the inscription declares that the *hiera* money belonged to the tribe of Aiantis and not to any god or even to the tribe's eponymous hero, Ajax. Therefore, all that this text shows us is that the two levels of the state could treat *hiera* wealth rather differently with respect to penalties, but in no way does it even suggest that Demosthenes' citation of the ten-fold penalty for debts on *hiera* owed to gods at the level of the *polis* is anything but perfectly accurate.

7. E.g., Dem. 24.99.

to render his case absurdly in error.[8] The orator does not merely substitute *hosia* for *dêmosia* everywhere. Throughout the speech, Demosthenes clearly acknowledges that the debts in question are owed either to the gods (as *hiera* funds) or to the public treasury, but he emphasizes by his frequent citation of the debtors' legal position that the debts with which he is practically more concerned are those owed directly to the public treasury.[9] The only solution by which the two implicit claims, namely, that the funds owed are either *hosia* or *dêmosia*, might be reconciled is to assume once again that *hosia* funds are derived from those that are, in origin, *dêmosia* and that Demosthenes has here employed the more emotionally charged term to cover them both. As for the origin of those public debts, Demosthenes does not describe how they might have arisen, whether by fines (as with *hiera*, surely) or some other method, but his speech in no way precludes that the debts originated either in loans of money, such as those offered by the *hieropoioi* of Nemesis, or from leases of land. As Demosthenes characterizes it, debts owed to the *dêmosion* would, with his opponent's plan, diminish the money accruing as *hosia* not necessarily in the form of lost principal but in the form of lost penalties when payments were late or not paid at all. The speech thus leaves open whether some debts might have been owed for which *hosia* was (notionally) lent out in principal and payable to the public treasury, or that they were merely contracted on *dêmosia* lent as principal, but which incurred the same penalty as *hosia*. The latter option is more difficult to accept since there is no evidence that *dêmosia* as an explicit category of funds was ever lent. On Demosthenes' logic, therefore, it can fairly be said that *hosia* simply encompasses, at a minimum, funds that *originated* as *dêmosia*, but without any further elaboration on when and how the financial structures necessary for that branching took shape institutionally. Since such

8. Since laws concerning murder, for example, were considered *hosia* (see Rudhardt [1992], 30–31 and 33–34), it is conceivable that the pay for jurors was labeled *hosia* by extension, and so, too, with the other kinds of state payments that Demosthenes claims would be threatened by lack of that kind of income. As noted earlier (see chapter 6 n. 7), the *kôlakretai* were in charge of paying jurors prior to their abolition, after which that and other such expenditures fell to the *hellenotamiai* for the brief period commencing in 411/10 when they then had control over the public treasury and prior to their abolition at the defeat of Athens, for which see Samons (2000), 259–60 and 274–75. Shortly after the reestablishment of the democracy, the Athenians situated the *tamiai* of Athena over a very large fund that at least partly covered these kinds of expenditures (explicitly attested for the inscription of *stêlai*, but not for jury pay); see ns. 39 and 42 below. While one should not in the least dismiss a priori the possibility that technical, administrative concerns drove these various arrangements, it seems well within the realm of possibility that the expenditures were *hosia* and not *dêmosia*, and thus deserving of a higher order of managerial oversight than usual.

9. Dem. 24.45 (gods or *dêmosion*), 50, 54, 71–72, 79, 123, 168, 200. A law inserted in the text at 22 also specifies particular crimes whose payments in "*hierai drakhmai*" were payable to Athena; cf. *IG* I^3 59 and chapter 5, n. 24.

debts could arise also from failure to pay rent on leased property, *hosia* could in principle apply equally well to real property as to money. In other words, the *hosia* designation might generally attach to any property that was collected or designated and then set aside for some limited set of "sanctioned" purposes.

The derivative nature of *hosia* money suggests that the public treasury need not have supported religious life directly through expenditure of *dêmosia* funds and so routed income from taxes and other sources in this manner, although it might have done so on occasion. The documents and texts discussed hitherto illuminate how the *polis*, tribe, or deme might also supply still other resources or money that the magistrates, including sacred treasurers of one or another sort, would then exploit in particular ways to generate, in effect, steady profits for the cult over a longer period of time. The money or those resources must fall in the category of *hosia* since, as the accounts show, they cannot also be *dêmosia* though originally derived from it, and as has been shown throughout this chapter, clearly *hosia* could not be described as falling into the static, terminal category of *hiera*. In other words, the principle that one can detect underlying these various sources is that that which was *hosia* was supplied initially by the *polis* (or its constituent parts acting on their own authority and initiative) and managed by it (or them) thereafter on behalf of a god as money or resources kept distinct from that which was *dêmosia*, whether in physically separate treasuries or in different accounts and the like. The *hosia* money in the case of Ikarion, to cite one earlier case, thus might well have emanated from the Ikarian public treasury, whereas the money transferred to the *hieropoioi* of Nemesis c. 500 might well have come from that pan-Athenian public treasury, and after which it might well have functioned as *hosia* funds.

Further Specialization in Hosia

Within the field of *hosia*-centered administration, two large classes of operation are nevertheless easy to discern, one of which concerns loans of money, the other the lease of land or other real property. With respect to loans, of which Nemesis' marble account is the earliest evidence known, many generic aspects of the operation remain unknown.[10] But it is clear enough that the relevant

10. One obvious reason for our ignorance is that since the gods and their treasurers were always, it appears, in the position of creditor and never as debtors they produced for posterity only that information which was both relevant to the general conduct of their loans and worthy of being inscribed on

treasurers served as creditors to other parties, most of whom must have been private individuals, from whom they collected interest at rates akin to those available commercially and over which they presumably retained full legal right to execute on default.[11] Similar legal rights are easier to identify with respect to the leases of land (whether agricultural, residential, quarries, and the like) for which the treasurers set the contracts to last for lengthy periods of time (sometimes decades) and included strict guarantees that the land would be returned in a suitable condition (allowing it to be leased profitably again).[12] Although often termed "sacred land" by modern scholars without respect for the ambiguity of our texts, and implying perhaps that it was *hiera*, the land was likely *hosia* in all cases. Only a very small number of properties were considered *hiera* and so could not be cultivated or used under any circumstances.[13]

This other kind of property was to be left entirely alone, regardless of whether this consecration incidentally deprived a cult or, rather more exactly, its sacred treasurers of income to use on behalf of the worship of the gods. Especially fertile properties like the Sacred Orgas on the border of Eleusis with Megara was considered so inviolate that its perceived cultivation by Megarians was a major cause of friction before the Peloponnesian War and nearly caused

---

stone in the form of accounts, decrees relating to interest, and so on. Conversely, it was the debtors who would have had to supply information regarding surety, guarantors, and so on, and then only on ephemeral media (to be destroyed or cancelled on fulfillment of the loan). On the legal asymmetry between these parties, and some of the ramifications arising therefrom, see Finley (1985), 90–95.

11. Despite a number of problematic claims with regard to the economic ramifications of these loans and leases (especially on the matter of credit and its commercialization), Finley (1985), 88–100, remains a useful précis of the legal rights that demes as well as private groups are known to have possessed. One should note that since Finley the often vitriolic debate over credit in the ancient economy has largely avoided discussion of these loans and the financial structures of which they were a part: e.g., Cohen (1992) and, from the opposing view, Millett (1991) *passim*, but see especially Millett, 171–77.

12. Papazarkadas (2011) provides the most recent and most extensive treatment of Athenian sacred land, both *hosia* and *hiera*, but Lambert (1997) offers a still critical comprehensive treatment of the fourth-century leases or sales of land (known to scholars as the *rationes centesimarum*) administered by the *polis* on behalf of a number of deities or cult groups who received compensation for resources used in other ways. See also Williams (2011) and Horster (2004) for other recent advances in our knowledge. On some of the legal and economic practices of leasing sacred land in general, see also Osborne (1998).

13. Out of convenience alone, the land or other resources in question is customarily called "sacred" (or its equivalents in other modern languages), but the legal quality of the connection between a god and some real property is hardly explicit in our evidence. Was a god considered to be a legal owner of property who could, through its treasurers, actually alienate it by sale, gift, or transfer? Or did the *polis* assume, in effect, ownership of that nature and simply, through its same treasurers, execute those transactions, or was the *polis*' custody of a more limited nature? On these matters, Papazarkadas (2011), 1–15, offers an interesting (and bibliographically thorough) but largely inconclusive treatment, except that he believes that the gods were thought to own all of the land in question, which I hold must only have been the case with regard to that which was *hiera*.

war again in the mid-fourth century.[14] Fundamentally unlike the leasable properties, whose status as *hosia* is plausible but unattested, these other lands (which must have been very small in total extent) were explicitly labeled as *hiera*.[15] In point of fact, the question that the Athenians posed to Apollo concerning the Orgas in the mid-fourth century illustrates abundantly well the difference between *hiera* and *hosia*, and with what seriousness the Athenians approached the matter:[16]

γρά[ψαι δὲ τὸ]ν γραμματέα τῆς βουλῆς εἰς δύο κα-
[ττ]ιτέρω ἴσω καὶ [ὁμοίω, εἰς μὲν] τὸν ἕτερον, εἰ λῶιον καὶ ἄμει-
[νό]ν ἐστι τῶι δήμ[ωι τῶι Ἀθηναίων μισ]θοῦν τὸμ βασιλέα τὰ νῦ-
[ν ἐ]νειργασμ[έ]να [τῆς ἱερᾶς ὀργάδος τὰ ἐκ]τὸς τῶν ὅρων εἰς οἰ-
[κ]οδομίαν τοῦ προ[στώιου καὶ ἐπισκευὴν το]ῦ ἱεροῦ τοῖν θεο-
ῖν· εἰς δὲ τὸν ἕτερον κ[α]ττίτ[ερον, εἰ λῶιον καὶ ἄμει]νόν ἐστι
τῶι δήμωι τῶι Ἀθηναίων τὰ ν[ῦν ἐκτὸς τῶ]ν ὅ[ρων ἐ]νειργ[α]σμέν-
α τῆς ἱερᾶς ὀργάδος ἐᾶν ἄνετα [τοῖν θ]εοῖν·

[The secretary of the Boule is to inscribe on two (pieces) of tin that are equal and alike, on one: "If it is more agreeable and better for the Demos of the Athenians that the (*arkhôn*) *basileus* lease out the land of the Hiera Orgas that has been worked recently outside of the boundary markers for the construction of a *prostoion* and the equipping of the shrine of the Two Goddesses." On the other: "If it is more agreeable and better for the Demos of the Athenians that the land of the Hiera Orgas that has been worked recently beyond the boundary markers be left uncultivated for the Two Goddesses."]

---

14. Fifth century: Thuc. 1.139.2. Harding (1994), 126–27, provides a reconstruction of the events and a more thorough appraisal of the evidence than can be offered here, but see now the more detailed analysis offered by Papazarkadas (2011), 244–59.

15. Reflecting also the fourth-century concern with raising income for religious purposes, the *Rhet. ad Alex.* 1425b19–25 states that it was common for communities to raise money by selling or leasing land that is neglected (τόπους τινὰς δημοσίους ἀμελουμένους) but not consecrated to the gods (τοῖς θεοῖς ἐξαιρετόν). Elsewhere (as in the roughly contemporary *IG* II^2 47), the term ἐξαιρεῖν was also used only very occasionally as a technical term in sacral finance (in this text, for income derived from a quarry consecrated to Asklepios); cf. Wilhelm (1942), 110. Likewise, the ps.-Aristotelian text *Oec.* 1346b13–20 points to the example of the people of Byzantion who sold or leased public and "cultic" (θιασωτικά)—but not necessarily sacred (*hiera*)—plots of land for varying lengths of time depending on their productivity.

16. *IG* II^2 204 (= Rhodes/Osborne 58; *I.Eleusis* 144), with Papazarkadas (2011), 244–59. The text explicitly identifies the territory as *hiera* (ἱερὰ ὀργάς): *ll.* 8, 16, 26 [restored], 69, 74.

The choice submitted to Apollo's decision allows for no middle ground: either the land that was currently, and quite illegally, being worked was to be let out formally so as to produce rental income, which could be directed then to construction projects at the shrine of Eleusis, or it would be permanently taken out of cultivation and fully consecrated to the Two Goddesses. Without deploying the discrete terms of *hiera* and *hosia*, the question put to Apollo nevertheless gives a remarkably clear description of what can only be these two categories. This oracular inquiry reminds us again that the term *hosia* signifies merely that which is "sanctioned" by the appropriate authority. In short, the Athenians applied the same basic distinctions to land as to money.

Both leases and loans were administered in a lucrative manner in several different ways that sometimes commingled with one another. In some cases, the deme or *polis* might direct the treasurers to use one kind of fiscal instrument to generate capital for the other, usually leases so as to provide capital for loans.[17] This kind of tactically bifurcated fiscal strategy is evident already in the inscribed accounts for the tiny deme of Plotheia (c. 420), which was able to engage in both leases and interest-bearing loans, and the monies that they generated for its religious festivals are impressive, for the sums available for lending (and in all but one case directed to specific festivals) mounted to 22,100 *drakhmai* for expenditures of perhaps two thousand *drakhmai*.[18] The costs, and opportunities, for other demes of far greater size must have been correspondingly significant. The common goal for which these various methods were applied was to provide as much regular income as could be had to purchase as many animals as possible, whose sacrifice would provide for a great banquet for all the people who made up that community. While Isokrates, furthermore, explicitly states that such leases *directly* supported a cult's sacrificial banquet (*hestiasis*), his audience can hardly have expected anything else.[19] Out of the many

17. For example, the deme Halai Aixonides (*IG* II² 2492, *ll.* 31–47, of 345/4) decreed that a number of (unproductive) olive trees be cut down from land (known by the name Phelleis and of unclear religious status, but possibly linked to Hebe, *l.* 22) then under a forty-year lease. The cut wood was to be auctioned to provide capital with which to make loans equivalent to 12 percent per annum, the proceeds of which would in turn be deducted from the amount owed on the lease.

18. *IG* I³ 258. Whitehead (1986), 166–69, and followed by Millet (1991), 173–74. The one exception noted above is that of the 5,000 dr. for *ateleia* (i.e., tax-immunity). This *ateleia* is surely a safeguard for those other funds lest the deme vote honors to someone such as would cost it future capital that it otherwise would have gained through tax (but nowhere mentioned in the inscription). Blok (2010), 75, acknowledges that the term ought to indicate tax-immunity (as it does everywhere else) but suggests unpersuasively that the fund was to be used by the *dêmarkhoi* to defray "unexpected collective expenses."

19. Isoc. 7.29. Rosivach (1994), 54–55, takes this passage as evidence that such leases (ἀπὸ μισθωμάτων) were a mainstay of earlier Attic practice.

preserved leases, some go so far as to state that their explicit purpose is to provide income for these sacrificial banquets.[20] That purpose is likely implicit in the great majority of other cases since the demes would have had little need for anything else other than that which served their religious life. The Ikarian accounts, too, are paired with a decree concerning the deme's financial support and organization of major sacrifices and banquets, whose expenses Blok suggests were to be backed by the *hosia* funds.[21] Of course, we cannot forget that, as shown in chapter 3, politically ambitious men were still offering in this era their own banquets parallel to those of tribes and demes in time-honored tradition. It is remarkable that the *polis* never required those wealthy men to stage a deme's sacrifices, say, as a liturgy.

In short, these various texts point to the complex and robust array of methods by which Athenians funded much of their religious life, or at least one of its most costly dimensions, that of sacrifice. It is not difficult to grasp the principles by which the Athenians conceived of the three categories of property under their collective control. In no instance is there evidence that the money generated ever reverted back to the public treasury as *dêmosia*. This money did not go back to repay, in effect, the treasury (or coffers of a deme, and so on) for the seed money that the relevant institution had earlier provided. Once earmarked as *hosia* or as *hiera*, any and all money or other property retained that designation and could not, it would seem, be put to a use inconsistent with that designation insofar as these various properties remained under the stewardship of the appropriate authority. Since *hosia* money was meant to be spent on sacrifice and the like, that concept would be easy enough to apply since it became *idia* (private) as soon as it entered the hands, say, of a man selling goats for sacrifice—but only then. Of course, if *hosia* money was used to commission a dedication to a god on behalf of the Boule, for example, it would ultimately be turned into a form of *hiera* wealth, minus that amount due to those fashioning and transporting the object, and so on. Wealth in that form, too, would not reenter the fiscal picture since it could not become *hosia* or *dêmosia*: it belonged permanently to the deity in question.

With regard to the public treasury, such a transfer of funds (or even its mere designation) was similarly permanent, so that that which was marked as *hosia* remained such and did not, it seems, become *dêmosia*, while that which be-

---

20. For example, a lease of a quarry for Herakles in Akris (*SEG* 26.134, of 332/1) directs the money to be used for a sacrifice (in the sanctuary of Theseus by the demesmen of Eleusis).
21. *IG* I³ 254. Blok (2010), 82–87.

came *hiera* all the more so could not become *hosia*, *dêmosia*, or of course *idia* (private) since it was not meant to be spent and could not, it seems, have its sanctity reduced. In ascending levels of importance and sanctity, these three categories of non-private wealth—*dêmosia*, *hosia*, *hiera*—therefore stood in a kind of fiscal hierarchy with regard to one another. But the financial tasks incumbent in *hosia* property, as has been evident throughout this chapter, were markedly different from those for *hiera*, which required almost no financial management but the most basic accounting and inventorying such as was the province of the *tamiai* of Athena. Consequently, the special loans of *hiera* for Nemesis in the mid-fifth century are best understood as hallmarks of a transitional period in which *hiera* had not come to mean a universally untouchable type of wealth as it was understood in the era when specialization in loans and leases reached its apogee. With that specialization came even greater numbers of sacred treasurers whose activities are documented only in relation to the property that they managed on behalf of the gods.

The Boule and the Funding of Athena Polias' Cult

Notwithstanding the abundance of evidence for *hosia* property as support for many lesser Athenian deities, there is next to no evidence concerning such holdings for the major gods and their cults, especially for what was surely the wealthiest and most important deity, Athena Polias. This constitutes a major problem in need of resolution, for if *hosia* was not used for Athena, then how did the Athenians fund her cult? And would the answer alter the essential contours of what we might now consider the likely historical development of sacred property in Athens?

Once again, it is fortunate that her financial affairs are at least sufficiently knowable in other respects to allow some attempt at a general understanding of what is likely to have been the means by which the Athenians funded her cult, and by extension perhaps the other major cults of the Athenian pantheon. Apart from the fines and penal sources of income, discussed in the last chapter, which likely accrued only to the goddess' *hiera* property in the control of her *tamiai*, it is especially difficult to identify what presumably ought to have been very extensive *hosia* properties. Notwithstanding Papazarkadas' recent survey of properties that are known to have belonged to Athena in the fifth and fourth centuries, they appear to have been quite minor in scale, even in comparison with the holdings of noticeably lesser deities like Artemis Agrotera.[22] Athena's properties appear to have been simply incapable of funding the customary round of sacrifices owed to her, quite apart from anything as major and costly as a Panathenaia. Even the most promising, though fragmentary, *stêlê* listing dozens of leases for land belonging to the gods in 343/2 contains no sign that Athena owned or benefited from any such property, although it includes her name prominently fixed in the heading of the text.[23] In principle, it is quite possible that once extensive epigraphic evidence for numerous properties of Athena has simply vanished, but it is nevertheless surprising that to date nothing has turned up for this wealthiest of Athenian gods.

Part of the difficulty may be that the relevant properties functioned on an entirely different basis than the leases whose documentation, though very fragmentary, does survive in relative abundance. Athena's own olive trees need not constitute leasable property but could certainly provide income. Although modern scholars have usually considered these trees to have been especially sacred to Athena (and thus *hiera* by implication), the few ancient sources relevant to this question suggest that even if that were true for some individual trees it did not necessarily apply to the whole class of trees, or at least the income produced by the trees' oil. After all, it is not at all assured that the oil supplied for the Panathenaic prize amphorae must also have been *hiera* even if the trees were, much less that *hiera* oil could be given away at all, even to victors in Athena's contests.[24] While the groves do not seem to have contained signifi-

22. Papazarkadas (2011), 18–22, 26–27.

23. *Agora* XIX L6, *ll.* 2–3: ʾΕπὶ Πυθοδότου [ἄρχοντος . . . c. 45 . . .] | [ʾΑ]θηνᾶς Πολιάδο[ς . . . c. 51..]. In republishing the text in the *Agora* volume, Langdon does not accept the earlier suggestion of Walbank (1983), 115, that the following lacuna might have continued [καὶ τῶν ἄλλων θεῶν]; cf. Williams (2011) on her fr. a of "Stele I" of four that she now identifies as constituting a series of inscriptions occasioned by a general reform of sacred finances c. 346/5). Of note also is the proposal by the seer Lampon, offered in the context of a reform of the sacral administration of Eleusis (*IG* I^3 78 [= *I.Eleusis* 28a], *ll.* 59–60), to investigate whether *aparkhai* should be collected of olive oil just as was collected of barley and grain (for which see the discussion in chapter 4). Nothing further is known of the effort, but, as Papazarkadas (2011), 276–77, rightly points out, the *aparkhai* would surely be due to Athena and not to Demeter and Kore. Moreover, Papazarkadas makes the interesting suggestion that this decree would have placed the *tamiai* of Athena in much the same position as the *hieropoioi* of Eleusis. If so, then we would not only have more evidence for the close typological relationship between these two boards but also evidence for an attempt at reversing the use of the *tamiai* earlier in the fifth century as a model for the *hieropoioi*, which I discussed in chapter 4.

24. In its note concerning the collection of the oil, *Ath.Pol.* (60.1 [= Pollux 8.87, 8.93], 60.3) never employs the vocabulary of sanctity in relation to these olives and their oil. Accused of harming such a tree, the defendant of Lysias 7 (who, likewise, employs neither *hiera* nor *hosia*) claims (4) that such olives (*moriai*) grew on privately owned land that the *polis* had sold after having confiscated it, and that the land subsequently was leased to a variety of individuals, including a freedman. It is difficult to imagine that the *polis* would ever alienate that property, or allow it to be owned privately, which it

cantly more trees than those required to supply the fifteen hundred to twenty-one hundred amphorae regularly awarded as prizes in the Greater Panathenaia in the fourth century, they would conceivably have been available to produce income for Athena's cult in years outside of the festival cycle, though this might not have been true much before the late fifth century.[25] As noted earlier, the disbursements handled by the *tamiai* in the late fifth century for the Greater Panathenaia amounted to about nine *talents* on each of two occasions, giving us thereby some rough indicator of what that festival must have cost. This figure, strikingly, seems well within range of what one could expect to receive from the (hypothetical) sale of surplus oil gathered in those years that did not directly supply the prizes. At least from the turn of the fourth century, there seems to have been enough sacred and private trees together to overcome the olive's own strong tendency toward biennial fruiting, which significantly reduces yield every other year.[26] Moreover, it is well within the realm of possibility that the sale

---

determined or was commonly known to possess such trees unless their degree of sanctity allowed such an act. Thus, Foxhall (2007), 118–21, argues that each enclosure constituted a "mini-*temenos*," while Papazarkadas (2011), 264–66, characterizes them as possessing a "haphazard distribution" across Attica that nevertheless received frequent inspections by special magistrates (ἐπιγνώμονες) by at least the beginning of the fourth century (when, too, the death penalty for serious offenses against the trees had also been changed to exile and loss of one's property). In her attempt to reconcile the seemingly conflicting evidence between Lysias and *Ath.Pol.* 60.2 concerning punishment for harm to the trees (exile and confiscation of property, and death [thus later altered to exile], respectively), Horster (2006) denies that the trees were secularized somewhat by the time of *Ath.Pol.* and thus rejects its evidence without demonstrating that the trees were in fact *hiera*. If we are to take seriously *Ath.Pol.*s' claim (60.2) that the Areiopagos once punished offenses of damage against the trees as carrying the death penalty but later altered that to exile, then we would have good reason to think that the sanctity of the trees was downgraded over time, hence occasioning the offense of sacrilege to be altered to one of damage (i.e., to *hosia* property) and meriting a lesser, though still severe, penalty. See also Todd (2007), 484 n. 30 on the economics of that change, and 477–540 with extensive commentary, text, and translation.

25. Based on the number of amphorae cited by a fragmentary inscription listing panathenaic prizes (*IG* II^2 2311, with text of J. Shear [2003]), Papazarkadas (2011) estimates that the festival required 1,200–2,150 amphorae and adds that (apparently hewing to the high end of that range) nearly 200,000 trees would be required (covering some 56.8km^2, but including, he concedes, a great number of trees that cannot also have been sacred). However, it should be noted that Papazarkadas, 269, dates the text to 391/0 and that this list shows a doubling of the prizes over what they had been even in the late fifth century (as *IG* I^3 1386 reveals; see Papazarkadas, 268–69). A relatively conservative estimate is that of Bentz (1998), who estimates the number of amphorae for the Greater Panathenaia at 1,500. Using Foxhall's (2007), 117–18, assumptions and the data provided by Shear on the number of amphorae in *IG* II^2 2311 (she estimates a maximum of 2,100 amphorae), Bentz's estimate would require only as many as c. 74,000–88,000 trees (covering, if massed together, c. 674–944ha). That estimate applies only to the fourth century, and it is not out of the question that the Athenians expanded (by grafting) the number of sacred olive trees to meet this demand, supplementing the sacred oil with high quality private oil from the market until the young trees could fully contribute.

26. With regard to the number of trees, see n. 25 above. On biennial fruiting, see Foxhall (2007), 7–9. Data concerning prices in classical Athens simply do not survive in any statistically meaningful quantity, and so to determine the likely price range for the trees' oil in years when it was not collected

of such oil would have been sufficient to cover, if not to defray, in any significant manner the aggregate expenses of all the goddess' festivals, such as the Lesser Panathenaia, which must have cost several more *talents*. One must always bear in mind, nonetheless, the possibility of severe drought, depression of prices for Attic oil, and other factors that would further lower the possible value of whatever oil could be put onto the market. In such instances, the Boule would have had to provide for significant funding on an emergency basis if it was not the regular practice of that body to make up for any and all shortfall. Although it is conceivable that a change in the management of the sacred olive trees for the express purpose of producing such oil occasioned the change in their legal status to a type of *hosia* property, there is simply no direct evidence that the Athenians did sell off the olive oil in order to raise *hosia* income for Athena, though this seems plausible enough.[27] In short, the absence of clear evidence for significant holdings of *hosia* money intended for Athena's worship, or land or other resources meant to support her cult—by far the most costly of Athens—seems surprising.

For those reasons, we might hypothesize that the cult's expenses were met by much more direct means than appears to be the case for those smaller cults

for the Panathenaia is an almost insoluable problem, in no small part because of our complete inability to measure the relevant price trends over time. Nevertheless, as to whether the oil in question could possibly have reached nine *talents* at all, an interesting proxy are the figures from independent Delos (307–167) as assembled and indexed by Reger (1994). Those figures show considerable fluctation amidst a decline in prices over that period. If we were to take the highest known prices (4.5 Attic dr./*khous*), which are very near also the earliest recorded (304/3: see Reger, 295), as the basis for testing whether Panathenaic oil could have supplied the nine *talents*—thus, using the highest known figure in a sort of "devil's advocacy" to test the hypothesis that the oil could not have supplied this sum—then at the rate of twelve *khoes* to the amphora, the 1,500 amphorae (i.e., as per Bentz's low estimate, for which see n. 25 above) would have a value of 81,000 dr., or thirteen and one-half *talents*, while that of Papazarkadas at 2,150 amphorae begets a value of 116,100 dr., or nineteen and one-third *talents*. Thus, at a price of even three dr./*khous* the oil could have supplied the sum of nine *talents* even on Bentz's low estimate.

However, with biennial fruiting, we must also average in the low yields (i.e., approximately half of the high yield, I assume). With that factor in mind, each estimate should over the course of any two successive years (and assuming, also, both the same price as used above from Delos in 304/3 and maximal oil yield with respect to each part of the cycle) be lowered by 25 percent: Bentz's figures correspond to 60,750 dr. (just over ten *talents*), while Papazarkadas' provide 87,075 dr. (fourteen and one-half *talents*). Even if one were then to cut the notional price of olive oil in half again simply for the sake of argument, it remains clear that a sale of such quantity of oil every year could supply the majority of what was needed to fund the Panathenaia.

27. In accord with Papazarkadas' discussion (n. 25 above), there appears to have been a significant change in the production of olive oil that the Athenians mandated in the late 390s. Moreover, he suggests (2011), 275–76, that to meet this demand the Athenians took a tithe of private olive oil for the panathenaic prizes, and no longer collected the oil simply from the most sacred trees (the *moriai*), whose status as *hiera* (as I take it) remained assured, 277–84, despite the lessening of punishments at about this time, 265–66.

whose accounts do occasionally survive. Why this question is so important for the story of Athens' sacred treasurers arises from a likely correlation between control over particular kinds of property and the prestige that a sacred treasurer enjoyed—matters central to understanding Solon's impact on these offices and indeed on the religious life of Athens more broadly. With regard to that connection, one cannot discount how different the administration of Athena's cult and properties was from those of other, lesser gods about which we have some information. In no way does our evidence, for one thing, even broker the possibility that Athena's sacred treasurers might have loaned out her money to private parties as did those serving the lesser goddess Nemesis. The more revealing point of comparison, nonetheless, is Delian Apollo, whose wealth, cultic importance, and position within the framework of Athens' imperial ideology in the fifth century render the god a close peer of Athena, but whose diversity and sophistication of financial operations constitute a significant difference.

That difference, moreover, is one for which the Athenians alone were responsible since, as V. Chankowski has recently shown in abundant detail, it was they who established quite rapidly a relatively elaborate and efficient structure of financial administration that was centered, ultimately, on cultivating *hosia* income for the cult of Apollo through a wide array of loans and leases. That development, on Chankowski's reading of the evidence, only commenced some time after 454, when the Athenians moved the treasury of the Delian League from Delos to Athens and integrated it partially with the domestic financial structures of Athens, properly speaking.[28] Yet Chankowski argues that it was the first-fruits (*aparkhê*) siphoned from allied tribute from 478 to 454 that, minus the expenses for certain major temples and related sacred structures, provided the capital (c. fifty *talents*, less true reserves of c. five *talents*) that then generated what I would categorize as *hosia* wealth.[29] Her proposal thus gives rise to an obvious and interesting dilemma. Since the *aparkhê* was treated by the Athenians in other cases as *hiera* wealth wholly and exclusively, if the Athenians designated such property as *hosia* (though the word is unattested in the relevant Delian and Athenian texts) that act would undoubtedly constitute a counter-example to the principle that *hiera* was a static category that admitted no reduction of sanctity and no management beyond guardianship. Either

28. On the circumstances of the move and its date, see, for example, Samons (2000); Chankowski (2008), 37–39; see also chapter 4, n. 56.
29. Chankowski (2008), 32–44, 317–23.

Chankowski must be wrong about the origin of the funds in question or we have before us a possible, and important, instance where the Athenians made a very different choice about the monies under their control that belonged ostensibly to the gods, for which Nemesis does provide a compelling parallel.

Given that the transfer of the treasury remains largely obscure to us except for the profound nature of its consequences for Athenian imperial ambition, it is conceivable that either alternative might be correct, and that the Athenians committed themselves to a remarkable act: either they made an exception for Apollo (and must have believed that they had the god's blessing to do so) or they provided some other (surely very expensive) means or capital by which the *hosia* funds could be generated.[30] Although both options cannot simultaneously be accepted, either must have been irregular and demanded by the unique circumstances that the move presented commensurate with the capacity of the Athenians to make choices about the property in their care. The abundant documentation relating to Apollo's property reveals that, notwithstanding inevitable differences in administrative technique and protocols, the god's sacred treasurers operated on broadly similar lines to their peers in purely Attic cults. As Chankowski suggests, the fact that many of the Delian texts were discovered only in Athens (such as the earliest known, which documents leases and loans to individuals spanning 434/3–431/0) or have duplicates in both locations argues for close interest by the Boule and Ekklesia in the management of Apollo's property. Thus, differences in how the colleges published the data for which they were responsible, some of which Chankowski details there, is not easily attributed to neglect or accident.[31] In other words, there is no obvious administrative reason why Apollo's cult should have been managed so differently from that of Athena. That the Athenians chose to manage Apollo's wealth, and that of many other divinities, in such a manner underscores that by this point the Athenians possessed ample capacity and experience to do the same for Athena,

30. Chankowski (2008), 41, notes further that 454/3 marks an administrative rupture between two colleges of magistrates that had handled affairs for Apollo, the *hellenotamiai* and the *amphiktyones*. After 454/3 it was the *amphiktyones* who managed the *hosia* properties for Apollo, while the *hellenotamiai* handled the *aparkhai* for Athena (instead of Apollo as had likely been the case since 478/7). Each college thus operated at the apex of sacral finance but on wholly different lines. While the nomenclature of the *amphiktyones* is redolent of ancestral claims of authority, Chankowski, 44–49, points out that there is no evidence that any such league (i.e., an Amphiktyoneia), of which these sacred treasurers would ostensibly have been representative (as with Apollo's shrine at Delphi), ever existed. Was such legitimizing nomenclature intended to make up for the sheer novelty of just whatever it was that the Athenians decided to do with respect to the stewardship of Apollo's treasure?

31. Chankowski (2008), 144–45. Earliest text: *IG* I^3 402; = *ID* 89; Chankowski 1.

whose wealth and cultic demands were of the scale and complexity of Apollo's, but chose to provide for Athena's worship by quite different means.

Budgeting by Prytany?

With respect to Athena, one route by which to account for the apparent absence of major standing assets of *hosia* wealth that had to meet great costs is to consider whether the Boule met the needs of the goddess' cult by allocating *dêmosia* funds as *hosia* monies out of the public treasury on some sort of scheduled basis, whether annual or by one of the ten *prytany* months in the civic calendar, and if need be, on an emergency basis as well. In other words, the matter at hand is whether the Boule took primary (or exclusive) responsibility for earmarking funds for the cult and whether it made its budgetary allocations in such a manner that the process would also not produce any permanent documentation. The Boule's direct involvement would be eminently sensible given the significance of the goddess' worship to the life of the community, thus demanding and deserving the greatest level of official attention. Moreover, the scale of money involved would surely have invited such fraud, waste, and abuse as the Boule would find intolerable and dangerous. That the *tamiai* of the sacred treasure took custody over their charge in front of the Boule, as stated by *Ath. Pol.* (47.1), betokens that kind of oversight and involvement, as do the numerous decrees of the Boule concerning the finances and administration of cults of all sizes and financial needs.[32]

In his important work on ancient Athenian fiscal practices, M. Faraguna has suggested that the system of budgetary allocation known as *merismos* originated gradually well before it is first attested in 386, and he points in this regard to the decree of 418/7 (*IG* I^3 84, *ll.* 14–18) mandating that the *arkhôn basileus* lease out the shared *temenos* of Neleus, Basile, and Kodros so as to benefit their shrine, but that the rent be paid to the *apodektai* in charge of the public treasury, who then distributed it to the sacred treasurers responsible for the shrine: the *tamiai* of the Other Gods.[33] Furthermore, Faraguna suggests that no single law likely established the *merismos* itself but that the Boule conducted its allocation on the basis of an accumulation of laws, whose net effect was to provide

32. For a general assessment of the Boule's financial oversight, see Rhodes (1972), 88–113, especially 91–99.
33. Faraguna (1992), 180–81, 183. First attestation: *IG* II^2 29, *ll.* 18–23.

some stability even if there was no single, unitary legislation to follow. But we can go still farther back, I believe. Allocation of some portion of income as *hosia* as it was received by the Boule must mean that there had already been in place an institutional pathway by which all of the relevant magistrates would carry out their responsibilities with that money in a constitutional and orderly manner. Therefore, the *merismos* system itself might well have its own origins close to that of *hosia*, and therefore in the sixth century.

There are, of course, simply the logistical and accounting problems posed by the scale of funds required, most of all with regard to the Greater Panathenaia. Also in his speech against Timokrates, for example, Demosthenes records an incident where the funds were found to be grossly insufficient only weeks before the festival, and so the Boule empowered a special group of 1,001 jurors to convene with itself and promulgate any laws needed to ensure funding.[34] For reasons such as that, it should perhaps be no surprise that *Ath.Pol.* (43.6) notes that the Boule's regular agenda encompassed matters that were, aside from other things, *hiera* and *hosia*:[35]

> αἱ δὲ δύο περὶ τῶν ἄλλων εἰσίν, ἐν αἷς κελεύουσιν οἱ νόμοι τρία μὲν ἱερῶν χρηματίζειν, τρία δὲ κήρυξιν καὶ πρεσβείας, τρία δὲ ὁσίων
>
> [Two meetings (held each year) concern other matters, in which the laws instruct the heralds to inquire three times about *hiera*, three times about embassies, and three times about *hosia*.]

While *Ath.Pol.* does not specify that *hosia* here must perforce be limited to anything budgetary, we should not forget that it was the *kôlakretai* who once funded cults as well as sacred embassies at the direction of the *naukraroi*. Therefore, *Ath.Pol.*'s three categories could well be fully budgetary in nature. At the very least, the appearance of *hosia* here likely marks the opportunity granted to all Athenian citizens to raise questions or advance proposals that have at least something to do with the administration of *hosia* properties and all that that might entail.

With regard to how the Boule might have done this in practice, several points are in order. First of all, there can have been no special budget for *hiera*

34. Dem. 24.26–29, with Lewis (1959), 245–47.

35. Cf. Aeschin. 1.23; Pollux 8.96. No source elaborates further on what *hiera* and *hosia* meant in this particular context, for which see Rhodes (1993), 529.

since, as shown earlier, this was not an active fiscal category but rather a terminal one into which money might only rarely be allocated, since it would thereafter not be spent for any purpose.[36] In principle, therefore, the Boule would only have undertaken action regarding how much *dêmosia* funds to designate as *hosia* and for which cults, festivals, and the like. But a potentially significant problem facing the Boule at any moment was the availability of money, concerning which it may also be helpful to return briefly to the question of public debt raised by Demosthenes. From at least the late fifth century onward, the Boule is known to have supervised the collection of debts to the public treasury more broadly and punished defaulters by depriving them of full civic rights (the records of which were in the custody of the *tamiai* of Athena).[37] Irrespective of the origins of those debts, close supervision of the magistrates entrusted with collecting them would place the Boule in a strategic position to determine precisely what funds would in fact be available, and on what schedule they would become available, for any expenditure or schedule thereof. In principle, the Boule could earmark incoming *dêmosia* funds to serve as *hosia* funds upon collection and allocate those funds to specific outlays. There need be very little delay in making those allocations, carried out by the *kôlakretai* and later by others taking their place, once sufficient funds or indications of promised payment were available.

For some lesser religious ends, the allocation might well have been set annually, but given the extensive needs of Athena Polias and the other major gods, one can imagine that the allocation would probably be easier to handle on the basis of every *prytany*. The major quadrennial festivals would have required, by all rights, much greater planning over the longer term, and it is surely no accident that our two fifth-century texts recording loan-like transfers from the *tamiai* to the *hieropoioi* and *athlothetai* relate to stop-gap payments necessary to put on the Panathenaia. As argued in chapter 4, in those instances the most

36. Rosivach (1994), 116 n. 31, thus rightly notes that there is no evidence for a separate budget for *hiera* in the fourth century, contrary to Schlaifer's (1940), 233, contention that the budget for *hiera* and *hosia* were treated separately. Rosivach, nonetheless, may go too far in suggesting that Demosthenes' mention of what Rosivach takes to be a common administration (*dioikêsis*) in his speech against Timokrates (24.96–97) vitiates Schlaifer's argument. The mutually exclusive distinction of *hosia* from *hiera*, to be sure, seems to have broken down by the late Hellenistic period, so that in advancing that particular claim Schlaifer would rely too heavily on inscriptions (*IG* II^2 1035; 3503) denoting a separate administration for *hiera* (ἡ ἱερὰ διατάξις) that are far too late (first century BC) and evince too great a degree of change to be of much help with regard to the fourth century.

37. Drawing extensively (but not exclusively) on Demsothenes' speech (24) against Timokrates, Rhodes (1972), 148–51, discusses the extent and nature of the Boule's involvement with public debt. With regard to the documents themselves, see Fischer (2003), 239–40.

likely scenario is that another board, such as the *athlothetai*, could not make the necessary payments on relatively short notice, and so the *tamiai* fulfilled a special mandate of the Boule to act in that capacity uniquely.[38] If the income fell short for any outlay, accordingly, the Boule (or the magistrates to whom it delegated authority) would then have had to apportion the available funds accordingly, sometimes bypassing normal protocol if a board found itself without funds for some reason.[39] Several fourth-century inscriptions, moreover, show that it was these same *athlothetai* who were the magistrates enjoined with spending money granted by the Boule in order to fund the Greater Panathenaia.[40] In point of fact, this primary level of allocation and distribution, which the Athenians termed *merismos*, has long been identified as the operative principle by which the Athenians handled their budget in the fourth century (that is, aside from such entities as the so-called Theoric and Stratiotic funds), but its substantial connection with *hosia* funding for cults has remained obscure due to the lack of explicit testimony or documentation about those funds that are labeled as *hosia*.[41] Nevertheless, it seems clear enough that the Boule would surely have retained ultimate authority over *hosia* funds and directed boards to handle funds on an emergency basis without need of inscribed decree. It is likely for that reason, I suggest, that early in the fourth century the *tamiai* of Athena's *hiera* treasure were nevertheless put in charge of a ten *talent* fund from which, among many other things, the inscription of Athenian decrees could be funded.[42] Without recourse to this hypothesis, such duties would be difficult to

---

38. In discussing these very transactions, Pritchett (1977), 300–301, likewise draws out the fact that boards who found themselves without adequate funds but committed to expenditures in excess of what they did possess would have had to come forward and make known their difficulties. In addition, Pritchett points also to the account of 410/09 (*IG* I³ 375) as reflecting the decision to dispense income in a particular way as made by the Ekklesia, not just the Boule, if at all (*l.* 3: ἐκ τôν ἐπετείον φσεφισαμένο τõ δέμο).

39. This is known to have happened with respect to other boards of magistrates. For example, Henry (1982), 104–07, points out the function of paying for the inscription of decrees (normally in the fourth century the duty of the *tamias* of the Demos) could also be assumed by the *apodektai* in times of financial crisis so as to avoid delays with their *merismos*; the one known instance is a text from 386/5 (*IG* II² 31, *ll.* 14–17).

40. *IG* II² 212, 380, 784, 1060+1036. It is perhaps because the duties of the *athlothetai* grew so extensively that, as *Ath.Pol.* indicates, they thus transferred to the custody of the *tamiai* the sacred olive oil until it was needed to fill the amphorae given as prizes for victories won during the festival. This practice would seem to be reminiscent of the transfers or rerouting that the earlier texts reflect: *Ath.Pol.* 60.1 (= Pollux 8.87, 8.93), 60.3, with Nagy (1978); Rhodes (1993), 670–75; Foxhall (2007), 117–21.

41. Faraguna (1992), 179–83, provides what still remains the best overview of the *merismos* and its operation in the fourth century. On the major funds noted above, which clearly belong to the fourth century, and their relationship to the *merismos*, see Faraguna, 184–94.

42. On this particular fund, see Faraguna (1992), 187–94; Henry (1982); Rhodes (1972), 103 n. 7. The fund might not have been solely devoted to paying for such inscriptions, even though that is in fact

explain given how little connection the *tamiai* otherwise had to non-*hiera* wealth. Not only would such oversight by the Boule, in sum, explain the disbursements discussed earlier as constituting a response to administrative crises but it would also be consistent with the lack of permanent surviving documentation concerning *hosia* money used for Athena's cult.

One further issue to be worked out concerns the magistrates responsible for carrying out the allocations set by the Boule. In a number of instances, the *tamiai* of Athena were entrusted with fulfilling an uncustomary financial role, which tells us very little about what should normally have happened and whether any other sacred treasurers might have carried out the duties of receiving or transferring *hosia* money. If indeed there were no *hosia* properties that could be managed in such a way as to produce enough income to fulfill running festival needs, it is sensible that the *kôlakretai*, prior to being deprived of critical duties in 415 and then ultimately abolished in 411, took care of this task. Under the direct supervision of the Boule, the *kôlakretai* distributed the *hosia* money from the public treasury to the legion of sacred treasurers responsible for various cults or for various religious undertakings like sacred embassies, and so on. This would easily account for the amalgam of financial and religious tasks that the sources credit to the *kôlakretai*.[43] After the *kôlakretai*, and in turn the *hellenotamiai* in 404, were abolished, still other magistrates were available to take up that basic duty, and it is in the subsequent period, namely the fourth century, that the evidence points to the *apodektai* (whom, once more, Androtion or his excerptors understandably confused with the *kôlakretai* in the time of Kleisthenes) as the primary distributors.[44] Such an error might well reflect how early *hosia* wealth originated, but it is not difficult to imagine how the precise mechanics of this larger operation might have changed considerably over time, namely, with regard to how much physical coin had to be moved and whether the sacred treasurers could merely reconcile accounts with the treasury if it

the only purpose for which it is attested. Hansen (1991), 156, estimates that the Ekklesia passed nine to ten decrees per meeting, of which there were thirty to forty per annum (in the fourth century), and thus c. 270–400 decrees per annum. If, say, 270 decrees were inscribed per annum at, say, 20 dr., the cost would run to nearly a *talent* (i.e., 5,400 dr.), leaving the fund to run out within a dozen years if not replenished. Although other disbursements cannot be identified, perhaps the fund served as a fiduciary stop-gap in which the *tamiai* would have the funds for certain emergencies always on hand, rather than having to make loans out of Athena's *hiera* wealth or receive funds from still another board in order to make payments.

43. Ed. Meyer (1899) vol. 2, 136–37, seems to have been the first scholar to recognize the importance of these officers to the whole of the Athenian fiscal structure, and wrote, 136, "ursprünglich gehörten sie also zu den höchsten und wichtigsten Beamten des staats."

44. On the *apodektai* and their budgetary role, see Faraguna (1992), 179–83; Papazarkadas (2011), 64.

acted as the ultimate paymaster for the whole of the state. Indeed, that is an essential lesson of the lead sheet of Nemesis' sacred treasurers. Yet the fundamental roles of those involved need not have changed much: the Boule allocated money, the magistrates in charge of the public treasury distributed that money, sacred treasurers took possession of it and carried out their tasks, in turn. In the end, some sacred treasurers must finally have received the funds and then spent them to meet the sundry needs of the cult, from purchasing the services of butchers to merely purchasing the fuel needed for sacrificial fires. We should not, however, assume that the Boule or those in charge of the public treasury retained very much oversight of the funds once they passed beyond their immediate control, for otherwise the strenuous system of accountability installed by the democracy, in which accounts are mainly checked at the end of the year, would perhaps be superfluous.[45] After all, the use of *ekhein* and *analiskein* in the Nemesis accounts, which I explored in chapter 5, might suggest that demarcated legal responsibility over property of one or another sort already had a long history. On that reading of the evidence, then, perhaps the *merismos* budgetary system that Faraguna explicated really did have some precedent in sixth-century practices.

The classical centuries, nonetheless, were an era in which the Boule could act with speed and flexibility as well as with foresight when it came to allocating income from various sources for the costly, ongoing, complex, and multilayered demands of the *polis*' religious life. For the Athenians not to have developed the *hosia* wealth of Athena very much at all, and yet do so for Delian Apollo, raises any number of questions. Given the costs of the Panathenaia, were the Athenians afraid that Athena would need properties so extensive in nature as to crowd out the other gods or even themselves from economic activity? The answer is hardly forthcoming, but in the Athenians' constant attention to the goddess' needs through their Boule we may glimpse practices close to the origins of *hosia* wealth itself, for the Athenians converted public income to the goddess' needs almost immediately. While they were willing to continue that practice for her, and likely for her alone, they discovered that to do so was to invest great energy and risk on an ongoing basis in complex matters of finance, whereas to create *hosia* wealth not only allowed them to defer many fiscal decisions but to transfer the labor involved to magistrates whose duty was to cultivate that wealth for the future.

---

45. Faraguna (1992), 184.

The budgetary mechanisms with which the Boule operated represent a high point in the development of Athenian institutions, but for all of their complexity and sophistication they required also new magistracies to manage the money and other property. Beginning already with the lead account of Nemesis c. 500, these officers appear at once to have been numerous and empowered to carry out intricate financial operations. And yet these magistrates remain almost entirely unknown to us politically or socially, just as the finances they handled were far more abstract and anonymous than such tasks as stewarding gold and silver *kosmos* for the *polis*' most important occasions, which long remained the preserve of the *tamiai* of Athena and their ilk. We have nothing comparable to Khairion's altar and we cannot identify the tasks of these other sacred treasurers as having any prestige at all. They were not called from among the wealthiest of Athenians, and so far as we know they did not serve on the akropolis or in any similarly august space like the Pinakotheke. They did not, finally, have any connection with the major political figures of the day. They are known to us only through the documentary residue of the property that they managed. This bifurcation of sacred treasurers into two great classes is as much an outcome of Solon's reforms and the politics of the sixth century as is *hosia* property itself.

Conclusions

In answer to the central question with which this exploration began, the foregoing chapters have found in Solon a figure whose laws did indeed shape much of the Athenian state with regard to its sacred treasurers and the organization of its religious life but whose own presence is often fugitive. It is as a catalyst that Solon's service as lawgiver is most meaningful here, while the successive regimes of the Peisistratidai and the democracy alike exercised with much greater intention their capacity both to execute the blueprints established by him and to add their own contribution and thus inexorably encourage the state's growth. Few instances are evident where one of those succesors decidedly abandoned that blueprint, and indeed much of the evidence assayed in this book, especially the Calendar and the Law, manifests the long adherence to it over the better part of three centuries.

What the Law established was, in a broad sense, that sacred treasurers mattered so much to the *polis* that they had to be treated differently. It mandated that the *tamiai* of Athena would henceforth be drawn only from a new census class, the *pentakosiomedimnoi*, of super-wealthy Athenians, that granted them prestige and exclusivity in return for a partially randomized "complex" process of selection that might have been intended to quench the more disruptive behaviors of those seeking this office. The Law, nonetheless, allowed the competitive spirit to thrive, and it was at the tribal level that archaic Athens was most politically vibrant. But this was not the only such law, for the evidence of the Calendar and associated materials point to an array of measures that Solon promulgated with respect to other sacred treasurers and magistrates whose duties concerned religious life. Considering that the archaic treasury was also organized around the tribes, in the decades following Solon elite Athenians sought all the more strenuously to gain such offices for the resources and prestige that they would bring. Furthermore, given how expensive electoral banqueting might be, even a relatively junior office might bring enough rewards to lower the cost needed to impress one's *naukraria* at the time of the next election. It was this dynamic that transformed Athenian finance.

Systemic pressure to come up with more resources only mounted in the sixth century, under the Peisistratid tyranny and the early democracy, because the underlying link between electoral success and access to the *polis*' treasure went undiminished. By the end of the century, the Athenians appear to have taken crucial steps to create greater wealth for the *polis*' religious life by a combination of outright taxes and the transformation, by fiat, of strictly public wealth (*dêmosia*) into a sanctified form (*hosia*) that could be more easily managed in relation to the growing costs of religious life. This transformation was necessary because even as the treasure (*hiera*) of the gods grew over time, it remained an economically immobile form whose sanctity rendered it off-limits. Whereas *dêmosia* was susceptible to the vagaries of tax receipts and the like, *hosia* could be used as liquid cash or used to develop the capital needed for loans that in turn brought in interest, or even as land of one sort or another that could be leased. But *hosia* wealth was not a solution for all fiscal problems, and where the costs of great festivals such as the Panathenia were concerned, the Boule applied public revenues directly to the relevant colleges of magistrates. Even in the Peloponnesian War, when the *tamiai* had to handle large amounts of cash for the Panathenaia or to melt Athena's *hiera* for the war effort, they did so out of emergency only and never adopted the duties or techniques of those who were customarily responsible for *hosia*.

In no small part, then, the sacred treasurers of Athens were magistrates whose offices encoded in their duties and prestige the larger history of Athenian governance, politics, and religious life, from Solon's laws through the fourth century. The inexorable separation of these officers into two broad categories whose difference springs from the very development of *hosia* wealth and the *polis*' commitment to fund and organize communal religious events and interests must also reflect the traditional, even conservative, manner with which the Athenians seem to have regarded these offices. The historical process by which this distinction became manifest, however, was largely one of addition, and only very rarely one of significant alteration much less subtraction. Perhaps one might suggest that new offices and boards were created so as to allow, in effect, the ritually centered ones like the *hieropoioi* of the Semnai to survive without novel and inappropriate burdens involving matters of logistics, accounting, and the like being placed on them. By that same token, it is not difficult to explain the striking prominence of the *tamiai* of Athena as being by far the best known of those officers in every category of surviving evidence.

Notwithstanding how its particular strands developed and came to precipitate much of the superstructure of Athenian institutions, property of one kind or another, at all times, was indispensable for religious life, whether the *hiera* of the gods or the *hosia* of the *polis*. As the touchstone for the honor, power, and dignity of those most visible of sacred treasurers, nonetheless, the mercurial alloy of property and ritual ought to possess a correspondingly prominent place in our understanding of Athenian institutions, especially in matters of governance and religion. No mere catalogue of tasks, modes of selection, and administrative what-not could adequately explain largely ritual offices like the *hieropoioi* of the Semnai under the fourth-century democracy when viewed alongside those offices bereft of immediate religious significance and consequently lost almost entirely from view except for the mute testimony of their fiscal management.

What this book has offered is far from a mere wealth of detail about those two great categories of sacred treasurers and the whole of the framework in which they operated, though those details should be of signal value to students of Athenian religion and politics. Rather, to assay the institutions of ancient society allows us to get at both its underlying historical development and the mentalities that accompanied that process, to say nothing of the intrinsic value of understanding the constitutional structures to which the Athenians, in this case, devoted so much of their energy and attention. Indeed, a central lesson of this study is that we cannot divorce consideration of such pragmatic phenomena as institutions and property from the domains of politics and ritual, or else we risk an intellectual shipwreck, as it were, on shoals of ignorance. Otherwise, there could be no hope of situating Khairion's great altar in one and the same historical stream as the marble inventories of Athena's *kosmos* and the Solonian Calendar, or the lead sheet of Nemesis and Demosthenes' illustrious thrice-fold service as a *hieropoios* of the Semnai, much less Euripides' evocative description of the mythological Athenian prince Ion (*ll.* 54–56), with which I close as a fitting salutation to the sacred treasurers of ancient Athens:

Δελφοί σφ ' ἔθεντο χρυσοφύλακα τοῦ θεοῦ
ταμίαν τε πάντων πιστόν, ἐν δ ' ἀνακτόροις
θεοῦ καταζῇ δεῦρ ' ἀεὶ σεμνὸν βίον.

[The Delphians made him the gold-keeper of the god, the trustworthy *tamias* of all things, and he lives out an ever-hallow life here in the chambers of the god.]

Appendix

Khairion and Alkimakhos

On display in the Epigraphical Museum in Athens, the altar of Khairion has not received any systematic study since its discovery in the late nineteenth century. The altar consists now of only two nonjoining fragments from a single massive block of moderately soft, ochre-colored, *poros* limestone (whose length can be restored as c. 2.75m).[1] The altar still exhibits on its underside the marks of the adze used to trim the stone, but where visible, the block's other sides betray much greater care. Upon the altar's front side, just below the upper edge, its dedicatory text proclaims in very large, deeply carved letters in retrograde script (*IG* I[3] 590):[2]

1. The monument (EM 13288) is now tilted vertically in the Epigraphic Museum so that the lettered, front edge is facing directly upward, while the altar's top faces the wall and cannot be accessed. With the very generous permission of Dr. Kharalambos Kritzas, the director of the Epigraphic Museum, I conducted a detailed examination of the altar (but could not view the altar's original top surface) in the spring of 2005. The current position of the monument renders some measurement difficult, but I was able to confirm those provided by Raubitschek in *DAA* (this text is his no. 330): preserved length, 2.30 m.; height, 0.32 m. (but 0.29 on the front, inscribed face); width, 0.70m. (but I do record 0.71m. here); depth of two grooves on underside for supports, 0.03m.; width of grooves, c. 0.18m; distance from left-hand groove to left lateral face, 0.44m.; distance between the grooves 1.51m. Based upon the position of the two cuttings for supports and the distance of the right-hand one from the right side of the altar, I calculate (again, with Raubitschek) that the original length of the altar was c. 2.75m., but it should be clear that it is difficult from the published photographs (see n. 4 below) and the presentation of the monument in the museum to see just how much of the fragments' surfaces originally joined. The height of the missing supporting blocks, of course, cannot be directly ascertained, also, but their maximum width (0.18m.) might suggest something in the range of 0.24–0.36m.
2. *IG* provides a somewhat incomplete or possibly misleading record of the letters, noting only "a. 0,06–0,07 (litt. rot. minores)." The largest completely preserved letter is that of the initial *alpha* in 'Αθεναίαι, whose height I recorded in 2005 (see n. 1 above) as 0.072m. The letters of the dedicatory verb were higher still (i.e., up to 0.078–0.08m.) but are incompletely preserved, while the height of all letters decreases as the inscription procedes in sinistrograde fashion. Even the remaining letters of Athena's name decrease in size, as the second *alpha* in the goddess' name measures only 0.064m.

[------- ⁝ ἀνέθ]εκεν ⁝ ᾿Αθεναίαι ⁝ Χα[ι]ρίον ⁝ ταμιεύον ⁝ Κλε[δ]ί̣[ϙο ⁝ hυιός] ←.

[Khairion, while serving as *tamias*, the son of Kleidiqos, dedicated to Athena . . .]

Discovered in the akropolis excavations during the course of the 1889 season, the monument lacks an original context given that it was recovered from fill for the terracing of the akropolis' southeastern edge, near the terrace wall and approximately where the courtyard of the (now-defunct) Akropolis Museum was later built.[3] The altar's form, additionally, might be suitable to many areas of the akropolis since the monument appears to be nothing other than a massive *trapeza*-type altar, in which case this block must have rested upon two smaller stones (now lost) to give the simple shape of a table or bench, albeit one of great proportions and weight.[4] Given its complete lack of ornamentation like molding or akroteria, and its apparent similarity to the pillars erected by several different colleges of *hieropoioi* and an *arkhôn basileus* in the mid-sixth century (as discussed in chapter 3), the altar was initially thought to be a freestanding *stêlê* whose script might as well be placed at a 90 degree angle to the viewer just as those other *stêlai* were inscribed and situated.[5] Alternatively, it was occasion-

---

though completely preserved. The remainder of the inscription continues to diminish in size (e.g., the *alpha* in Khairion's name measures just 0.056m.) but does rise when the first few letters of his patronymic occur (e.g., both the *kappa* and *lambda* measure 0.066m.). The overall effect is to emphasize the act of dedication to Athena at the righthand side of the block; no traces of color were evident in the letters at the time of my autopsy.

3. Lolling (1899), 35 no. 8 (this text), describes the findspot as being close to the steps of the akropolis museum. In his initial report (1889) of this text (no. 2 there), 10, Lolling relates no information concerning the precise findspot but merely publishes the monument as one of a large number of inscriptions recovered, 6, from an area very close to the southern terrace wall of the akropolis at a spot where there was a rather large embankment or pile of earth, and does not mention anything in relation to the museum since it was not yet begun. The other inscriptions contain an intriguing mixture of sixth-century votive dedications, a fifth-century account of the *tamiai*, fourth-century decrees (often relating to the tribes), and several Roman honorific dedications, the totality of which points to a post-antique deposition.

4. Kirchner (1948), no. 4, provides good photographs of the front side for the two fragments recovered (but cuts a portion of the right-hand fragment where it would have extended toward the other fragment). Kirchner seems to support Raubitschek's earlier supposition (see n. 5 below) also ignoring Hiller von Gaertringen's label of "*stela*" in *IG* I² (this text as no. 467). Raubitschek in *DAA* (this text as no. 330) abandoned his earlier attribution and identified the monument as an altar, though without further discussion of its specific form and hence the basis of its identification.

5. Although initially described as a *stêlê* recovered from the area along the South Wall of the akropolis in the vicinity of the Brauronia precinct, it was immediately thought to belong to a building such as a *tamieion*. Kavvadias (1899), 10, paraphrases Lolling extensively, who notes in his own catalog with Wolters (1899), 35 no. 8, only that the stone had originally been constructed as part of a wall (of unknown identity), as its cuttings suggested. Yet Lolling, 10, actually describes the monument as a *stêlê* but suggestes that, by virtue of what one would now consider the bottom, it had been later adapted for use in a wall or a building, perhaps a *tamieion*. It is not clear why the original suggestion

ally thought that the block was a part of one of the Schatzhäuser, and perhaps even a *tamieion* such as the structure known from Hekatompedon Decree B.[6]

Often dated to the early sixth century (for example: *IG* I^3: "c. a. 600–575?") and thus implicitly contemporary or nearly so with the Athenian lawgiver Solon, the altar's inscription has relatively few comparanda and none that date so early.[7] If the inscription's letter-forms are anything to go by (and that is not assured), the altar might be more plausibly dated to c. 565 or perhaps as late as c. 550, when a few inscriptions evince some rough degree of similarity.[8] The name

---

was later modified. Raubitschek "Weihinschriften" (1939), 46, likewise describes the stone as a "Porosplatte, vielleicht die Weihinschrift eines kleinen Gebäude, sicher keine Stele!" However, in another publication that appeared the same year, Raubitschek "Votive" (1939), 17, described the monument as "a large poros altar" and only offered later in *DAA*, 365, that "it is assumed that the preserved slab was the crowning member of an altar construction." However, Raubitschek does not offer a reconstruction of the monument he envisages, nor do the few comparanda he offers provide sufficient parallels, namely, the altar depicted on the Busiris vase (which possesses volute akroteria for which there are no corresponding cuttings on this monument). On the broken left corner of the stone, there is enough room for restoration of a possible τὲν τράπεζαν, or even the more remote τόνδε ταμιε͂ον or τὸν θησαυρόν, and more than enough than for Raubitschek's τὸν βομὸν (1949, 365), which was not accepted by *IG*. On whether or not Khairion's dedication is metrical, see Peek in *Zeitschirft d. Martin-Luther Universität Halle-Wittenberg* 4 (1954/5), 233 n. 158 (*non vidi*) to the effect that the dedication is not metrical, *pace* Gallavotti (1979), 148–49.

6. The findspot of the altar (see n. 3 above) is likely unreliable for any hypothesis suggesting a location in the southeast area of the akropolis, given the propensity of those involved in the terrace work for the Kimonian walls and Parthenon (not to speak of other efforts) to move materials around quite freely to their ultimate burial as rubble.

7. Perhaps following Kirchner (1948), 9 no. 4, Jeffery (1990), 71 (this text as no. 12), dated the text to just after 600 (and is given to c. 600–575? in *IG* I^3; cf. Morris [2000], 275), but her parallel was a Naxian and not an Athenian dedication. Figueira (1984), 454, suggests "*ca.* 550" without elucidating the reason, but perhaps based upon Raubitschek's discussion and similar dating of the text in *DAA* (this text is no. 330).

8. The approximate date of the monument can only be determined by recourse to comparable letterforms on four other monumental dedications, since the altar was found without sufficient context and lacks any diagnostic molding. The Moskhophoros (*IG* I^3 593: c. 570–60?) offers a very close parallel due to the shared use of several letterforms that are also found on Khairion's altar, namely, the slanted *epsilon* with tail, crossbar *theta*, and long-legged *nu*. Without citing any specific elements, Lolling (1889), 10, already noted the Moskhophoros as a close comparandum. The crossbar of the *alphas* on the altar does not meet the foot of the opposite leg, as it does on the Moskhophoros. Yet the slightly later(?) altar of Athena Nike (*IG* I^3 596: c. 550) likewise shows a close affinity, in that while it employs the same *epsilon* as the other two monuments, it also uses one without the tail. An early Eleusinian dedication (*IG* I^3 990 [= *I.Eleusis* 2]: c. 550?) also displays the same kind of *nu* and *epsilon* as does Khairion's, but its *alpha*'s crossbar does meet the opposite foot. One other dedication from the akropolis (*IG* I^3 602: c. 540?) also uses much the same *epsilon* and *alpha*. As Jeffery (1990), 71, pointed out, if as early as she dated it, the monument would be the earliest Athenian inscription to carry punctuation.

Among the other monuments discussed at some length in this monograph, the three pillars offered by colleges of *hieropoioi* (*IG* I^3 507–09) and that of Alkiphron (*IG* I^3 991) exhibit the key features where those letters are represented or surviving (but where 509, dated by *IG* "c. a. 550?" possesses a "cartwheel" *theta*, and there is a greater mixture of letterforms on 508, dated by *IG* "c.a. 562?–558?"). Therefore, these four monuments appear to be nearly contemporary with Khairion's altar.

of Khairion's father, Kleidiqos, is best restored with the *qoppa* as would be consistent with early to mid-sixth-century conventions in Attic script, but other names, and thus orthography, might also be possible.[9]

Aside from this altar, Khairion is known also from a second monument that, in the eyes of some scholars, placed him amidst the major political questions of mid- to late sixth-century Athens. This second monument consists of the grave marker that adorned his burial in Eretria, about which little is known given the early date of its discovery and publication except that his burial in a *pithos* was topped with a marble disc that bore his epitaph. The text appears to be Attic script and bears a message that for all of its brevity offers unusual testimony:[10]

Χαιρίον
᾿Αθεναῖο̣ς
εὐπατριδõν
ἐνθάδε κεῖ-
τα‹ι›.

[Khairion, an Athenian of the Eupatridai, lies here.]

Comparison of letter-forms on the epitaph with other archaic inscriptions offers the best possibility for establishing the date independent of historical considerations, despite the paucity of securely dated comparanda and the idiosyncrasies of individual letter-cutters, especially within a specific genre of text. The

9. Personal autopsy (see n. 1 above) indicated a very small part of a vertical stroke at approximately the bottom center of where a letter should be expected two letters over from the *epsilon* of the patronymic. For reasons of sense this cannot represent anything but a *iota*, which I underdot in my text above. Therefore, the name must be something like Kleid- and thus Kleidiqos is a reasonable restoration that should be spelled with a *qoppa*, as that of the nearly contemporary *tamias* Eudiqos provides a clear parallel (*IG* I^3 510, *l.* 3). Later renderings are more properly spelled with a *kappa*. The form with *qoppa* is retained here for the sake of clarity and accuracy. On the phonological significance of *qoppa* (as distinct from *kappa*), see Threatte (1980) vol. 1, 22–23, who also notes, 21–22, that it had begun to disappear from Attica c. 570–50, which makes the plaque with the *tamias* Eudiqos in his estimation one of the last (Athenian) documents known to carry this letter; nevertheless the date of that graphic (and phonological) shift remains consistent with the proposed date of the altar.

10. *IG* I^3 1516 (= XII [9] 296, but text reprinted here is that of I^3). Kourouniotes (1899), 144, suggests that the stone (blue-grey in color, but otherwise not identified) originally covered a *pithos* burial (hence its circular shape), which is typical of archaic Eretria, but mentions nothing of its original archaeological context nor how it came to his attention. Kourouniotes immediately suggested the connection with the Peisistratidai that has since served as a critical element in many historicizing reconstructions of the period's monuments. For note and photograph, see Nilsson (1955) vol. 1, p. 563, and pl. 33, no. 4.

forms of the *theta* and *delta* would suggest that this inscription belongs at the beginning of that range, therefore c. 550–25 (and perhaps even more precisely, c. 540).[11] The span of time between Khairion's altar and epitaph suggests that he need not have been a young man when he dedicated the altar to Athena Polias while *tamias*, although later, secondary interment of his remains in Eretria (or at least the inscription of the epitaph) cannot be ruled out. What seems to have been the particular form of Khairion's burial in a *pithos* with a stone lid was very rarely if ever practiced in Attica, where *tumulus* burials for the elite dominated the mortuary landscape. In both Attica and Eretria, a *pithos*-with-lid form of burial resonates somewhat with practices typical of elite burials, but only of an earlier age.[12] In aggregate, these features present a puzzle that might,

11. The *khi* on the epitaph is Attic, but of the cross type that is more typical after 520, and not typical of archaic Euboean inscriptions. But the exclusivity of script there is not absolute. The Attic alphabet is also found at Eretria for the late archaic ("500–480?") gravestone of Philon (= *IG* XII 9 287; *SGDI* 5302; *LSAG* 14), and perhaps in a slightly later ("500–475?") proxeny decree also from Eretria (*IG* XII Suppl. 549; *LSAG* 15). Jefferey (1990), 67, suggests that this particular form of *khi* dominates in Attic script in the second half of the sixth century although there are other forms used as well; cf. Jeffery (1938–39) on *IG* I^3 972 (c. 550?). The *alphas* are positioned so that the left leg is made vertical, but the crossbar does not angle down to the opposite foot of the right leg and remains perpendicular to the left leg. This particular letterform first appears in the middle of the sixth century (e.g., *IG* I^3 508, 510, 546–47, 972) and is also known from several examples from the 520s to the end of the sixth century, when it is very well attested by the akropolis dedications. Nevertheless, Jeffery (1990), 66, attributes the form in question only to the period approximately "525–500" and cites the herm of Hipparkhos (*IG* I^3 1023) as a parallel. The herm appears to be reliably identified with those of the tyrant Hipparkhos (Pl. *Hipparch.* 229a-b), and therefore ought to have been erected before his death in 514. By way of parallel, a cup by Epiktetos of c. 515 clearly supports the attribution, because of its inscription Ἵππαρχος καλός together with the image of a young man crafting a herm, for which see Shapiro (1989), 126. For its part, the stone herm does have a similar *alpha* to that of Khairion's epitaph, and the *theta* is pointed, while the *epsilon* is slightly tailed and therefore comparable to the downward angle of the *epsilon* in *l.* 2 of the epitaph. The second group appears at the end of the sixth century and continues into the very early fifth century, attested by numerous examples (e.g., *IG* I^3 526–27, 618–19, 641, 679, 706, 730, 907, 973, 1015, 1088, 1229, 1230bis, 1231, 1277, 1337 [late fifth century]). Another important parallel is *IG* I^3 683 (the dedication by Iphidike) from perhaps the last decade of the sixth century, which possesses very similar letterforms of *alpha*, *delta*, and potentially *nu* as well, except that it possesses the pointed *theta* only. Khairion's epitaph has both the cross-barred and "cartwheel" *theta*, which are still found together in the same contexts (e.g., *ostraka*) in the early fifth century. The *delta* also appears to be tipped up slightly on the right angle, which is usually a very early feature in both Euboic and Attic scripts.

12. The earliest and best known Eretrian burials within large vessels of some sort are those of the adult cremations in *lebêtes* at the family plot at the West Gate subsequently venerated as a heroön, for which see Bérard (1970), who also, 13, considers the burial of Khairion merely to be an example of a "continuité du système, qui semble par ailleurs assez primitif." Analysis of Attic burial patterns in sixth century is hampered by a lack of reliably excavated and published remains except the Kerameikos and the agora. Boardman and Kurtz (1971), 71, suggest that use of large coarseware *pithoi* for adults was exceptional throughout the archaic period in Attica and note, 88, that five inscribed and painted marble discs are indeed known from Attica, but their precise interpretation is difficult in part because three of them use the obscure term "from the *êrion*" and apparently none have a secure context.

from one point of view, be best explained as reflecting the death and burial of an elite Athenian in exile from Peisistratid Athens.

Nonetheless, for the epitaph to present Khairion not merely as an Athenian but as indeed a member of the Eupatridai is not obviously or even necessarily consistent with a narrative of exile. Otherwise, we must wonder why those burying Khairion chose to make so public his status and Athenian identity, especially when Peisistratos seems to have had his own ties to Eretria and so could all the more easily have discovered and disturbed the grave of an opponent, if that indeed is what Khairion was.[13] Yet, Khairion's status as one of the Eupatridai complicates matters because it would seem to tie him to the politics of Athens, not Eretria. As noted in the introduction, some scholars like H. T. Wade-Gery (working from mainly post-classical sources such as Plutarch) argued that the Eupatridai might be best thought of as at least a section of the elite endowed with a caste-like constitutional hold over certain powers.[14] Indeed, others have gone so far as to identify the Eupatridai with the whole of the pre-Solonian elite, and thus as the main target of Solon's laws.[15] As I first suggested in the introduction, however, there is no reliable evidence that the Eupatridai constituted a discrete and coherent order endowed with defined and broad constitutional or other prerogatives, such as the Solonian census classes. Furthermore, even the supposition of some ancient sources that the Eupatridai constituted a single *genos*, no less, clearly goes too far in ascribing to them the status of a single kin-group.[16]

---

13. Peisistratos and Eretria: Hdt. 1.61.2, followed perhaps by *Ath.Pol.* 15.2. On the strength of Peisistratos' connections with Eretrians (possibly involving their various colonial ventures in northern Greece), see Lavelle (2005), 116–23, 134–41. Stanton (1990), 206–07, goes so far as to suggest that the Peisistratidai had actually sent Khairion to Eretria to take care of some business on their behalf.
14. Wade-Gery (1958), 108–10. See, for example, the critique of Figueira (1984), 453–58, who also accepts the genealogical tie of Khairion and Alkimakhos first suggested by Raubitschek, thus argues strongly against the idea that the Eupatridai formed anything like a caste, suggesting instead that it was a merely a subjective attribution of identity without any legal basis or implications. See also the discussion in chapter 1.
15. E.g., Stanton (1990) no. 105; see also the introduction, nos. 11–14, 16; chapter 1, nos. 3, 24, 44.
16. Toepfer (1889), 176ff., follows the reading by Hilzer of Sophokles (*El.* 160–63, 1070–81) as evidence that the *genos* of the Eupatridai could claim descent from Orestes despite (or even because) of his blood guilt; cf. Parker (1983), 202–03. Polemon claims (ap. Σ *OC* 489 = *FHG* vol. 3 F49 [text of Müller is in error]) that the Eupatridai did not have a share in the celebrations for the Erinyes conducted in part by the *genos* of the Hesykhidai (text of de Marco [1952]: τὸ δὲ τῶν Εὐπατριδῶν γένος οὐ μετέχει τῆς θυσίας ταύτης). Parker (1996), 299, goes too far in describing this relationship as one of exclusion, as the wording seems only to refute the assumption or claim that the Eupatridai would naturally have participated in the cult, not that they were forbidden from attending the procession or observing the public sacrifices. The source of that claim (in favor of the Eupatrid participation or control) is obscure, but may have been prompted by the ritual topography of the cult itself. Given that a shrine of the ritually important hero Hesykhos was located beside the Kyloneion(?) (Κυδώνιον in ms. L, but Κλυδωνιον in mss. M and R) yet outside of the "nine gates," it is possible that one of the

But a simpler explanation should proceed first from the observation that the burial did occur in Eretria, and not in Attica, and thus that the epitaph ought to have performed its function relative to that fact alone.

An interesting difficulty, nonetheless, is that a number of the later sources suggest that the Eupatridai were defined both by their religious prerogatives, on the one hand, and, on the other, by virtue of being one of the main political groupings of early Athens, if they did not have, in fact, an exclusive hold upon certain high offices of the state. Some high offices do seem to have been hereditary, after all. As discussed first in chapter 2, the Solonian Calendar does list the prerogatives due the *phylobasileis* and one specific *trittys*, the Leukotainioi, long past when this magistracy and its associated bodies ought to have ceased to exist by dint of the reforms of Kleisthenes. Again, we do not know who held these positions or were considered rightful members of the Leukotainioi, but the logic by which they are included in the Calendar is most consistent with hereditary office. Perhaps, then, at least some families (or even their *genê*?) really could claim to have a monopoly upon political power (that is, by virtue of an office with religious as well as political duties), though in no way could this extend to the whole of the elite. At most, the Leukotainioi ought to have represented a notional 1/12 of the pre-Kleisthenic body of Athenians.[17] Since there is

---

Atthidographers inferred (falsely) that the Eupatridai must have had a role in making a propitiary offering to the vengeful spirits of Kylon's executed supporters, perhaps under the impression that the Alkmaionidai, who are regularly associated with that guilt and under a curse, were of course Eupatridai.

Some aspects of the Eupatridai as they appear in the Atthidographer Philokhoros might even suggest that this identity owed something to an aetiology developed so as to explain why the *hieropoioi* of the Semnai (i.e., the Erinyes) existed as they did. In a claim that seems to anticipate Philo's much later ascription of great wealth and zealously good behavior to the *hieropoioi*, which I discussed in chapter 4, Philokhoros (*FGrH* 328 F 4) clearly states that at some point in its early history the Areiopagos was constituted solely of Eupatridai, even after its membership was increased in number, and that these were men who were "distinguished for their wealth and moderate life." Philokhoros says nothing of ritual purity, as Rhodes (1993), 183, suggests that Hammond (1961), 78 n. 9, assumed in a difficult interpretation of *Ath.Pol.* 13.2. Wallace (1989), 14 (cf. 188ff.), appears to translate St. Maximus the Confessor's paraphrase of Philokhoros in such a way as to suggest that the Areiopagos was formed from two distinct groups, the Eupatridai "and men distinguished by wealth and sober life." However, Wallace seems to have translated the first καί twice, but it only coordinates with the second one to help define the preceding phrase by apposition, namely, to describe who the Eupatridai were. In any case, it is difficult to avoid the sense that Philokhoros might have identified the *hieropoioi* as taking the place of the cursed and disgraced Eupatridai, and thus subject to the same essential criteria of wealth, standing, and behavior by dint of ritual necessity, just as the *arkhôn basileus* might have been thought to have assumed functions once the prerogative of the Attic kings.

17. Lambert (1998), 256 n. 50, does note the linguistic oddity that the term *trittys* ought originally to have singled a body made up of three parts, and not the opposite sense that it regularly has in Greek texts as indicating a third of some other body, but suggests that the former, standard, sense must have been in place well before the Kleisthenic reforms. In that case, the Leukotainioi should represent

no reason to suspect that the elite were confined to certain *trittyes*, this one *trittys* ought to have included men who were of lesser station and means.[18] My hypothesis would make some sense, perhaps, out of both Pollux's statement that these *phylobasileis* were indeed drawn from the Eupatridai and also of Strabo's claim that it was the Athenian king Ion who divided the Athenian population into four parts and granted to one of those parts the sole power to act as *hieropoioi*.[19] It is natural that the heads of the *phylai* should have responsibility

---

one-third of their tribe, and twelve such bodies will have made up the whole of the Athenian citizenry prior to those reforms. Papazarkadas (2007), 29–30, however, prefers the former interpretation with respect to a group that he identifies as another pre-Kleisthenic *trittys*, the Epakreis, but does not reconcile that notion with the constitutional requirement of a tribe being made up of three such *trittyes*.

18. That particular *genê* might also have associated directly with the Eupatridai is a complicating factor, and one need only look at Isocrates' identification (16.25) of the Eupatridai as a distinct family line of Alkibiades (and parallel to the Alkmaionidai) apparently in contradiction of the *skolion* that makes the Alkmaionidai merely part of the Eupatridai, whatever they were. Despite Dickie's conclusive argument (1979) that the Alkmaionidai constitute an *oikos*, Parker (1996), 318–19, still equivocates over their identity. But Parker (1996), 323–24, helpfully elucidates that the evidence for whether or not the Eupatridai are a caste or *genos* reflects overlapping definitions in which the two dimensions, status and ritual prerogative, are frequently paired together but the definition as *genos* is particularly weak, even when for the Hellenistic period there is some assertion of the Eupatridai as a single *genos*. Welwei (1992), 108 n. 66, (following Bourriot [1976]) also maintains that the later identity of the Eupatridai is a false lead. Given the eclipse of the term from Athenian life for several centuries spanning the Athenian democracy, such claims seem plausibly interpreted as a later, archaizing creation and another attempt at grounding one's nobility.

19. Strabo 8.7.1 C383. The principal, but highly obscure, source for those hereditary aspects of the four Ionian tribes is *Ath.Pol.* (fr. 2 Chambers; = fr. 3 Kenyon; fr. 385 Rose; *PatmLex.* p. 152 s.v. γεννῆται; cf. Σ Plat. *Axioch.* 371d and Harp. s.v. τριττύς; cf. Rhodes [1993], 67) that ascribes to Aristotle's *Ath. Pol.* the claim that each of the tribes were divided into twelve *phratriai* and *trittyes* to correspond to the months of the (sacral) year, and that each *phratria* was then divided into thirty *genê*, each of which contained thirty men to correspond with the thirty days of the month. While the calendrical correspondance is clearly obtuse, and the passage ignores the twelve *naukrariai* into which each tribe was actually divided (unless it has confused them with the *phratriai* and *trittyes*), it is the notion that all Athenians were part of *phratriai* that is of most interest, since under the democracy these bodies determined the fundamental legitimacy of boys as prospective Athenian citizens, for which see Lambert (1998). In addition, the passage delineates the early (i.e., mythical) division of the Athenians into *genê* (and whose priesthoods [specifically citing the Eumolpidai, Kerykes and Eteoboutadai] it alleges were allotted: αἱ ἱερωσύναι . . . ἐκληροῦντο). Most recently, Blok and Lambert (2009) have cited this passage as direct support for their argument that Athenian *genê* in the fourth century, including the Eteoboutadai, employed sortition as the means by which priesthoods were filled when left vacant by death or any other cause. Blok and Lambert, 96–97, describe this passage as "the clearest statement in the literary record that *genos* priesthoods were appointed by lot," but the prevalence of simple election as the method used for magistracies in archaic Athens alone ought to serve as caution against accepting the passage at face value on this or any other point.

Likewise, Plutarch's paraphrase of another now lost portion of *Ath.Pol.* (*Thes.* 25.1–3 [= *Ath.Pol.* fr. 3 Chambers]) reports another division of the citizen body into thirds. Accordingly, it is another king, Theseus, who concedes almost total divine and political power to the Eupatridai but arranges it so that while the Eupatridai appear to excel in *doxa*, the Geomoroi do so in *khreia*, and the Demiourgoi do so in numbers (*plêthos*)—"as if in equal proportion" to the role granted to the Eupatridai. Such patterns do not encourage confidence in the underlying historicity of what they purport to record.

for certain rituals for no other reason than to secure through ritual the well-being of their group. Some hereditary claims to religious privilege, therefore, recognized as essential by the *polis* and thus grandfathered into the democracy that followed those reforms, would seem to offer the least complicated reason for their appearance. Yet, we need hardly ascribe to the whole of the archaic elite before or after Solon a caste-like hold upon political authority even if some offices, and the offices of those akin to sacred treasurers, were in truth hereditary in nature.

But such a religious *cum* political identity need not have arisen at all in the time of Khairion, even if its historical seeds had already long been sown in archaic offices like that of the *phylobasileis*. The Eupatridai also appear in a *skolion* preserved by *Ath.Pol.* (19.3) that is of uncertain date except that the event it commemorates (an unsuccessful battle by the Alkmaionidai against Peisistratos at Leipsydrion) must have occurred sometime after c. 546, and is therefore roughly contemporary with Khairion's epitaph:[20]

αἰαῖ Λειψύδριον προδωσέταιρον,
οἵους ἄνδρας ἀπώλεσας μάχεσθαι
ἀγαθούς τε καὶ εὐπατρίδας,
οἳ τότ ' ἔδειξαν οἵων πατέρων ἔσαν.

[Ah, Leipsydrion, traitor of comrades!
You destroyed such men, noble in battle and Eupatrid alike,
Who showed then of what sort of fathers they were (truly born).]

What the *skolion* delineates as being characteristic of the Eupatridai is little more than of illustrious ancestry and bravery in war. In no way does the *skolion* give us to think of anything pertaining to religion or to political power. Whatever the origins of those other traditions that attribute to the Eupatridai such extensive powers in those very fields of endeavor, the *skolion* does not suggest that we should read Khairion's epitaph with such issues in mind at all.

Familial connections to elite Eretrians, moreover, might better explain the mere fact of Khairion's burial at Eretria in conjunction with his epitaph's unusual claims. Since Khairion's identity as an Athenian perforce reflects his pa-

20. Concerning the other textual sources for the *skolion*, and also on the action at Leipsydrion, see Rhodes (1993), 235. On what little is known concerning the date of the incident, see Robinson (1994), 363; cf. Rhodes (1976).

ternal descent, any such connection with Eretrians can only have gone through his mother, but about this the epitaph is of course silent since neither the Athenians nor the Eretrians commonly indicated such or used a matronymic. But we need not presume that the epitaph was intended to make any more lasting or profound a statement than was to be communicated to an immediate audience of Eretrians. The circular form of the marble could hardly have been meant to be a permanent memorial; it was made to lie flat and cannot have remained visible for very long unless assiduously cleared of soil, weeds, and the like. The epitaph, it seems, was not intended to be visible for a very long period, but it might have sufficed to meet a more immediate need, namely, to identify Khairion as a person whose remains should not be disturbed by those unsure of his identity when, say, digging a new grave in the immediate vicinity. Moreover, Eretrians also employed names that shared the *Khairi-* stem, in which case confusion with an Eretrian seems like a plausible hazard.[21] Thus, the epitaph's Attic script, ethnic designation of the deceased as an Athenian, and perhaps even the antiquated form of burial might serve to protect him from being too easily confused for a common Eretrian interloper. Are we perhaps allowed to imagine that Khairion's Eupatrid status was intended to further that end by demarcating him even from common Athenians in a very general manner? All that can be said, then, for the political implications of his claim to Eupatrid status is that those who interred him at Eretria expected that this indication of some or another kind of status in Athens would be met positively enough at Eretria to ensure his grave be undisturbed. Beyond that, we cannot say what Khairion's claim would have meant to contemporary Athenians, but it was probably not for them that the epitaph's message was intended.

Nonetheless, the narrative of exile has also relied upon a third monument naming Khairion, but which was erected in late archaic Athens. As first discussed in chapter 3, a group of at least three, possibly four, late archaic statuettes have often been thought to represent *tamiai* or some other important magistrates in the very act of carrying out their duties. The whole basis for ascribing this type of statuette to *tamiai* in the first place rests upon the identification of the best preserved and largest example, whose dedicator is an Alkimakhos the son of Khairion, as the son of the very same Khairion whose altar and epitaph are at issue.[22] At a sheer minimum, the late sixth-century votive in question

21. The pronominal element Χαιρι- is reasonably well attested in Eretria, for which see *LGPN Aegean* s.vv.

22. Raubitschek "Votive" (1939), 17–18, is the first to attribute this particular statuette to the column of

comprises a marble Ionic column that bears an epigram inscribed in the flutes, and which was originally crowned by a relatively small statue or other object. Although some objections have been raised against the attribution of the column to the statuette long restored atop it, since they do not actually join (due, at a minimum, to damage to both elements), the statuette is described simply as a sculptural representation in the round of a bearded man, wearing a full *himation* and sandals, seated upon a chair and holding what was probably a writing board or pair of wax tablets in one hand and a stylus in the other (its left hand is missing; the right hand grips a now lost object).[23] For this basic reason the statuette and those like it are often deemed "scribes" or some type of magistrate upon the unarticulated presumption that no truly private figure would thus be depicted.[24]

Insofar as the monument can be reconstructed (and accepting the pairing of figure with column), the figure itself would have been situated above eye-

---

Alkimakhos, as well as to identify the figure as a *tamias*. Trianti (1994), 83–86, assigns the Fauvel head to this statue, and suggests that the marble is from Asia Minor, but also rejects Raubitschek's identification of the figure as a *tamias*. Angiolillo (1997), 204–6, accepts Raubitschek's sculptural identification and provides a photograph of the statue placed on the column (reproduced in color at p. 110) that no longer reflects the display of the statue alone in the (old) Akropolis Museum; cf. Keesling (2003), 184 fig. 59. In the museum, this and the other two sure examples of the type are all now displayed in close proximity to one another. Keesling (2003), 182–85 and (her) Appendix no. 3, also provides an extensive discussion of this monument, based likewise heavily upon that of Raubitschek and agreeing that it represents Khairion as a *tamias*, and suggests that even if Trianti's restoration of the plinth is correct (disassociating the "scribe" from the inscribed column, and positing an equestrian figure instead) the figure would probably represent Khairion. Day (2010), 197, 227, 230, likewise accepts the attribution, as does Shapiro (2001), 94–96.

23. This statuette differs noticeably not only in being rather large and slanting but also for the fact that it does not have a small chest or box placed upon the lap, as does at least one other of the statuettes, as easily seen in Krumeich (1997), pl. 1, of Akropolis Museum no. 144. Schuchhardt (1939), 207ff., nos. 309–11, provides a more detailed description and photographs of the three certain statues including this one (i.e., Akropolis Museum nos. 146, 629) and that attributed to Alkimakhos, to which a fragmentary fourth example may be added, for which see Schuchhardt (1939), 333, no. 455.

24. It is not clear on what grounds, for example, Angiolillo (1997), 204–5, thinks that it possible that the sculpture represents a *grammateus* or even a *hieropoios*. Faraguna (2005), 68, accepts the identification with *grammateis*. Cahn (1973), 15ff., suggested a *katalogeus* inspecting the cavalry, if not a *tamias*. Shapiro (2001), 94–96, suggests that they represent *khrêsmologoi* and thus connects the statues with the Peisistratidai, known for their interest in oracles and those who purveyed them. Doubtful of Raubitschek's connection of the monuments of Khairion and Alkimakhos and thus of the identification of any of the figures as *tamiai*, Krumeich (1997), 22–23, adopts the more neutral designation "Beamter."

If in fact they are dedications of writing instruments and not instruments of another kind, some twenty-five bone styluses known from the early akropolis might constitute another form of *ex officio* dedication. Although Trianti (1994), 85, provides a photograph of five of the styluses (all in good condition) and the corresponding museum numbers and current storage locations, she does not discuss their function. Stubbings (1962), 445–46, briefly discusses the similarly early examples of stylus dedications from Perachora and provides a short list of others from around Greece known to have been excavated.

level (Raubitschek restored the whole as c. 2.5m in height), while the epigram would have been clearly visible due to its deep chiseling and paint.[25] To judge from the position, height, and posture of the statue (it leans noticeably to its right), the figure would probably have gazed down at the viewer over his writing implements(?), twisting slightly and ostensibly engaging the attention of a viewer sharply.[26] Moreover, the extensive remains of paint on the surface point further to the visual splendor and expense of Alkimakhos' monument.[27] The dedicatory inscription (*IG* I³ 618) inscribed upon the column's flutes proclaims Alkimakhos' affiliation in a manner that is visually complicated, appearing almost like a "T" or the profile of an ionic capital with each of two long lines flanked by a pair of two-letter sequences: [28]

1	ʽΑλ-	←↓
2	κίμαχός μ ᾽ ἀνέ{σ}θε͂κε Διὸς κόρει τόδ ᾽ ἄγαλμα	←↓
4–5	ε|ὐ-	←
3	χολέν, ἐσθλο͂ δὲ πατρὸς *h*ὺς Χαιρίονος ἐπεύχεται ‹ε͂›να[ι].	←↓

[Alkimakhos dedicated me, this object of delight, as a vow to the daughter of Zeus, and boasts that he is the son of a noble father, Khairion.]

25. Raubitschek reconstructs the monument so that the capital would have been at eye level and provides in *DAA*, 10–11 (no. 6), extensive notes on the dimensions of the relevant fragments.

26. Although the epigrammatic dedication does not address the viewer to look at it, as is sometimes found on votives (but more typically on funerary epitaphs), the form of the monument suggests strongly that it was created in such a manner as to engage the viewer strongly. Keesling (2003), 181, notes that while the "stand and look" formula of inscribed address is limited in archaic Attica to funerary epitaphs, it is found on the fifth-century portrait statues of Olympia. The odd posture of the figure suggests that perhaps it was designed with foreknowledge as to where it would be situated. Hence, the figure would have been crafted with this slanting pose so that when situated next to some other monument or structure, which would otherwise crowd its space toward the head the figure, the figure would appear less awkward.

27. McGowan (1997), 219–20, suggests that the text continued into the missing flutes at the bottom of the column, but that the final NA or NE belongs to a participle (thus, the final word of *l.* 4 would read not ‹ε͂›να[ι] but να- or even νε-) somehow indicating the act of offering a dedication. But McGowan does not identify what word this could actually be (since it could not be a form of ἀνατιθέναι unless one assumes a similar omission of the initial letter: e.g., ‹ἀ›να[θείς]) and why it would be somehow preferable to εἶναι. The text appears to be complete, therefore.

28. Note that the syllable of *ll.* 4–5 (εὐ-) is actually distributed across two flutes, and that it is also the only part of the inscription that can be upright with respect to the viewer's eyes. But this syllable is actually positioned to the right of *l.* 3, whereas the two-letter syllable (᾽Αλ-) of *l.* 1 is positioned to the left of *l.* 2. For that reason, I arrange (and number) the text differently from *IG*. On the visual and spatial dynamics of the text as laid out vertically upon the flutes of the column, see the extensive comments of Day (2010), 50–57, 76, 81, 114.

If Raubitschek's hypothesis proves to be correct, Alkimakhos' epigram could be read to indicate that the figure atop his monument was his father, since he boasts (*epeukhetai*) that he is the son of a "noble father" (*esthlou patros*) while the column and its crowning statue are offered in fulfillment of a vow (*eukhôlen*).[29] Few if any parallels are forthcoming for a clear case in which the subject of an archaic Athenian image can even be shown to be a parent of the dedicator.[30]

Even if we were to concede that such unusual language and the monument's identification of Khairion as especially worthy of praise render it most likely that the figure atop it was none other than Khairion, and that Khairion was depicted as a *tamias*, there is no satisfactory basis upon which to suggest that the monument has very much at all to do with the Peisistratidai. Likewise, attempts to connect politically this family with the Alkmaionidai, with whom there may have been some distant familial links, fail to persuade.[31] No evidence is known, however, that can demonstrate Khairion or his son were *not* allies or supporters of the Peisistratidai, as such a connection with the Alkmaionidai might well suggest. Keesling, who accepts Raubitschek's and others' identification of Alkimakhos and Khairion, and the narrative of exile, thus downdates

29. The phrase extends far beyond the usual patronymics of other dedicators and echoes a passage in the *Iliad* (5.246–48) where the heroes Pandaros and Aineias boast to be the sons of their respective fathers, which their foe Sthenelaos takes to be a sure sign of their prowess. Friendländer and Hoffleit (1948), 51, also suggest a parallel phrase in Sophokles *Phil.*, 96 that "may show that this formula was almost an aristocratic catchword in Athens," but do not cite any other examples of similar phrasing.

30. Apparently unaware of Alkimakhos' monument as a possible analogue, Rhodes (1993), 143, suggests (but provides no reason) that *Ath.Pol.* 7.4 is in error (*pace* Pollux 8.131) when *Ath.Pol.* describes the dedication of Anthemion the son of Diphilos as an "image of Diphilos" (εἰκὼν Διφίλου), which would (in principle) be the only other example of such parental representation. Keesling (2003), 182, 187–95, notes other fifth-century examples of fathers represented by dedications offered by their children, which should offer important comparanda.

31. For instance, McGowan (1997), 219 n. 50, suggests that it was this Alkimakhos who dedicated a Doric votive column in Delphi c. 525–500 during exile from Athens but relies upon Jeffery (1990), 102–03, who restores the name extensively, and dates the putative statue of Khairion to the end of the sixth century. The editors of *LGPN Central Greece* apparently do not accept the identification, if aware of the hypothesis, and there is no reason to think that to offer a dedication at Delphi must signify one's exile.

Raubitschek in *DAA*, 12, is the first to assert a connection between this family and that of the Alkmaionidai through his identification of Khairion. Davies (1971), 12–15, argues against Raubitschek's idea on the basis of a conservative reading of the evidence and the probabilities of prosopographic confusion. In favor of identification of the two families as related is the appearance of the 'Αλκ- stem in the name of Alkimakhos, given the (reasonable, but impossible to prove) supposition that pronominal elements tend to be repeated, often with very high frequency, throughout a family's descent much more so than with terminal elements. The resulting patterns of some, but not all, families is that the pronominal element may be associated with a particular family line, although ostensibly available to all other families.

this and most other late archaic sculpture atop the akropolis to the period of the democracy's first decades (510–480), that is to say when it would be safe to express anti-Peisistratid values through sculpture, but the consensus has otherwise been to place the bulk of related archaic statuary in the earlier range of c. 525–500.[32] A funerary epitaph (*IG* I^3 1234) from the Kerameikos for one who is likely to be the same Alkimakhos probably dates, on the basis of its letter-forms, to c. 500(?), and so provides a *terminus ante quem* for his votive moment. Yet in either case, the monument does not allow one to argue for a connection to the Peisistratidai, for if it occurs within the period of their hegemony (that is, to 510) then we must read into it an almost secretive text that somehow escaped detection while proclaiming resistance to them; but if it occurs afterward, then we must wonder why it does not lash out against the tyrants more obviously.[33] Nevertheless, Alkimakhos' dedication asserts merely a strong claim of filial devotion and offers no objective sense that this devotion possessed a political character at all.

32. Keesling (2003), 66ff., argues that it is only in the early fifth century that victorious Athenian athletes first begin to offer dedications in which they represent themselves. One might well wonder whether that kind of self-representation underlies the offerings of seated magistrates that are at issue here, and which, on Keesling's dating, would commence a decade or two earlier than those of athletes. For the alternative view, see, for example, Karakasi (2003), 139ff.

33. Davies (1971), 13, makes the problematic connection between chronology and politics more explicit but still opts to characterize Khairion as an exile.

Works Cited

Aleshire, Sara B. *The Athenian Asklepieion: The People, Their Dedications, and the Inventories* (Amsterdam: 1989).

Allen, Danielle S. *The World of Prometheus: The Politics of Punishing in Democratic Athens* (Princeton, NJ: 2000).

Amyx, D. A. "The Attic Stelai. Part III. Vases and Other Containers." *Hesperia* 27 (1958), 163–254.

Amyx, D. A., and W. Kendrick Pritchett. "The Attic Stelai. Part III. Vases and Other Containers." *Hesperia* 27 (1958), 255–310.

Anderson, Greg. *The Athenian Experiment: Building an Imagined Political Community in Ancient Attica, 508–490 B.C.* (Ann Arbor, MI: 2003).

Anderson, Greg. "Before *Turannoi* Were Tyrants: Rethinking a Chapter of Early Greek History." *CA* 24 (2005), 173–222.

Andrianou, Dimitra. *The Furniture and Furnishings of Ancient Greek Houses and Tombs.* (Cambridge, UK: 2009).

Angiolillo, Simonetta. *Arte e culture nell'atene di Pisistrato e dei Pisistratidi. 'Ο ἐπὶ Κρόνου Βίος* (Bari: 1997).

Arnush, Michael F. "The Career of Peisistratos Son of Hippias." *Hesperia* 64 (1995), 135–62.

Barucchi, Laura. "Il metodo di selezione degli arconti in Atene arcaica." *MEP* 9/10 (2004–05), 69–85.

Beekes, Robert. *Etymological Dictionary of Greek* (Leiden: 2010).

Bentz, Martin. *Panathenäische Preisamphoren. Eine athenische Vasengattung und ihre Funktion vom 6.–4 Jahrhundert v. Chr.* Antike Kunst Beiheft 18 (1998).

Bergquist, Birgitta. *Herakles on Thasos: The Archaeological, Literary, and Epigraphic Evidence for His Sanctuary, Status and Cult Reconsidered*. Boreas 5 (Uppsala: 1973).

Bieber, Margarete. "Two Attic Black-Figured Lekythoi in Buffalo." *AJA* 48 (1944), 121–29.

Blamire, Alec. "Athenian Finance, 454–404 B.C." *Hesperia* 70 (2001), 99–126.

Blok, Josine H. "Deme Accounts and the Meaning of *Hosios* Money in Fifth-Century Athens." *Mnemosyne* 63 (2010), 61–93.

Blok, Josine H. "Perikles' Citizenship Law: A New Perspective." *Historia* 58 (2009), 141–70.

Blok, Josine H. "Solon's Funerary Laws: Questions of Authenticity and Function." In Blok and Lardinois (2006), 197–247.

Blok, Josine H., and André P. M. H. Lardinois, eds. *Solon of Athens: New Historical and Philological Approaches*. Mnemosyne Suppl. 272 (Leiden: 2006).

Blok, J. H., and S. D. Lambert. "The Appointment of Priests in Attic *gene*." *ZPE* 169 (2009), 95–121.

Boardman, John, and Donna C. Kurtz. *Greek Burial Customs* (Ithaca, NY: 1971).

Böckh, August. *Die Staatshaushaltung der Athener*. 2 vols. (Berlin: 1817).

Boersma, Johannes Sipko. *Athenian Building Policy from 561/0 to 405/4* (Groningen: 1970).

Boersma, Johannes Sipko. "Peisistratos' Building Activity Reconsidered." In Sancisi-Weerdenburg (2000), 49–56.

Boisacq, Emile. *Dictionnaire étymologique de la langue grecque. Etudiée dans ses rapports avec les autres langues indo-européenes* (Heidelberg and Paris: 1916).

Börker, Christoph. *Festbankett und griechische Architektur*. Xenia 4 (Konstanz: 1983).

Bourriot, Félix. *Recherches sur la nature du genos. Etude d'histoire sociale athènienne-periodes archaïque et classique*. 2 vols. (Paris: 1976).

Brock, Roger, and Stephen Hodkinson, eds. *Alternatives to Athens: Varieties of Political Organization and Community in Ancient Greece* (Oxford: 2000).

Bubelis, William. "Athenian Community and State" rev. of Paulin Ismard, *La cité des réseaux. Athènes et ses associations VI*[e]*—I*[e] *siècle av. J.-C.* (Paris: 2010). *Classical Review* 62.1 (2012), 205–7.

Bubelis, William. "Dignity and Power: Athenian Sacred Treasurers from Solon to the Persian Wars." PhD. diss., University of Chicago, 2007.

Bubelis, William."The Sacred Triremes and their *Tamiai* at Athens." *Historia* 30 (2010). 1–27.

Buck, Carl D. "Discoveries in the Attic Deme of Ikaria, 1888. VII. Inscriptions from Ikaria. No. 8–17," *AJA* 5 (1888), 304–19.

Buck, Carl Darling, and Walter Petersen. *A Reverse Index of Greek Nouns and Adjectives Arranged by Terminations with Brief Historical Introductions* (Chicago: 1945).

Buck, Robert J. "The Reform of 487 B.C. in the Selection of the Archons." *CP* 60 (1965), 96–101.

Buschor, Ernst. "Heraion von Samos: Frühe Bauten." *AthMitt* 55 (1930), 1–99.

Buschor, Ernst, and Hans Schleif. "Heraion von Samos: der Altarplatz der Frühzeit." *AthMitt* 58 (1933), 146–73.

Butz, Patricia A. "Early Publications of Bronze Inscriptions from the Akropolis." In *From the Parts to the Whole, vol. 1. Acta of the 13*[th] *International Bronze Congress,*

Held at Cambridge, Massachusetts, May 28-June 1, 1996, eds. Carol C. Mattusch, Amy Brauer, and Sandra E. Knudsen (Portsmouth, RI: 2002), 151–56.

Cahn, Herbert A. "Dokimasia." *RA* (1973), 3–22.

Camp, John M. *The Archaeology of Athens* (New Haven, CT: 2001).

Carawan, Edwin. "Eisangelia and Euthyna: The Trials of Miltiades, Themistokles, and Cimon." *GRBS* 28 (1987), 167–208.

Carey, Christopher. "The Shape of Athenian Laws." *CQ* 48 (1998), 93–109.

Carlier, Pierre. *La royauté en Grèce avant Alexandre* (Strasbourg: 1984).

Cartledge, P. A., and F. D. Harvey, eds. *Crux: Essays in Greek History Presented to G. E. M. de Ste. Croix on His 75th Birthday* (London: 1985).

Cavanaugh, Maureen B. *Eleusis and Athens: Documents in Finance, Religion and Politics in the Fifth Century B.C.* (Atlanta: 1996).

Chaniotis, Angelos. "Priests as Ritual Experts in the Greek World." In Dignas and Trampedach (2008), 17–34.

Chankowski, Véronique. *Athènes et Délos à l'époque classique. Recherches sur l'administration du sanctuaire d'Apollon délien*. BEFAR 331 (Athens: 2008).

Chankowski, Véronique. "Les places financières dans le monde grec classique et hellénistique des cités." *Pallas* 74 (2007), 93–112.

Chantraine, Pierre. *Dictionnaire étymologique de la langue grecque. Histoire des mots*. 2nd rev. ed. (Paris: 2009).

Clinton, Kevin. *The Sacred Officials of the Eleusinian Mysteries*. Transactions of the American Philosophical Society n.s. 64 pt. 3 (Philadelphia: 1974).

Cohen, Edward E. *Athenian Economy and Society: A Banking Perspective* (Princeton, NJ: 1992).

Cole, Susan Guettel. "Professionals, Volunteers, and Amateurs: Serving the Gods *kata ta patria*." in Dignas and Trampedach (2008), 55–72.

Connor, W. Robert. "'Sacred' and 'Secular': Ἱερὰ καὶ ὅσια and the Classical Athenian Concept of the State." *AncSoc.* 19 (1988), 161–88.

Connor, W. Robert. "Tribes, Festivals, and Processions: Civic Ceremonial and Political Manipulation in Archaic Greece." *JHS* 107 (1987), 40–50.

Cooper, Guy L. III, after K. W. Krüger. *Attic Greek Prose Syntax*. 2 vols. (Ann Arbor, MI: 1998).

Davies, J. K. *Athenian Propertied Families, 600–300 B.C.* (Oxford: 1971).

Davies, J. K. *Democracy and Classical Greece*. 2nd ed. (Cambridge, MA: 1993) [Hassocks: 1978].

Davies, J. K. "Demosthenes on Liturgies: A Note." *JHS* 87 (1967), 33–40.

Davies, J. K. "Religion and the State," in *Cambridge Ancient History*. Vol. IV 2nd ed. (1988), 368–88.

Davies, J. K. *Wealth and the Power of Wealth* (New York: 1981).

Davis, Gil. "*Axones* and *Kyrbeis*: A New Answer to an Old Problem." *Historia* 60 (2011), 1–35.

Davison, J. A. "Notes on the Panathenaea." *JHS* 78 (1958), 23–42.

Day, James, and Mortimer Chambers. *Aristotle's History of Athenian Democracy*. University of California Publications in History 73 (Berkeley: 1962).

Day, Joseph W. *Archaic Greek Epigram and Dedication: Representation and Reperformance* (Cambridge, UK: 2010).

De Ste. Croix, G. E. M. *Athenian Democratic Origins and Other Essays*, David Harvey and Robert Parker eds. (Oxford: 2004).

De Waele, Jos. *The Propylaia of the Akropolis in Athens: The Project of Mnesikles* (Amsterdam: 1990).

Deubner, Ludwig. *Attische Feste* (Berlin: 1932).

di Cesare, Riccardo. "Intorno alla Stoa delle Erme." *ASAA* 79 (2001), 17–36.

Dickie, Matthew W. "Pindar's Seventh Pythian and the Status of the Alcmaeonids as *Oikos* or *Genos*." *Phoenix* 33 (1979), 193–202.

Dignas, Beate. *The Economy of the Sacred in Hellenistic and Roman Asia Minor* (Oxford: 2002).

Dignas, Beate, and Kai Trampedach, eds. *Practitioners of the Divine: Greek Priests and Religious Officials from Homer to Heliodorus* (Cambridge, MA: 2008).

Dillon, Matthew. "Was Kleisthenes or Pleisthenes Archon at Athens in 525 BC?" *ZPE* 155 (2006), 91–107.

Dindorf, W. *Scholia Graeca in Euripidis Tragoedias*. 4 vols. (Oxford: 1863).

Dinsmoor, William B., and William B. Dinsmoor Jr. *The Propylaia to the Athenian Akropolis*. Vol. 2: *The Classical Building*, Anastasia Norre Dinsmoor ed. (Princeton, NJ: 2004).

Dinsmoor, William Bell. "The Hekatompedon on the Athenian Akropolis." *AJA* 51 (1947), 109–51.

Dittenberger, Wilhelm. "Die eleusinischen Kerykes." *Hermes* 20 (1885), 1–40.

Dittenberger, Wilhelm. "Zur Hekatompedon-Inschrift." *Hermes* 26 (1891), 472–73.

Dow, Sterling. "The Athenian Calendar of Sacrifices: The Chronology of Nikomakhos' Second Term." *Historia* 9 (1960), 270–93.

Dow, Sterling. "The Law Codes of Athens." *Proc. Massachusetts Hist. Soc.* 71 (1953–57), 1–35, pl. 1.

Dow, Sterling. *Prytaneis: A Study of the Inscriptions Honoring the Athenian Councillors*. Hesperia Supplement 1 (Athens: 1937).

Dow, Sterling, and David H. Gill, S.J. "The Greek Cult Table." *AJA* 69 (1965), 103–14, pls. 25–26.

Dreher, Martin. "Antwort auf Léopold Migeotte." In *Symposium 2003* Hans-Albrecht Ruprecht ed. (Wien: 2006), 247–54.

Duplouy, Alain. "Les Eupatrides d'Athènes 'nobles défenseurs de leur patrie.'" *CCG* 14 (2003), 7–22.

Duplouy, Alain. "L'aristocratie et la circulation des richesses. Apport de l'histoire économique à la définition dés élites grecques." *RBPh* 80 (2002), 5–24.

Ebert, Joachim. *Griechische epigramme auf Sieger an gymnischen und hippischen Agonen* (*Abh. Akad. Leipzig* 63 [2]) (Berlin: 1972).

Ehrenberg, V. "Losung." In *RE* "Lokroi-Lysimachides" vol. 13 (1927), cols. 1451–1504.

Ekroth, Gunnel. *The Sacrificial Rituals of Greek Hero-Cults*. Kernos Suppl. 12 (Liège: 2002).

Faraguna, Michele. *Atene nell'età di Alessandro. Problemi politici, economici, finanziari*. Mem. dei Lincei ser. 9, vol. 2, fasc. 2 (Roma: 1992).

Faraguna, Michele. "Scrittura e amministrazione nelle città greche: gli archivi pubblici." *QUCC* 80 (2005), 61–86.

Feaver, Douglas D. "Historical Development in the Priesthoods of Athens," *YCS* 15 (1957), 123–58.

Ferguson, William Scott. "The Salaminioi of Heptaphylai and Sounion." *Hesperia* 7 (1938), 1–74.

Ferguson, William Scott. *The Treasurers of Athena* (Cambridge, MA: 1932).

Figueira, Thomas. "The Ten *Archontes* of 579/8 at Athens." *Hesperia* 53 (1984), 447–73.

Finley, Moses I. *Politics in the Ancient World* (Cambridge, UK: 1983).

Finley, Moses I. *Studies in Land and Credit in Ancient Athens, 500–200 B.C.: The Horos Inscriptions*. Corr. ed. with new introduction by Paul Millett (New Brunswick, NJ: 1985) [originally published New Brunswick, NJ: 1951].

Fischer, John E. "Sanides and Sanidia." In *Gestures. Essays in Ancient History, Literature, and Philosophy Presented to Alan L. Boegehold*, Geoffrey W. Bakewell and James P. Sickinger, eds. (Oxford: 2003), 237–50.

Flensted-Jensen, Pernille, Thomas Heine Nielsen, and Lene Rubinstein, eds. *Polis and Politics: Studies in Ancient Greek History Presented to Mogens Herman Hansen on His Sixtieth Birthday, August 20, 2000* (Copenhagen: 2000).

Floren, J. *Die griechische Plastik. I. Die geometrische und archaische Plastik* (München: 1987).

Fornara, Charles W. *The Athenian Board of Generals from 501 to 404*. Historia Einzelschrift 16 (Wiesbaden: 1971).

Forsdyke, Sara. *Exile, Ostracism, and Democracy: The Politics of Expulsion in Ancient Greece* (Princeton, NJ: 2005).

Fouchard, Alain. "*Dèmosios* et *dèmos*: sur l'État grec." *Ktéma* 23 (1998), 59–69.

Foxhall, L., and A. D. E. Lewis, eds. *Greek Law in Its Political Setting: Justifications Not Justice* (Oxford: 1996).

Foxhall, Lin. *Olive Cultivation in Ancient Greece* (Oxford: 2007).

Foxhall, Lin. "A View from the Top: Evaluating the Solonian Property Classes." In Mitchell and Rhodes (1997), 113–36.

Furtwängler, Andreas E., and Hermann J. Kienast. *Samos*. Vol. III. *Der Nordbau im Heraion von Samos* (Bonn: 1989).

Gagarin, Michael, and David Cohen, eds. *The Cambridge Companion to Ancient Greek Law* (Cambridge, UK: 2005).

Gagarin, Michael. *Drakon and the Early Athenian Homicide Law* (New Haven, CT: 1981).

Gallo, Luigi. "Le imposte dirette nelle poleis greche: un istituto tirannico?" *MEP* 3 fasc. 4 (2000), 17–36.

Georgoudi, Stella. "Les magistrates au service des dieux: le cas des démarques en Attique." In *Athènes et le politique dans le sillage de Claude Mossé*, Pauline Schmitt-Pantel and François de Polignac, eds. (Paris: 2007), 83–109.

Gill, David. *Greek Cult Tables* (New York: 1991).

Gill, David. "*Trapezomata*: A Neglected Aspect of Greek Sacrifice." *HThR* 67 (1974), 117–37.

Glotz, Gustave. "Sortitio." In C. Daremberg and E. Saglio *Dictionnaire des antiquités grecques et romaines après les textes et les monuments*. Vol. 4 part 2. *R-S* (Paris: 1907), 1401–17.

Haensch, Rudolf. "Amtslokal und Staatlichkeit in den griechischen Poleis." *Hermes* 131 (2003), 172–95.

Hägg, Robin, ed. *Ancient Greek Cult Practice from the Epigraphical Evidence. Proceedings of the Second International Seminar on Ancient Greek Cult, Organized by the Swedish Institute at Athens, 22–24 November 1991* (Stockholm: 1994).

Hall, Lindsay G. H. "Ephialtes, the Areopagos, and the Thirty." *CQ* 40 (1990), 319–28.

Hamel, Debra. *Athenian Generals: Military Authority in the Classical Period*. Mnemosyne Suppl. 182 (Leiden: 1998).

Hamilton, Richard. Review of D. Harris (1995), *BMCr* 7.8 (1996), 690–93.

Hamilton, Richard. *Treasure Map: A Guide to the Delian Inventories* (Ann Arbor, MI: 2000).

Hammond, N. G. L. "Land Tenure in Attica and Solon's *Seisachtheia*." *JHS* 81 (1961), 76–98.

Hammond, N. G. L. "Strategia and Hegemonia in Fifth-Century Athens." *CQ* n.s. 19 (1969), 111–44.

Hannel, Krister. "Neokoroi." In *RE* 2nd ser. vol. 16, 2 "Mystagogos-Nereae" (1901), cols. 2422–28.

Hansen, Mogens Herman. *The Athenian Democracy in the Age of Demosthenes: Structure, Principles and Ideology*, J. A. Crook trans. (Oxford: 1991).

Hansen, Mogens Herman. *Polis and City-State: An Ancient Concept and Its Modern Equivalent. Symposium, January 9, 1998*. Acts of the Copenhagen Polis Centre 5 (Copenhagen: 1998).

Hansen, Mogens Herman. "Seven Hundred Archai in Classical Athens." *GRBS* 21 (1980), 151–73.

Hansen, Mogens Herman. "When Was Selection by Lot of Magistrates Introduced in Athens?" *C&M* 41 (1990), 55–61.

Harding, Phillip. *Androtion and the Atthis: The Fragments Translated with Introduction and Commentary* (Oxford: 1994).

Harris, Diane. *The Treasures of the Parthenon and Erechtheion* (Oxford: 1995).

Harris, Edward. *Democracy and the Rule of Law in Classical Athens: Essays on Law, Society, and Politics* (Cambridge, UK: 2006).

Harrison, Thomas. "Religion and the Rationality of the Greek City." In Goldhill and Osborne (2006), 124–40.

Heberdey, Rudolf. *Altattische Porosskulptur* (Wien: 1919).

Hedreen, Guy. "The Return of Hephaistos, Dionysiac Processions, and the Creation of a Visual Narrative." *JHS* 124 (2004), 38–64.

Hellström, Pontus. "The Asymmetry of the Pinacotheca—Once More." *Op.Ath.* 11 (1975), 87–92.

Hellström, Pontus. "A Pre-Mnesiklean *Hestiatorion* on the Athenian Akropolis?" In *Vltra Terminarum Vagari: Scritti in onore di Carl Nylander*, Börje Magnusson et al., eds. (Roma: 1997), 119–27.

Henry, Alan S. "Polis/acropolis, Paymasters and the Ten Talent Fund." *Chiron* 12 (1982), 91–118.

Hermann, Hans-Volkmar. "Zanes." *RE* Suppl. 14 *Aelius bis Zone* (1974), 977–81.

Hignett, C. *A History of the Athenian Constitution to the End of the Fifth Century B.C.* (Oxford: 1952).

Hölscher, Tonio. "Schatzhäuser—Bankethäuser?" In Stephanie Böhm and Klaus-Valtin von Eickstedt, eds. *ΙΘΑΚΗ: Festschrift für Jörg Schäfer zum 75. Geburtstag am 25. April 2001* (Würzburg: 2001), 143–52.

Horster, Marietta. *Landbesitz griechischer Heiligtümer in archaischer und klassischer Zeit* (Berlin: 2004).

Horster, Marietta."Die Olivenbäume der Athena und die Todesstrafe." In *Symposion 2003. Vorträge zur griechischen und hellenistischen Rechtsgeschichte (Rauischholzhausen, 30. September—3. Oktober 2003)* Hans-Albrecht Rupprecht, ed. (Wien: 2006), 167–85.

How, W. W., and J. Wells. *A Commentary on Herodotus*. 2 vols. (Oxford: 1912).

Humphreys, S. C. *The Strangeness of Gods: Historical Perspectives on the Interpretation of Athenian Religion* (Oxford: 2004).

Hunter, Virginia. "Pittalacus and Eucles: Slaves in the Public Service of Athens." *Mouseion* 3rd ser. 6 (2006), 1–13.

Hurwitt, Jeffrey M. *The Athenian Acropolis: History, Mythology, and Archaeology from the Neolithic Era to the Present* (Cambridge, UK: 1999).

Huxley, George. "Madvig on Hellenotamiai." *RFIC* 118 (1990), 319–22.

Ismard, Paulin. *La cité des réseaux. Athènes et ses associations VIe-Ier siècle av. J.-C.* (Paris: 2010).

Jacob, O. "Les esclaves publics à Athènes." *Musée Belge* 30 (1926), 57–106.

Jacobsthal, Paul. *Diskoi*. Winckelmannsprogramm 93 (Berlin: 1933).

Jacoby, Felix. *Atthis: The Local Chronicles of Ancient Athens* (Oxford: 1949).

Jacoby, Felix. "ΓΕΝΕΣΙΑ: A Forgotten Festival of the Dead." *CQ* 38 (1944), 65–75.

Jacquemin, Anne. "'Hiéron', un passage entre 'idion' et 'dêmosion.'" *Ktéma* 23 (1998), 221–28.

Jameson, Michael. "Sacrifice and Animal Husbandry in Classical Greece." In Whittaker (1988), 87–119.

Jameson, Michael. "Theoxenia." In Hägg (1994), 35–57.

Jeffery, L. H. *The Local Scripts of Archaic Greece: A Study of the Origin of the Greek Alphabet and Its Development from the Eighth to the Fifth Centuries B.C.* (orig. publ. 1961) rev. ed. with suppl. by A. W. Johnston (Oxford: 1990).

Jeffery, L. H. "A Sixth-Century Poros Inscription from Attica." *ABSA* 39 (1938–39), 90–93.

Jones, Nicholas F. *The Associations of Classical Athens: The Response to Democracy* (Oxford: 1999).

Jones, Nicholas F. *Public Organization in Ancient Greece: A Documentary Study* (Philadelphia: 1987).

Jordan, Borimir. "Herodotos 5.71.2 and the Naukraroi of Athens." *CSCA* 3 (1970), 153–75.

Jordan, Borimir. *Servants of the Gods: A Study in the Religion, History and Literature of Fifth-Century Athens* (Göttingen: 1979).

Judeich, Walther. "Hekatompedon und Alter Tempel." *Hermes* 64 (1929), 391–415.

Judeich, Walther. *Topographie von Athen*. 2nd ed. (München: 1931).

Jüthner, Julius. "Diskoi." *JÖI* 29 (1934), 32–43.

Kallet, Lisa. "*Dêmos Tyrannos*: Wealth, Power, and Economic Patronage." In K. A. Morgan, ed. *Popular Tyranny, Sovereignty and Its Discontents in Ancient Greece* (Austin, TX: 2003), 117–53.

Kallet-Marx, Lisa. "Money Talks: Rhetor, Demos, and the Resources of the Athenian Empire." In Osborne and Hornblower (1994), 227–51.

Kapparis, K. A. "Assessors of Magistrates (Paredroi) in Classical Athens." *Historia* 47 (1998), 383–93.

Karakasi, Katerina. *Archaic Korai* (Los Angeles: 2003).

Kavoulaki, Athena. "Processional Performance and the Democratic Polis." In *Performance Culture and Athenian Democracy*, Simon Goldhill and Robin Osborne, eds. (Cambridge, UK: 1999), 293–320.

Kavoulaki, Athena. "The Ritual Performance of a Pompê: Aspects and Perspectives." In *Δώρημα. A Tribute to the A. G. Leventis Foundation on the Occasion of Its 20th Anniversary* (no ed.). (Nicosia: 2000), 145–58.

Kavvadias, G. "᾿Επιγραφαὶ ἐκ τῆς ᾿Ακροπόλεως." *AD* (1899), 6–21.

Keaney, John J. "The Date of Aristotle's *Athenaion Politeia*." *Historia* 19 (1970), 326–36.

Keaney, John J. "Hignett's *HAC* and the Authorship of the *Athenaion Politeia*." *LCM* 5 (1980), 51–56.

Kearns, Emily. "Change and Continuity in Religious Structures after Cleisthenes." In Cartledge and Harvey (1985), 194–207.

Kearns, Emily. *The Heroes of Attica*. BICS Suppl. 57 (London: 1989).

Keesling, Catherine M. *The Votive Statues of the Athenian Acropolis* (Cambridge, UK: 2003).

Kolbe, Walter. "Zur athenischen Schatzverwaltung im IV Jahrhundert." *Philologus* 38 (1929), 261–67.

Kosmetatou, Elizabeth. "The Athenian Inventory Lists: A Review Article." *AC* 71 (2002), 185–97.

Kosmetatou, Elizabeth. "A Numismatic Commentary of the Inventory Lists of the Athenian Acropolis." *RBN* 147 (2001), 11–37.

Kroll, John H. "Silver in Solon's Laws." In *Studies in Greek Numismatics in Memory of Martin Jessop Price*, Richard Ashton and Silvia Hurter, eds. (London: 1998), 225–32.

Krumeich, Ralf. *Bildnisse griechischer Herrscher und Staatsmänner im 5. Jahrhundert v. Chr.* (München: 1997).

Kurke, Leslie. "The Economy of Kudos." In Carol Dougherty and Leslie Kurke, eds. *Cultural Poetics in Archaic Greece* (Cambridge, UK: 1993), 131–63.

Lambert, Stephen D. "Athenian State Laws and Decrees: 352/1–322/1: II Religious Regulations." *ZPE* 154 (2005), 125–59.

Lambert, Stephen D. *The Phratries of Attica*. 2nd ed. (Ann Arbor, MI: 1998).

Lambert, Stephen D. "A Polis and its Priests: Athenian Priesthoods Before and After Pericles' Citizenship Law." *Historia* 59 (2010), 143–75.

Lambert, Stephen D. *Rationes Centesimarum: Sales of Public Land in Lykourgan Athens*. ΑΡΧΑΙΑ ΕΛΛΑΣ 3 (Amsterdam: 1997).

Lape, Susan. "Solon and the Institution of the 'Democratic' Family Form." *CJ* 98.2 (2002–03), 117–39.

Ledl, Artur. *Studien zur älteren athenischen Verfassungsgeschichte* (Heidelberg: 1914).

Lehmann-Haupt, C. F. "Schatzmeister- und Archontenwahl in Athen." *Klio* 6 (1906), 304–22.

Lewis, D. M. "After the Profanation of the Mysteries." In *Ancient Society and Institutions. Studies for Victor Ehrenberg on His 75th Birthday*, E. Badian, ed. (Oxford: 1966), 177–91.

Lewis, D. M. "Cleisthenes and Attica." *Historia* 12 (1963), 22–40.

Lewis, D. M. "The Deme Ikarion." *ABSA* 51 (1956), 172.

Lewis, D. M. "An Inventory in the Agora." *ZPE* 36 (1979), 131–34.

Lewis, D. M. "Law on the Lesser Panathenaea." *Hesperia* 28 (1959), 239–47.

Lewis, D. M. "A Note on *IG* i² 114." *JHS* 87 (1967), 132.

Lewis, D. M. "Notes on Attic Inscriptions." *BSA* 49 (1954), 17–50.

Lewis, D. M. "Public Property in the City." In *Selected Papers in Greek and Near Eastern History*, P. J. Rhodes, ed. (Cambridge, UK: 1997), 60–76.

Linders, Tullia. *Studies in the Treasure Records of Artemis Brauronia Found in Athens* (Lund: 1972).

Linders, Tullia. *The Treasurers of the Other Gods in Athens and Their Functions*. Beiträge zur klassischen Philogie 62 (Meisenheim am Glan: 1975).

Lolling, H. G. "᾿Επιγραφαὶ ἐκ τῆς ᾿Ακροπόλεως." *Deltion Arkhaiologikon* 5 (1889), 6–21.

Lolling, H. G. "Inschrift aus Kyzikos." *Ath.Mitt.* 13 (1888) 304–09.

Lolling, H. G. ΚΑΤΑΛΟΓΟΣ ΤΟΥ ΕΝ ΑΘΕΝΑΙΣ ΕΠΙΓΡΑΦΙΚΟΥ ΜΟΥΣΕΙΟΥ. Vol. 1 ΕΠΙΓΡΑΦΑΙ ΕΚ ΤΗΣ ΑΚΡΟΠΟΛΕΩΣ (Athens: 1899).

Loomis, William T. *Wages, Welfare Costs and Inflation in Classical Athens* (Ann Arbor, MI: 1998).

Lougovaya-Ast, Julia. "Myrrhine, the First Priestess of Athena Nike." *Phoenix* 60 (2006), 211–25.

MacDowell, Douglas M. *The Athenian Homicide Law* (Manchester: 1963).

Maffi, Alberto. "Τὰ ἱερὰ καὶ τὰ ὅσια. Contributo allo studio della terminologia giuridico-sacrale greca." In *Symposion 1977: Vorträge zur griechischen und hellenistischen Rechtsgeschichte (Chantilly, 1.-4. Juni 1977)*, Joseph Modrzejewski and Detlev Liebs, eds. (Köln: 1982), 33–53.

Makres, Andronike K. "The Rediscovery of *IG* I[3] 253–4." In *Αττικαί Επιγραφαί· Πρακτικά συμποσίου εις μνήμην Adolf Wilhelm (1864–1950)* Angelos P. Mathaiou, ed. (Athens: 2004), 123–40.

Marco, Vittorio de. *Scholia in Sophoclis Oedipum Coloneum* (Rome: 1952).

Markle, M. M. "Jury Pay and Assembly Pay at Athens." In Cartledge and Harvey (1985), 265–97.

Mazarakis-Ainian, Alexandros. "Ein antikes Heiligtum auf Kythnos." In *Neue Forschungen zu griechischen Städten und Heiligtümern. Festschift für Burkhardt Wesenberg zum 65. Geburtstag*, Heide Frielinghaus and Jutta Stroszeck, eds. (Möhnesee: 2010), 21–53, pls. 12–24.

McGowan, Elizabeth P. "The Origins of the Athenian Ionic Capital." *Hesperia* 66 (1997), 209–33, pls. 55–60.

Meiggs, Russell. *Trees and Timber in the Ancient World* (Oxford: 1982).

Meritt, Benjamin D. "Greek Inscriptions." *Hesperia* 8 (1939), 48–82.

Meritt, Benjamin D. "Notes on the Decrees of Kallias." *AJP* 55 (1934), 263–74.

Meyer, Eduard. *Forschungen zur alten Geschichten*. 2 vols. (Halle: 1892–99).

Migeotte, L. *L'emprunt public dans les cités grecques. Recueil des documents et analyse critique* (Québec and Paris: 1984).

Migeotte, L. "La gestions des biens sacrés dans les cités grecques." In Rupprecht (2006), 233–46.

Migeotte, L. "Sur l'emploi de 'Prodaneizein.'" *Phoenix* 34 (1980), 219–26.

Migeotte, L. "Sur les rapports financiers entre le sanctuaire et la cité de Locres." In Knoepfler (1988), 191–203.

Mikalson, Jon D. "Prothyma." *AJP* 93 (1972), 577–83.

Mikalson, Jon D. *The Sacred and Civil Calendar of the Athenian Year* (Princeton, NJ: 1975).

Millett, Paul. *Lending and Borrowing in Ancient Athens* (Cambridge, UK: 1991).

Mitchell, Fordyce W. *Lykourgan Athens: 338–322* (Cincinnati: 1970).

Moreno, Alfonso. *Feeding the Democracy: The Athenian Grain Supply in the Fifth and Fourth Centuries BC* (Oxford: 2007).

Morris, Ian. *Archaeology as Cultural History: Words and Things in Iron Age Greece* (Malden, MA: 2000).

Morris, Ian. "Early Iron Age Greece." In *The Cambridge Economic History of the Greco-Roman World*, W. Scheidel, I. Morris, and R. Saller, eds. (Cambridge, UK: 2007), 211–41.

Morris, Ian. "The Strong Principle of Equality and the Archaic Origins of Greek Democracy." In Ober and Hedrick (1996), 19–48.

Nagy, Blaise. "The Athenian Athlothetai." *GRBS* 19 (1978), 307–13, pl. 2.

Neils, Jennifer, ed. *Goddess and Polis: The Panathenaic Festival in Ancient Athens* (Hanover, NH: 1992).

Nelson, Max. "The Phantom Stelai of Lysias, *Against Nichomachus* 17." *CQ* 56 (2006), 309–12.

Németh, György. "Μεδ ' ὄνθον ἐγβαλε̃ν." In Hägg (1994), 59–64.

Ober, Josiah. "Aristotle's Political Sociology: Class, Status, and Order in the Politics." In Lord and O'Connor (1991), 112–35.

Ober, Josiah. "The Athenian Revolution of 508/7 B.C.E.: Violence, Authority, and the Origins of Democracy." In Dougherty and Kurke (1993), 215–32.

Ober, Josiah. *Democracy and Knowledge: Innovation and Learning in Classical Athens* (Princeton, NJ: 2008).

Ober, Josiah. *Mass and Elite in Democratic Athens: Rhetoric, Ideology, and the Power of the People* (Princeton, NJ: 1989).

Ober, Josiah. *Political Dissent in Democratic Athens: Intellectual Critics of Popular Rule* (Princeton, NJ: 1998).

Oehler, Johann. "῾Ιεροποιοί." In *RE* vol. VIII *Hestiaia-Hyagnis* (1913), cols. 1583–88.

Oehler, Johann. "Κύαμος." In *RE* vol. XI *Katoikoi-Kynegoi* (1922), cols. 2233–34.

Ohnesorg, A. *Ionische Altäre. Formen und Varianten einer Architekturgattung aus Insel- und Ostionien* (Berlin: 2005).

Oliver, G. J. *War, Food, and Politics in Early Hellenistic Athens* (Oxford: 2007).

Oliver, James Henry. *The Athenian Expounders of the Sacred and Ancestral Law* (Baltimore: 1950).

Oliver, James Henry. "From *Gennetai* to *Curiales*." *Hesperia* 49 (1980), 30–56.

Oliver, James Henry. "Greek Inscriptions." *Hesperia* 4 (1935), 5–32.

Oliver, James Henry. *Marcus Aurelius: Aspects of Civic and Cultural Policy in the East.* Hesperia Suppl. 13 (Princeton, NJ: 1970).

Osborne, Robin. "Social and Economic Implications of the Leasing of Land and Property in Hellenistic Greece." *Chiron* 18 (1998), 279–323.

Osborne, Robin, and Simon Hornblower, eds. *Ritual, Finance, Politics: Athenian Democratic Accounts Presented to David Lewis* (Oxford: 1994).

Ostwald, Martin. *From Popular Sovereignty to the Sovereignty of Law: Law, Society, and Politics in Fifth Century Athens* (Berkeley, CA: 1986).

Pafford, Isabelle A. "*IG* I^3 6 and the *Aparche* of Grain?" *ZPE* 177 (2011), 75–78.

Page, D. L. *Further Greek Epigrams: Epigrams before A.D. 50 from the Greek Anthology and Other Sources, not Included in Hellenistic Epigrams or the Garland of Philip* (Cambridge, UK: 1981).

Papazarkadas, Nikolaos. "IG II[2] 2490, the Epakreis and the Pre-Cleisthenic Trittyes." *CQ* 57 (2007), 22–32.

Papazarkadas, Nikolaos. *Sacred and Public Land in Ancient Athens* (Oxford: 2011).

Parker, Robert. *Athenian Religion: A History* (Oxford: 1996).

Parker, Robert. *Miasma: Pollution and Purification in Early Greek Religion* (Oxford: 1983).

Pernin, Isabelle. "L'impôt foncier existait-il en grèce ancienne." In Andreau and Chankowski (2007), 369–83.

Petrovic, Andrej. *Kommentar zu den simonideischen Versinschriften*. Mnemosyne Suppl. 282 (Leiden: 2007).

Pringsheim, Fritz. *The Greek Law of Sale* (Weimar: 1950).

Pritchett, W. Kendrick. "The Attic Stelai. Part I." *Hesperia* 22 (1953), 225–99.

Pritchett, W. Kendrick. *The Choiseul Marble*. University of California Publications in Classical Studies 5 (Berkeley, CA: 1970).

Pritchett, W. Kendrick. "Expenditure of Athena, 408–406 B.C. and the Hellenotamiai," *BCH* 88 (1964), 455–81.

Pritchett, W. Kendrick. *The Greek State at War*. 5 vols. (Berkeley, CA: 1971–91).

Pritchett, W. Kendrick. "The Hellenotamiai and Athenian Finance." *Historia* 26 (1977), 295–306.

Pritchett, W. Kendrick, and Anne Pippin. "The Attic Stelai. Part II.

Raaflaub, Kurt A. "The Breakthrough of *Demokratia* in Mid-Fifth-Century Athens." In Raaflaub, Ober, and Wallace, eds. (2007), 105–54.

Raaflaub, Kurt A., Josiah Ober, and Robert W. Wallace, eds. *Origins of Democracy in Ancient Greece* (Berkeley, CA: 2007).

Raaflaub, Kurt A., and Robert W. Wallace. "'People's Power' and Egalitarian Trends in Archaic Greece." In Raaflaub, Ober, and Wallace, eds. (2007), 22–48.

Reger, Gary. *Regionalism and Change in the Economy of Independent Delos, 314–167 B.C.* (Berkeley, CA: 1994).

Reitzenstein, R. *Geschichte der griechischen Etymologika. Ein Beitrag zur Geschichte der Philogie in Alexandria und Byzanz* (Leipzig: 1897).

Rhodes, P. J. *The Athenian Boule* (Oxford: 1972).

Rhodes, P. J. *A Commentary on the Aristotelian "Athenaion Politeia."* 2nd rev. ed. (Oxford: 1993).

Rhodes, P. J. "Documents in the Greek States: Archives and Inscriptions, Part I." *G&R* 48 (2001), 33–44.

Rhodes, P. J. "Documents in the Greek States: Archives and Inscriptions, Part II." *G&R* 48 (2001), 136–53.

Rhodes, P. J. "Peisistratid Chronology Again." *Phoenix* 3 (1976), 219–33.

Rihll, T. E. "Classical Athens." In *The Cambridge World History of Slavery, Vol. 1: The Ancient Mediterranean World*, Keith Bradley and Paul Cartledge, eds. (Cambridge, UK: 2011), 48–73.

Roberts, Jennifer Tolbert. *Accountability in Athenian Government* (Madison, WI: 1982).

Robertson, Noel. "Athens' Festival of the New Wine." *HSCP* 95 (1993), 197–250.

Robertson, Noel. "The Laws of Athens, 410–399 BC: The Evidence for Review and Publication." *JHS* 110 (1990), 43–75.

Robinson, Eric W. "Reexamining the Alcmaeonid Role in the Liberation of Athens." *Historia* 43 (1994), 363–69.

Rosivach, Vincent J. "Notes on the Pentakosiomedimnos' Five Hundred Mediminoi." *CQ* 55 (2005), 597–601.

Rosivach, Vincent J. "The Requirements for the Solonic Classes in Aristotle, AP 7.4." *Hermes* 130 (2002), 36–47.

Rosivach, Vincent J. *The System of Public Sacrifice in Fourth-Century Athens* (Atlanta: 1994).

Rotroff, Susan I. "An Anonymous Hero in the Athenian Agora." *Hesperia* 47 (1978), 196–209.

Roussel, Denis. *Tribu et cité. Etudes sur les groupes sociaux dans les cités grecques aux époques archaïque et classique.* Annales littéraires de la université de Besançon 193 (Paris: 1976).

Rudhardt, J. *Notions fondamentales de la pensée religieuse et actes constitutifs du culte dans la Grèce classique.* 2nd ed. (Paris: 1992).

Rupprecht, Hans-Albert, ed. *Symposion 2003. Vorträge zur griechischen und hellenistischen Rechtsgeschichte (Rauischholzhausen, 30. September—3. Oktober 2003)* (Wien: 2006).

Rups, M. "Thesauros: A Study of the Treasury Building as Found in Greek Sanctuaries." PhD. diss., Johns Hopkins University, 1986.

Ruschenbusch, E. "Der sogenannte Gesetzescode vom Jahre 410 v. Chr." *Historia* 5 (1956), 123–28.

Salmond, Paul D. "Sympathy for the Devil: Chares and Athenian Politics," *G&R* 43 (1996), 43–53.

Samons, Loren J., II *Empire of the Owl: Athenian Imperial Finance* Historia Einzelschriften 142 (Stuttgart: 2000).

Sancisi-Weerdenburg, Heleen. "Cultural Politics and Chronology." In Heleen Sancisi-Weerdenburg, ed., *Peisistratos and the Tyranny: A Reappraisal of the Evidence* (Amsterdam: 2000), 79–106.

Sartori, Cristiana. "I 'tamiai' di Delfi," *MEP* 2 (1999), 157–75.

Scafuro, Adele C. "Identifying Solon's Laws." In Blok and Lardinois (2006), 175–96

Schaefer, Hans. "Das Problem der griechischen Nationalität." In *Probleme der alten Geschichte. Gesammelte Abhandlungen und Vorträge*, Ursula Weidemann and Walter Schmitthenner, eds. (Göttingen: 1963), 269–306.

Schlaifer, Robert. "Demon of Paenia, Priest of Asclepius." *CP* 38 (1943), 39–43.

Schlaifer, Robert. "Notes on Athenian Public Cults." *HSCP* 51 (1940), 233–60.

Schmitt-Pantel, Pauline. *La cité au banquet. Histoire des repas publics dans les cités grecques* (Paris: 1992).

Schubert, Charlotte. "Die Naukrarien: Zur Entwicklung der attischen Finanzadministration." *Historia* 57 (2008), 38–64.

Schuchhardt, Walter-Herwig. "Rundwerke ausser den Koren Reliefs." In Hans Schrader, ed., *Die archaischen Marmorbildwerke der Akropolis* (Frankfurt am Main: 1939), 187–342.

Schwahn, Walter. "Tamiai." In *RE* 2nd ser. vol. 4, A2 "Symposion-literatur—Tauris" (1932), cols. 2099–136.

Sealey, Raphael. "Aristotle, *Athenaion Politeia* 57.4: Trial of Animals and Inanimate Objects for Homicide." *CQ* 56 (2006), 475–85.

Sealey, Raphael. "Constitutional Changes in Athens in 410 B.C." *CSCA* 8 (1975), 271–95.

Shapiro, H. A. *Art and Culture under the Tyrants in Athens* (Mainz am Rhein: 1989).

Shapiro, H. A. "Zum Wandel der attischen Gesellschaft nach den Perserkriegen im Spiegel der Akropolis-Weihungen." In *Gab es das Griechische Wunder? Griechenland zwischen dem Ende des 6. und der Mitte des 5. Jahrhunderts v. Chr.*, Dietrich Papenfuß and Volker Michael Strocka, eds. (Mainz: 2001), 91–100.

Shear, Julia Louise. "Polis and Panathenaia: The History and Development of Athena's Festival." PhD. diss., University of Pennsylvania, 2001.

Shear, Julia Louise. *"Polis" and Revolution: Responding to Oligarchy in Classical Athens* (Cambridge, UK: 2011).

Shear, Julia Louise. "Prizes from Athens: The List of Panathenaic Prizes and the Sacred Oil." *ZPE* 142 (2003), 87–108.

Shear, T. Leslie, Jr. "The Athenian Agora: Excavations of 1980–1982." *Hesperia* 53 (1984), 1–57.

Sickinger, James P. *Public Archives and Records in Classical Athens* (Chapel Hill, NC: 1999).

Sihler, Andrew L. *New Comparative Grammar of Greek and Latin* (Oxford: 1995).

Sinos, Rebecca H. "Divine Selection. Epiphany and Politics in Archaic Greece." In Dougherty and Kurke (1993), 73–91.

Slings, S. R. "Literature in Athens. 566–510 BC." In Sancisi-Weerdenburg (2000), 57–77.

Snodgrass, Anthony M. *Archaic Greece: The Age of Experiment* (Berkeley, CA: 1980).

Snodgrass, Anthony M. "The Economics of Dedication at Greek Sanctuaries." *ScAnt* 3–4 (1989–90), 287–94.

Stahl, Michael. *Aristokraten und Tyrannen im archaischen Athen* (Stuttgart: 1987).

Stanton, G. R. *Athenian Politics c. 800–500 BC: A Sourcebook* (London: 1990).

Stein-Hölkeskamp, Elke. *Adelskultur und Polisgesellschaft. Studien zum griechischen Adel in archaischer und klassischer Zeit* (Stuttgart: 1989).

Straten, F. T. van, ed. *Faith, Hope, and Worship: Aspects of Religious Mentality in the Ancient World* (Leiden: 1981).

Straten, F. T. van, ed. *Hiera Kala: Images of Animal Sacrifice in Archaic and Classical Greece* (Leiden: 1995).

Strauss, Barry S. *Athens after the Peloponnesian War: Class, Faction and Policy 403–386 BC* (Ithaca, NY: 1986).

Strauss, Barry S. "Democracy, Kimon, and the Evolution of Athenian Naval Tactics in the Fifth Century BC." In Flensted-Jensen, Nielsen, and Rubinstein (2000), 315–26.

Stroud, Ronald. "Adolf Wilhelm and the Date of the Hekatompedon Decrees." In *Αττικαί Επιγραφαί· Πρακτικά συμποσίου εις μνήμην Adolf Wilhelm (1864–1950)*, Angelos P. Mathaiou, ed. (Athens: 2004), 85–97.

Stroud, Ronald. *The Axones and Kyrbeis of Drakon and Solon* (Berkeley, CA: 1979).

Stroud, Ronald. *Drakon's Law on Homicide* University of California Publications: Classical Studies 3 (Berkeley, CA: 1968).

Stubbings, J. M. "Ivories." In Humfry Payne *Perachora: The Sanctuaries of Hera Akraia and Limenia. Excavations of the British School of Archaeology at Athens 1930–1933. Vol. II Pottery, Ivories, Scarabs, and Other Objects from the Votive Depost of Hera Limnaia* (Oxford: 1962), 403–51.

Swoboda, Heinrich. "Über griechische Schatzverwaltung." *WS* 10 (1888), 278–307.

Tanoulas, Tassos. "The Pre-Mnesiclean Cistern on the Athenian Acropolis." *AthMitt* 107 (1992), 129–60.

Taylor, Claire. "From the Whole Citizen Body? The Sociology of Election and Lot in the Athenian Democracy." *Hesperia* 76 (2007), 323–45.

Thompson, Dorothy Burr. "The Golden Nikai Reconsidered." *Hesperia* 13 (1944), 173–209.

Thompson, Homer. "A Golden Nike." *HSCP* Suppl. 1 *Athenian Studies Presented to W. S. Ferguson* (Cambridge, MA: 1940), 183–210.

Thomsen, Rudi. *Eisphora: A Study of Direct Taxation in Ancient Athens* (Copenhagen: 1964).

Threatte, Leslie. *The Grammar of Attic Inscriptions*. 2 vols. (Berlin: 1980–96).

Todd, S. C. *A Commentary on Lysias, Speeches 1–11* (Oxford: 2007).

Todd, S. C. *The Shape of Athenian Law* (Oxford: 1993).

Tomlinson, R. A. "Perachora: The Remains Outside the Two Sanctuaries." *ABSA* 64 (1969), 155–258, pls. 45–59.

Tomlinson, R. A. Review of J. Servais' "Aliki I. Les deux sanctuaires." *JHS* 101 (1981), 210–11.

Tomlinson, R. A. "Two Notes on Possible Hestiatoria." *ABSA* 75 (1980), 221–28.

Tréheux, Jacques. "L'aménagement intérieur de la Chalkothèque d'Athènes." *Études d'archéologie classique* 1 (1955–56), 133–46.

Tréheux, Jacques. "L'inventaire des clérouques d'Imbros," *BCH* 80 (1956), 462–79.

Tréheux, Jacques. "Retour à Imbros et à Samothrace." In *Hellènika Symmikta: Histoire, archéologie, épigraphie*, Paul Goukoswky and Claude Brixhe, eds. (Nancy: 1991), 143–49.

Trianti, Ismini. "Παρατηρήσεις σε δύο ομάδες γλυπτών του τέλους του 6ου αιώνα από την Ακρόπολη." In Coulson et al. (1994), 83–91.

Van Wees, Hans. "Mass and Elite in Solon's Athens: The Property Classes Revisited." In Blok and Lardinois (2006), 351–89.

Van Wees, Hans. "Megara's Mafiosi: Timocracy and Violence in Theognis." In Brock and Hodkinson (2000), 52–67.

Verdeles, N., M. Jameson, and Io. Papakhristodoulou. "'Επιγραφαὶ Τίρυνθος." *AE* (1975), 150–205.

Vickers, Michael. "Demus's Gold *Phiale* (Lysias 19.25)." *AJAH* 9 (1984), 48–53.

Vollgraff, Guilielmus. "Inscriptio in Arce Argorum Reperta." *Mnemosyne* 57 (1929), 206–34.

Wade-Gery, H. T. *Essays in Greek History* (Oxford: 1958).

Wade-Gery, H. T. "The Financial Decrees of Kallias (I. G. I^2, 91–92)." *JHS* 51 (1931), 57–85.

Wade-Gery, H. T. "Studies in the Structure of Attic Society: II. The Laws of Kleisthenes." *CQ* 27 (1933), 17–29.

Walbank, Michael B. "The Confiscation and Sale by the Poletai in 402/1 B.C. of the Property of the Thirty Tyrants." *Hesperia* 51 (1982), 74–98, pls. 27–28.

Walbank, Michael B. "Leases of Sacred Properties in Attica, Part I." *Hesperia* 52 (1983), 100–35.

Wallace, Robert W. *The Areopagos Council, to 307 B.C.* (Baltimore: 1989).

Wallace, Robert W. "Revolutions and a New Order in Solonian Athens and Archaic Greece." In Raaflaub, Ober, and Wallace (2007), 49–82.

West, Allen B., and A. M. Woodward. "Studies in Attic Treasure-Records (Continued)." *JHS* 58 (1938), 69–89.

Whibley, Leonard. *Greek Oligarchies: Their Character and Organisation* (New York: 1896).

Whitehead, David. *The Demes of Attica. 508/7-ca. 250 B.C.: A Political and Social Study* (Princeton, NJ: 1986).

Wilamovitz-Moellendorff, Ulrich von. *Aristoteles und Athen*. 2 vols. (Berlin: 1893).

Wilhelm, Adolf. "Attische Urkunden. V. Teil." *Sitz. ber. Akad. Wien*. 220.5 (1942), 1–192.

Wilhelm, Adolf. "Inschriften aus Erythrai und Chios." *JÖAI* 12 (1909), 126–50.

Williams, Arden L. "Leasing of Sacred Land in 4th-Century Athens: A Reassessment of Six Inscribed Fragments." *Hesperia* 80 (2011), 261–86.

Wilson, Peter. *The Athenian Institution of the Khoregia: The Chorus, the City and the Stage* (Cambridge, UK: 2000).

Wolff, Hans Julius. "The Origins of Judicial Litigation among the Greeks." *Traditio* 4 (1946), 31–87.

Woodhead, A. G. "The Institution of the Hellenotamiae." *JHS* 79 (1959), 149–52.

Woodward, A. M. "Treasure-records from the Athenian Agora." *Hesperia* 25 (1956), 79–121.

Index Locorum

Texts with multiple references are found under the principal reference, for which a concordance is supplied below with the relevant lemma. Abbreviations are those of *SEG* and *LSJ* wherever possible or commodius.

A. Inscriptions

B. Literary Sources

Index Rerum